STATE OF NEW YORK, } ss.
ULSTER COUNTY,

SURROGATE'S OFFICE.

I, Arthur C. Connelly, Clerk of the Surrogate's Court of Ulster County, New York, do hereby certify that the following abstracts from the records of Wills in this office are correct and true and have been compared with the said original records.

Witness my hand and seal of said Court, at the City of Kingston, N. Y., this 15th day of November, 1905.

ARTHUR C. CONNELLY,
Clerk of the Surrogate's Court of
(L. S.)   Ulster Co., N. Y.

STATE OF NEW YORK, } ss.
ULSTER COUNTY,

ULSTER COUNTY CLERK'S OFFICE,
Kingston, N. Y.

I, John D. Fratsher, Clerk of Ulster County, New York, do hereby certify that the following abstracts from the records of Wills recorded in the Books of Deeds in said office are correct and true and have been compared with said original records.

Witness my hand and seal of said office at the City of Kingston, N. Y., this 10th day of August, 1905.

JOHN D. FRATSHER,
(L. S.)   Ulster County Clerk.

ULSTER COUNTY, N. Y.

PROBATE RECORDS

IN THE OFFICE OF THE SURROGATE, AND IN THE
COUNTY CLERK'S OFFICE AT KINGSTON, N. Y.

A CAREFUL ABSTRACT AND TRANSLATION OF THE DUTCH AND
ENGLISH WILLS, LETTERS OF ADMINISTRATION AFTER
INTESTATES, AND INVENTORIES FROM 1665, WITH
GENEALOGICAL AND HISTORICAL NOTES, AND LIST
OF DUTCH AND FRISIAN BAPTISMAL NAMES
WITH THEIR ENGLISH EQUIVALENTS

BY

GUSTAVE ANJOU, Ph. D.

Member of the American Historical Association; The National Geographic Society;
The American Scenic and Historic Preservation Society; New York Historical
Society; New York Genealogical and Biographical Society; National Arts Club;
Royal Societies Club; Catholic Record Society; Société Suisse d'Héraldique;
Herold Verein, Berlin; K. K. Heraldische Gesellschaft, Vienna;
R. Accademia Araldica Italiana, Bari; British Numismatic
Society; Yorkshire, &c., Parish Register Societies, etc.

WITH INTRODUCTION BY JUDGE A. T. CLEARWATER, LL.D.

VOLUME I.

EXHAUSTIVE INDEXES OF PERSONS AND LOCALITIES,
FAC-SIMILES OF WILLS, ETC.

Southern Historical Press, Inc.
Greenville, South Carolina

This volume was reproduced
from a personal copy located in
the Publishers private library

All rights reserved. No part of this publication may be reproduced,
stored in a retrieval system, transmitted in any form, posted
on the web in any form or by any means without the
prior written permission of the publisher.

Please direct all correspondence and book orders to:
**SOUTHERN HISTORICAL PRESS, Inc.
1071 Park West Blvd.
Greenville, SC 29611**

Published 1906 by:
  Gustave Anjou
ISBN #978-1-63914-661-1
Printed in the United States of America

INTRODUCTION

By Alphonso Trumpbour Clearwater, LL.D.

The History of Ulster County may be said to consist of four periods. The first began with the establishment of a Dutch trading post at Ponckhockie, the junction of the Hudson and the Rondout, in 1614. The second with the settlement at Kingston of Christoffle Daavis, Mattys Hendrix and Johan DeHulter, Dutchmen, and Thomas Chambers, an Englishman, in 1652. The third with the treaty of Paris in 1763. The fourth with the inauguration at Kingston of George Clinton, the first Governor of the State under the Constitution, on the 30th day of July, 1777. During each of these periods the County played an important part, and so influential were the people of Ulster in swinging the colony into line with the patriot cause that in October, 1777, the British under Sir John Vaughan wantonly burned Kingston in retaliation. Down to 1683 the only civil divisions of the Province of New York were Manors, Towns or Cities and Patents. On the first of November of that year, Dongan being Governor, the following Act was passed by the Governor, Council and Representatives:

> "An Act to divide the Province and Dependencyes into Shires and Countyes, passed November 1st, 1683. Having taken into consideration the necessity of divideing the Province into respective Countyes for the better governing and settling Courts in the same.
>
> Bee it enacted by the Governor and Councell and Representatives, and by the authority of the same, the said Province bee divided into twelve Countyes as follows * * * * * *
>
> The Countye of Ulster to contain the Townes of Kingston, Hurley and Marble Towne, Ffox Hall and the New Paltz and all the villages, neighborhoods and christian habitacions on the west side of the Hudsons River from the Murderer's Creek near the Highlands to the Sawyer's Creek."

Of these Kingston, Hurley and Marbletown were towns, Fox Hall was a manor and New Paltz was held by patent. Since the granting of this charter, the County of Sullivan, and parts of the Counties of Greene, Delaware and Orange have been taken from the territory it described. Situate upon the west bank of the Hudson, practically midway between New Amsterdam and Fort Orange (New York and Albany), and in many respects the rival of those places, having for its whole eastern front the great natural highway of the Hudson, and traversed by three large streams, the Esopùs, the Rondout and the Wallkill, along which passed the constantly traveled Indian trails connecting the North (The Hudson) with the South (The Delaware) river, Ulster early became and always has remained prominent, if not pre-eminent, in historical interest. Its early settlers principally came from Holland. Many of them were the younger sons of well-to-do Dutch families who, inspired by that spirit of adventure common to the youth of all times and all lands, sought a broader sphere of action in the new world than was afforded by the old. To Ulster came also the Huguenots who, exiled from France because of their religious faith, found among the Dutch of Esopus an hospitable welcome and the right to a free and open Bible. Thus it is that for more than two and a half centuries the men who have been most prominent and potent in the affairs of the County have, as a rule, borne Dutch or Huguenot names. To the Dutch more than to any other people America owes its civil and religious liberty, and its wise and tolerant system of laws, the Pilgrims first learning of the strength and advantage of a republican form of government during their sojourn in Holland. To the Dutch also the world is indebted for the system of recording deeds, mortgages and wills, and from the earliest settlement to the present the records of Ulster have been scrupulously and accurately kept, running back in unbroken succession for over two hundred and fifty years. The early records are written in Dutch and, aside from those of marriages and baptism, consist of six classes :—

1. The record of the transfers of lands by deed.
2. The record of the mortgaging of lands for debt.
3. The record of wills, and the succession of estates.
4. The record of the acknowledgement of debt, as distinct from that creating a lien on lands.
5. The record of judicial transactions.
6. The record of agreements with the Indians.

The original records are contained in a number of well worn and much thumbed volumes, originally bound, some in vellum, some in sheepskin, and have had rather a remarkable history. They remained in the office of the County Clerk at Kingston from the time they were written until about fifty years ago, when suddenly they disappeared. Many efforts were made to find them. The Grand Jury instituted an investigation, the Board of Supervisors offered a liberal reward for their return, but nothing could be learned of their whereabouts or by whom they had been taken. One day during the summer of 1895 a large box was delivered to the County Clerk by an Express Company. It contained the long lost records, carefully covered with a waterproof wrapper and closely packed with cotton wool. They had been shipped from an obscure village on the southern shore of Long Island by a person whose name and address were not given. It is not known who took them, in whose possession they were during their absence, or who returned them. Various explanations have been suggested. Among others that they had been sent to Brooklyn for translation by a Dutch scholar who died before he began the work; that after his death his family sent them to the old City Hall of that City; that when the new City Hall was erected they were returned to Kingston. This, however, does not account for all the known facts. After they were returned they were carefully examined by my father, Isaac Clearwater, who spoke and read Dutch as readily as he did English. He recognized their great importance and advised their translation into English. When the Board of Supervisors of the County met the following November, I called its attention to the character of the material they contained, and suggested that they be translated at the expense of the County. The Board at once by unanimous resolution requested me to act as commissioner for the purpose, and a translation was made of the early Dutch records not recorded in the Deed Books, which translation is now contained in three large folio volumes of over six hundred pages each, and with the original records preserved in the office of the County Clerk. Among the most interesting of the old records are those containing the proceedings and adjudications of the Dutch Court of Schout and Sheppens from 1658 to 1684. That Court was the predecessor of the Court of Common Pleas, of the Court of Sessions and of the existing County Court, and for strict impartiality, jealousy of the rights of the individual, the equitable administration of justice, soundness of judgment and compression and lucidity of statement its proceedings and decisions rarely have been surpassed, while its records portray the life of the early settler in a picturesque and interesting manner. A partial index of them recently has been printed by the County of Albany as part of its own early records which that County is now putting in print, this index being included because the intimate relations which existed between the people of the settlements of Fort Orange, Beverwyck and Rensselaerwyck and those of Esopus, Wiltwyck and Kingston during the seventeenth and eighteenth centuries resulted in many transactions the record of which was indifferently kept at one place or the other.

Dr. Anjou, omitting only the ornate legal formulas which form part of the deeds, mortgages and wills of the period, presents all that which is of interest alike to the student and the general reader, particularly noting any entry of unusual character. The seals attached to the documents, of which rubbings have been made and engraved in many cases, are private seals. Official seals were not early used. Most well-to-do Dutchmen used seals engraved according to their fancy, a few used their family arms, but this was the exception. A novice always experiences difficulty in tracing the ancestry of Dutch families, in examining the documents signed by Dutchmen and in following the proceedings of Dutch Courts in America, arising from the fact that, while the French and English invariably used their surnames, the Dutch, as a rule, were indifferent about this and usually are designated by others, and designate themselves, by their Christian names alone, even in important legal documents. This answered every purpose in a primitive and small community where everyone was known, but now leads to much confusion. For instance,

Lambert Huyberts is Lambert Huyberts Brink.
Tjrick Claessen—Tjrick Claessen De Witt.
Jan Wilhemsen—Jan Wilhemsen Hooghteyling (Houghtaling).
Jan Mattys—Jan Mattys Jansen.
Teunis Jacobse, or Jacobsen—Tunis Jacobsen Klaarwater (Clearwater)
Peter Cornelius—Peter Cornelius Low.
Albertse Heymans—Albertse Heymans Roosa.
Hendrick Jochemsin—Hendrick Jochemsin Schoonmaker.
Aaert Jacobsen—Aaert Jacobsen Van Wagonen.

The first statutory provision for the probate of wills and the granting of letters of administration was enacted by the Governor, Council and Representatives convened in general assembly on the 11th day of November, 1692. The preamble recited that the rights of orphans and the estates of such as died intestate throughout the Province were often concealed, wasted, embezzled and destroyed to the utter ruin of many orphans and to the prejudice of the next of kin for want of having good and sufficient persons in each county to enquire after the same, and the Act provided that on or before the 25th day of March, 1693, there should be elected and appointed in each town throughout the counties within the Province two able and sufficient freeholders who should, upon the death of any person in their respective towns, repair to the place of habitation where the deceased resided within forty-eight hours after the interment and make enquiry if the deceased made any will, or had any real or personal estate not devised by him at the time of his death, and if upon enquiry it was found that he had made no will, but had died intestate, then it should be lawful for such freeholders to make strict and diligent search and enquiry into all the real and personal estate that the intestate died possessed of, and inventory the same and bring or cause to be brought unto such person or persons in the county where the intestate died who should be appointed by the Governor to supervise the intestate's estates, and file with him upon their oath an inventory of the estate, whereupon the supervisor of estates should issue his warrant to two good and sufficient freeholders within the town where the intestate died for the appraisement of the goods and chattels left by the intestate, and upon the return of the same he should cause the goods and chattels to be secured or sold, the proceeds to remain in his hands or to be placed into good and sufficient hands who should be able to produce the same again when the next of kin should appear in right to claim the same. It further provided that if the intestate at the time of his death left a wife and children behind him, then, in such case, the wife only should have the right of administration, but if he left only orphans and had no relations or kindred who would administer upon his estate, then the supervisor of each county should have the administration and care of the estate, and the same should be secured for the use, benefit and behoof of the orphans, and should be secured and improved until the orphans married or came to the age of twenty-one years. It further provided that the supervisor of estates should take effectual care of the education and instruction of the orphans in the Holy Protestant Religion, and that they should be honestly maintained according to the capacity of the estate. It was further enacted that the several Judges of the respective Courts in remote counties in open Court, and on extraordinary occasions or, if necessary, out of Court, assisted with two Justices of the Peace, might grant probate of any will or letters of administration to any person where the estate exceeded the value of fifty pounds.

Testamentary dispositions of property were made before a judicial officer during the lifetime of the testator, and consequently probate after the testator's death was unnecessary. The method was primitive, but effective. The testator appeared in Court and stated to the Judges, who were the Schout and Sheppens, the disposition he wished to make of his property. This was entered upon the minutes, and, unless revoked, when he died the property was disposed of according to his recorded wishes. Beginning in 1685, wills were recorded in the book of deeds indiscriminately with grants of land and mortgages, and this practice continued down to 1778, nearly a year after the adoption of the first constitution. Hundreds of wills, however, were recorded in New York and Albany, and apparently it was the custom to have them recorded in either or both offices until 1786, when testamentary dispositions were proved before the Court of Common Pleas and an entry of the record was made in a book kept for that purpose, "agreeable to an Act of the Legislature of the State of New York, passed on the Fourth day of April, 1786." A Surrogate's Court was established in 1787, and the first will proven in that court bears date January 5th, 1787, and was recorded on the 10th day of May of that year. The first Surrogate was Joseph Gasherie, whose seal, now the seal of the Surrogate's Court, was an oblong oval after the pattern of the seals of the old Ecclesiastical Courts, and contained the figure of a woman, holding a child by the hand, standing near a monument the finial ornament of which was a mortuary urn. A device evidently intended to furnish in realistic suggestion what it lacked in artistic conception.

I can hardly speak too highly of the care taken by Dr. Anjou in preparing this work. Every precaution seems to have been taken against error. Not only is the work authentic, but official, and a properly certified copy of any of the records it contains can at any time be obtained from the official in whose custody the original record is kept at an insignificant cost without the long, laborious and expensive search which the effort to find records of this character usually involves, and when thus procured and certified it will be admissible in evidence in any Court of justice in any civilized country of the world, while the work itself can be cited as authoritative and decisive upon genealogical questions by all applicants for membership in the great patriotic and historic societies of this country. Thus it is and will be invaluable not only to the historians, antiquarians and genealogists of the day and of all time, but to every person descended from those ancestors who gave to Ulster a unique distinction among the counties of America.

PREFACE.

*

The first two volumes of ULSTER COUNTY PROBATE RECORDS, now presented, consist of careful, verbatim abstracts of wills, letters of administration after intestates, bonds of administrators, renunciations, and inventories from 1663 to 1766, 1792 and 1827, respectively, on file or deposited in the offices of the County Clerk of Ulster County, at Kingston, the Surrogate of Ulster County, at Kingston, the Surrogate of New York, the Library of the Long Island Historical Society, or in hands of private individuals, who courteously have permitted a transcript to be taken for publication.

A large proportion of these records were written in the Dutch language, and a few wills were in French. Of all these a careful copy has been made, comparison made with the original records, and a literal English translation given. In the translation of the Dutch records, the compiler has had the assistance of several Dutch scholars.

The official translation of the Dutch records at Kingston includes only a small part of the wills and deeds, written in the Dutch language, and not one of those recorded in the Deed- or Will-Books.

Ulster wills, filed in the office of the Surrogate at New York, have ben rendered in a new translation, as the abstracts thereof, which were issued by the New York Historical Society, are neither correct nor complete, or in any way reliable.

About 250 wills relating to Ulster, and not included in these volumes, are filed in Albany; a careful abstract, Dutch and English, will be printed in the third volume of Ulster County Probate Records, which will also contain wills probated in New York from 1766, and in Kingston from 1793.

In the compilation of the list of Dutch and Frisian baptismal names, the compiler has had the assistance of several Dutch scholars, and it is believed this list is the most complete so far issued.

The genealogical and historical data can, in the main, be accepted as reliable, as the compiler has depended principally upon public documents, i. e., parish registers, land-papers, and similar records. The words "married after" indicate that banns were issued on that date, the marriage probably taking place soon after. It is curious to note, however, that the Secretary's papers frequently contain statements from which it would appear as if the marriage was performed previous to the publication of banns.

Variations of surnames have been properly noted, and carefully indicated, both in the text and in the indexes; married daughters have been indexed both under the paternal surname and the names of their husbands. Children have, as a rule, been indexed under all the surnames which the Dutch system of nomenclature permitted them to adopt, unless known by a certain name, under which they then will be found.

The separate index of instruments, with name of testators, or intestate, character of document, date of issue and date of probate, all arranged alphabetically, will be found useful. Surnames relating to the same family, although the spelling may vary, have been placed under one heading and proper cross-references made to this heading.

The compiler is indebted to Messrs. Gerritt H. Van Wagenen, Thomas G. Evans, B. Fernow, Wm. Gordon Ver Planck, Eugene F. McPike, H. O. Collins, Frank J. Conkling, and Geo. A. Morrison, Jr., for genealogical data; to Messrs. Arthur C. Connelly and John D. Fratsher for assistance in comparing these abstracts with the original records, and to many others for help and encouragement.

The Inventories, it is hoped, will throw much new light upon the home life, the habits and possessions of the early inhabitants of Ulster County. As a rule, few books were found in the colony, and these consisted mainly of the great Bible, generally Dutch, psalm-books, and sermons. In only one inventory do we find a Virgil, Young's Night Thoughts, and other books of similar character. "A Pair of Humspun Breeches" gives us an idea of the industrial life among the early inhabitants. Spinning wheels, evidently, were found in every family. The necessity for protection against the Indians, and the hunt, made "guns" of all descriptions necessary. Every family of any importance had slaves, male and female, and it is curious to note that one testator, called to New York to fight against the "oppressors (the English) who wish to place them under slavery," should continue his tirade with the statement that his "slaves are not to be free."

Rent was paid in "marketable winter or summer wheat." "Green rugs" frequently occurs in the inventories. Pewter, or "puter," was the most common metal used, but silver spoons and forks were not uncommon. Knee breeches and knee-buckles, waistcoats, and shoe buckles for the men, petticoats, short gowns, check aprons, white linen stockings, and black hoods for the women, were the garments most frequently mentioned. After the Revolution, we find mention of guns, swords, "baginets," conduce boxes, and powder horns.

The old English system of giving to the eldest son some small personal property, as "his right for being my first born," prevailed until late. The testators, as a rule, were deeply religious, and their testaments invariably contain a long religious preamble, in which the testator gives his soul to his "Redeemer and Saviour," trusting that, notwithstanding his sins, he will arise on the day of judgment. Outfits for the unmarried daughters were frequently provided for, and a careful perusal of these documents will convince the reader of the generous sense of justice to all related to the testator, which prevails. In only a few cases, some member of the family has been cut off with the proverbial shilling.

From a letter, written by Lord Cornbury to Secretary Hodges, we find that

"The trade of the Province, in 1705, consists chiefly of flower and bisketts, which is sent to the Islands in the West Indies, in return they bring Rum, Sugar, Molasses, and sometimes pieces of Eight, and Cocoa, and Logwood; to Europe Our people send Skins of all sort, Whale Oyle and Bone."

(Extract from Lord Cornbury's letter to Secr. Hodges, London Documents, XVI.)

Governor Moore, in an official letter to the Lords of Trade, written in 1767, stated that "every family makes a coarse cloth called lindsey-woolsey, the warp being of linen and the woof of wool. Every family is furnished with a loom, and the itinerant weavers who travel about the country, put a finishing-hand to the work."

Looms were frequently mentioned in the wills and inventories, as well as izer, or wafer-irons, which were favorite wedding presents, and often decorated with the coat-of-arms of the groom, together with his initials and those of his bride, and the date of their marriage.

The compiler would be indebted for any genealogical or historical data, relating to families mentioned in Ulster County Probate Records, which have not been brought out in the text, particularly baptisms, marriages and deaths. Wills in the hands of private parties, if placed at the disposal of the compiler, will be copied, properly translated, if necessary, and printed in the third volume of these records.

GUSTAVE ANJOU.

New York, 1906.

FAC-SIMILES OF SIGNATURES.

FAC-SIMILE OF SIGNATURES.

1784 Gilbert Livingston	Dirck Swart 1788
1788 Cor.s E. Schoonmaker	Peter Coutant 1791
1791 Samuel Wyatt	Samuel Finley 1791
1791 James M. Hughey	Cadwallader Colden 1792
1792 Alex.r Colden	Thomas Colden 1792
1792 Margaret Bell	Cornelius Schout 1792
1791 Corn.s Roosa	Nicholas Hardenbergh 1787
1791 David Rinehart	Jacob Rinehart 1795
1788 Abraham DeLameter	Elias Lunsbery 1791
1789 Rich.d Lounsbery	Simon Dubois 1789
1748 Mattys Persen	Abraham Persen 1763
1771 Johannis Snyder	Cornelius Persen 1771
1771 Stephanus Fero	Corneles N. Persen 1781
1781 Huybert Ostrander	Jacobus Depuy 1778
1780 W.m Legg	

VOL. II. FAC-SIMILES OF SIGNATURES.

DUTCH AND FRISIAN BAPTISMAL NAMES AND THEIR EQUIVALENTS IN ENGLISH.

A

Aaghie, Agatha,
Aagje, Agatha,
Aagt, Agatha,
Aaltje, Alice,
Aart, Arthur,
Adda, Alice,
Adelheyd, Adelaide,
Adriance, Adrienne,
Adriaantje, Adrian,
Aefje, Eva,
Aeltje, Alice,
Aert, Arthur,
Aetje, Eve,
Agnietje, Agnes,
Agt, Agatha,
Alberick, Alberic,
Aldert, Albert,
Aletta, Alice,
Alewijn, Alwin,
Alyd, Adelaide,
Alta, Alida,
Annatje, Anne,
Andreas, Andrew,
Andries, Andrew,
Anghe, Agnes,
Angeniete, Agnes,
Annechet, Anne,
Anneken, Anne,
Annetje, Anne,
Antie, Anne,
Antje, Anne,
Arendt, Arnold,
Ariaan, Adrian,
Arie, Adrian,
Arriaantje, Adrian,
Augustijn, Austen,

B

Badeloch, Beatrice,
Balt, Balthazar,
Baltje, Balthazar,
Baltus, Balthazar,
Barber, Barbara,
Barend, Bernard,
Barent, Barent,
Bart, Bartholomew,
Bartel, Bartholomew,
Bartelmus, Bartholomew,
Bartje, Barbara,
Bastian, Sebastian,
Batje, Bathilde,
Beeltje, Neeltje, Cornelia,
Beletje, Arabella,
Bell, Isabella,
Bella, Isabella,
Bernd, Bernard,
Bert, Gilbert,
Bertus, Albertus,
Beth, Elizabeth,
Betje, Elizabeth,
Blaas, Blasius,
Boudje, Baldwin,
Boldwijn, Baldwin,
Bonifaas, Boniface,
Boudewyn, Baldwin,
Bram, Abraham,
Bregje, Bridget,

C

Carel, Charles,
Case, Cornelius,
Casper, Jasper,
Catrijn, Catharine,
Ceerles, Charles,
Celia, Cecilia,
Cheerelz, Charles,
Cheiltje, Cornelia,
Chime, James,
Christoffel, Christopher,
Christyntje, Christina,
Claasje, Clasine,
Claes, Nicholas,
Coen, Conrad,
Coenraad, Conrad,
Coenraadt, Conrad,
Cornelis, Cornelius,
Crispijn, Crispin,

D

Daaf, David,
Daam, Adam,
Daatje, Alice,
Denys, Dionysius,
Derrick, Theodoric,
Desin, Gerardina,
Diederick, Theodoric,
Dientje, Bernardina,
Diewertje, Debora,
Dina, Bernardina,
Dirk, Theodoric,
Dirkje, Theodoric,
Dolf, Adolphus,
Door, Dorothy,
Doortje, Dorothy,
Doostie, Theodosia,
Dort, Dorothy,
Dortchen, Dora,
Dorus, Theodore,
Dries, Andrew,

E

Eefje, Eve,
Eelet, Helena,
Eike, Agnes,
Els, Aletta,
Elsje, Aletta,
Emmetje, Emily,
En, Anne,
Engel, Angelica,
Engelina, Angelica,
Engeltje, Angelica,
Enrik, Henry,
Epje, Egbert,
Ethilrede, Awdry,
Evert, Everard,
Eyntje, Annie,
Eytie, Ida,

F

Femmetje, Frances, Fanny,
Fick, Sophia,
Fletje, Sophia,
Floortje, Florentina,
Florentijntje, Florentina,
Floris, Florian,
Francijntje, Frances, Fanny,
Francina, Fanny,
Frans, Francis,
Fransje, Frances, Fanny,
Freek, Frederick,
Frem, Ephraim,
Frerk, Frederick,
Friko, Frederick,
Frits, Frederic,
Fytje, Sophia,

G

Garret, Gerard,
Geerje, Gertrude,
Geert, Gerard,
Geertie, Gertrude,
Geertje, Gertrude,
Geertrui, Gertrude,
Geertruida, Gertrude,
Geertruyd, Gertrude,
Geesje, Gerarda,
Geleyn, Giles,
Gellis, Giles,
Gepje, Rachel,
Gerrit, Gerard,
Gerritje, Geraldina,
Giel, Michael,
Gijs, Gilbert,
Gijsbertus, Gilbert,
Godfried, Godfrey,
Goris, George,
Goverd, Godfrey, Timothy,
Griet, Margaret, Madge, Peg,
Grietje, Meg, Peggy,
Guido, Guy,
Gysbert, Gilbert,
Gyslbert, Gilbert,

H

Hannes, John, Jackie,
Hans, John, Jack,
Hansje, Joan, Johanna,
Harck, Hercules,
Harmen, Herman,
Hein, Henry,
Heintje, Henry,
Hendrica, Henriette,
Hendrikje, Henriette,
Hentje, Henriette,
Heyltje, Helena,
Hieronimus, Jerome,
Hilligond, Hilda,
Hilletje, Hilda,
Hiskia, Hezekiah,
Huigen, Hugo,
Huybert, Hubert,

I

Ifje, Eve,
Ikcc, Agnes,

J

Jaantje, Jane,
Jaap, Jacob,

Jaapje, Jacob,
Jacob, James,
Jacoba, Jacobina,
Jacobje, Jacob,
Jacobus, James,
Jacomyntje, Jemima,
Jaepje, Jacob,
Jan, John,
Janneken, Jane,
Jannetje, Jane,
Janotje, Jane,
Jansje, Jane,
Jantina, Jane,
Jantje, Johnny,
Japic, Jacob,
Jeremias, Jeremiah,
Jeronimus, Jerome,
Jetje, Henriette,
Joannes, John,
Joaptie, Jacob,
Jobje, Jacob,
Jochem, Joachim,
Johannes, John,
Joost, Justin, Joseph,*
Joris, George,
Josyntje, Josine,
Juliaantje, Juliana,
Jurgen, George,
Jurian, George,
Jurn, George,
Jurrian, George,
Jury, George,
Justin, Justin,
Justje, Jenny,

K

Kaat, Catharine,
Kaatje, Kate, Kitty,
Karel, Charles,
Kareltje, Charles,
Katrijn, Catharine,
Katryntje, Kate, Kathleen,
Kee, Cornelia,
Kees, Cornelius,
Keesje, Cornelius,
Keetje, Cornelia,
Kersten, Christian,
Kesia, Kathleen,
Klaar, Clare,
Klaartje, Clare,
Klaas, Nicholas,
Klaasje, Nicholas, Nick,
Krelis, Cornelius,
Ko, James, Jemmy, Jem,
Koba, Jacobus,
Koosje, Jacobina,
Koris, Cornelius,
Korsten, Christian,
Krelius, Cornelius,
Kris, Christian,
Krischan, Christian,
Krisje, Christina,
Kristel, Christina,
Kristijntje, Christina,
Kruschen, Christian,
Kyrn, Quirine,

L

Lambrecht, Lambert,
Laurens, Lawrence,
Leen, Leonard,
Leendert, Leonard,

Leentje, Magdalena,
Lena, Magdalena,
Lenoor, Eleanor,
Letje, Adeline,
Lezart, Elise,
Lieve, Leo,
Lijsbert, Lisbet,
Lijsje, Lise,
Lodewijk, Lewis,
Lotje, Charlotte,
Loures, Lewis,
Louw, Lawrence,
Lucia, Lucy,
Ludovicus, Louis,
Lukas, Luke,
Luytje, Luke,
Lys, Lisbet,
Lysbet, Lisbet,
Lysje, Lise,

M

Maaicke, Mary,
Maarten, Martin,
Maartje, Martina,
Maas, Bartholomew,
Machiel, Michael,
Machteld, Mathilda,
Magdaleentje, Magdalen,
Magtelt, Mathilda,
Manus, Herman,
Margit, Margaret,
Margriet, Margaret,
Margrietje, Margaret,
Marij, Maria, Mary,
Maritje, Mary,
Mariken, Mary,
Marregante, Magdalena,
Marritius, Morice,
Martijn, Martin,
Martijntje, Martina,
Mattheus, Matthew,
Matthys, Matthew,
Maybe, Maria, Mary,
Mayken, Maria, Mary,
Mayacca, Mary,
Meewes, Bartholomew,
Menassus, Myndert,
Metie, Matilda,
Metjen, Martha,
Michiel, Michael,
Micheltjen, Michael,
Mie, Mary,
Mietje, Mary,
Mijntje, Wilhelmina, Mimmi,
Morice, Maurice
(but in one instance, Maria),

N

Na, Nanny,
Naatje, Anne,
Neeltje, Cornelia,
Niesje, Dionyse,
Nol, Arnold,

O

Obadja, Obadiah,
Olivier, Oliver,
Oeycke, Agnes,
Oetje, Agnes,
Orselina, Ursula,
Outie, Agnes,

P

Paultje, Pauline,

Paylyntie, Pauline,
Phlip, Philip,
Piet, Peter,
Pieter, Peter,
Pietje, Petronella,
Pouw, Paul,
Powles, Paul,

R

Randolph, Randal,
Reimond, Raymond,
Reindert, Reynold,
Reinier, Reynold,
Reinoud, Reynold,
Resyntje, Rosina,
Rijkaard, Richard,
Rijkerd, Richard,
Rip, Rupert,
Ritsert, Richard,
Robbert, Robert,
Roedolf, Rudolphus,
Roeland, Rowland,
Roelof, Rolph, Ralph,
Rogier, Roger,
Rolfe, Ralph,
Rombout, Rumbold,
Roosje, Roseta,
Rozemond, Rosamund,
Ruben, Reuben,
Rut, Roger,
Rutgert, Roger,
Rutsjert, Richard,
Rykaard, Richard,

S

Saal, Solomon,
Saam, Samuel,
Saar, Sarah,
Saartje, Sally,
Sander, Alexander,
Sanna, Susannah,
Sanneke, Susanna,
Santje, Susanna,
Sannertje, Susanna,
Sasze, Sara,
Sefia, Sophia,
Seletje, Cecilia,
Selie, Cecilia,
Servaas, Gervas,
Seytie, Cynthia,
Shaan, Christian,
Sierrity, Charity,
Sijmen, Simeon,
Simson, Samson,
Sitske, Cynthia,
Smiaa, Hezekiah,
Staats, Eustace,
Stans, Constance,
Steven, Stephen,
Stijntje, Christina,
Stoffel, Christopher,
Styntje, Christina,

T

Taatje, Sara,
Tanna, Anna,
Tanneken, Anne,
Teeuw, Matthew,
Teeuwis, Matthew,
Teunis, Anthony,
Teuntje, Antonia,
Thys, Matthias,

---

* See Joseph German's will.

Tiebout, Theobald,
Tientje, Albertina,
Tietje, Albertina,
Tijmen, Timothy,
Tijs, Matthias,
Tiletje, Albertina,
Tit, Tietje, Albertina,
Tjaatje, Charity,
Tjerck, Theodorick,
Tobias, Toby,
Toff, Christopher,
Toffels, Christopher,
Tomatius, Timothy,
Tonjes, Anthony,
Tonnes, Anthony,
Tool, Anthony,
Toon, Anthony,
Toontje, Antoinette,
Tressje, Theresa, Tracy,

Trijn, Catherine,
Trui, Gertrude,
Truitje, Gertrude,
Tryntje, Catharine,
Tsassen, Christian,
Tziasso, Christian,
Tymen, Timothy,

U

Urseltje, Ursula,
Ury, George.

V

Valentijn, Valentine,
Veltje, Valentine,

W

Willem, William,
Willemintje, Wilhelmina,

Willempje, Willy,
Willemtje, Wilhelmina,
Willemyn, Wilhelmina,
Wim, William, Willy,
Wimpje, Wilhelmina, Mimmi,
Wout, Walter,
Wouter, Walter,
Wyntje, Wilhelmina, Mimmi,

Y

Ydtje, Ida,
Yke, Agnes,
Yzaak, Isaac,

Z

Zanneke, Susan,
Zjarritjen, Charity,

ABBREVIATIONS.

Adm............. administration,
b................born,
bt............... baptized,
d................died,
dau.............daughter,
d. inf............died in infancy,
d. y............. died young,
E............... east,
int.............. intestate,
j. d..............young woman,
j. m.............young man,
Jr................Junior,
K................Kingston,
m................married,
               (m.—name of wife, or husband, within a parenthesis, indicates a probable, but not absolutely proved marriage),
m. 1.............married, first,
m. 2.............married, secondly,
N................ north,
N. Y.............New York,
N. Y. Sur........New York Surrogate,
p................page,
prob............. probably,
q. v............. quo vide (which see),
s................son,
S............... South,
Sr...............Senior,
supra............before,
w............... wife,
W...............West,

Abstracts of Wills on File in the County Clerk's Office, City of Kingston, N. Y.

*

(The Dutch records of Ulster County from 1663 to 1684 consist of six volumes of court proceedings, and five volumes of secretary's papers, containing deeds, mortgages, wills, etc., all kept in a square wooden box, under lock and key. A translation of these records was made in 1896, which was subsequently bound in three large folio-volumes. Unfortunately, there is no index to these volumes, which makes them practically inaccessible to the general searcher. In the Report of the Public Archives Commission of the American Historical Association, 1900, II., p. 77, attention was called to a few errors, "as a rule unimportant" and "easily corrected" in case the translations should be printed." While the official translation has been utilized, a careful comparison with the original records has been made, and great care has been observed in securing the proper meaning intended by the testators).

SECRETARY'S PAPERS.

Translations of Dutch Records, Liber l., p. 91.

Sept. 18, 1663.—The Court resolved: Whereas persons were killed during the troubles on June 7th last, which persons had no relatives, therefore the Court will administer their property:

SEBA, WILLEM JANSEN, servant.
LOOMAN, HENDRICK JANSEN, brewer's assistant.
WILLEMSEN, DIRRICK, inhabitant.

The Court appoints as administrators: *Albert Gysbertsen* and *Tjerck Claesen De Witt*, commissaries.

"Inventory of the estate of *Hendr. Looman:* A horse, being a gelding, a brewing kettle, 1 sword and belt, 1 trunk without key, with contents: 1 letter case with book of accounts, 1 old gray suit, 1 old gray-colored pair of pants, 1 new gray suit, 2 pair of black woollen stockings, 1 new black hat, 1 hat box, 1 pipe of lead, 4 small pieces of *Haarlem* cloth, 1 cloth brush, 1 square cravat, 2 ties, 3 handkerchiefs, 1 package of about 1 pound lead, 1 wagon frame with iron tires."

Page 93.—*Cornelius Barentsen Slecht,* refusing to give an account to the local court of the estate of *Willem Jansen Seba,* was arrested by order of said court, and confined at the house of the Schout, *Roelof Swartwout,* until willing to render an account. Dated Oct. 9, 1663.

Page 272.—On March 3, 1665, *Jacob Burhans* was appointed curator for the estates of *Hendrick Jansen Looman* and *Willem Jansen Seba.*

※

Page 120.—October 30, 1663.—*Aeltje Claes* requested that the estate of deceased *Claesje Teunissen* be administered. The Court appoints *Matthew Capito* to make an inventory. On repairing to the house of the deceased, *Roeloff Swartwout* and *Matthew Capito* were told by Aeltje Claes and "the eldest daughter of the deceased," that "the domine had arranged everything" and that they "ought to go to the domine."

※

Page 127.—*Tjerck Claessen De Witt,* on Nov. 26, 1663, deposits with the court an inventory, taken on Nov. 14, 1663, of the estate of his brother-in-law, *Jan Albertse Van Steenwyck,* requesting that a curator be appointed and a guardian over the minor children. This was first referred to the Domine, *Hermanus Blom,* and the court afterwards appointed *Tjerck Claessen De Witt,* and *Evert Pels* curators, and *Hendrick Jochemsen, T. C. De Witt, and E. P.,* guardians.

※

Page 184.—July 10, 1664.—*Sweerus Teunissen,* successor of *Jan Barentsen Wemp,* deceased, requests his money from *Aert Pietersen Tack,* who has left this place, because he is the principal creditor of said Aert Pietersen Tack, and further requests that the estate of Aert Pietersen Tack be sold to satisfy a mortgage.

Page 227.—Dec. 18, 1664.—*Aeltje Wygert,* widow of *Albert Gysbertsen,* deceased, appeared before *Gysbert Van Imbrock, Jan Willemsen Hoochteylingh,* Scheepens, about a heifer which her husband had bought from the estate of *Aert Pietersen Tack.*

※

Page 237.—Jan. 27, 1665.—Petition of the guardians of the minor children of *Mattys Jansen,* deceased.

Page 254.—*Roeloff Swartwout* appears as guardian of said children.

Page 354.—*Roeloff Swartout* and *Cornelius Barentsen Slecht* appear as guardians of above children.

※

Page 300.—Sept. 7, 1665.—*Jacob Kip,* brother-in-law of Mr. *Gysbert Van Imbrock* (surgeon of *Wildwyck,* widower of *Rachel Monjeur de la Montagne* (who died Oct., 1664), who also died Aug. 19/29, last, leaving three minor children, a daughter named *Lysbet,* now about 6 years old, two small sons, the eldest named *Johannes,* about 4 years old, and *Gysbert,* about 1 year old), deceased, brought to the court "the last wishes of said deceased, signed by said deceased, and also an authorization from *Johannes La Montagne, Sr.,* father-in-law of said deceased, that they administer to the estate, the deceased having left three minor children." The court appointed Jacob Kip and Johannes la Montagne guardians of the children.

Inventory taken September 1st, 1665, of the effects of Mr. *Gysbert Van Imbroch* in the presence of the Hon. Heer *Willem Beeckman*, Schout, *Jan Willemsen Hoochteylingh* and *Jan Joosten*, deacons at *Wildwyck*, having been requested to do so by the aforesaid *Gysbert Van Imbroch* during his life.

Two beds, Two head-pillows, Four cushions, One child's bed, Two new green blankets, belonging to *William Montagnie*, Three green worn out blankets, Three white blankets, Two curtains with a top piece (valletje) on the bed-stead, One bed-stead (ledecant) half surrounded by curtains.

IN AN OLD CHEST.

Two pieces of black cloth, together 4 ells, One "ninocent" of black cloth. One pair of trousers, made of black cloth, One man's suit of clothes, made of gray cloth, One leather coat, with silver and gold bands, A black turkish coarse grained (grof greyne) man's suit of clothes, An old suit of clothes made of black cloth, (man's), A pair of half worn black silk man's stockings, An orange colored sarsenet sanative girdle (orangie armosyne gesondheyt), A cloak made of black cloth, A cloak made of grey cloth, Five silver spoons, One silver head dress, found in a green box, One silver thimble, Two pieces of silver and gold ribbon, One piece of blue silk ribbon, One child's chain (kinderkettinje) of braided black and white seewan, in a small white box inside the little green box, Two diamond rings, Two womens knives made of silver in a tube (kooher), A silver platter (may also mean scale) (schaele), Four (4) pieces of narrow silk ribbon, bordered with lace, A small piece of narrow silver and gold band wound around a small piece of wood, belonging to *W. Montagnie*. A colored coarse grained skirt with green lining, A colored reversible skirt with green lining (weereshynde vrouwerock), A red scarlet (roode scharlaken) skirt, A black coffee waist or jacket, A colored coarse grained waist with nonpareil binding (or jacket), A black coarse grained tabard, made of silk, with the bottom piece (methetonderote), stuff for an apron black sarsenet (kind of cloth), Two black sarsenet capes or hoods, A colored sarsey waist, (probably jersey), A colored sarsey apron, a beaver muff, An old beaver muff, A woman's testament (bible) with silver clasps, A velvet cape or hood, A wig with a wreath, A woman's fan, A white woolen swaddling cloth, (cap-luyer), Two white woolen dipers, One black colored. stomacher, One old "bornlyf" (probably "bovenlyf" meaning waist), Two cosmetics, one black, one pair white leather woman's gloves, Another woman's fan, Five white hoods.

IN AN OLD NAPKIN.

Two round handkerchiefs, bordered with lace, A round handkerchief of cambric bordered with lace, A white round handkerchief of velvet (vloers) A square handkerchief, Three gowns (nederstucken) with bands, Five gowns (nederstucken) without bands, Two night neck kerchiefs.

TIED IN A NAPKIN.

Two white child's hoods with little flaps, Five child's over-hoods (boven mutsjes) Two child's kerseys, Five breast-shirts (Borst hemdjes) Eight white child's hoods. Seven child's ruffles, Two child's bibs, One white swaddle (swachteltje), Two old sanatory girdles, Two pairs of woman's ruffles, Four child's beast-coats, One pair of child's stockings.

One pair of gray woolen stockings, Two pair of Frieze stockings, Four sheets, Nine bands, Three ruffles, Two man's linen caps, Six pillow cases, Three woman's shirts, Two white woman's aprons, Three more pillow cases, Seven man's shirts, One sheet, Three cravats, Four man's handkerchiefs, Seventeen small napkins, Two large napkins, One table cloth, Two shaving towels, Another old man's shirt, Another small napkin, Another cravat, Three old white linnen capes (capers) or hoods, five more man's handkerchiefs, One colored towel, (bont hand doeckje), Two colored (bont) pillow cases, A box made of silk and ribbons for female utensils (vrouwen gereetschap), Another small napkin, An old velvet lamp covering (lamper) perhaps lamfer meaning crape or mourning hat-band. 11¼ ells of white linnen, 34 ells of ossenbrugs linen, A small psalm book with silver clasps, A little bag containing in seewan one hundred twenty five gldrs nine stivers Some papers in a little white bag with the directions to have them examined Seven books being debtors accounts and memorials besides some papers covered with writing, A yellow medicine chest with some contents, in which medicine chest are deposited in the lower second portion the separation, division, settlement and valuation of the estate and income belonging to the orphans of *Rachel DeFereest*, dec'd. Further account and declaration of the receipts and expenditures before the orphan chamber of the City of *Leydenhad* and made in regard to the effects and revenues belonging to the children left by *Rachel DeForeest* and her husband *Jan Mony DelaMontagne*, A white medicine chest with some contents, a plate with eight razors and five pairs of scissors, Three firelocks, One gun-barrel, Two swords, One game-bag, One shot bag with a powder horn and belt, One comb-holder with five combs.

IN A SMALL KEG COVERED WITH DEER-SKIN.

Three small bags with fine shot, A small bag with bullets and flints, Three small bags with powder,

One box with senna leaves and other herbs, A skin-iron (velyrer), A box with wafers, A barber's saw, A desk with a few papers, Two tick tack tables, An old leather doublet with a pair of red drawers, A pair of old serge pants, A old vest of red cloth, Three hats, A pair of woman's shoes, Two pairs of children's shoes, Two pair of man's shoes, One pair of skates, One little bag with pepper, One little basket with white starch, Eight large tankards, Two window panes in two detached frames, Four small staves of lead, Thirty six small tankards, A saddle and bridle and a pair a straps and a pair of old man's shoes, A cellar with a bottle wherein there is a little oil.

DEPOSITED IN A TRUNK.

A keg with papers and letters, Nine pair of stockings, One pair of gloves, One blue truss, One perpetual almanac, One gray fur cap, (written carpuysin in the original evidently meaning karpoets), one beaver, One otter, Five old pictures, Six tin dishes, One tin bowl, Twelve tin plates, A wine glass with pewter foot, A tin mustard pot, A small tin saucer, A mustard saucer, A tin salt-cellar, A mortar with the stamper, A small tin beaker with a small liquor glass, A pot-hook, A copper frying pan, A grid-iron, A tong, An iron chandelier with two branches (or candlestick), A ladle, Two iron candle-snuffers, A hatchet, A skimmer, A copper candle-stick, A tin plate, olive oil can, a large carving knife, a carrying strap (draeghband) or shoulder belt, A glass or window washer, A small hammer, A pair of ice spurs, A whet stone, A riding-spur, A pad lock without key, Two gimlets, A copper compass, A pot, Two small boxes with some black lace, Another carrying strap, or shoulder belt, A piece of cotton, Another small hammer, Some red paint in a piece of cloth, In a leather bag some blue starch, Two child's hoods or roller, A child's coat as made by the savages (wilde Kinderrockje), Two "carpoese" as used by the savages (karpoets—fur cap), A small basket with some sundry articles and patch work or remnants, A bag containing eleven sacks, a copper kettle, a can filled with oil, A pall, A half aem (20 gallons) of anisette, belonging to *W. La Montagnie*, A small keg with French wine it being sour, A barber's grind stone with its frame, A pulley (block) with a rope, A keg with butter, A butt-end or stick of a musket (kolve), A cane, A East India bedspread, A little keg about half filled with soap,

ON THE LOFT.

5½ sch. wheat, 130 sch. of oats, One sch. of rye,

SEPT. 2.

A bear skin, Two hairy deerskins used for chair cushions, One prepared deerskin, Three white earthen-ware cups, A white earthen-ware basin for shaving, or shaving dish, A copper basin used for shaving, or shaving dishes, A elyster syringe, Three pair of copper scales with the balances, A flat lead ink stand, (platte loode inct kooker), a pocket pistol, A beer faucet, A tin pump, A leather suspender, A broken glass lantern, Six grey hats, Two ink stands of lead, Three pounds of copper house-weights (huisgervicht), One pound of lead weights, Five pairs of cargo shoes, Another faucet,

A DUTCH BIBLE IN FOLIO.

Folio
- History of *Emanuel Van Meteren*
- *Titus Livius*, in Dutch
- Medicine book of *Christopher Wirtsungh*.
- Medicine book of *Ambrosius Paree*.
- Medicine book of *Johannes De Viga*
- Book on the mixing of wine
- A Versaly & Valuerda Anatomy.
- Frederick Henry of Nassau, his life and works.

Quarto
- *Johan Sarcharson*, General exhibit (vertoninge) of Holy Writ
- Bacchus Wonderworks (Wonderwercken)
- *Bernhard Van Zutphen* Practice.
- *Sebastian Frank's* World's mirror.
- Receuil of *Amsterdam*.
- A German (work on) medicine and products of art (Kunststucke).
- A written medicine book.
- Another written medicine book.
- A German manual of the Catholic Faith.
- Another written medicine book.
- Redress of the nobility of Holland by *Johan Geul*.

Octavo
- Two books on the perfection and perspicuity of the Word of God by *Albert Hutteman*.
- A French catechism.
- Bee-hive of *Aldegonde*.
- Arithmetic by *Jan Belot Dieppois*.
- Chronicles of the lives and works of the Kings of England.
- Medical remarks by *Nicolaes Tulp*.
- German medical manual by *Q. Apollinaren*.
- d'Argenis by *J. Barcklaj*.
- Confession of faith by *P. Paulus Van Venetien*.
- Treatise on the faith by *Henry Hexman*.
- Examination of Surgery by Mr. *Cornelis Herls*.
- A written medicine and student book.
- German song book.
- Book on surgery without a title.
- Arithmetic by *Sybrand Hansen Cardinael*.

Secretary's Papers. 25

Duodecimo	Characteristics of the children of God, *Jan Taffin*. The Golden harp. Royal road to heaven. Two tracts by *Petrus Molinej*.
16 mo.	Meditations on the 51st Psalm. Twelve "Devotions" by *Philip Kegel* in German.
School Books in Quarto	8 Stories of David. 3 Last Wills. 7 Hours of death. 17 Beautiful (heerlycke) (or exquisite) proofs of man's Misery (ellende). 3 General Epistles.
School Books in Octavo.	100 Catechisms. 23 Stories of Joseph 102 A. B. C. books 27 Arts of Letters. 19 large "Succinct Ideas" 20 small "Succinct Ideas" 9 "steps" (trappen) of youth. 13 proofs of human misery. 8 Books of the Gospel and the Epistles. 48 "Succinct Ideas" by *Jacobus Borstius*. 1 "Short way" by Megapolensis.	These were "question books" to teach children religion and in some quarters are even yet used in Holland.

8 small A. B. C. books on parchment, Three small gardener's manuals, Two writing books which are clean and without writing, Two paintings for chimney coverings wrapped in gray paper, 15 unframed pictures, One picture book, 38 small metal mirrors, 37 wooden combs in 2 small boxes, One barber's case with instruments, One penknife, One bottle of tragacanth vinegar, One bottle with perfumery or fumigating matter (fumative goet), Five molds for casting bullets, A little glass with juniper oil, A small glass with yellow medicine, A tankard, Three pressed woman's bonnets, Some nails and iron work, A bar of Spanish soap, Some candle grease, A large powderhorn with powder, Some pints, Three medical syringes, One clothes bush, Two old table books (tafelbockjes), 17 figuring pens, A box with sundry articles, consisting of needle, thimbles, bullets, and other small things, A small keg with some hops, Some papers in a drawer in the stove room.

IN A ROUND BOX RESERVED FOR THE CHILDREN INTRUSTED TO THE CARE OF ALBERT JANSEN VAN STEENWYCK.

Eleven shirts, A small waist, A yellow and a white breast coat or guernsey shirt, apron, a pair of pants, two small round handkerchiefs, a serge bodice, three more sanative girdles, a yellow apron a white apron, serge bodice, two pair ———, two small ruffles, small stockings, a hood for a girl, two collars, five bibs, three bands, four handkerchiefs, two pair of front ruffles (voormouwtje), five pocket handkerchiefs, A small red night gown.

A mirror in the stove room, A till, A copper shaving basin, A watch, Three wood bins, A schepel (Dutch measure equal in those days to 2/5 bushel), a scoop, a clothes line, some wood in a barrel, A church pew, A pipecan (pypkan) without screw, A flour sieve, A bar of iron used for the purpose of suspending pots and kettles above the fire, in the hearth fastened in the chimney (hang yser), Some whale oil in an open keg, as well as a tin half pint and a tin pint, Two iron pots full of whale oil, A faience can with some grape seed oil in it, A calabas with bear grease, A empty pot, an ancker of whale oil or other oil (an ancker—1/6 of a hogshead) Two axes, Two wash tubs one large and one small one, An oil can, Two milk tubs, One small empty iron pot, Two can cleaners, Two boxes of bunkers as made by the savages (wilde backen), A stone oil can, A tin half mud (measure), A tin funnel, A stone faience can, without handle, A tin saucer and two earthenware saucers, Two water-pails, An iron mortar with the stamper, A cooking pan, A large kettle, A high iron pot, An iron frying pan, A chain pot hanger, Two hearth irons, Two white iron lamps, another small copper kettle, A pair of tongs, An ash scoop, An old mole, A gridiron, A meat barrel, A round table, A bird cage, A water cask, A spade, A pepper drawer (peperlae), A salt barrel, Four earthenware saucers, An earthenware platter, An earthenware salt cellar, Two benches, Seven chairs, A barber's chair, A square table,

AFTERWARD SEPARATED FROM THE OTHER WASH AND PUT IN A BASKET.

Five small napkins, A blue shaving towel, Two white shaving towels, Two pillow cases, Two pocket handkerchiefs, Two pair of "povretten," Five bands (a kind of tie), Another man's handkerchief, A man's hood, A cravat, Two sheets, Three table cloths, Three napkins.

Two boars, one year old (twee jarige bergen), Three hogs, or sows, Two milch cows, An old buck, A young buck, A cow, Some pigeons, Some chickens, A fringed border and one made of colored ribbon around the mantle piece, A shovel or adre (schop ofte dissel), Three milk tubs sawed of ankers (a measure in the care of *Albert Jansen Van Steenwyck*), A yoke, A tin beaker, holding a half pint, Four tin spoons,

All of which aforenamed articles have been found and are stored in the deceased Mr. Gysbert Van Imbroch's own house, standing and situated in the village of Wildwyck with a garden annexed to it, surrounded with good palisades.

And taken at Wildwyck by us, the undersigned this 2d. day of September N. S. of the year 1665.

                            (Signed)   Will Beeckman,
In presence of me   Jan Willemsen. Hoochteylinch,
    (Signed)   Mattheus Capito,   Jan Joosten.
                 Secretary.

CONDITIONS AND TERMS

Whereupon the effects of the deceased *Mr. Gysbert Van Imbroch*, Surgeon, will be publicly sold to the highest bidder, by the appointed guardians of the minor children.

1st. The purchaser of any of the effects shall pay cash for said effects, or at least within six weeks.

2nd. The payment shall be made in good current sewan or in grain, at the following prices:
    The sch. of wheat at six gldrs.
    The sch. of rye at four gldrs. and a half.
    The sch. of buckwheat at three gldrs.
    The sch. of oats at two gldrs.
    The sch. of barley at four gldrs.
    The sch. of white peas at four gldrs.
    The sch. of gray peas at five gldrs.
And said grain to be delivered at the house where the deceased *Mr. Gysbert* died.

3rd. If any body pays within 24 hours (said purchaser) shall be entitled to a five percent. reduction, if not, shall be obliged to pay the full purchase money.

4th. The purchaser shall be obliged to furnish two sufficient sureties to the satisfaction of the sellers, and in case the purchaser cannot produce the same, similar effects shall be again put up for sale, and the expense for the same shall be borne by the first purchaser, and in case they should bring a higher price he shall not profit by the same.

5th. The stiver money shall fall and come to the charge of the purchaser in accordance with the local custom.

Thus done at Wildwyck this September 9th, N. S. of the year 1665.

WAS PUT UP.

A milch cow, for which was offered by *Jacob Kip*................................150 gldrs.
These remain fixed, and are (by the auctioneer) increased with 50 gldrs. and
    Hendrick Cornelissen Lyndraeyer became purchaser for....................180 gldrs.
Two milch goats and a young buck about 1 year old bought by) *Albert Govertsen*,
    securities, *Jan Willemsen* and *Walran*, for................................ 64 gldrs.
Thomas Chambers, a gelded buck for.. 22 gldrs.
Hendr. Cornelissen Lyndr. A Haymow with privilege of choice.................. 56 "
Rut Jacobsen another hay mow... 50 "
Willem Beeckman, Three winter hogs being two males and one female............ 21 "
Jan Jansen V. Oosterhout, Some chickens, as many as shall be found.............. 9 "
Willem Beeckman, Some pigeons under condition that they shall remain in the cot until the guardians shall find that they become a nuisance (dat de voogh-den bevinden haer hinderlyckte syn)... 15 "
Willem Montagnie, A flint lock with the game bag and mold for balls........... 68 "
Albert Jansen, A flint lock with the mould for casting mall.................... 55 "
Evert Pels, a flint lock... 37 "
Hend. Albertsen, A pocket pistol... 15 "
Albert Jansen, A sword with a belt... 12 "
Albert Jansen, A sword with a belt... 17 "
Cornelis Slecht, A small bag with powder... 45 "
Aert Martsen Doorn, A small bag with powder...................................... 17 "
Antoni Delva, Four small bags with small shot, ball and some flints............ 30 "
Henderick Albertsen, A piece of white linen, 11¼ ells at 8; 11................. 96 "
Aert Martensen, Ossenbrugs-linen 24 ells at 4; 6...............................103 gldrs. 4 st.
Long Jacob, A copper kettle.. 24 "
Jan Joosten, A large copper kettle... 40 "
Albert Govertsen, A small mended copper kettle................................... 6 "
Capito, A small iron pot... 18 "   10 st.
Albert Covertsen, A small flat iron pot.. 13 "
Tjerck Claesen, A suspending iron with a copper frying pan..................... 30 "
Joris Hael. An iron frying pan.. 7 "
Tjerck Claesen, A pair of tongs with a shovel.................................... 8 "
Roelof Swartw., A gridiron with a pair of tongs................................. 18 "   10 st.
Jan Jansen V. Amersfort, A schimmer or ladle, hatchet and iron spoon............. 9 "
Jan Willemsen, A candle stick, two irons and some cotton......................... 8 "   5 st.
Tjerck Claesen, Two beer faucets, two gimlets, a wine pump, a tin oil can...... 20 "
Walran DuMont, Two hearth irons, one chain pot hook............................. 41 "
J. Jansen, V. Amersfort, A wooden bunker with a lot of nails................... 12 "
Aert Martensen, A wood bunker with a lot of nails............................... 16 "   10 st.
Jan Joosten, A bunker, as used by the savages, with a lot of nails............. 28 "   10 st.
Albert Jansen, A flint lock.. 36 "
Jan Brabander, Two forest axes and adze a spade................................. 19 "
Lambert Huyberts, a black hat.. 31 "
Lambert Huyberts, A gray "carpoes" or fur cap................................... 16 "   10 st.
Jan Willemsen, An old gray hat... 5 "
Arent Jansen, A gray hat... 27 "
Jan Buyr, A leather coat with a pair of serge pants............................ 21 "
Lambert Huyberts, An old pair of red drawers, small old red coat, and an old black small coat... 18 "
Mrs. Bloems, A small Bag with pepper, and a small box with thimbles, needles and other (things)... 13 "

Secretary's Papers.   27

Jurioen Westphoel, A wooden bunker with a small gridiron.................... 11 gldrs. 10 st.
Jan Willemsen, Four small earthenware saucers, earthenware table plates and an
    earthenware salt cellar... 6 " 10 st.
Albert Jansen, Three pair of old man's stockings............................... 20 " 10 st.
Jan Willemsen, Three pair of old man's stockings............................... 15 " 5 st.
Tjerck Claesen, Three pair of old man's stockings.............................. 10 "
Evert Pels, Three pair of *Iceland* stockingc, old.............................. 10 "
Lambert Huyberts, A pair of filled (gevulde) stockings......................... 16 " 5 st.
Henrick Palingh, Two fur caps, one small coat, both as worn by the savages and
    one piece of cloth... 25 "
Daniel Botterwout, surety *Thomas Chambers*, A saddle, a bridle, a pair of old
    boots, a skin iron, a spur and a suspender..................................... 50 "
Long, Jacob, A new gray hat.. 29 "
Old Michiel Verbrugge, A new gray hat.. 30 "
Pieter Hillebrants, A new gray Hat... 23 "
Jacob Burhans, A new gray hat.. 28 "
Aert Martensen, A little new gray hat.. 25 "
W. Hoorenbeeck, A new gray hat... 32 "
Pieter Hillebrants, A mirror with a bird cage.................................. 12 "
Capito, An ancker of whale oil... 70 "
Henry Palingh, An empty half aem, with a faucet, and in a keg some old whale
    oil and axle grease... 8 "
Aert Martensen, An iron pot filled with whale oil.............................. 15 " 10 st.
Jan Joosten, An iron pot half filled with whale oil and an empty iron pot...... 10 "
Jan Willemsen, A can with rape seed oil, and a small calabas with bear-grease.... 15 "
Antoni Delva, A couple of cannons (een paer canons) two powder horns, a shot
    bag with a belt.. 15 "
Lambert Huyberts, Two water pails, a yoke and a flour sieve.................... 23 "
Willem Beeckman, Two clothes lines in a firkin................................. 6 "
Capito, A keg containing some.. 10 "
Arent Teunissen, Two small tubs made from an ancker, a milk can and a firkin, a
    buttermilk keg and a milk pan.. 21 "
Arent Teunissen, Two empty barrels... 6 " 10 st.
Jan Brabander, A wash tub, a chopping board an empty keg....................... 6 "
Jan Cornelissen Smits, An old chest.. 5 "
J. J. V. Amersfort, A meat barrel.. 8 " 5 st.
Arent Teunissen, Four empty kegs... 1 " 15 st.
Lambert Huyberts, An ancker and a tun.. 3 "
Lambert Huyberts, A bier barrel at *Cornelis Slecht's* and another one at *Swart-
    wout's* containing 3 anckers... 6 " 10 st.
Roelof Swartwout, a keg filled with hops....................................... 3 " 5 st.
Lambert Huyberts, A firkin and a flower keg.................................... 4 " 15 st.
Lambert Huyberts, An empty keg, a salt barrel and a pepper box................. 6 " 5 st.
Tjerck Claesen, a keg with vinegar... 14 "
Jan Willemsen, A cellar with a bottle of oil................................... 8 "
Capito, A tube and a cane cudgel... 6 "
Roelof Hendericks, A window cleaner, a brush, two pot-cleaners................. 3 "
Evert Pels, a bottle of vinegar and a can with oil, not known what kind of oil.... 11 "
Jan Cornelissen Smits, A prepared deer skin and two hammers.................... 8 "
Albert Jansen, A perpetual almanac, an East Indian bed-spread, a fringed border
    for the mantel-piece, and seven small maps..................................... 16 "
Aert Martensen, Three deer skins for chair cushions............................ 1 " 10 st.
Roelof Swartw., A pair of new shoes.. 12 "
Aert Martensen, Four small tankards and a pint tankard......................... 3 "
Ridsert Cage, Four small tankards and a pint tankard........................... 4 " 5 st.
Aert Martensen, A pair of woman's shoes.. 11 " 10 st.
Ridsert Cage, 8 small tankards and a pint tankard.............................. 5 " 5 st.
Albert Jansen, a copper scale with the balance 3 lb. of house-weights, and 1 lb. of
    lead-weight.. 24 "
Henderick Jochems, Two pairs of old shoes...................................... 18 "
Evert Pels, Eight small tankards and a pint tankard............................ 4 " 10 st.
Willem Beeckman, Four small tankards and a pint tankard........................ 2 "
Michiel Verbrugge, A pair of new shoes... 10 "
Evert Pels, Four small staves of lead.. 9 "
Willem Beeckman, An old broken waffle-iron..................................... 2 "
Roelof Swartwout, A tick tack board with the pieces............................ 8 "
Capito, A tick tack board with the pieces...................................... 18 "
Jan Cornelissen Smits, A pair of new shoes..................................... 12 "
Lambert Huyberts, A pair of new shoes.. 12 " 5 st.
Jan Willemsen, Two pairs of old shoes.. 7 " 10 st.
Albert Jansen, A small box with wafers, a small bag with red paint and a pair of
    ice spurs.. 4 "
Evert Pels, A lantern with a broken pane and a mob............................. 4 "
Jan Joosten, 15 tankards and a pint tankard and 3 moulds for balls............. 4 " 10 st.
Albert Jansen, Two paper chimney plates (papieren schoorsteen borden)......... " 10 st.
Walran Dumont, Two small boxes with 33 wooden combs............................ 3 "

Walran Dumont, 17 mirrors made by the savages (wilde spiegeltjes)............	6	gldrs.	10 st.
Heyman Allerts Roos, 18 mirrors made by the savages.........................	8	"	
Henderick Palingh, 46 Succinct ideas by Borstius.............................	10	"	
Henderick Palingh, 34 School books in 4"...................................	20	"	
Henderick Palingh, 29 School books in 4"..................................	13	"	10 st.
Jacob Barents Cool, 3 pressed women's hoods................................	1	"	15 st.
Hend. Palingh, 24 School books in 4"......................................	12	"	
The same 31 School books in 4"...	13	"	
Hend. Palingh, 33 School books in 8"......................................	2	"	
The same An old French catechism....................................	1	"	
The same 12 school books in 8"...	3	"	
J. Jansen V. Amersfort, 19 writing pens (cyffer pennen) some pictures, three old ink stands, a pair of old gloves..	2	"	5 st.
Hend. Palingh, A package of A. B. C. books.................................	5	"	10 st.
Henryck Palingh, 25 school books in 8"....................................	6	"	10 st.
The same 22 school books in 8"...	6	"	
The same 24 school books in 8"...	5	"	10 st.
The same 13 school books in 8"...	5	"	
The same 24 school books in 8"...	5	"	5 st.
The same 26 school books in 8"...	5	"	
The same 21 school books in 8", and 3 gardeners books..................	9	"	
Hend. Cornelissen Lyndr, Two tracts by *Petrus Moling*.......................	3	"	
Albert Jansen, Life and Works of Prince Henderick............................	16	"	
Jan the Smith, The gaining of land (landwinninghe) and the wonders of mountain-mining...	7	"	
Jan Joosten, Beehive by Aldegonde, and the chronicles of the Kings of England..	10	"	5 st.
Roelof Swariw., Bernhard Van Zutphen, practice and the Recueil of Amsterdam...	15	"	
Capito, World's mirror by *Sebastian Frank,* and d'Argenio by *J. Barcklaj*........	7	"	
Henderick Aertsen, Treatise on the faith by *Henry Hexman,* Perfection of the Word of God by *Albert Huttenis,* and Meditation on the 51st Psalm.......	8	"	
Pieter Hillebrants, Redress of the Holland Nobility............................			
Johan Sarseharson General exposition of Holy Writ, another book by the same...	3	"	
Henderick Aertsen, Perfection of Holy Writ by *Albert Huttenis,* Characteristics of the children of God, Royal road to heaven, Golden hary..............	13	"	5 st.
Capito, German Song book, 12 Meditations, Manual of the Catholic faith, an old memorial, a lot of "piet"..	3	"	5 st.
Albert Jansen, A watch...	70	"	
Christoffel Davids, Two chairs..	4	"	5 st.
Fat Henderick Hend., Two chairs...	5	"	
Albert Govertsen, Three chairs...	8	"	10 st.
The same Six printed pictures belonging to DuMont.....................	5	"	
Tjerck Claesen, A round table..	10	"	
Albert Jansen, A church pew...	3	"	
Christoffel Davids, Two benches and a small square table.....................	9	"	15 st.
The same Six printed pictures of *Walran Dumon*.......................	4	"	
Hender. Albertsen, Six printed pictures belonging to Du Mont.................	5	"	

* Mr. Versteeg's translation, slightly modernized, has been used for the abstract of this instrument.—Child's childrens.

✿

Page 440.—Apr. 16, 1667.—*Aert Martensen Doorn,* and his wife, *Geertruyd Andriessen,* request that the Hon. *Willem Beekman,* Schout, and *Roelof Swartwout,* commissary, be appointed guardians over Geertruyd's son by a former marriage, viz., *Jan Jacobs Slyckkoten.* So ordered. ✿

Page 441.—May 14, 1667.—*Guert Hendricksen,* uncle and blood-guardian (i. e., natural guardian) over the minor children of *Jan Hendricksen,* his deceased brother, living at Albany, requests that a guardian may be appointed for said children. *Jan Willemsen Hoochteylingh,* elder, and *Hendrick Aertsen,* deacon, appointed by the court.

✿

Translations Dutch Records, vol. II.

Page 53.—*Roeloff Swartwout* and *Jan Willemsen,* guardians of the children of *Albert Gysbertsen,* deceased, and the mother of said children, request permission to render an account of the estate to the children, they having attained majority, except *Jan,* who is "one year short thereof." Permission granted.

Page 94.—Marriage contract, and testamentary disposition by

HILLEBRANTS, PIETER.

"In the name of the Lord, Amen. Be it known by these, that on March 20, 1665, N. S., appeared before *Mattheus Capito,* Secretary of *Wildwyck, Pieter Hillebrants,* young man, accompanied by his mother, *Femmetje Alberts,* and *Aeltje Wygerts,* widow of *Albert Gysbertsen,* accompanied by *Roeloff Hendericks,* her son-in-law, who in this manner have stipulated these marriage conditions. 1. The marriage to be concluded in accordance with the canons of the reformed religion. 2. All the property, belonging to either party, to be used in common, in accordance with the custom of *Holland,* with the exception that the bride sets apart for each of her children 50 gilders heavy money, viz. for *Aeltje* and *Jan,* children of *Lubbert Jansen,* and for *Lysbet* and *Gysbert,* children of *Albert Gysbertsen.*—*Roeloff Swartwout* and *Jan Willemse Hoochteylingh* to be appointed guardians over said children, who are to be instructed in reading, writing, and, if possible, learn a trade.—In case of death of either party, the property to be divided." Signed Pieter Hillebrants, *Aeltien Hybersen,* Femmetje Alberts (her mark), *Roeloff Hendricks, Wilh. Beeckman,* Jan Willemsen Hoochteylingh, and Roeloff Swartwout.

SECRETARY'S PAPERS, Liber A., p. 20 (Translations of Dutch Records, II., 102).

VERMEULEN, JOOST ADRIAENSEN, of Pynacker.

Testamentary disposition, dated Sept. 2, 1665, and written in Dutch.

"Before me, *Mattheus Capito,* Secretary of the village of *Wildwyck,*" "appeared personally (in proprie persoon) the worthy Joost Adriaensen Vermeulen of Pynacker."—After a long religious preamble, the testator disposes of "six schepels of wheat" "to the poor at Wildwyck" "syn huysvrouw (his wife) *Femmetje Hendericks* and "his little daughter *Marietje* by his said wife" "shall take possession of the estate gained and acquired here by him" and of "all such estate as he has in the old country (Vadreland) or might inherit."—As executors in Wildwyck "the worthy persons *Albert Jansen Van Steenwyck* and *Roeloff Hendericksen,* both his brothers-in-law," they to "send any balance" to his "lawful wife and child in the old country."—As executrix of property in the old country, the testator appoints his wife Femmetje Hendericks."

JAN JANSEN VAN OOSTERHOUD   JOOST ADRYAENS.
JAN BROERSENS

Joost Adriansen of Pynaker in Holland, came from Leerdam, Apr. 16, 1663, in the 'Spotted Cow' m. l. March 20, 1663-4, Femmetje Hendricks of *Meppelen, Prov. Drenth, Holland*, res. Wiltwyck, m. 2., "of *Opynen*, near *Tiel, Gelderland*, Holland, widower of Femmetje Hendricks", Oct. 28, 1668, *Elisabeth Willemsen Krom*, of Pynacker, in *South Holland*, near *Delft*, m. 3., "molenear (miller), Wedower van *Lysbeth Croeing"*, July 9, 1681, *Marritje Heys*, widow of *Philip Lieuw*, of *New York*, and d. of *David Jochemsen* and *Christina Cappoens* (who in her will refers to her 'dau. *Marya Hays*, m. to *Peter Praa*" "at her death without lawful issue" "the property not to go to the children of Joost Adriansen, deceased"). On Oct. 17, 1683, the will of Joost Adrians, deceased, was proved at *Fort James* before *Thomas Dongan*, Lieut. General, Governor and Vice-Admirall, and Jan Joosten being therein appointed as tutor or overseer, was confirmed as such. (N. Y. Sur. Office, Wills, Liber 1-2, p. 279). "Joost Adrians, of Bushwick, L. I., in his will, dated July 27, 1683, recorded, but not proved, in Albany (Clerk of the Court of Appeal's Office, Liber A., p. 2), mentions "wife Mary Hay sole heiress."—Joost Adrian's widow, m. 3., March 15, 1684, *Capt. Pieter Praa*, b. in *Leyden*, 1655.

Joost Adriansen and Lysbet Willems Crom had issue:
i. *Jannetie*, bt. Apr. 5, 1672; ii. *Willem*, bt. Oct. 13, 1678; iii. *Hendrick*, bt. Apr. 24, 1681, all in New York.

Joost Adriaanze, molenner, and Maritje Heys had issue:
iv. *Sara*, bt. June 18, 1682, in *Kingston*.

Roeloff Hendricksen, j. m. of *Almedo* in Overyssel, m., Nov. 30, 1664, *Aeltje Lubbers*, of *Elburgh*, Gelderland, res. Wiltwyck.

Joost Adriansen & Co., on Apr. 30, 1658, petitioned for permission to build a saw mill and grist mill at *Turtle falls* on the *South River*, and the petition was granted on May 6th (Dutch MSS., Albany, Council Minutes, VIII., p. 872).

Joost Adriansen had on May 8, 1677, a grant from the Court of Kingston for 6 acres of land over the Mill Kill (N. Y. Land Papers I., p. 113), and on Sept. 27, 1677, there is a conveyance from *Jan Borhans* to Joost Adryansen of a house and lot in Kingston (Ibid., p. 126).

Jan Jansen van Oosterhout in *Brabant*, widower of *Annetje Hendricks* (one of the witnesses), m., Febr. 18, 1663, *Annetjen Jelles* of *Bommel*, Gelderland, res. Wiltwyck.

John Joosten, administrator to the estate of Joost Adrians, late of Boswick upon Long Island, deceased, on Apr. 23, 1685, agreed to arbitration regarding some land in *Hurley*, called the *Wasmaker's Land*, sold to *Derrick Schepmoes* by Joost Adrians in his lifetime. (See Ulster Deeds, under John Joosten).

See also *Jan Joosten Van Meeteren*).

Liber A., page 92. T. D. R., Liber 2, p. 104.

GERRETSEN, ALBERT, from Embderland.

Testamentary disposition, dated Sept. 3, 1665, and written in Dutch.

"To the poor of *Wildwyck* 8 schepels of wheat."—"Lawful wife, *Willemtje Jacobs*, shall rightfully "hold" the whole estate "for the love, chastity, faithfulness and affection manifested towards him during their married life, and for other reasons." Signed by the testator, and witnessed by *Jan Willemsen Hoochteylingk* and *Jan Joosten Van Meteren*, both Commissaries in the village of Wildwyck.

(Willemtje Jacobs, widow of Albert Gerretsen, m. 2, May 11, 1668, *Jan Cornelissen*, of *Gottenburgh, Sweden*, and m. 3, Dec. 24, 1679, *Jan Broerse Decker*, widower of *Heyltje Jacobs*, res. Marbletown.

Liber A., page 114. T. D. R., Liber 2, p. 122.

BLANCHAN, MATTHEUS.

Testamentary disposition, dated Sept. 7/17, 1665, and written in Dutch.

"Before me, *Mattheus Capito*" "appeared the worthy Mattheus Blanchan, born in the village of *Noeuville o corne* in the parish de la paroise *Ricame* de la conté de *S: Paul* in the province of *Artois*."—Long religious preamble.—"*Magdalen Joire*" "lawful wife, shall possess the whole estate" "here in America, as long as she remains a widow" also "all the land in Artois" "where the testator was born" and in *"Armentiers* and other places" she to keep the "three children, *Magdalena, Elizabeth* and *Mattheu*" "minors" "until they reach their majority or marry." "When they marry, she to act towards them as she treated the two other married daughters, *Catarinen* and *Marien.*"—After remarriage, wife to have only one half of the property, for the purpose of bringing up the three minors.—"Wife being present, consents to these conditions." Signed by the testator, and witnessed by *Wallerand Du Mont* and *Pier Nuee*.

(Matthys Blanshan, from Artois, farmer, and his wife, *Maddelen Jorisse,* and their son-in-law, *Anthony Crispel,* with his wife, *Maria Blanshan,* and three younger children of Mattheus Blanchan, sailed for the new world in the *'Gilded Otter',* April 27, 1660, arriving at *Wiltwyck* before Dec. 7, 1660.
On Oct. 8, 1666, Jan Jansen van Oosterhout conveyed to M. B. a house and lot in W. (English MSS., xxii., p. 11).—On June 18, 1667, there is a deed of confirmation from Gov. Nicolls to M. B. for a house and lot of ground at W., at *Esopus.* (N. Y. Land Papers, I., p. 21).—On Oct. 16, 1666, *Roeloff Swartwout* and *Jurien Westphael* make a declaration respecting the arrival of M. B. and family and his application for a place to settle. (Ibid., p. 12.—On June 7, 1673, there is a deed of confirmation from Gov. Lovelace to M. B. for 63 acres land in Hurley. (N. Y. Land Papers, I., p. 51).—On May 20, '1686, there is a description of a survey of a lot of land, of about 63 acres, part of *Hurley great piece,* on the north side of *Esopus Kill,* laid out for M. B. by *Philip Welles,* surveyor (N. Y. Land Papers, II., p. 186).—On Oct. 11, 1686, M. B. had a Patent for 62¾ acres 36 rods land in Hurley. (Engl. MSS., xxxiii, p. 60).—On June 17, 1697, *Mathias Blansan* petitioned for a patent for 100 acres of land, south of the *Cale Bergh,* in *Marbletown.* (N. Y. Land Papers, II., p. 249). Magdalena B., m., Sept. 28, 1667, *Jan Matthysen Jansen,* of *Fort Orange,* when she is described as "of *England."* (q. v.)
Elizabeth B., m. Oct. 27, 1668, *Pieter Cornelisen Low* (q. v.).
Cattery Blancsan, d. of M. B., m. at *Manheim, Germany,* Oct. 10, 1655, *Louis Du Bois,* b. Oct. 27, 1627 at *Wicres, France* (q. v.).
Matys Blanjan, Jr., of Manheim, m. March 30, 1679, *Margrietje Claas Van Schoonhoven (Margriet Claasen)* of *Nieu Albanien (Albany).*
See also his later will, dated Apr. 30, 1688).

Liber B., page 260.   T. D. R., Liber 2, p. 243.

DU JOU, CHRISTIAEN, of Horly.

Testamentary disposition, dated Aug. 10, 1676, and written in Dutch.

"To his children, three of whom, viz. *Anna, Pieter,* and *Elizabeth,* are married, and two of whom, viz., *Maria* and *Margrieta,* are unmarried" "the unmarried to receive as much as the married children received, i. e. 100 Rixdollars" also "50 Rixdollars" worth of clothing for Mary", "Margerita, being the youngest", "to receive during her minority 70 Rixdollars."*—"For Pieter's wedding-suit (Bruilofts Kleeding) 15 Rixdollars." —Residue to be divided among the children.
Witnessed by

<table>
<tr><td>Louys Du Bois</td><td>Christian Du Jou (his mark).</td></tr>
<tr><td>Hugo Freer (his mark)</td><td>Testus: Wm. La Montagne, S.</td></tr>
</table>

(*Christian Deyo,* from near *Calais,* came in the *'Gilded Otter',* Apr. 27, 1660, from *Manheim, Germany.*—See his later will, under *Christian Deijou,* of New Paltes, dated Febr. 1, 1687-8.
i. Anna, b. 1644, m. *Jean Hasbrouck* (q. v.); ii. Pierre (Peter), m. *Agatha Nickel* (both in honor living in *Curr Pfaltz, Mutterstadt,* circuit of *Newstadt,* in the Palatinate), as appears from a certificate by *Jacob Amoyot,* Pastor there, dated Jan. 21, 1675); iii. *Maria,* b. 1653, m. "of *Moerstadt, Rhenish Bavaria, Palatinate,"* at *Manheim,* 1676, *Abraham Hasbrouck,* of *Calais, France;* iv. Elisabeth, m. *Simon Le Fevre;* v. Margaret, m. March 6, 1681, *Abraham*

(*) Rijksdaalder (Rixdollar), a Dutch coin, worth about $1.

Du Bois, s. of *Louis* (and *Catharine Blanchan*).—In his later will (q. v.), he mentions "my soones soon", *Christian Deijo*. He was son of Peter D., and m., Febr. 1, 1702, *Marytje De Graaf (du Cont).*)

Liber B., page 261. T. D. R., Liber 2, p. 244.

WYNKOOP, CORNELIUS, of Kingston.

Testamentary disposition, dated Aug. 11, 1676, and written in Dutch.

"Lawful wife and seven children" "the survivors to possess the whole estate." "In case husband or wife should remarry, then he or she" is "to divide one half with the children as their patrimonial share."—Note: "What has not been perfectly expressed above is that one child shall not receive more at the division than the rest of them."—Signed by the testator and witnessed by WESSEL TEN BROECK and DIRCK JANSEN SCHEPMOES.

(Cornelius Wynkoop was in *Albany* as early as 1655; came to *Kingston* prior to 1671. His wife was *Maria Janse Langendyck* (q. v. under Maria Wynkoop). They had issue:—i. *Johannes* (Major), m., June 7, 1687, *Judith Blodgood*, and 2., 1696, *Cornelia*, d. of *Dirck Wessel Ten Broeck* (see Cornelius Wynkoop's will); ii. *Maria*, m. *Moses*, s. of *Nicholas Depuy*; iii. *Evert*, b. in *New Albany*, m. Aug. 26, 1688, *Gertrude*, d. of *Jacobus Elmendorf* and *Grietje Aertse van Wagenen*, and 2., *Antje*, d. of *Roeloff Kierstede* and *Eiche Roosa*; iv. *Gerrit*, m. *Hillitje*, d. of *Gerrit Fokker* and *Jacomyntje Slecht*; v. *Nicholas*, bt. K. Oct. 15, 1668; vi. *Catherine*, bt. June 18, 1671; vii. *Benjamin*, bt. Apr. 18, 1675, m. Oct. 20, 1697, *Femmetje*, d. of *Abr. Vanderheul* and *Tryntje Hendrick Kip*).

Liber B., p. 262. T. D. R., Liber 2, p. 244.

BARENTSEN, TRYNTIE, wife of Cornelius Barentsen.

Testamentary disposition, dated Aug. 17......(year not mentioned), and written in Dutch.

"Cornelis Barentsen, her husband, co-testator" and herself "desire that the whole estate" "shall be inherited by the survivor" and at their deaths by "the children: *Jacomeyntie, Hendrick, Annetie, Mattys*, and *Petronella*. "If any of the testators should re-marry, one half of the property is to be divided immediately among the children.—"A linen-chest made by *Jan Jansen*, which Petronella has, is above her portion (Een Kasse gamaakt door Jan Jansen" "voor linen kasse date Petronella voor uyt heeft boven haar portie").

WESSEL TEN BROECK
JAN HEYNDERICKSZ.

Signed CORNELIS BARENTSE SLECHT by me TRYNTYE TYSEN BOSCH

(Cornelis Barentsen Slecht, widower of Tryntie Bos, of *Woerden, Holland*, m. 2., after Sept. 26, 1684, *Elsie Janse*, of *Breestede, Danmark*, d. of *Jan Jansen Breestede*, and widow of *Adrian Petersen Van Alcmaer*; she m., 3., *Hendrick Jochemsen Schoonmaker* (see Jochem Schoonmaker's will, dated Dec. 9, 1729).

On July 23, 1664-7, Cornelis Barentsen Slecht had a deed of confirmation from Gov. Nicholls of 40-50 acres of land at *Esopus* (N. Y. Land Papers, I., p. 23)—Cornelis Barentsen (*Borensen*) "convicted upon oath and affirmance for taking of arms in a riotous and illegal manner upon the 16th of Febr., 1666, to awe, terify and supress his Majesty's English Garrison established at Esopus" "deserves to be put to death" but the Governor sentences him "to be banished for three years, giving him liberty to sell his estate at the Esopus."

Petronella m., Aug. 16, 1679, *Jochem Hendrick Schoonmaker*, oldest s. of the above Hendrick Jochemsen Schoonmaker (see Jochem Schoonmaker's will).—Jacomyntie m. 1., Apr. 29, 1663, *Jan Barentsen Kunst* (when she is called *Jakemyntje Cornelis*) and had a. *Jannetje*, bt. Febr. 24, 1664, b. *Barent*, bt. Jan. 30, 1667; m. 2., after Oct. 27, 1668, *Gerrit Focken*, of *Ritsen, East Friesland*, and had c. *Hillitje*, who m. *Gerrit*, s. of *Cornelius Wynkoop* and *Maria Janse Langedyk*

(q. v.); m. 3., 1677, *Jan Eltynge* (*Elting Roelofsen*, q. v. (*), d. *Jacomyntje*, m. *Henry Pawling*; e. *Tryntje*, m. *Solomon Du Bois*.—Annetie m. *Cornelis Hoogeboom* (q. v.).— Mattys Cornelis Sleght m. *Marya Maddeleen Crupel* (*Crispel*), and had issue: a. *Maria Maddelen*, bt. Aug. 28, 1681; b. *Tryntie*, bt. Jan. 27, 1684, m. March 5, 1703, *Matthys Mattysen, Jr.*; c. *Antoni*, bt. May 25, 1690, m. Nov. 1, 1715, *Neeltje Boogaard*; d. *Jan*, bt. Nov. 1, 1694, m. Aug. 6, 1716, *Elizabeth Smedes*; e. *Cornelis*, bt. Oct. 10, 1697; f. *Petrus*, bt. Sept. 21, 1701; g. *Hendricus*, bt. Dec. 22, 1706, m. Jan. 3, 1736, *Zara Kierstede*).

Liber B., page 263. T. D. R., Liber 2, p. 245.

HOOGEBOOM, CORNELIS, and wife, Annetie Cornelisen Sleght.

Testamentary disposition, dated Aug. 17...... (year not mentioned, but probably 1676), written in Dutch.

"The whole estate shall be inherited by the survivor." "If they both should die without having re-married, the estate to be inherited by the nearest relatives (bloet verwant) on both sides."—"The eldest son (named *Peter*, in the margin), of the brother of Cornelis Hoogeboom shall receive Cornelis Hoogeboom's cloak (Mantell)."—*Jacomentie's*** daughter, sister of *Annetie Cornelis*, named *Jannetie Jansen Kunst*" "a sum of 100 guilders light money, to be paid by the survivor. Signed by both testators, as above, and witnessed by WESSEL TEN BROECK and JAN HEYNDERICKSZ.

(A gulden is a Dutch silver coin, worth about 41 cents.
Cornelis Pieterse Hoogeboom, tile and brickmaker, was in *Manhatans* 1656, at *New Amstel* on the *Delaware*, 1657, when he had a son in the same trade at *Beverwyck*; was in 1660 at Beverwyck, attempted brickmaking at Manhatans, with *Jan Andries De Graef*, 1661; engaged in 1664 to make tiles at Beverhorst for *Gerrit Van Slichtenhorst* from Jan. to Nov. for 60 beavers, half in tiles.
Cornelius Hoogeboom's brother, *Bartholomews*, a skipper on the *Hudson* in 1680, between New York and Albany, who died Febr. 15, 1702, had with wife, *Catryn*, a son, *Peter*.
Annetie Cornelisen Sleght was dau. of *Cornelis Barentsen Slecht* (see *Tryntie Barentsen*).
Cornelius Hoogeboom on Apr. 1, 1672, received a grant from the Trustees of *Kingston* for a lot of ground for a brick-yard. (N. Y. Land Papers, I., p. 45).

Liber B., page 265. T. D. R., Liber 2, p. 246.

TYSEN, JAN, and his wife, Madelena Blansjan.

Testamentary disposition, dated Sept. 25, 1676, and written in Dutch.

"The estate "after re-marriage of either party" to be divided, one half to go to the children, begotten by them." "If they should die simultaneously, the children are to inherit the entire estate." Survivor to retain possession of the estate until the majority of the children. "Our son, *Matthys* is entitled to a piece of land, which was given to him by Father *Thoomas Chambers*." "If either party should re-marry, and have children, one fourth of the estate is to be divided, but the real estate shall belong to the children of the first marriage."

JOOST ADRYAENS	JAN MATTYSEN
DIRCK SCHEPMOES	MATELEN BLANCHN.

(*Mattys Janse van Keulen* had on Aug. 18, 1646, a grant of 50 morgens land at Harlem by Director *Kieft*, became a trader, removed to *Fort Orange*, and thence to *Esopus*, where he died prior to Febr. 15, 1663, on which day the deacons loaned 1000 guldens from his estate. M. J. married *Margaret Hendricks*, who m. 2., *Thomas Chambers*, Lord of the Manor of *Foxhall* (q. v.). M. J. and Margaret, his wife, had issue:

---

* See Elting Roelofsen for Jacomyntie's children, and their marriages.
** *Jacomyntje Focken*, dau. of *Cornelis Barentse Slecht*.

i. Jan Mattysen (Tysen), above, born at Fort Orange, who m. after Sept. 28th, 1667, Madelena Blanchan, of England (see Matthys Blanchan), and had issue:
a). *Marreganto (Magdalena)* bt. Oct. 15, 1668, m, *Richard Broadhead;* b. *Mattys Jansen,* bt. June 18, 1671, m. 1 June 7, 1695, *Anna Elmendorf,* m. 2. June 13, 1703, *Rachel Popinga,* m. 3. *Annetjen Masten* (see his will under Mattys Jansen, dated August 21, 1727); c. *Hendrick,* bt. April 6, 1679, m. Nov. 28, 1724, *Anneken Schoonmaker;* d. *Davit,* bt. Apr. 24, 1681; e. *Margriet,* bt. Jan. 14, 1684, m. March 5, 1704, *Barent Burhans;* f. *Sara,* bt. Oct. 8, 1686, m. 1705, *Elias Van Bunschoten;* g. *Catheryn,* bt. Sept. 30, 1688, m. *John Crook, Jr.;* h. *Maria,* bt. Apr. 20, 1692, m. Oct. 23, 1729, *Thomas Betty,* s. of *John Beaty* and *Susanna Ashfordby* (q. v.); i. *Thomas Jansen,* m. Nov. 22, 1702, *Mayken Bogaard* (q. v. under *Hendericus Jansen;* j. *Jan,* who went to England and died there.
All surnamed JANSEN.

ii. *Mattys Mattysen* (s. of Mattys Janse van Keulen), a Captain in 1685, and later on serving against the French on the northern frontier, m. Tjatje, dau. of Tjerck Claesse De Witt (q. v.), and had issue:
a. *Sara,* b. *Hurley,* bt. Apr. 16, 1678, m. Jan. 17, 1697, *Matthew Du Bois;* b. *Lea,* bt. *Hurley,* May 11, 1679; c. *Mattys,* bt. Apr. 24, 1681, m. March 5, 1704, *Tryntje Sleght* (see *Hendrickus Van Keuren*); d. *Tierck,* bt. Dec. 24, 1682, m. Febr. 1, 1702, *Marytje Ten Eyck* of *Hurley* (see *Tyrck Van Keuren,* of *Kingston*); e. *Thomas,* bt. Nov. 1, 1684, d. y.; f. *Barbara,* bt. Oct. 11, 1685, m. 2. Nov. 5, 1727, *Peter Tappen;* g. *Klaes,* bt. Dec. 4, 1687; h. *Thomas,* bt. Oct. 13, 1689, m. Apr. 11, 1730, *Mary Paling;* i. *Hasuel,* bt. Jan. 28, 1692, m. *Mary,* dau. of *Abr. Riker;* j. *Cornelis,* bt. June 3, 1694, m. Dec. 29, 1718, *Kezia Hoogteeling,* d. of *Willem Jansse H.* and *Ariaentie Samuels* (see *Jan Willemse Hooghtyling*); k. *Benjamin,* bt. Oct. 18, 1696; l. *Nicholas;* m. *Gerardus;*
All surnamed VAN KEUREN.

iii. *Catrina Mattysen,* m. Oct. 3. 1660, *Jan Jansen,* carpenter from *Amersforrt, Utrecht.*
iv. *Anneke Mattysen,* m. after March 25, 1668, Sergt. *Jan. Hendricks* (*Buur*) of *Fort Orange.*

See Jan Tysen's later will under Jan Mattysen, of Kingston, dated Oct. 7, 1719.—On Febr. 18, 1673, Jan Mattysen received a grant from the Court at Kingston of a lot of ground. (N. Y. Land Papers, I., p. 49).—In 1686, there is a survey of 600 acres lands on *Hudsons River,* north of *Callicoone Hooke,* Kingston limits, laid out for *John Tyson and Company,* by *Philip Welles,* surveyor. (Ibid., II., p. 167. See also xlviii, pps. 73—74.)

Liber B., page 266. T. D. R., Liber 2, p. 246.

DU BOOYS, LOWIES, and his wife Chatharina Blansjan.

Testamentary disposition, dated Oct. 13, 1676, and written in Dutch.

"After their deaths, the whole estate shall go to their children" "the minors first to be educated until they can earn a living. If either should re-marry, he or she shall pay one half to the children, begotten by them, and in case of death, one fourth of the remaining half shall be divided among the children.—If the survivor remains unmarried, he or she shall not be compelled to pay out anything more to the children than it may please the survivor, either as a marriage portion, or in some other way. At death of both parties, the children shall inherit the entire estate. In case of re-marriage of either party, without lawful issue, the children shall have one half of the estate.

WESSEL TEN BROECK   LOUYS DU BOIS
                        CATELEN BLANCAN.

(Louis Du Bois, b. Oct. 27, 1627, at *Wicres, France,* m. at *Manheim, Germany,* Oct. 10, 1655, *Katryn,* dau. of *Matthys Blanshan* (q. v.), and emigrated, April 27, 1660, in the '*Gilded Otter.*'—His brother-in-law, *Pierre Billou,* came from *Artois* in the '*St. John the Baptist,*' Aug. 6, 1661.—The widow m., 2., *Jean Cottin* (q. v.).—Louis Du Bois and Catheryn, his wife, had issue: i. *Abraham,* b. Manheim, Dec. 26, 1657, m. K. March 6, 1681, *Margriet,* d. of *Christian Deyo* (q. v.); ii. *Isaac,* b. Manheim, 1659, m. K., June, 1683, *Maria Hasbrouck,* b. *Moudestad, Paltz;*. iii. *Jacob,* bt. Oct. 9, 1661, m. March 8, 1689, *Lysbeth Varnoye;* iv. *Sarah,* bt. Sept. 14, 1664, m. Dec. 12, 1682, *Joost Jansz,* of *Marbletown;* v. *David,* bt. March 13, 1667, m. March 8, 1689, *Cornelia Varnoye;* vi. *Solomon,* b. *Hurley,* 1670, m. 1692, *Tryntje Gerritsen;* vii. *Rebecca,* bt. June 18, 1671, d. y.; viii. *Ragel,* bt. Apr. 1675, d. y.; ix. *Louis,* b. 1677,

m. Jan. 19, 1701, *Rachel Hasbrouck* (see *Jonathan Du Bois*); x. *Matthew*, b. Jan. 3, 1679, at Hurley, m. Jan. 17, 1697, *Sara Matthysen*, d. of Mattys M.
See Du Bois Re-union, Philadelphia, 1876; N. Y. Gen. Reg., 1896, pps. 190—.
See also his later will, dated March 27, 1694, and codicil, dated Febr. 22, 1695/6.—Letters of administration were granted to Katharine Du Bois, July 13, 1697. (N. Y. Sur. Office, Liber 5—6, p. 172).—See also his will, dated March 30, 1686, and a complete copy thereof printed in "History of New Paltz," by Ralph Lefevre, p. 283.
On May 26, 1677, the Esopus Indians conveyed to Louis Du Bois and associates a tract of land over the *Rondout Kill*, beginning at the high hill called *Moggonck*, thence southeast to *Juffrons Hook* in the *Long Reach* on the *Great River* (*Magaat Ramis*), thence north to the Island called *Rappoos*, on the *Kroonme Elbow*, at the commencement of the Long Reach, thence west to the *High hill* to a place *Waracahaes* and *Tawaeretagne*, along the High hill southwest to Moggonck, with free access to the Rondout Kill (New, Paltz); (N. Y. Land Papers, I., p. 114).—On Oct. 22, 1677, there is a petition from L. Du B. and others for a Patent at the Esopus (Ibid., p. 132), and on Dec. 28, 1678, an Indian deed for land at Esopus, embracing "ye land on both sides of ye creeke, and ye land called in ye Indian tongue *Pawachta* to *Pakasek*, *Wakaseeck*, *Wakankonach* (Ibid., p. 152).

Liber B., page 274.   T. D. R., Liber 2, p. 250.

CORNELISSEN, PETER, and Elisabeth Blansjan.

Testamentary disposition, dated Nov. 1, 1676, and written in Dutch.

"The survivor shall possess the entire estate; at re-marriage, one half thereof shall go to the children. If both parties should die without having re-married, the children are to inherit the property, the minors first being brought up. If either party should survive, and not marry, such survivor shall have the use of the estate until death. Signed in the presence of MATYS BARENTSEN and Hendrick Rycke by

HEYNDERYCK RYCKE   PETER CORNELISEN (his mark)
MATTYS CORNELIS SLECHT ELISIEBETH BLANSAN.

(Pieter Cornelisse, for whose later will see *Pieter Cornelisse Low*, came from *Holstein*, Febr. 1659, in "*Faith*," and m., 1668, *Elisabeth*, d. of *Mattys Blanchan* (q. v.), and had issue: i. *Cornelius*, b. 1670, of *Esopus*, m. in *New York*, July 5, 1695, *Margaret Borsum*, dau. of *Tymen Van Borsum*, of N. Y., cordwainer, who in his will, dated July 22, 1702, proved Jan. 4, 1702—03, mentions wife *Gritie* (*Fockens*) and "my daughter, Margareta, wife of *Cornelius Low*, shall have the other half" "of the estate" "remainder to the widower of my daughter, whether it be Cornelius Low or any other husband." (N. Y. Sur. Office, Liber 7, p. 76).—See also Col. N. Y., by Geo. W. Schuyler, II., p. 435, History of Kingston, p. 483, *Steven's* Chamber of Commerce; ii. *Madeline*, m. *Benjamin Smedes* (q. v.); iii. *Antje*, m. July 20, 1701, *Philip Viele*, b. Albany; iv. *Marytje*, m. 1705, *Aert Van Wagenen*; v. *Matthys*; vi. *Peter*; vii. *Abraham*, bt. July 15, 1683; viii. *Jacob*, bt. June 24, 1688; ix. *Johannis*.
All surnamed LOW.
On Dec. 20, 1719, a draft of warrant of survey was issued for 3292 acres of land for Cornelius Low et al, in Ulster County, on the west side of Hudson's river, about 12 or 14 miles backwards, in ye woods, being part of the resumed lands lately belonging to Capt. *John Evans* (N. Y. Land Papers, vii., p. 98—).—Survey laid out by *Allane Jaratt*, surveyor general (*New Windsor, Orange Co*). (Ibid., p. 110).

Liber C., page 10.   T. D. R., Liber 2, p. 327.

TROPHAGEN, WILLEM.

Deposition, dated Aug. 26, 1671, and written in Dutch.

"Before me, *W. Montagne*, Secretary for the Hon. Court, this day appeared *Willem Trophaegen*, Doctor and medical officer (Medisini Amptman) (*) of the manor (huijis) of *Hemelycke* in the Diocese (sticht) of *Minnen* under the Count *Van der Lip*, born in the city (stat) of *Lemmichor*.—*Hendrick Trophaegen* is brother of deponent's father. His

---

* Or physician and bailiff.

son, *Anthony Trophaegen,* is preacher for the Calvinists at *Almina.* The sister of deponent's father (is named) *Anna Trophaegen,* her husband is *Johannes Willemsen Cooperslaeger.* Deponent's mother, *Eeledt Delandal.* Her sister had a daughter, Stoeten (*) and Mayor (Burgemeester) within *Lemigo.* Her brother is *Johanes* Delandel, prebendary within *Herfort* and her other sister had a husband by the name of *Johanes Niehosen,* councillor within Heerfort. The guardians of the said Willem Trophaegen *Willem Schellinck—Jan Willems: Harmen Sproedt—Johannes Nichousen,* this *Willem Jansen* being at Lemigo in the year 1647, when he issued a power of attorney to Johannes Nichoesen and Anthony Traphaegen, preacher.

"I married *Jannetie Claesen Groenvis* of *Meppelt,* with whom I had a daughter whom I named *Eelet Trophaegen.* After my wife's death, I married *Aeltie Dirrecks Meermans,* and had with her a son, named *Johannes Trophaegen.* At her death, I married *Joosje Willemsen Noortryck* of *Amsterdam,* with whom I had a daughter, *Rebecca* and a son, *Willem* and *Hendrick Trophagen.*

"Whereas the aforesaid Willem Trophagen is considering the approach of death, he has deemed it proper to make known his familyconnections (de gelegenheit van syn geslaecht), that the children, when of age, may inquire at *Minnen Corpus Christy fief* (leengoederen), paying annually 100 Rixdollars (**) and other fiefs called *Maria Vergina* in the church of Lemigo, paying annually 80 Rixdollars; another fief at *Billeveldt,* called *Anna Salutes,* paying annually 60 Rixdollars. I pray, that the Lord will protect these children, when I shall have left them, in their good rights, and that they may be educated from said income. Signed by the deponent, and witnessed by ALBERT JANSEN.

(See William Trophagen's will, dated Febr. 16, 1685.)

Liber D., page 20.   T. D. R., Liber 2, p. 353.

HOOGHTEYLINGH, JAN WILLEMSEN, and his wife, Barbara Jans.

Testamentary disposition, dated Nov. 8, 1671.

"Barbara Jans, being weak and sick in bed" "the survivor shall remain in full possession of the entire estate. If either party should happen to marry, their only son, *Willem Jansen,* having no other children, shall then have half of the real estate and the personal property."

CORNELIS BARENTS SLECHT (Commissary)   JAN WILLEMSEN
CORNELIS WYNKOOP (Ex-Commissary)   BARBARY JANS (her mark).

(Jan Willemse Hooghtyling died previous to 1702. He and his wife, Barbara Jans, had a son, *William Jansse Hooghtaelingh,* who married *Ariaentie Samuels* (*doghter*), and had issue: i. *Samuel,* bt. June 8, 1679; ii. *Philippus,* bt. Sept. 4, 1681; *Dina* (*Desia*), bt. Oct. 14, 1683; *Hiskia,* bt. Jan. 31, 1686; v. *Kesia* (*Trezia*), d. of *Willem Hoogstyler* & Ariaentie Samuels, bt. Sept. 4, 1689, in New York, m., Dec. 29, 1718, *Cornelis Matthysen Van Keuren* (q. v.), all men-

---

(*) Evidently something is missing in the original. Opposite Stoeten appears in the margin: "having yet two sisters, *Elsebus Trophagen* and *Catharina Trophagen.*"

(**) See note, page 31.

tioned in Jan Willemse Hoghtyling's later will, which see. Philippus m. before 1704, *Jannetje Rosa.* Another son of Willem Jansse, named Jan Willemse, Jr., d. y.

On May 8, 1677, *Jan Williamsen Hooghtig* received from the Court at Kingston a grant of about 8 acres of land (N. Y. Land Papers, I., p. 111). He was schepen, deacon, and commissioner to treat with the English).

Liber E., page 87. T. D. R., p. 418.

PARYS, EVERDT, of Hurly.

Will dated March 26, 1678, and written in Dutch.

"Wishing to dispose during his life of his estate, makes known by these present his debts and possessions:

Mr. Notticham owes 10 schepel of wheat on the first instalment in May, and 60 schepel on the last instalment, as per contract.

Mr. Quynel owes 40 gilders in wheat.

Gerret Lambertsen owes 10 or 12 gilders.

Am indebted to *Mr. Hall,* according to his books of account.

To *Jacob Lusena* for the purchase of a mare, 30 schepel of wheat and some wine.

Hyman Allessen 14½ schepel of wheat.

To *Mr. Roelof* (*) 4 schepel of wheat.—Plow at *Swachenhal's*, where there is still coming to *Prys* one half.

Warnaer Hoornbeerg 3 schepel of wheat.

Nicolaes De Majer 11 schepel of wheat.

Maycken, the wife of *Jan Joosten,* 1 schepel of wheat.

Joost Adriaensen, linen for a shirt and some wine.

Am indebted to *Gorge Davits* to the amount of 40 gilders.

Benjamin Provoost 6 schepel of wheat.

Jan the smith 3 schepel of wheat.

Lowies Du Booys 2 schepel of wheat.

Benjamin Provoost 6 schepel of wheat.

Peter Hillebrants owes me 2 schepel of corn.

Jan Bigs owes me 2 schepel of wheat.

I owe *Jacob Ruts* 3 schepel of oats (haver).

"If anything should be overlooked, *Marie Hals,* eldest daughter of Mr. Hall, is appointed legatee of everything."

EVERT PARYS (his mark).

WILLIAM ASFORDBIE
JOHN BIGGS   Testus: W. LA MONTAGNE, Secretary.
N. ANTHONY

Liber E., page 98. T. R. D., Liber 2, page 425.

ELMENDORP, JACOBUS.

Will dated June 2, 1678, at Kingston, and written in Dutch.

"Wife shall possess the entire estate." "If she should happen to marry" one half thereof is to go to the children. At her death, the entire

---

(*) *Roelof Kierstede,* in the official translation, but not in the original record. There is nothing to indicate that Roeloff Kierstede is referred to, as *Roeloff Swartwout* also was styled "Mr."

estate to go to the children. Also everything in Holland with the testator's father, *Coenraedts Elmendorf*, living at *Rynborch* in the *Rynstraet* in the Gilded Cable (vergulde Cabeltouw), viz. 450 gilders, belonging to the testator, and his two brothers and two sisters, children of a former marriage of Conraedt Elmendorp, deceased, and *Janneken,* their mother, before the distribution to the other children. To wife also everything else he may inherit.—*Gommert Poulussen* authorized to receive the money in Holland, and to pay it to testator's wife, in whatever money it may consist of. Signed by the testator and witnessed by *Dirck Schepmoes* and *Joost Adryaens*.

(See his later will, dated Aug. 27, 1685, under *Jacobus Van Elmendorp*.
Jacobus Van Elmendorp m., after Febr. 28, 1668, *Grietje Aertsen*, daughter of *Aert Jacobsen van Wagonen*, from *Utrecht* (see *Gerrit Aartse*), and has issue: i. *Coenraet*, bt. March 12, 1669, who m. "jong man van *Kingston*", at *Albany*, June 28, 1693, *Ariantje Gerritse Van den Bergh*, widow of *Cornelius Martinsen Van Buren*, and m. 2., Nov. 25, 1704, at Kingston, *Blandina*, daughter of *Roeloff Kierstede* and *Eycke Albertse Roosa*; ii. *Geertje*, bt. June 18, 1671, m., Aug. 26, 1688, *Evert*, s. of *Cornelis Wynkoop* and *Maria Janse Langendyk*; iii. *Anna*, m. June 7, 1695, *Matthyse*, s. of *Jan Matthysen Jansen* and *Magdalena Blanshan*; iv. *Jacobus*, bt. Nov. 24, 1678, m., after Oct. 9, 1706, *Antje*, dau. of *Cornelis Cool* and *Jannetje Lambertsen*, and had a dau., *Margaret*, who m., Dec. 22, 1732, *Thomas*, s. of *Abraham Gaasbeck Chambers*.

Jacobus Elmendorp (Van Elmendorp), the testator, was son of *Coenraedt Elmendorf* of *Rynborch, Holland*.

See also the will of Gertie Elmendorf).

Liber E. (turned upside down, but running page 180. T. D. R., 2, p. 468.

WYNKOOP, MARIA, widow of CORNELIUS WYNKOOP.

Deposition, dated May 16, 1679.

"On this 16th day of May, anno 1679, Maria, widow of the deceased Cornelis Wynkoop, at present sick in bed, very weak, and considering the certainty of death. In conformity with the Christian nature of love, she has therefore appointed Wessel Ten Broeck and Mr. Willem De Majer guardians or overseers over her children, during their minority, they to conform with the provisions of the will made by her late husband, unless otherwise provided for in this instrument. Eldest son, *Johannes*, shall have, in advance, a piece of silver from *Piet Heyn's* (*) fleet.—To her eldest daughter a painted ward-robe, a red skirt, a silver bell with the chain, two silver spoons, all the silver money, a gold ring, some furniture, a tick, and a bed with its belonging. A cow, previously given to her by her father, is at present at Walraven's.—To her youngest daughter, *Catharina,* a chest (cofter), all the clothing, except the red skirt (or petticoat, "Rock") given to *Marrytie,* a gold ring, a tick bed with its belongings.—To the sons their father's clothing.—To the youngest son, *Benjamin,* two silver spoons, and the cow, at present at Teunes Eellesen's. —Recommending said guardians to guide her children in the fear of the Lord, and to take care of her estate; desiring that this instrument shall be carried out after her death, legally and inviolably. In the presence of two (members) of the Court at *Kingston*.

(*) Admiral Piet Pietersen Heyn.

Note. All the silver money was Marrite's—as well as some furniture.

Maria Van lange dyck, widow of Cornelis
Wynkoop, deceased (her mark).

(Witnesses did not sign the instrument.)

Liber E., running page 177. T. D. R., Liber 2, p. 470.

ROELOFSEN, ELTING.

Testamentary disposition, dated Sept. 30, 1679, and written in Dutch.

"Being now ready to depart for Holland, and considering the perils of the sea, the injuries from heaven, the certainty of death."—Wife *Jacomyntie Sleght* shall remain in the full possession of lands, and all other property, she to pay to the children by her marriage with *Gerrit Foocken*, deceased, 200 schepels of wheat. Jan Elton binds himself to do the same, should he be the survivor. The lands at *Horly* to remain mortgaged, as security for the said 200 schepels of wheat. Both parties agree to these conditions.

Joost Adryaens
Benjamin Provoost
	Jan Eltynge
	Jacomyntie Slecht
	Cornelis Barents Slecht and
	    Roelof Swartwout, as
	    guardians.

(Written in English.)

"The Executors of the Abovementioned Instrument have desired before Thomas Chambers & Capt. Henry Beekman, Esqrs., and Justices of the County Court or Court of Sessions, that the same might be Renewed. The Justices Refer the same to the Court of Oyer And Determiner. Kingston, 3d of March, 1685.

John Ward.

(Jan Eltinge, son of *Roeloff Eltinge* and *Aaltjen Eltinge*, was born at *Swichtalaer*, a dependency of *Beyla*, in the Prov. of *Drenthe*, on July 29th 1632 old style, and hath received Christian Baptism at the hands of our Rev. Mr. and Father in Lord, Dr. Johannis Beeltsnyder, and was named Jan Eltinge, born of honest and virtuous parents, who have always sustained a good reputation among us and whose kindred is still numerous. Dated at Bayle, Jan. 20, 1680, and signed by *Guiljemus Hofstede*, Cecle Beylensis et Classis Meppelanae, pt. Deputatus.

Maria Eltinge, his sister, was born Febr. 28, 1630,

Bartelt Eltinge, his brother, was born Dec. 18, 1631, as all appears from a certificate, which Jan Eltinge brought with him from Beyle.

He resided first at *Flatbush, L. I.*, where he was paid 25 guilders for carpenter's work on the church; bought on Nov. 27, 1663, of *Derrick Jansen*, cooper, a farm and building plot in Flatbush, on the east side of the road (Flatbush Records, B., p. 150). Declared in 1679, under oath, that he was son of *Roeloff Elton* and *Aeltie*, his mother (*Steven Coerten, Willemtje Roelofs, Jan Strycker*, armorer, *Jan Seebringk, Goert Stevensen* of *Flatlands*, all natives of Drenten, made declarations, on Oct. 10, 1679, as to the identity of Jan Elten, a native of same place, but now of Kingston. (English MSS., Albany, xxviii, pps. 135-136).

Jan Eltinge m., 1677, *Jacomyntie*, dau. of *Cornelis Barentsen Slecht* and widow of *Jan Barentsen Kunst* and of *Gerrit Focken* (see *Tryntie Barentsen*), and had issue: i. *Geertje*, m. July 6, 1699, *Thomas Hall*, of *Marbletown*; ii. *Aeltje*, m. Oct. 20, 1695, *Aert Gerretse Van Wagenen* (see *Gerrit Aartse*); iii. *Roeloff*, b. Hurly, bt. Oct. 27, 1678, m. June 13, 1703, *Sarah*, dau. of *Abram Du Bois* and *Margaret Deyo* (see his will, as well as Dubois Reunion, p. 97); iv. *Cornelis*, bt. Febr. 29, 1681, 's. of *Jan Ente*', m. Sept. 3, 1704, *Rebecca*, dau. of *Joost Janse Van Meeteren* and *Sara Du Bois* (see *Jan Joosten*); v. *William*, bt. Jan. 19, 1685, m. *Jannetje*, dau. of *Hillebrand Le Sueur* and *Elsje Jurian Tappen* (see his will, under William Eltinge, dated Dec. 7, 1743).

On Sept. 15, 1719, *Peter Hoganboom, Ruleif Elting, Cornelius Elting, Thomas Noxon* and *Jacobus Brown* petitioned for a survey of the *Great Vly* in *Kingston*, inherited by them from *Cornelius Hoganboom*, deceased, and *Janita*, his wife, and *Severyn Tenhout*, late of Co. Ulster. (Engl. MSS. lxi, p. 182).

"Jan Eltinge, late of Hurley, by his last will devised to his five children, Roeloff, Cornelius, Willem, Geertje (now widow of Thomas Hall of *Raretan Co. Somerset, N. J.*) and Altje Eltinge (mother of *Gerrit Van Wagenen* of Kingston), half of his Estate, and the other half to his wife's 9 children: *Jannetje* (now widow of *Cornelius Newkerk*, of *Hurley**), *Hillitje* (wife of *Gerrit Wynkoop* of *Philadelphia*), *Jacomyntje* (wife of *Henry Pawling*, of Philadelphia), Roeloff, Cornelius, and William Eltinge, Gerrit Van Wagenen, Geertje (as above), *Tryntje* (late wife of *Solomon Du Bois* of *New Paltz*)—said heirs now grant to the children of said Du Bois the 1/9 part of lot No. 5 in *Dutchess* Co., over against the *Rondout Creek*, also 1/18 part in a meadow called *Jacomyntje's fly*, dated Aug. 2, 1729." (See Ulster Deeds).

Court Records

or "Esopus Records," as they previously were called, contain a mixture of Court Records and Secretary's papers. Volume V. is evidently composed of stray leaves from other books, collated and bound together. On page 1 is a "Lijste van all de Boeeke van het Prottocol Soo als het is bevonden bij ons ondergeschreeve Persoone geauthoriseert bij de Justices" (List of all the books of the protocol, as the same have been found by us, the undersigned, authorized by the justices). No signatures were attached, but, at a later date, the following, written in English, was added in a different handwriting:

Present:

    Coll. Jacob Rutsen   Kingstowne this 19th of Febr. 1700/1
    Major Jacob Aertsen   at a meeting of Justices.
    Mr. Jan Mattyse
    Mr. Abram Haesbroeck
    Mr. Arion Gerritse
    Mr. Roelif Swartwout
    Mr. John Heermans
       Esquires, Justices of the peace.

Liber V., page 149. T. D. R., Liber 2, page 561.

JOOSTEN, JACOB.

    Testamentary disposition, dated Aug. 1, 1680, and written in Dutch.

"Sick in bed," "considering the certainty of death" "wishing to dispose of what God will permit him to leave." "As soon as it pleases God to take his soul, his body shall receive Christian burial."—*Gerrit Cornelissen* shall possess everything left by him, viz. from *Jan Joosten's* 32 schepels of wheat, from *Roelof Swartwoudt's* 13 schepels and 2 gilders. From *Wyntie Roosae's*, not knowing how much.—From this to be deducted: For the poor 4 schepels of wheat. In *Midwout* was due 170 guilders, of these, he has received some linen from *Cornelis Barntsen Van der Wyck*, also stockings, shoes, two knives, ten pounds of tobacco. Has yet a running account with *Jacob Kip*; thinks there is still something coming to him, but gives to said Kip, out of gratitude, because Kip had him nursed

---

(*) See *Cornelis Gerritse*.

when he was sick, one half of what may be due him. Owes 6 guilders to *Tyntie Kip*. Wishing all his friends happiness and blessings, and desires that the provisions of this instrument be complied with after his death. Signed, as above, by the testator, and witnessed by *Jan Joosten* and *Johannes De Hooges*.—(Red sealing-wax, evidently from a ring, or a seal; no devices can be clearly distinguished, but in the upper left corner appears to be the impression of a 'J').

(Jacob Joosten (*van Vovelens*) on July 18, 1657, proposed to sell, by auction, his house and lot in *Beverwyck*.. (Albany Co. Records).—*Adriaentie Cornelise Van Velpen*, wife, and attorney, for Jacob Joosten (van Covelens), conveyed, on Oct. 13, 1671, her house and lot in Albany to Jan Connell (Ibid.).—Jacob Joosten took the oath of allegiance to the English in New York, 1664. —Jacob Joosten was town-clerk of the five Dutch towns from 1670—1673, and Schoolmaster of *Flatbush*.

Jacob Joosten of *Raagh*, on the *Moesel, Germany*, Presenter of the Church and Schoolmaster in *Wiltwyck*, m., Sept. 19, 1662, at Albany, *Arriaentjen Verschuer*, of *Welpe, Gelderland*, widow of *Marckes Leendersen*, res. at Fort Orange, and on (blank day) of August, 1663, Jacob Joosten and *Ariaentje Van Wolpen* had a daughter, Neeltje, bt. in Kingston.

On July 12, 1661, Jacob Joosten was appointed a messenger for the Court of Wiltwyck and the church, with an annual salary of 200 guilders in sewan. He occupied lot No. 7 in Wiltwyck.)

Liber V., page 221. T. D. R., Liber 2, page 590.

JOOSTEN, JAN, van Meeteren.

Testamentary disposition, dated Dec. 16, 1681, and written in Dutch.

"Wife *Maycken* shall retain full possession (of the estate). She consents that the survivor shall possess everything, lands, houses, personal property, money, gold, silver, coined or uncoined. After their decease, the property to be inherited by their children, *Joost* to have one half of the entire estate first. Joost and *Gysbert* to have the land at *Marbletown*, Joost one half, and then the other half to be divided between them. *Geertie Crom* to have the land at *Wassemaker's land*. Children of *Lysbeth*, deceased, to have their portion, in money, from the other children.

BENJAMIN PROVOOST   JAN JOOSTEN
LEVERYEN TEN HOUT   MAYCKEN HENDRIX (her mark)

(Jan Joosten came from *Tiederwelt* with wife and five children, aged 15, 12, 9, 6, 2½, on Sept. 2, 1662, in the ship 'Fox.' J. J. had, March 30, 1671, from Gov. *Lovelace*, a deed for a lot in *Marbletown* (N. Y. Land Papers, I., p. 37), and on Oct. 11, 1671, a confirmation of 30 acres lot of ground in M. (Ibid., p. 42). (See also Joost Adriaensen Vermeulen).—Jan Joosten van Meeteren and *Mayke Hendrix*, his wife, had issue: i. *Joost Jansen*, van Meeteren, *Gelderland*, m., Dec. 12, 1682, *Sara Dubois*, of *Kingston*, res. *New Paltz* (see *Louis Du Bois*), and had: a. *Jan*, bt. Jan. 14, 1683, b. *Rebecca*, m. Sept. 3, 1704, *Cornelis Eltinge* (see *Elting Roelofsen*); ii. *Gysbert* (m. *Catharina*, and had *Hester Jans*, who m. Lourents Barentse, and had, Helena, bt. N. Y., Dec. 5, 1712); iii. Lysbeth.—Jan Jooste, Jooste Jansen and Geertje Krom frequently appear as witnesses to the baptisms of children of *Gysbert Crom* and *Geertie Van Vliet*, dau. of *Dirck Aryensse Van Vliet* and *Machteld*, his wife, and to the baptisms of children of *Jan Hamel* and *Geertrud Crom*.)

Liber VI., part A., page 28. T. D. R., Liber 2, p. 616.

TEN BROECK, WESSEL, and Maria Ten Eyck, his wife.

Testamentary disposition, dated March 7, 1681, and written in Dutch.

Survivors to inherit everything. If the children should marry, the survivor is entitled to present claim for dowry, in whatever sum he or she sees fit, depending upon the children's deportment, but the survivor cannot be forced to do so. If the survivor should marry, one half of the property is to go immediately to the children. Real estate, lands, houses, gardens cannot be alienated except to the family, i. e. the children and their descendants down to the third generation (in de darde gelidt).—The eldest son, *Wessel Ten Broeck, Junior,* shall have first interest in the house and lot, provided he pays proper value therefor.—All the children to receive equal shares, sons as well as daughters, but not until the youngest child (de jongster) is full grown, he to be maintained until then. If the estate should be sufficient, and the children could be well educated, the full grown children are to receive every year their share of any residue of the estate. Signed, as above, and witnessed by *Jan Joosten,* Justice, and *Tierck Claesen (De Witt).*

(See his later will under *Wessel Ten Broeck, Senior,* of *Foxhall.*
Wessel Ten Broeck was born about 1636 in *Munster, Westphalia,* and emigrated in *'Faith,'* Dec. 1659, m., in *New York,* Dec. 16, 1670, *Maria,* dau. of *Coenradt Ten Eyck* and *Maria Bode.* She died Nov. 15, 1694, and Wessel Ten Broeck, who had removed to Kingston about 1675, m. 2., Sept. 26, 1695, *Laurentia Kellenaer,* widow of Dominie *Van Gaasbeck* and of *Thomas Chambers* (q. v.)—Issue: i. *Wessel,* b. March 28, bt. Apr. 30, 1672, m. June 6, 1694, *Jacomyntje,* b. *Leyden, Holland,* Nov. 26, 1673, dau. of *Laurentius Van Gaasbeck* and *Laurentia Kellenaer.* She d. Jan. 29, 1741, and he died Febr. 7, 1744 (see his will, dated Apr. 27, 1743); ii. *Maria,* b. 1674, m. Nov. 14, 1693, *Charles,* s. of Capt. *Daniel Brodhead.* She d. July 9, 1717. iii. *Elsie,* b. 1676, m. Dec. 22, 1695, *Cornelis Jansen Decker.* She d. June 9, 1725. iv. *Gertrude,* bt. Dec. 8, 1678, d. unm. Aug. 13, 1716; v. *Sarah,* bt. Dec. 14, 1679, m. Nov. 22, 1702, *Cornelis Vernooy.* She d. Jan. 2, 1716. vi. *Coenraat,* bt. Apr. 2, 1682, d. inf.; vii. *Conrad,* bt. Nov. 29, 1683, d. Febr. 18, 1703; viii. *John,* bt. July 19, 1685, d. inf.; ix. *John,* bt. Nov. 28, 1686, m. Dec. 9, 1715, *Rachel,* dau. of *Hyman Roosa* and *Anna Margaret Roosevelt.* He d. March 5, 1775. x. *Jacob,* bt. March 25, 1688, m. Jan. 17, 1712, *Elisabeth,* dau. of *Johannis Wynkoop* and *Judith Bloodgood.* He d. Apr. 1746.
See *Matthys Ten Eyck's* will for data relating to Coenraedt Ten Eyck and his children.—See *Thomas Chambers* for data relating to Laurentia Kellenaer and her former husbands.—See *Hyman Roosa's* will for his other children.—See *Cornelius Wynkoop* for his son, Johannes, and his two wives.—Capt. Daniel Broadhead came from England in the expedition sent out by the *Duke of York,* 1664, under command of Col. *Nicholls.* He commanded the English garrison at Kingston.—Wessel Ten Broeck had, Sept. 21, 1676, a grant from the Court of Kingston, of a certain marsh containing 14 acres (N. Y. Land Papers, I., p. 86). On Nov. 13, 1676, a survey was made of about one acre land at Esopus (Ibid., p. 96). On Apr. 13, 1678, he had another grant for a lot of wild land (Ibid., p. 151). On Apr. 4, 1682, an additional grant for 8 acres land in addition to 12 acres conveyed to him by *Wm. Ashfordby,* over the mill dam, between the path of the great valley and the small valley (Ibid. II., p. 4).

Liber VI., page 65. T. D. R., Liber 3, p. 1.

SCHEPMOES, DIRCK JANSEN.

Testamentary disposition, dated Nov. 1, 1682, and written in Dutch.

Survivor to remain in full possession of the entire estate, money, goods, houses, lands and personal property, unless the survivor should happen to marry, in which case he or she is to act according to conscience, appointing two guardians besides the survivor, to secure the interest of the children. The entire property to be divided among the children, when of age or at marriage.

W. D. MEYER　　　　　　　　　　DIRCK JANSEN SCHEPMOES
HENDRICK VAN DE WATER　　　　MARYA WILLEMS

(Jan Janszen Schepmoes m. in New York, *Sarah Pieters,* who, after his death m. 2., Sept. 7, 1656, *William Couch (Koech)* from *England.* Letters of administration were granted, Jan. 29,

1690-1 after Jan Jansen Schepmoes, of New York, to *Abraham, Dirck, Anna,* widow of *Henry Coyler, Sarah,* wife of *Johanes De Wandeloer, Aeltie,* wife of *Johanes Van Giesen, Sarah,* wife of *Dirck Jansen,* and *Joaptie,* wife of *Gerrit Hortenburg.* (N. Y. Sur. Office, Wills, Liber 3-4, p. 134). Jan Jansen Schepmoes and Sarah Pieters had issue: i. *Annetje,* bt. Febr. 16, 1642, m. *Henry Coyler;* ii. *Abraham,* bt. Nov. 25, 1643 (witn. *Theunis Janssen,* sailmaker, and *Eltje Hendricks);* iii. *Aeltje,* bt. Sept. 3, 1645 (*Simon Joosten* and *Marritje Lievens,* witn.), m. 1. *Jan Everts Ketelkas,* and 2., in N. Y., June 24, 1687, *Johannes Van Giesen,* of *Bergen;* iv. *Jobje,* bt. Jan. 6, 1647, m. *Gerrit Hortenburg;* v. *Dirck,* bt. Sept. 2, 1648 (of whom presently; vi. *Wesel,* bt. Jan. 1, 1650; vii. *Tryntie,* bt. June 23, 1652; viii. *Sara,* bt. Apr. 12, 1654, m. Johanes De Wandelever.
    v. Dirck Jansen Schepmoes m. *Maria Willems (doghter),* and had issue:
        i. *Jan (Johannes),* bt. N. Y., Apr. 7, 1672, m. Febr. 18, 1697, *Neeltje Gerritsen,* b. *Hurley,* widow of *Pieter Crupel;* ii. *Ragel,* bt. March 31, 1678 in *Kingston,* m. May 19, 1700, *Bernardus Swartwout,* of Hurley; iii. *Lea,* bt. Sept. 4, 1681; iv. *Willem,* bt. Hurley, June 9, 1684, m. 1. *Geertruy Davis,* m. 2. June 24, 1711, *Catryntjen Tappen* (see his will); v. *Rebecca,* bt. Nov. 6, 1687.
    Dirck Jansen Schepmoes and *Margariet Tappen* had issue:
        vi. *Anna,* bt. Sept. 3, 1704, m. July 8, 1725, *Johannes Jansz;* vii. *Ariaantje,* bt. Nov. 17, 1706; viii. *Dirck Willemse,* "*klyn son.*"

Liber VI., page 66. T. D. R., Liber 3, p. 1.

VAN BORSUM, BARENDT.

Testamentary disposition, dated Nov. 19, 1682, and written in Dutch.

Wife *Machtel Adriaensen* shall remain in full possession of the entire estate, houses and money, unless either should marry, when the survivor is to pay one half of the property to the children, when of age or at marriage. The children to receive a Christian education from the income of the estate.—If remaining "unmarried" (ongetrouwt), the children are not to lay claim to anything before the death of both their parents.—Tools, a gun, as well as man's apparel to go in advance to the little son (soontien).

JACOP RUTGERSEN	BARENDT VAN BORSUMS
JOSHEM ENTHELBERT	MACHTEL VAN VLYET
van namen	

(In the margin, opposite the last provision: "but they shall all be appraised and their value deducted from his share in the estate." This was evidently written afterwards, as it appears in a darker ink, and is witnessed by *C. Hoogenboom*).

    (Barendt Van Borsum was son of *Egbert Van Borsum,* y. m. van *Embden,* who m. Dec. 11, 1639, *Annetje Hendricks,* y. d. van *Amsterdam,* and brother of *Tyman Van Borsum,* of N. Y. cordwainer, who in his will, dated July 22, 1702 mentions "my two brothers and sisters, *Janetie,* wife of *Peter Adolph, Annette,* wife of *Andrew Brestede,* children of my brother, *Hendrick van B.,* children of my brother *Barent Van Borsum,*" etc.—See also *Pieter Cornelisen Low.* Barent Van Borsum and Machteld Adriansen Van Vlied had issue: i. *Annetje,* bt. May 31, 1676; ii. *Egbaert,* bt. in *Kingston,* Sept. 15, 1678; iii. *Neltie,* bt. Apr. 9, 1683 (witn. *Gysbert Crom, Jan Joosten, Hermanus Van Borsum,* and *Geeritie Van Vlied);* iv. *Aefje,* m. 1. Oct. 10, 1703, Andries de *Wandelaar,* s. of Johannes de W., m. 2., Oct. 8, 1707, Louis Anthony van Niewenkuyzen.)

Liber VI., page 86. T. D. R., Liber 3, p. 14.

VAN SLEGHTENHORST, GERRIDT.

Testamentary disposition, dated Febr. 16, 1682/3, and written in Dutch.

Survivor to possess everything until death or remarriage, (wife's name being *Aeltie Lansinck*), when one half of the estate, whether houses, land, gold, silver, coined or uncoined is to go to the children; the minors to be brought up in an honest and Christian manner. Children to divide equally at death of both parents, if survivor had remained unmarried. In the latter case, he or she to be entitled to keep possession of the entire estate, unless inclined to share with the children. After the death of both the minors, *Hillegont* and *Gerrit, Ragel* and *Gouda* are to receive, in advance, and above their share, fifty beavers or the value thereof.

| WM. FISHER | G: V: SLICHTENHORST |
| WESSEL TEN BROECK | AELTYE LANSYNCK |

Quod attestis: WM. DE LA MONTAGNE, Secr.

(In the margin: It was forgotten in the above will that the minors are to be brought up from (the proceeds of) the estate. On attaining their majority, they are to divide in accordance with the provisions in the will. Dated Febr. 22, 1682/3.

| WM. MONTAGNE, testis | GERRIT VAN SLICHTENHORST |
| HINDERICK KIP | AELTIE LANSINCK |

(Aeltie Lansinck was dau. of *Gerrit Lansick*, who came from *Hassell*, near *Swoll* in *Overysell*, and died previous to Oct. 3, 1679, having also had sons *Gerrit, Hendrick, Johannes*, and daughters, *Gysbertje*, w. of *Hendrick Roseboom*, and *Hillitie*, widow of *Storm Van der Zee*.
Gerrit Van Slichtenhorst was son of *Brandt Arentse Van Sclichtenhorst*, of *Niewkerk* in *Gelderland*, who was appointed a director of the *Rensselaerwyck Colony* in 1646, but returned to Niewkerk, where he died about 1668. Gerrit Van Schleghtenhorst was one of the magistrates of Schenectady in 1672, and died in Kingston, Jan. 9, 1684).

Liber VI., page 95. T. D. R., Liber 3, p. 21.

VERNOOY, CORNELIS, and his wife, Annetie Cornelis.

Testamentary disposition, dated Febr. 23, 1682/3, and written in Dutch.

Survivor to possess everything until death or remarriage; in the latter case, one half of the estate to go to the children.—If the survivor should remain unmarried, nothing shall be paid out to the children, except at the pleasure of the survivor. Children to inherit everything at death of both their parents, the minors to be educated out of the estate. The mother gives to her eldest daughter (de moeder maecht aen haer outste dochter) *Selie* all her apparel.

| ABRAHAM LAMESENK (LAMBERTSE?) | CORNELIS VERNOOY (his mark) |
| | ANNETIE CORNELIS (her mark) |

(*Cornelis Cornelissen Vernooy* with wife, *Annatje Cornelis* (dau. of *Cornelis Barentsen Van de Cuyl* and *Lysbet Arents*), and children, came in the 'Faith,' Jan. 1664.—They had issue: i. *Lysbeth*, m. March 8, 1689, *Jacob Du Bois*; ii. *Geertruy*, m. Jan. 11, 1702, *Pieter Louw*; iii. *Rachel*, m. after Febr. 8, 1707, *Abram Bevie*, of *Hurley*, res. *Rochester*, when "½ of a piece of 8 for the poor" was given; iv. *Seletje* (*Selie*), bt. March 22, 1665, m. after June 17, 1682, *Abraham la Matre* of *Midwoud* (*Flatbush, L. I.*); v. *Cornelia*, bt. Apr. 3, 1667, m., March 8, 1689, *David*, s. of *Louis Du Bois* and *Cathryn Blanshan;* vi. *Cornelis*, bt. Jan. 5, 1679, m., Nov. 22, 1702, *Sarah*, dau. of *Wessel Ten Broeck* and *Maria Ten Eyck* (q. v.); vii. *Johannis*, bt. Apr. 24, 1681, m., Nov. 26, 1724, *Janneken Louw;* viii. *Jacob*, bt. Febr. 10, 1684, m. after Apr. 28, 1728, *Annaatjen Du Bois;* iv. (child not named), bt. Jan. 2, 1687; x. *Greetje*, m. before March 15, 1695, *Jacob*, s. of *Tjerck Claessen De Witt* and *Barbara Andriesen;* xi. *Marritje*, m. July 9, 1696, *Lodewyck*, s. of *Warnaar Hoornbeck* and *Eva De Hooges*. (It is probable that the children were not born in this order, and that Greetje and Marritje were born soon after arrival).

Liber VI., part B., (the book turned upside down) running page 227. T. D. R., Liber 3, p. 190.

MEYDERSEN, EGHBERT.

Testamentary disposition, dated April 9, 1684, and written in Dutch.

"Not feeling very well (niedt wel te passe)."—Wife, *Femmetie Alberts,* to have everything at his death, whether house, lots, etc. After her death all to go to the children of Eghbert Myndersen, to be divided equally, except the little closet or chest (kasje), which is to go to the eldest daughter.

MARTEN HOFFMANN   EGBERT MEYNDERSEN (his mark)
Testis: WM. DE LA MONTAGNE, Secretary.

(Egbert Meyndertszen and *Jacobje (Jaepje) Jans* had issue: i. *Mayken,* bt. in N. Y., Apr. 27, 1661 *(Annetje Jans,* witn); ii. *Jannetie,* bt. Jan. 11, 1664, m., March 7, 1682, *Andries,* s. of *Tjerck Claessen De Witt* (q. v.), and d. Nov. 23, 1733; iii. *Meyndert,* bt. July 3, 1667).

Liber VI., running page 226. T. D. R., Liber 3, p. 191.

JANS, GRITIE, widow of Jan Lembertsen.

Testamentary disposition, dated June 27, 1684, and written in Dutch.

"Her daughter (haer dochter) *Annetie Adriaensen* shall have, in advance, the bed, pillow and two small cushions (kleyne kussens), and *Geesje* is to receive the two large cushions (groote kussens), also the silver top-iron (ovryser). Residue to be divided between them.

GRIETIE JANSEN (her mark)
(No witnesses).

(Jan Lambertszen and Gritie Jansen had: i. *Geesje,* bt. N. Y., June 4, 1653 (witn. *Pieterje Jans,* et al).
End of "Testamentary Dispositions" in the Volumes called "Dutch Records."
The Dutch wills which follow, are on file in the County Clerk's Office, have not been translated before, and are not included in the "Translations of Dutch Records," vols. i-iii, from which the above dispositions have been transcribed.

Abstracts of Wills on File in the County Clerk's Office, City of Kingston, N. Y.

BOOK OF DEEDS I (AA)

Page 29.—TROPHAGEN, WILLIAM, of Kingston.

Will dated Febr. 16, 1685.

"My soule to Almighty God." "To my three sons namely *Johannes Trophagen, William Trophagen* and *Henry Trophagen*, all my Land which I att present enjoy withall houses barns" also "three horses with a plow and a wagon and other implements with the proviso that my said three sons shall work upon the land" "and Likewise to maintain me And my wife *Joosie* so long as both or Either of us shall live."—"My eldest son Johannes Trophagen 50 gilders and my Eldest Daughter *Helena* wife of *Jan Boerhanse* 50 gilders being Allotted to them before I married my Last wife Joosie." "The rest of my Estate whether in horses cows hogs either young or old or household stuff shall be equally divided amongst my three sons And my two daughters (to witt) Helena who is married unto Jan Boerhans of Kingston And *Rebecca* who is married unto *Peter Peterson* of *Hurley*."—Wife appointed executor, and after her death "my three aforesaid sons joyntly Executors. Signed by the testator, and witnessed by WARREN DU MONT and WILLEM JACOBS.

(*William Jansen Trophagen* (or *Traphagel*, as his name also was written), van *Lemgo*—see his declaration—m. 1. *Justje* (*Jannetie*) *Claes Groenvis* (*Willems*), of *Boswyck*, in the Dutch Ref. Church, Brooklyn; m. 2., June 1, 1658, in *New Amsterdam*, *Aeltie Dirck* from *Steenwyck* in *Overyssel*, (or *Aeltie Dirrecks Meermans*, as she is named in his declaration); m. 3., Jan. 15, 1661, *Joosje Willems Norrtryck* of *Amsterdam*, widow of *Jan Verkinderen*. On May 7, W. T. moved with his family into the first house erected near the Pond in *Bushwick*. On May 12, 1664, he was sentenced as punishment for abusing the magistrates of the town 'to be tied to a stake, with a paper on his breast inscribed "Lampoon Carrier" (Dutch MSS., Albany, X., p. 216).—On Apr. 15, 1676, W. T. received a grant of 20 acres land by the Court of Kingston (N. Y. Land Papers, I., p. 74).—On Oct. 2, 1676, there was granted to W. T. from Gov. *Andros*, a piece of land at *Esopus*, north east from Capt. *Thomas Chamber's* farm, of about 10 acres, also a piece of land of 10 acres north and south along the *Great Creek* or Kill to the Water Kolch (Ibid., p. 90·1).
Eelet (*Helena*) T., 'eldest daughter,' m. 1675, *Jan Burhans* of Kingston; *Johannes T.*, bt. in N. Y., April 9, 1659, m. 1. *Aagjen Winne*, and had a. *Alida*, bt. Oct. 10, 1708, b. *William*, (see his will); *Johannes T.* m. 2., Jan. 25, 1718, *Eva Zout*, widow of *Hans Juriaan Louks*, b. Hoogduytsland (*Germany*), and had: c. *Aaltjen*, bt. Apr. 8, 1711, d. *Jannetjen*, bt. Sept. 27, 1713; (See Johannis T.'s will).—*Rebecca* T., bt. in *Bushwick*, June 19, 1662, m. *Peter Peterson* of *Hurley*; *William* T. m. 1. *Tryntje Peele*, and 2., Apr. 30,1699, *Gepje Pier*, widow of *Hendrick Ariaense*, and had: a. *Johannes*, bt. May 26, 1700, b. *Willem*, bt. Febr. 21, 1703, c. *Geesje*, bt. Apr. 15, 1705, d. *Aarent*, bt. June 20, 1707;—*Hendrick* T. m. *Sara Kierstede*, and had: a. *Willem*, bt. Sept. 11, 1698; b. *Eycke*, bt. July 14, 1700; c. *Roeloff*, bt. Aug. 9, 1702, d. *Joannes*, bt. Apr. 9, 1704, e. *Lucas*, bt. March 17, 1706, f. *Catryn*, bt. June 20, 1708, g. *Jonathan*, bt. Nov. 10, 1710.

Page 39.—DU BOIS, Lois of the New Paltz.

Will dated March 30, 1686.

"Estate (after payment of debts) to be Equally divided amongst my children: but my two Eldest sonns desiring to haue Each of them a part of the Land of the New Paltz and more than the other children by Reason their names are uppon pattent, but if they will be content to deale Equally with my other children whether in land houses or Any other sort of Goods whatsoever belonging to my said Estate As well the land of the Paltz that I have bought former And after my death And their mothers decease shall be dealt Equally Amongst them."—"My two Eldest sonnes will Each of them have part of the land lying in the New Paltz—on condition that they shall pay for the said land with interest unto the other of my children and shall not inherit any of the other land housing or Another sort of Goods belonging to my said Estate but them that have home-lotts And have built thereon shall keep the same upon condition that the other of my children shall have so much land in stead thereof in such convenient places As may be found most Expedient for them." "My wife their mother shall have the ordering of the Estate as long as she remains a widdow." "If she marry the Estate to be divided amongst the children aforesaid except my two eldest sons." Signed by the testator, and witnessed by

    ARENT TUNISEN   (Recorded May 5, 1686.)
    DIRCK SCHEPMOES
  (See his former and later wills).

Page 51.—ADREIJANSE, PETTER, of Kingston.

Will dated Febr. 30, 1686.

"To my brother *Hendrick Hendricks* of Kingston yeoman, All my hoole Estate of Lands Chatils & Goods.

    JOHANNES WYNKOOP   PETTER ADREIJANSE (his mark)
    HUMPHR. DAVENPORT

Page 52.—HENDRICKS, HENDRICK, of Kingston, yeoman.

Will dated Dec. 30, 1686.

"To my brother Petter Adreijanse of Kingston All my hooll Estate, Lands, Chattiels, and Goods." Signed by the testator. Same witnesses as above.
  (See Hendrick Aryansee).

Page 65.—DEIJOU, CHRISTIAN, of New Paltes.

Will dated Febr. 1, 1687/8.

"To my soon *Petter Deyou* 50 Ricksdallers yt my soon was In Debted to me; and then to deal Equally with ye Rest of my Childerin of all my Estate."—"To my soones soon Whos name Is *Christian Deijo* 40 pieces of Eight and A small Gunn."—"To my five children All ye Rest of my Estate of Lands housings Chattills and mouable Goods."—"My Corps may be buried att ye New Poalls."

    NICOLAS DEPEW   CHRISTIAN DEYOU (his mark)
    WALLROUEN DUMONT
    JNO DAVID   June 30, Humphrey Davenport and Wallrouen
    HUMPHREY DAVENPORT Demont appeared before Henry Beekman.
  (See his former will).

Page 71.—BLANCHAN, MATTHES & MAGDELEN JOORE.

"If Matthis Blanchan happens to dy first his wife shall continue in possession of all ye Goods so long as she lives and if Magdalen Joore happens to Deceas first her husband Matthis Blanchan shall continue in possession of ye Goods and Estates as long as he lives and if Either of them marry hee or Shee shall deliver to ye children ye Equall half part of ye whole Estat butt if both Matthis Blanchan and his wife happen to dy then their son *Matthis Blanchan* shall have ye farme lying in Hurley with house barns and appurtenances with four horses and four cows, and whatt Remains in Esopus and America their children shall Equally divide Among them yt is to say Chatharine Maria Magdalena Elizabeth Matthes." Dated Aug. 22, 1671, and recorded Apr. 30, 1688.

(Capt.) Thomas Chambers
Cornelius Barentse, Clarke   } Magistrates of ye Court.
Jno Williamse

Attestor, W. De la Montagne

(See his former will).

Page 93.—FFRANCKFORD, ABRAHAM, of Kingston, March'tt.

Will dated September 28, 1689.

"Ffirst being penitent & Sorroy from ye bottom of my hart for my Sins past most Humbly desiering forgivenness for ye Same."—"I will that my well beloved wife Sara Ffranckford Shall have all my whole Estate of Lands, houses & house hold Goods and all whattso Ever may bee Due & owing unto me" "my said wife only paying Unto My Eldest Sone *Jack* fifty & one pcs of Eight when by him demanded; and to my younger sone *Pearle* fifty pcs of Eight Uppon demand and no More and ye Rest of my said Estate, my wife *Sara* Shall keepe & Injoy for Ever." Signed by the testator.

Johanes Hardenbrock
Jockein Brannarne

Page 96.—HARMILLE, TOMAS.

Will dated March 12, 1688/9, and written in the Dutch language.

"In de name des Heere, Amen (In the name of God, Amen) "Kranck" (sick) "Ei dogh myn volle verstaent Hebbende" (but of perfect mind). "As executors of my whole estate I appoint the Deacons of the Reformed Church." "My whole estate to the poor of said church (de Arme Behoorende Aen Onse Kerrick).

Signed by the testator.

Jan Duke (his mark)   } (Apr. 21, 1690, appeared before *Jacob Artse,*
N. Anthony   } Justice of the Peace, proving the will).

Page 99.—CLAESSE(N), HENDERICK, Carpender.

Will dated November 12th, 1688.

"I Acknollig before ye After mentioned witnesses that *Cornelia Swartwout* my Espoued and truly belouwed Brid is and Schal bee And Remain the Only herriss of my whole Estaet" "And iy Schold please God to giueue Childeren to her and that she after my Death Shold Com to re-marry than Schall ye hallif of y Estaet Remaen inviolable to ye Children that hauf been proceated and Agriment Alder bout ouer "Children Schall Equilly inherit as well sons as Doghters only ye Eldest son Schall haufe an Engelish Schilling "And furdher to hinder And Scham All manner of troubbell that might Arrise by ye same So Schall be Give unto the Recerdit Basterd Child named *Claes* whoes modder is called *Debora* an English Schilling". "And to hold this my matrimony, Condisyon and Last will and testament, as by this written, I dissanull and revoke all manner of wills and testaments" and "Swere before ye Leving And Almeighty God" "that I Schall neuer fforsack nor Lefe Cornelia Swartwout" "my betroued bryd untill ye End of my death."

Signed by the testator, and witnessed by *Thomas Garton* (Justice of ye Pease), *Mattis Clarkson*, and *Jan Ward*.

(*Hendrick Claessen Schoonhoven* m. *Cornelia Swartwout*, dau. of *Roeloff S.* and *Eva Alberts*, and bt. March 13, 1667. They had issue:—i. *Ifje*, bt. Apr. 28, 1689; ii. *Cornelis*, bt. Oct. 4, 1691; iii. *Nicolaes*, bt. June 3, 1694; iv. *Fransyntje*, bt. Nov. 15, 1696; v. *Henricus*, bt. Aug. 5, 1699; vi. *Margriet*, bt. Jan. 22, 1702; vii. *Catharina*, bt. Oct. 12, 1707.)

Page 112.—LOMMENDIEU, PETER, of Kingstown, Marchant.

Will dated Febr. 10, 1691/2.

"Sick and weake in body".

"My dear Mother *Martha Lommendieu* all what goods Merchandise whatsoever that I have in Company and without Company, and that I doe will that all what goods yt is Left in ye hands of *Steven Valloo* pr. Inventory Shall be seen, Shall be Sent Downe to New Yorke and there delivered in ye hands of *Mr. Steven de Lance* merchant in New Yorke for to keep till *Mr. August Yea* (Jay) doth return, or on ordre from my said mother for the Delivery, also I do will yt Steven Valo Shall Receive from all and Every Person in the County of Ulster all what debts that is now Stending out, and what that shal be Received—he shall send unto the said Steven Delance, at Yorke for my mothers and my Parteners account August Yea." Signed by the testator.

JOHN DAVID
S. VALLEOU
H. DAVENPORT

(Probated March 30, 1692, John Davy, Stephen Valo & Humphry Devenport appeared before Henry Beekman & Philip Schuyler, Esqrs., Justices of the Peace).

(Letters of administration were granted to *Stephen De Luncy* and *Stephen Vulleuu* (N. Y. Surr. Office, Liber 3-4, p. 331).—*Benjamin L'Hommedieu* came from *New Rochelle, France*, had letters of denization, March 10, 1686-7, settled on *Shelter Island*, res. at *Southold, L. I.*, 1690, a merchant, m. *Patience*, dau. of Capt. *Nath. Silvester*, and had: *Benjamin, Jr.*, *Hosea*, *Silvester*, who m. Elisabeth Booth, Peter, Patience, and Susan, who m. Jonathan Tuthill.)

Page 129.—WITTAKER, EDWARD, of Kingstown.

Will dated Sept. 3, 1694.

"Sick and weak in body." (Long religious preamble). "To my Dear wife *Hanna Wittaker,* the Right third part of all my Real & personall Estate of what nature or kind Soever during her Naturall Life, Except a gray horse and a Colt hereunder bequeathed unto my Sonns, and after her decease yt ye same then in being shall bee to ye onely proper use benifitt & behoffe of my two sonns hereunder named," "to be Equally Devided between them, Except £ 20 yt shall bee for ye proper use of my Wives Daughters Children.—3dly, I give and bequeath unto my Sonn *James Wittaker"* "a gray Horse and ye Right third part of all my Reall and personall Estate of what nature or kind soever Except a gray Colt hereunder bequeathed unto my Sonn *Edward Wittaker."* 4thly. "To my son Edward Wittaker" "a gray Colt and the Right third part of all my Reall and personall Estate," "Except a gray Horse before Excepted." —Son James Wittaker and "my friend & Nabour *William Legg"* executors. Signed by the testator.

BOUDEWYN D' WITT (his mark)
ABRAM B. RUTAN
W. D. MEYER

(All witnesses appeared before Capt. Wessel ten Broeck & Lt. Jacob Aertse, Justices of ye Peace, Jan. 16, 1694/5. Prob. Jan. 21, 1694/5. Thos. Garton, Judge of ye Court of Common Pleas.

W. D. Meyer, Clark).

(Edward Whittaker was a soldier in the Duke of York's Regiment, and had with his wife, Hannah: i. Edward, who m. June 18, 1700 *Hillitje Burhans* (see his will), ii. James, bt. Apr. 24, 1674, m. Dec. 6, 1696, *Elisabeth Titsoort,* b. *Schenectady.*)

Page 167.—DU BOIS, LOWIES, of Kingstown.

Will dated March 27, 1694, and written in the Dutch language. "In deen Naeme Des Heeren, Amen."

"Voor Eerst bevele ick myn Ziel aen de almagtige godt myn schepper, En Jesus Christus myn Verlosser, En aende hylige geest myn hyligmaker, En myn Lichaem tot de aerde van waer het selve gecomen is, om op Eem Christelyke manier begraven to werden" (I bequeath first my soul to the Almighty God my shepherd and to Jesus Christus my saviour and to the holy ghost my redeemer, and my body to the earth from which it came, to be buried in a Christian manner).

"Soo geve ick aen myn huysvrouw *Catryna de boys* (to my wife Cathrina, all myn staat van Landen, huysen, goederer, Schulden, gelt, gout, silver gemünt of ongemünt (all my property in land, houses, goods, debts, money) "om gedürende haer leven to mogen gebrüycken En na myn" "huysvrouws" "alsdan in Weesen sal syn" met desen Verstande noghtans dat Indier myn huysvrouw wederom quam te hertrouwen, alsdan gehouden is om de helft vande geheele staat uyt te keeren aen myn Erfgenamen hier na beschreven; Ten Derden Soo geve ick aen myn outsten Soon (if the widow should marry, then to his eldest son) *Abraham du boys* ses pont in gelt voor het Recht van Eerst geboorte (£6 as his right being the first born).

"Soo geeve ick aen myn soon Abraham du boys of Erfgenamen de geregste agste part van myn gehelen staet alsdan in Weesen (the eight part of my whole estate).

"Aen myn soon *Jacob* De geregste aghste part van my geheele staat" (to my son Jacob an eight part of the estate).

"Aen myn soon *David*" an eight part of the estate.

"Aen myn soon *Salomon*" an eight part of the estate.

"Aen myn soon *Lowies*" an eight part of the estate.

"Aen myn soon *Matthew*" an eighth part of the estate.

"Aen de naergelaten Kinderen Van Wijlen," (children of deceased), *Isaacq du boys*," an eight part of the estate" met des Conditie dat Ingevallen de voors. Kinderen in haere onmondighyt mogle Comen te overslyden dat alsdann voors. part sal onder myn andere Erfgename hier ingeschreven Egaelyck gedeelt werden." (If any of the children should die before they become of age, then their shares to be divided among the other heirs mentioned).

"Aen de Kinderen van myn dogter *Sara*—getrout hebbende (to children of my daughter Sara, wife of *Joost Janse*, nü in *Wesen* an eight part of the estate."

Wife appointed executrix. Signed by the testator.

JAN WARD
S. VALLOAU
W. D. MEYER

(23 June, 1696. A true copy examined
W. D. Meyer, Clark).

(Codicil.)

Page 169.—DU BOIS, LOWIES, of Kingstown.

Will dated Febr. 22, 1695/6, and written in the Dutch language.

"Kennelick sy Een Jeder by Desen dat ick" "En Laast Will & Testem't hebbe gemacht Den 27 Dagh van maert 1694" by Dese approbeere En bevestige, En begerende data Deselve in alle Deelen sal opsevolgt Werde, Except met Dese Sondering als hier onder myn begeerte uytgedrückt Enbeschreven is te Weten" (Be it known that I on March 27, 1694 made a will, which is hereby approved and to be followed in all parts, except as here provided)—

"Myn soon *Jacob du boys* sal hebben in Regt & Waren Eydendom d' geregte helft van myn *bouwery* gelegen opt *horly* stück, tüsschen t' Landt van *hyman* & *Jan Rosa* En t' Lant van *Lammert huyberse,* om voor hem Daar te Disponeren na Welgevallen met dese Conditie dat myn soon Jacob du boys sal gehouden syn te betalen voor voors. Landt d' quantytyt van Een Duysent En fyf hondert schepel tarw, oock soo sal de voors. Jacob du boys d'andere helft van voors. Landt in huer gebruycken tot dat myn Jongste soon *Matthew du boys* tot mondigen dagen sal gekomen syn, En voor het' gebuyck Der selve te betalen vyftigh schepels tarw pr annum" (to my son Jacob half of my farm at Hurly adjoining land of Hyman and Jan Rosa and land of Lammert Huyberse" "on condition that he pays 1500 shepels wheat; Jacob to use the other half until my youngest son Matthew Du Bois becomes of age, for which he is to pay 50 shepels wheat yearly).

"Soo Verclaer ick, dat ick van Desen Dagh hebbe getransporteert aan myn Jongste soon Matthew Du booys Een huys En Erf in *Kingstowne* Een perceeltie wy Landt En de geregte helft van myn Landt gelegen op het *Horly* stück volgens Teneur van voors. traspoort mits dat my voors. soon Matthew du boys sal moeten uytkeeren En betalen de quantityt van vüftien hondert schepels tarwe nietlegenstaar de dat voors. transport vermelt dat de betalinge der selve geschiet is." (I have this day conveyed to my youngest son, Matthew Du Bois, house and land in Kingston, a parcel of meadow land, and one half of my land at Hurley, for which he is to pay 1500 schepels of wheat).

"Soo is myn will En Begeerte t'landt Door myn soon *David Du boys* van *Jan Wood* gecogt, Dat de betalinge sal uyt myn staat moeten geschieden als ick sül aan myn voors. soon David du boys belooft hebbe." (Payments for the land which my son David bought from Jan Wood to come out of my estate, as I had promised my son David).

"Myn soon *Salomon Du boys* En *Lowies du boys* sullen mogen in waren & Regten Eydendom to hebben voor haar & haar order of Erfgename myn landt gelegen onttrent d' *Paltz* volgens grontbrief van Coll. *Thomas Dongan* gedatert Den 2 dag van Junij 1688: en daar voor te betalen De quantityt van aghthondert schepels tarw." (My sons Salomon and Louis Du Bois are to have my land in the Paltz, conveyed to me by deed from Coll. Thomas Dongan, dated June 2, 1688, for which they are to pay 800 shepels of wheat).

"Myn Dogter *Sara* Huysvrouw van *Joost Janse* sal mogen in waren & Regter Eygen dom te gebben voor haar En haar order of Erfgename Een stück Landt gelegen onder de Jurridictie van *Horly* naest de grondt van *Corneles Cool* En Daer voor te betalen de quantityt van seven hondert schepel tarw te Vertaan dat Bos Lant gelegen omtrent voors. Landt, medec geinludert is voor voors. soomme." (My daughter Sara wife of Joost Janse to have a piece of land in Hurley adjoining the land of Corneles Cool, for which she is to pay 700 shepels of wheat. This includes the woodland adjoining. Signed by the testator.

W. D. Meyer	(Major Jacob Rutse and Mattys Slegt of
Jacob Rutsen	Kingstown appeared before *Capt. Dirck*
Jan Burhans	*Schepmoes* and Mr. *Johannis Wynkoof*, Jus-
Matthys Slegt	tices of the peace, March 26, 1696.

W. D. Meyer, Clark.

Henr. Beeckman, Judge of ye Court ot Common Pleas.

A true copy Examined 23 June 1606.)

BOOK OF DEEDS, Liber I.   53

Page 208.—POULSE, GOMMEN, of Kingstown.

Will dated April 6, 1699, and written in Dutch.
Religious preamble.

"So Stel ick tot Erfgename van myn geheele Staat *Gretie Elmendorf* Wedewe Van Wiljen *Jacobus Van Elmendorp* Om over t selve te Disponeere na haar Eygen goetduncken En believen, Sonder dat voors. Grietie Elmendorp gehouden Sal Syn Reecg: te geven wegens voors. Staat Aan Jemant."

(I appoint Gretie Elmendorf, widow of Jacobus van Elmendorp, deceased, heir to my entire estate, with right to dispose thereof, and without being obliged to give an account to any one).

Gritie Elmendorp appointed executor.

GOMMEN POULSE (his mark).

W. D. MEYER	(Witnesses, all of Kingstown, appeared
GERRIT AERTSE	before Jan Tysell & Jan Heemans, Justices
TEUNIS OOSTERHOUT	of the peace, June 19, 1699.

JACOB RUTSEN, Judge of the Court of Common Pleas.
A true copy examined. JOHN MARTIN.)

Page 212.—CORNELISE, MARTE & Mayke Cornelise, of Claverak, County Albany.

Will dated Aug. 13, 1685, and written in Dutch.

"Voor my (before me) *Robt. Livingston,* Secr. van Albany Colony *Renselaerwyck* en *Schinectady*" appeared "Marte Cornelisse huyeman woonende Aent (husbandman living at) Claverak in County van Albany & Mayke Cornelise."—Long religious preamble. "Tot haer Eenige & Uyterste Erfgename de Langst levende van her beyden (the survivor to be sole heir), en dat in alle de goederen Roerende & onrorende, Landereyen huys Skuyre Bestialien Actien Credyte, gelt, gout, Silver, juwelen, Cledeeren, Linnen, woollen, huysraat & anders niets gesonders noch gereseweert die d' Eerste oft livige van haer beyde (of all goods, real estate and movable, lands, houses, barn, cattle, negotiable paper, money, gold, silver, jewels, clothing, linen, wool, household goods, and everything else).

"En wanneer d. Langstlevende Sall Comente overlyden (and when the survivor dies) Soo is het Express Begeerte van d Testaurs dat d Staat die Alsdan bevonde Sal worden (it is the testators' wishes that the estate shall then) Egaeel Sal gedeelt worden (be divided equally) onder haer Seven Kinderen (among their seven children), met namen (by name) *Fannerie* huysvrowe (wife) van *Hendrick Cornelis Bogard,* out 28 Jaeren (28 years old), *Cornelis* out 26 Jaeren, *Teuntie* huysvrouw van *Livinus Winne* out 21 Jaeren, *Geertruy* out 18 Jaeren, *Marytie* out 16 Jaeren, *Cornelis* out 10 Jaeren & *Jacob Martense* out 8 Jaeren den Een met meerden als den ander (the one not more than the other) Exempt dat haer Soon Cornelis t' Beste Peert voor uyt Sall Trecken (except that son C. shall have the best horse first) & dan Egael deelen met d' andere kindere (and then to divide equally with the other children), Sullende vorders d' Langstlevende gehouden syn d kindern die mynderjaerigh zyn opte voeden ind vreese des heeren (the survivor to be bound to bring up the minors in praise of the Lord), en eeingh Konst off hantwerk laere leeren (and to teach them a profession or a trade) waennede zyte Syner tydt met Godt & met Eere aende Cost kunne geracken (so that they may be able to make a living in God and honor) & wanner zy ten mondigen daege off howelyken Staet Sall off Sullen gekome zyn (and when they become of age, or marry) So Sall d Langstlevende in Constientie Sall bevinden te behooren Sonder meer (the survivor shall be bound to give such child or children a proper marriage outfit, as good as the estate will permit and the conscience of the survivor dictates).

"En soo d Langstlevende mockte comen te behovelycken (if the survivor should happen to marry) his or her part is to be divided among the seven children.

"Maj. Abraham Staas en Jan Verbeeck" om hem off haer te Assistere" (to assist him or her (i. e. the survivor) in the proper discharge of this "laeste will & Testament."

ABRAHAM STAAT
JAN VERBEEK

MARTE CORNELISE (his mark).
MAYKE CORNELISE husvrouwe van
Marte Cornelise (her mark).

Hendrick Bogard of *Marbletown* appeared before *Jan Mattyse* & *Jan Heermans*, Justices of the peace, both witnesses being dead, and the will was probated June 19, 1699.—JACOB RUTSEN, Judge of the Court of Common Pleas.

(Henderik Cornelisen Bogaart, m. *Jannetje* (Fannerie) *Martensen*, dau. of *Cornelis Martensen* and *Marritje Martensen*, and had a daughter, *Sara*, bt. Nov. 6, 1692, and other children.—Cornelis Martenz, j.m. of *Albany*, res. at *Claverack*, m. after Febr. 23, 1685, *Cornelia Van Vredenburgh*, of *New York*, res. *Kingston*, and had: i. *Isack*, bt. Jan. 1, 1696, ii. *Jacobus*, bt. Nov. 6, 1698.—In the will, recorded at Albany, and dated 1676-7 "*Maerten Cornelissen*, of *Claverack*" is said to be "born in the city of *Yesselsteyn*, and wife Mayeke Cornelis, born at *Barrevelt*." (Albany Co. Rec., Notarial Papers, I., p. 606).—Livinus Winne was son of *Peter W.*, Commissary or Magistrate of *Bethlehem*, Albany Co., born at *Ghent*, who made his will, July 6, 1684, proved Febr. 22, 1695-6 (Ibid., Wills, I., p. 44.)

Page 215.—DE WITT, JAN CLAETZ, of Amsterdam In Hollandt.

Will dated March 31, 1699, and written in Dutch.

"Myn Neef *Evart Bogardus* en Myn Nicht *Tialie Bogardus* Sal hebben en genieten Alles wat Ick hier in America heb" (my nephew, E. B., and my niece, T. B., shall have all that I have here in America) on condition that they "Sal geven en Leveren Aen *Nicholas Hofman* myn neef Vyfen twentigh Stuck van Achten (give and deliver to N. H., my nephew, 25 pieces of eight (an old Dutch coin)."—"De kinderen van myn Suster *Tialie Heerekeus* Sal hebben Myn gehull Staet die Ick In' *Hollandt* heb, Roerende en onroerende (the children of my sister,

T. H., shall have all my real estate and personal property in Holland). Signed by the testator, and witnessed by

 STEPHEN GACHERIE
 MELLYSE VLECHT.

Jacob Aertse, Justice of the peace, Stephen Gacherie & Mallyse Vlecht appeared before *Arie Gerritse* & *Roeloff Swartwout,* Justice of the peace, June 26, 1699, proving the will.

 (Jan Claessen De Witt was a brother of Tjerck Claasen De Witt (q.v.), and died unmarried.)

Page 221.—VAN ELMENDORP, JACOBUS.

Will dated Aug. 27, 1685, and written in Dutch.

"Syn vrowe Sall de geheele staedt besitten soo lange als Sy Owhertroudt leeft." "Als Sy kompt tehertrowten dat sy de gerechte heeft vande Staet Sall uyt keeren aende kinderen" *"Coenraedt, Gertie, Anna, Jacobus, Jenneke, Tekla."* "Dat soo myn vrow kompt te hertrowen En dat naer haer doot de kinderen genoemt, haer Moeders Portie." (His wife shall have the whole estate for life, if unmarried. If she should marry, only one half of the property, the other half to go to the children (named), and after her death, all to go to the children.

"Myn zoon Coenraedt myn landt genaempt *Wassenmakers* landt met de Appendentie vandiewvoor daysent Scheepell Tarve, En of syn Erfnisse soo hoogh niet landt door gebraeck van myn vrow mochte worden verkocht all wat het meeder gelt als duysent Scheepell Tuverage daerop Sall hy moeter betalen." (My son Coenraedt shall have my land called Wassemaker's land, with the 4,000 schepels of wheat, and if his inheritance should not be large enough, my wife may dispose of sufficient for the purpose, except that all what is over 1,000 schepel of wheat shall belong to her).

"Alle kinderen sollen Egaell sonder onderscheyt delen" (all the children shall divide equally). "De Erftenisse van myn Patrimoniale goederen int Vater landt Sall mede Egael worde gedeelt doch de Jongste dochter genaempt Tekela Sall voor uyt hebbende hondert gulten hollandts (my paternal inheritance in the old country shall be equally divided, but my youngest daughter, called Tekela, shall have, in advance, 100 hollandish gulden).

"Soon Coenraedt Sonder Erfgenamen quam te Sterven heeft Jacobus Syn broeder Tselverecht in alles als Coenraedt in die Testament vermeelt (if C. should die without issue, his brother J. shall have the same interest in this will as C.). Signed by Jacobus Van Elmendorp (l. s.), and Grietien Elmendorp (l. s.). and witnessed by

 JAN HENDRIX
 GOMMERT POWLISSEN.

John Hendrix of Kingston appeared on Nov. 30, 1699, before *John Ward* and *John Herrmans,* Justices of the peace, proving the will.—All witnesses not being present, I have moved to the Widdow & Relict of said Jacobus Elmendorp & his heirs, viz. Coenraedt Elmendorp, *Mattyse Wynkoop*, husband of *Gaertie Elmendorp, Jacobus Elmendorp* & *Jenneke Elmendorp*, whom answered they approved of it.

JACOB RUTSEN, Judge of the Court of Common Pleas.

(See Jacobus Elmendorp.)

Folio 252.—DE WITT, TJERCK CLAESE, of Kingston.

Will dated March 4, 1687, and written in Dutch.

(Long religious preamble, similar to previous wills.) "Myn huysvrouw *Barbara d' Widt* sall blyven in posessie van myn geheele staet om geduerende haer Leeven." (My wife, B. de W., shall continue in possession of my whole estate, as long as she lives).

"Aen myn oudste Soon *Andres de Widt*" "de gerechte twaelfde part van myn geheele Staet, en dat myn voorsch. soon na het overlyden van myn voors. huysvrouw, sall hebben en genieten voor hem" "de gerechte helft van all t' Lant, huysing, etc. myn soebehoorende Mils gehouden naelselve by onpartydige parsonen op Eedt gepryseert is, uyt te Keeren en betalen aen myn andere Erfgenaemen als haer volgens dien Sullen Compiteeren ook so heb ick 't landt van *Cocksinck* betaelt en Naederlant Een grandt van de goveneur en Raeden van deese proventie voor Een groot bedeelte, geobtineert alsmede een stuck Landt omtrendt de *Klyne Soopis* in Compagnie met *Wm. de Meyer* gecoght Welcke Lande van *Korcksinck* en *Klyne Esoopeis* ick hebbe gegeven aen myn voors. Soon en Confermeere tselve sonder dat hy gehouden Sall syn Jetwes voor 'tselve aen myn andere Erfgenaeme te betalen." (To my oldest son, A. de W., 1/12 of my estate, and after the decease of my wife one half of all the land, houses, my mill, etc., to be appraised by impartial witnesses, he to pay to my other heirs whatever they may appraise it to. I have paid for my land at C., and also obtained a grant from the Governor and Council of this Province, as well as purchased a piece of land near the Little Esopus in company with Wm. de Mayer, which land I have given to my said son, and which conveyance I hereby confirm; he not to be obliged to pay anything further for said land to my other heirs).

"Aen myn Jongste soon *Tjerck de Widt*" "de gerechte twaelfde part van myn geheele Staet en dat myn voors. Soon na het overlyden van myn voors. huysvrouw sall hebben en genieten" "de geregte helft van all 't lant huysing Etc." (To my youngest son, T. de W., 1/12 of my entire estate, and after my wife's decease one half of all the land, houses, etc.).

"Myn Soon *Jan de Widt*" "de geregte twaelfde part van myn geheele State op maniere als boven ook dat myn voors. Soon uyt de penningen myn Competeerende weegens Koop van Landt Sall genieten vyf hondert Competeerende weegens Koop van Landt Sall genieten vyf hondert Schepels tarwe." (My son J. de W. 1/12 of my whole estate, as above, and out of the money due me for sale of land, 500 schepels of wheat).

"My son *Luycias D Witt*" "de gerechte twaelfde Part van myn geheele Staet" "ook so hebbe ick Een Sloep getimmert de voorlede Jaer de helft van voors. Sloep is en Sall Syn ten behoeven" (My son, L. de Witt, 1/12 of my estate, and half interest in a sloop which I built last year).

"Aen myn Soon *Dieck d Witt*" "de gerechte twaelfde part van myn geheele Staet." "Aen myn dogter *Tjatje* huysvrouw van *Mattys Mattyson*" "de gerechte twaelfde part van myn geheele Staet." "Aen myn dogter *Jannetie* huysvrouw van *Cornelis Swetts* de gerechte twaelfde part" (to son D., daughter T., wife of M. M., and daughter J., wife of C. S., 1/12 part of the entire estate each) met dese Conditie dat Indien myn voors. Dogter quam te overlijden Sonder Kindere" "voors. portie Sall Syn Ten behoeve van myn Erfgenamen om Egaelyck" "gedeelt Te Werden (on condition that if my daughter should die, leaving no children, her portion shall be equally divided among my other heirs).

"Aen myn dogter *Geertruy*" "de gerechte twaelfde part van myn geheele Staet," "ock soo heift myn voors. dogter een Negerinn" "in possessie myn toe behoerende Welch ick begeere Sall Syn ten behoeren van myn voors. dogter" (to my daughter G. 1/12 part of my whole estate, and the negress which she now has in her possession).

"Aen myn dogter *Ragel*" "de gerechte twaelfde part van myn geheele Staet" "mits dat gekort sal werden uyt myn voors. dogters portie tot benifitie van myn Erfgenamen Een hondert pondts die myn voors. dogters man *Cornelis Bogardus* Schuldigh Aen myn is voor Een Aghule van Een bercken tyn Aen him vercoght (to my daughter R. 1/12 of my whole estate, less £100, which my said daughter's husband, C. B., owes me for 1/8 interest in a brigantine, which I sold him) dogh begeerende dat t' Kint van voors. Bogardus met naeme *Barbara* Sall genieten nye voors. hondert pondt vyftigh Stuck van aghten" (the child of said B., called Barbara, to have 50 pieces of eight out of said £100).

"Aen myn dogter *Maritie*" "de gerechte twaelfde part van myn geheele Staet." "Aen myn dogter *Aegie*" "de gerechte twaelfde part van myn geheele Staet." (To daughters M. and A. 1/12 part each).

"Indien Eeniege van myn voors. Erfge. in haere onmondighyt quamen to overlyden dat als dan desselfs portie onder myn Erfgenaemen Eegaelyk sall gedeelt werden." (If anyone of my heirs should die during their minority, such portion shall be equally divided among my other heirs).

"Huysvrouw Barbara de Witt" appointed executrix. Signed by the testator, and witnessed by

  Jacob Rutsen Abraham Lamater W. D. Meyer.

Abr. Lamater & Wm. de Meyer of Kingston, appeared, March 6, 1700/1 before Jacob Rutsen, Judge of the Court of Common Pleas, proving the will. (A true copy examined with the original by *Ruth Bleeker*, Clark).

(Tjerck Claesse De Witt, from *Grootholdt*, in *Zunderland*, m. in *New Amsterdam*, Apr. 24, 1656, *Barbara Andriessen*, from *Amsterdam*. A sister of T. C. De W., *Emmerentie De Witt*, m.

at New Amsterdam, in 1662, *Martinus Hoffman*. His brother, *Jan Claetz De Witt*, made his will March 31, 1699 (q.v.).—He had in 1661 a brother-in-law, *Jan Alberse* in *Beverwyck*, and another, *Pieter Janse*, in *Oosterbemis*, in *East Friesland, Holland*.—Had in 1661 land there, which he had inherited from his father, from which he was receiving rents.—His widow, Barbara De Witt, died July 6, 1714, and the property was appraised, in accordance with the provisions in the will. (See Ulster Co. Deeds).—T. C. de W. died in Kingston, Febr. 17, 1700.—On June 25, 1657, Tjerck Claessen (De Witt) appeared before *Johannes La Montagne*, Deputy at *Fort Orange*, declaring that he had conveyed to Carsten Claessen and Jan Barensen (Wemys) 180 guilders to be paid in merchantable beavers, growing out of a sale of a stallion, at public sale, of which *Jan Roeloffse* remained the last bidder (Albany Co. Rec.).—On Sept. 10, 1660, Madame *Johanna De Laidt* and her husband, Hon. *Jeronimus Ebbinck* granted to T. C. (De Witt), inhabitant of the Colony of *Rensselarswyck* two pieces of land in *Esopus*, the north field comprising 35 morgens 155 rods, the other adjoining the west side 35 morgens 110 rods, in exchange for which T. C. has given his house 20 feet long and with a passage 30 feet broad, and lot 10 rods and 29 feet long, in Beverwyck, adjoining on the east side the street, on the west the garden of *Henderick Anderiessen* and *Lambert Van Neeck*, and on the south by the house of *Hendrick de Backer* (Ibid.).—Tjerck C. de W. and *Heymanse Roos* are to be punished if they continue to oppose authority.—Letter from Dir. *Stuyvesant*, July 30, 1663 (Dutch MSS., Corr., xv, p. 48).—On June 25, 1672, T. C. de W. had a deed from Gov. Lovelace, for a parcel of bush land, together with a house, lot, orchard, and calves' pasture, lying near Kingston, in Esopus (N. Y. Land Papers, Albany, I., p. 46).—On Oct. 8, 1677, he had a deed from Gov. Andros for a piece of woodland of about 50 acres, at Esopus, to ye west of the towne (Ibid., p. 128).—On May 14, 1694, he petitioned for an order for survey of 280 acres of land purchased of the Indians at *Coxinke* (English MSS., xxxix, p. 160).—On the Patent of T. C. de W., near the confluence of the Mombackus and Rondout Kills, stood, for a long time, a sycamore tree, in which had been cut a man's face, carved to commemorate a battle fought near the spot, Mombakkus (silent head from 'mom', silent, and 'bak or bakkus' head), which was named thereafter.—Tjerck C. de Witt's will is also recorded in N. Y. Sur. Office, Liber 7, p. 601, under *Dirck Claas De Witt* (wife Barbara).

They had issue: i. *Andries*, m. March 7, 1682, *Jannetje Egbertsen* (bt. N. Y. Jan. 11, 1664, d. Nov. 23, 1733, d. of *Egbert Meindertse* & *Jaepe Jans*). Captain Andries was accidentally killed, July 22, 1710; ii. *Taatje*, b. Albany ab. 1659, carried off by the Indians at the burning of Kingston, 1663, but rescued, m., 1677, *Matthys Mattysen Van Keuren*, s. of *Matthys Jansen* & *Marg. Hendrickse*; iii. *Jannetje*, bt. Febr. 12, 1662, m. *Cornelis Swits* (q.v.); iv. *Klaes*, bt. Febr. 17, 1664; v. *Jan*, bt. Febr. 14, 1666, m. *Wyntje Kierstede*, d. of *Roeloff K. & Ikee (Anghe) Roosa*, d. of *Albert Heymanse R.* (q.v.); vi. *Geertruy*, bt. Oct 15, 1668, m. March 24, 1688, *Hendrick Hendricksen Schoonmaker* (see *Hendrick Jochem S.*); vii. *Jacob*, m. before March 1, 1696, *Grietje Vernooy*, d. of Cornelius V. & Annatje Cornelis (q.v.); viii. Rachel, m. Cornelis Bogardus, (s. of *Cornelis B.* and *Helena Teller*); ix. *Lucas*, m. Dec. 22, 1695, *Annatje Delva* (d. of *Anthony D.* & *Jannetje Hillebrants* (q.v.); x. *Peek*, m. 1., Jan. 2, 1698, *Marytje Janse Vanderberg*, of Albany, and 2., Dec. 21, 1723, *Maria Teunis*, widow of *Jacob De Mott*; xi. *Tjerck*; xii. *Marritje*, m. 1., Nov. 3, 1700, *Hendrick Hendricksen Kortright*, s. of *Hendrick Jansen* (K.), and *Catharina Hansen Webber*, and 2., Sept. 6, 1702, *Jan Macklin*; xii. *Aagje*, bt. Jan. 14, 1684, m. Aug. 23, 1712, *Jan Pawling* (bt. Oct. 2, 1681, s. of Henry Pawling & Neeltje Roosa, d. of Albert Heymanse R.), rem. to Phila.)

Folio 262.—ARYANCE, HENDRICK, brewer.

Will dated Sept. 11, 1690.

(Long religious preamble.)

"I will that my well beloved wife *Gheppy* Shall have ye Just half of my whole Estate of Landt Chattles house and household goods" "and ye other half of my Estate of Landt Chattles house & house hold goods I will ut my oly Son *Arrie Hendricks* Shall have & injoy" "further I will yt my well beloved wife Shall injoy yt whole Estate as long as yt She Continues a widdow but when she shall Come to marry againe then ye half of ye Estate yt belongs to my my Son Arie shall be delivered to him or his assignes before marriage day of my wife."

HENDRICK ARYANCE (his mark).

ARENT TUENISSEN
CORNELIS MASTEN
HUMPHREY DAVENPORT

(Arent Tuenissen & Cornelis Masten appeared, June 16, 1701, before Jacob Rutsen.—A true copy examined, Rth Bleecker, Clark).

(*Henric Adriaans*, j.m. from *Gelderland*, res. Kingston, m., Jan. 19, 1685, *Gepie Arents Pier*, b. Kingston. *Henderic Arie* & *Gepje Aerts* had issue i. *Arie*, bt. Nov. 11, 1688. *Aarian Hen*-

dricks, m., before March 8, 1724, *Catrina Van den Bogaard*, and had with other children a daughter, Gepjen (Rachel).
See Hendrick Hendricks.)

Folio 273.—CORNELISON, GERRITT, of Hurley.

Will dated Febr. 3, 1686.

"To my eldest son *Cornelis*" "all my tools yt belong to his whole rights Trade & to my dear & Well beloved Wife I doe give & bequeath all my Lands goods, Chattles, houseings barnes orchards household goods & all Such my goods & tools & Nessersarys that belong to my ffarme now in my possession" "after her death to my ouldest son Cornelis & my second son *Arie* & my third son *Jan* & my daughter *Nettie*" to each an "Equall ffifth part of all my goods & Chattells" "to be equally devided among these my said ffive Children" "if any one or more Shall dye before my wife the said part shall be Equally devided amongst ye other brothers or sisters if nott married."

GERRITT CORNELISON (his mark).

HENRY PAULING
CORNELIS COLE

(Cornelis Cole of Hurly appeared before Coll. Henrius Beeckman, Judge, Capt. Dirck Schepmoes and Capt. Wessel Ten Broeck, Justices of the Court of Common Pleas, March 4, 1695/6).

(Gerrit Corneliszen m. *Chieltje Cornelis* (*Slegt*), came in Apr. 1659 in '*Moseman*' with wife and a sucking child, had issue: i. *Cornelis* m. *Jannetie Kunst*, see his will under *Cornelis Gerritse*; ii. *Arie* (*Gerretsen*) b. in *Midwoud* (*Flatbush, L. I.*), m. after Oct. 17, 1686, *Lysbert Lambertse*, b. *Kingston*, d. of *Lambert Huybertse* (q.v.) (witn. *Cornelis Kool & Neeltje Gerritsen*), and had a. *Hendrikje*, bt. Oct. 17, 1686; b. *Gerrit*, bt. May 30, 1697 (witn. *Cornelis Garritsen*, & *Gerritie Gerritsen*); iii. *Jan*, bt. N. Y., Sept. 8, 1666 (witn. *Theunis Cornelis*, and *Fytie*); iv. *Neeltje* (Neeltje); v. *Gerratje*, bt. March 12, 1669, m. Jacob Du Bois.—On Apr. 5, 1686, there is a survey of a tract of land of 85 acres, on the north side of *Esopus Kill*, *Hurley*, called '*Old Bouery*,' laid out for *Garret Cornelies*, by *Philip Welles*, surveyor (N. Y. Land Papers, II., p. 160).

Folio 273.—GERRITSE, CORNELIS, of Hurly.

Will dated Febr. 7, 1695, and written in Dutch.

(Long religious preamble.)

"Myn waerdi huysvrouw *Jannieti Kunst* sall hebben en besitten myn geheele Staat van huysen Landen goederen schulden paerden & beesten of 't Reght van Erfenisse door myn vaeder Zeligr *Gerrit Cornelisse* aen myn Volgens Testement gegeven gedurende haer Leven (my worthy wife, J. K. shall have my entire estate of houses, lands, goods, debts, horses and cattle, which were given me by my father, G. C., deceased, by his testament, during her life) Except indien myn voors. huysvrouw moght Coomen weederom te hertrouwen data alsdan gehouden is de gerechte helft van myn voors. Staat uyt te Keeren aen myn Kinderen Wettelyk myn voors. huysvrouw getrouweert met naeme *Gerrit Jan Arie Barent Gilie* en *Jacomyntie* om Egaelyk onder myn Ses Kinderen gedeelt to werden (except in case my said wife should happen to marry, when one-half of the estate shall go to the children, begotten by my said wife, by name G. J. A. B. G. and J., to be divided equally between them) alleenlyk dat myn oudste Soon Gerrit sall voornye genieten drie pondt (my eldest son, G., to have, in advance, £3). En alvoren myn voors. huysvrouw in den houwelyken Staat bevestight wert sall gehouden syn Staat" "en gehouden syn dat na haer overlyde di gerechte helft van voors. ses Kinderen om Egaalyk (if my wife should marry, half of the estate shall be secured for my six children after her death). "Doch indien van myn voors. Kinderen in haer onmondighyt moghte Coomen te overlyden Dat so daeniege overleeden Kindres portie sall door de Levende Egaalyk gedeelt werden (if any of the children should die during their minority, their shares shall be divided equally among the other surviving children).

"Sall myn voors. huysvrouw gehouden syn om myn voors. Kinderen te Alimenteeren En optevoeden En te Laeten Leeren En Schryven En een bequam Kunst of hantwerck te Laeten Leeren (my wife shall be bound to bring up my said children, to have them taught reading and writing, and to permit them to acquire a profession or a trade).

"So stell ick tot voogden ofte monbaeren over myn onmondrege Kinderen Coll *Henricus Beekman* En Major *Jacob Rutsen*. (As guardians over my children who are under age, H. B. and J. R.) Wife appointed executrix.—Cornelis Gerritse (his mark). Witnessed by *Roeliff Swartwout, Rich. Brodhead,* and *W. D. Meyer.*

Richard Broadhead and William d'Meyer appeared before the Court March 4, 1695/6, proving the will.

(Cornelis Gerritse (*Newkerk*), s. of *Gerrit Cornelissen* (*supra*), m. *Jannetie Kunst*, d. of *Jan Barentsen Kunst* and *Jacomyntje Sleght*, d. *Cornelius Barentsen Sleght*, and had issue: i. *Gerrit*, bt. July 28, 1684; ii. *Jan*, bt. Nov. 29, 1685; iii. *Adrian*, bt. Febr. 27, 1787; iv. *Barent*, bt. Oct. 13, 1689; v. *Gilles*, bt. Nov. 5, 1691; vi. *Jacomyntje*, bt. June 8, 1694; vii. *Cornelis*, bt. Aug. 30, 1696; (*Gerard Cornelis, Jacomyntje Sleght, Jan Elten, Chieltie Cornelis, Ary Gerritz, Hillitje Jans,* and *Gerrit Cornelis,* were witnesses to the baptisms of these children).—For Gerritz, see Gerrit Newkerk. For Jan, see Johannis Newkirk.)

Folio 274.—HUYBERTSE, LAMBERT, of Hurly.

Will dated Febr. 12, 1695/6, and written in Dutch.

Long religious preamble.

"Aen myn Jongste soon *Pieter Lammertse* twee paerde als meede dat syn huys door hem bewoont uyt myn Staat sall werden voltoyt als van Solder vloer deuren en vensters Etc. (To my youngest son, P. L., two horses; the house, in which he lives, shall be finished (completed) out of my estate with solid floors, doors and windows, etc.) "So geve ick aen myn voors. soon" "de geregte vyfde part van myn geheele Staat (to said son 1/5 of my estate).

"Aen myn Soons *Huybert Lammerse* En *Cornelis Lammerse* en myn schoon soons *Cornelis Cool* en *Arien Gerrets* en Jeder de gerechte vyfde part van myn geheele Staat" "met deese Conditie dat voors. Arie Gerritse sall hebben en genieten de gerechte vufde part van myn Lant naest aent 'lant geleege hem toe behoorende" "alle de andere Roerende Staat Egaelyk onder haer te deelen" (to my sons H. L., and C. L., and my sons-in-law C. C. and A. G. 1/5 each of my estate, on condition that Arie Gerritse shall have the 1/5 part next to his own land; all the personal property to be divided equally).

"Tot Executors" "Huybert Lammertse Cornelis Lammerse Pieter Lammerse Cornelis Cool En Arie Gerritse (as executors, persons named).

"Myn schoon soon Cornelis Cool sall mogen hebben Aen een Stuck twee porties vant Landt door myn bewoont t'weeten het Eene nu aen hem gemaecht ent 'ander door hem van myn Soon Lammert Huyberse gecoft" (My son in law, C. C., shall have one piece, two portions of land, where I live, one part now given to him, and the other part purchased of my son, L. H.).

Lammert Huybertse (his mark); witnessed by *Wessel ten Broeck, Jacobis Lameter,* and *Parre Noose (Pierre Noue).*

(Lambert Huybertse, of *Wageningen*, in *Gelderland*, sailed for this country, Dec. 1659, with wife and two children; a third was born on the passage. His wife was *Hendrickje Cornelis*. He afterwards assumed the surname *BRINK*. They had issue: i. *Huybert Lambertsen*, of Wageningen, m. March 16, 1679, *Hendrickje Swartwout*, from *Albany*, res. *Hurley*, and had: a. *Lambert*, bt. Jan., Febr. or March 4, 1680, b. *Roelof*, bt. Apr. 27, 1684, c. *Thomas*, bt. Dec. 6, 1685, d. *Hendrick*, e. *Eva*, bt. May 25, 1690, f. *Henricus*, bt. Nov. 18, 1694, g. *Henricus*, bt. Jan. 10, 1697, h. *Johannes*, bt. May 28, 1699; ii. *Jannetie Lamberts*, m. *Cornelise Teunisse Cool* (q.v.); iii. *Cornelis Lambertz*, "born at sea," (see Cornelis Lambertse); iv. *Lysbeth Lambertsen*, bt. Febr. 14, 1666, m. *Arye Gerrytsen* (see *Cornelius Newkirk*); v. *Hendrik Lambertsen*, bt. Dec. 5, 1663, m. *Geesje Jansen*, and had: a. *Rachel*, bt. Nov. 6, 1692; vi. *Pieter Lambertsen*, bt. June 24, 1670, m. *Geertruy Teunisen (Matthewssen)*, and had: a. *Henderik*, bt. Apr. 23, 1693, b. *Matthew*, bt. June 9, 1695, c. *Cornelis*, bt. July 25, 1697, d. *Lambert*, bt. Nov. 26, 1699, e. *Lambert*, bt. Jan. 15, 1702, f. *Antje*, bt. Apr. 2, 1704, g. *Lysbeth*, bt. Aug. 11, 1706, h. *Gerrit*, bt. Sept. 18, 1709; i. *Johannes*, bt. May 11, 1712; j. *Helena*, bt. Nov. 7, 1714; vii. *Gerrit Lambertsen*, m. *Antje Hooghlandt*, and had: a. *Breechje*, bt. June 10, 1694, b. *Teunis*, bt. Febr. 7, 1697, c. *Claertje*, bt. July 14, 1700, d. *Dirrick*, bt. Dec. 25, 1703.)

Page 283.—HOOGHTYLING, JAN WILLEMSE, of Kingstown.

Will dated Aug. 11, 1702, and written in Dutch.

Long religious preamble.

"Myn neger met name *Kieser* Sal vrij syn, van syn Slavereij, en moge gaan wadr het hern goet of gerade dienckt Sonder dat myn Erfgenamen hem Sullen Comen ofte mogen & hinderen (My negro, K., shall be free from slavery, and may go wherever the Lord, in his grace, permits, without being prevented by anyone of my heirs).

"So stel ick tot Erfgenamen over myn geheele Staat Soo wel Roerende als onroerende Sonder Exceptie met name *Willem Janse Hooghteyling* Soon van Wijlen *Jan Willemse Hooghtyling Junior, Samuel Hooghtyling, Philip Hooghtyling, Hiskia Hooghtyling, Desia* en *Kesia*, altsamen kinderen van Wijlen *Willem Janse Hooghtyling*, Eenigste kint vàn myn, om Egalyck onder haar allen gedeelt te werden, En In cas Eenige van myn voors. Erfgenamen mogte overleden syn alvoren dis myn laaste Will of testement in syn kragt is, als mede die geene die in haar onmondighyt Comen te overlyden dat alsdan des overlyden portie Sal syn ten behoove van myn andere Erfgenamen." (As heirs of my entire estate, real as well as personal, without exception, I appoint W. J. H., son of deceased Jan W. H., Jr., S. H., P. H., H. H., D. and K., all children of deceased W. J. H., my only child, to be equally divided between them, and if any of these heirs should die before the probation of this my last will and testament, or a minor, the survivors are to divide his share).

"Myn Executeurs" "sullen gehouden syn om uyt te keren en betalen uyt myn Staat aan *Sara Rosenkranz* voor haar getrouwe dienst in my Sieckte, de Somme van Een hondert Schepels tarw of vyftight Stuck van Agte" (my executors shall be bound to pay to Sara Rosenkranz, for her faithful service during my sickness, the sum of 100 schepels of wheat or 50 pieces of eight).

"Soo ist dat *Garrit Van Vliet* in het voorjaar syn huer tyt op myn Landt geepirceert is, En ick hem belooft heb dat alvoren hy van myn Landt Sal moet en Ver-Strecken, nogh twe Jaren daar toe Sullen, geaddert Werden, t' welck ick begeer dat na gekomen Sal Werde, Mits dat voors. Gerrit van Vliet de huer van voors. Landt gehouden is aan myn Erfgenamen te betalen." (As Gerrit Van Vliet has paid the rent for my land last spring, I have promised him that he may have two years more before he gives up said land, provided he pays the rent for the land to my heirs).

JAN WILLEMSE HOOGHTYLING (his mark)

JACOB SWAAN
RAY CROESWELT
TEUNIS ELISSE (syn merck)
W. D. MEYER, County Clark.

(Bay Croswelt and Jacob Swaan appeared, March 4, 1702/3 before Coll. Henricus Beekman, and Mr. Wm. Legg, Esq., Judges, and Capt. Dirck Schepmoes, Major Johannis Wynkoop, Mr. John Cock, Capt. Charles Broadhead, Esq., Justices).

(See his former will).

Page 286.—DE WITT, BOUDEWYN, of Kingston, Chirurgyn.

Will dated June 24, 1703, and written in Dutch.

(Long religious preamble).

"Aan myn huysvrouw *Maria d' Witt* myn gantsche Staat van huyse, Lande, goedere, Schulde, gelt gout, Zilver, gemünt, ofte ongemünt, En Wat verder aan d' Staat is Dependerende, met volkome maght aan myn voors. huysvrouw, om over voors. Staat te Disponeere na haar Welgevallen." (To my wife, M. de W., my entire estate of houses, lands, goods, debts, money, gold, silver, coined or uncoined, and whatever belongs to said estate, with full power to dispose thereof at her pleasure).

Wife appointed executrix. Signed by the testator.

DIRCK SCHEPMOES
TEUNIS ELISSE (his mark)
MOSES D' GRAAF
W. D. MEYER

(Witnesses appeared, July 15, 1703, before the Court).

(Boudewyn De Witt m. Marie De Witt, and had i. *Petronella*, m. *Hendrick Ten Eyck*.—On Oct. 11, 1699, B. de W. petitioned to be released from a fine (Engl. MSS., xliii, p. 62). B. de W. was Sheriff of Ulster Co., May 26, 1702 (Ibid., xlv, p. 127). March 18, 1703, *Barnes Cosens*, escheator-general, petitioned for his pay, he having seized the estate of B. de W., and others (Ibid., xlvii, p. 69).

Page 290.—HENDRICKE, DIRCK, " van de Mannor of Foxhall."

Will dated Jan. 8, 1699/1700, and written in Dutch.

(Long religious preamble).

"Aan myn huysvrouwe *Grietie Hendrix* alle myn geheele Staat van huyse, Lande, paarden, beesten, Negers, Schulden, etc." "Dogh met desen Verstande dat myn Neger Jongen met namen *Samson* die in myn huys geboren is, na het Overlyden van myn voors. huysvrouw Sal vry van Slaverny syn, Sonder dat Jemant Eenige pretentie sal komen maken, Dogh met dese Conditie dat Indien de voors. Samson op Eenige van de Leefsyt van myn voors. huysvrow quam qualyck te Comporteren En ongehoorsamenhyt aan haar betoonde, vat sy myn voors. huysvrouw Sal vermogen over hem te disponeren En vercopen voor de tyt van syn Leven sonder Eenige Contraduitie of verhindering van Jemant, of oock Sonder Reden Wegens syn ongehoorsam hyt of quaat Comportem 't Dieswegen aan Jemant te geven."

(To my wife, Gritie Hendrix, my entire estate of houses, lands, horses, cattle, negroes, debts, etc., on the understanding that my negroboy Samson, born in my house, shall be free from slavery after the death of my wife, without any objection from anyone, but on the condition that if he, during my wife's life has not shown her obedience, my wife may dispose of him and sell him, without objection from anyone, or else to give him away).

Wife appointed executrix.

DIRCK HENDRIX (his mark)

WILLEM TRAPHAGEN
JOHN LEGG
W. D. MEYER

(Witnesses appeared before the Court, Sept. 9, 1703).

(Dirck Hendricksen m. *Grietje Pieterse* (see her will under Gritie Hendrix), and had son: *Hendrick*, bt. March 8, 1665).

Page 294.—BOGARDIES, PIETER.

Will dated Febr. 3, 1701/2, and written in Dutch.

(Long religious preamble).

"Geen oudste soon of Jonger soon preverentie of dobbele portie van myn goedt of goederen Sal genieten of moegen begeeren, maar myn huysvrouw *Wyntie Bogardus* of de moeder van alle myn kinderen Sal over myn Nagelaten Staat & 'sy huysen ende Erven ende Jacht meubelen dat is Roerende ende onroerende goederen Landt ende grondt" "disponeeren" "ende dat so Lange als sy de naam van Bogardus draagt maar soo sy komt te hertrouwen soo sal sy soo veel hebben als de Wett haar geeft (neither the oldest son nor the youngest son shall have or claim a single or double portion of my estate, but my wife, W. B., the mother of all my children, shall dispose of (or possess) my estate, houses, grounds, ship, furniture, real and personal property, as long as she bears the name of Bogardus, but if she should happen to marry, she shall have what the law gives her). After her death "het landt dat van *Thomas Janse* of *Jacob Salamonse* gecogt is in de wy benoorden de Bever Kill aan *Anthony Bogardus* ende *Ephraim Bogardus* ende *Petrus Bogardus* myn drie Soonen by haar moeder Wyntie Bogardus geprocureert sal Eewighlyck & Erwelyck Eygen syn (the land which was bought from T. J. or J. S. on the meadow north of Beaver Kill shall go to A. B., E. B., and P. B., my three sons, begotten by their mother, W. B.) "Maer het Landt dat Van *Volekert* En *Jan Thomasse* haar Erfgename gekogt is Sal Ephraim Bogardus end Petrus Bogardus veernoont, Ick segge het Landt dat besuyde de Bever Kill lyt mot haar byde" "mits Conditie datse het selve Landt mit aan Vreemde sullen verkopen, maar soo het quam dat sy naae Een ander landt metter woon buyten het governm't quam te verstrecken soo sullen sy gesamentlyck aan haar broeders ende susters verkopen maar niet aan vreemde (but the land which was bought of Volekert and J. T.'s heirs, shall go to E. B. and P. B., that is the land which is south of Bever Kill, on condition that the land shall not be sold to strangers, but to their brothers and sisters). "Soo sal Anthony Bogardus en Ephraim Bogardus en Petrus Bogardus wel op myn begeeren staan om niet overtreden beveele verder dat dese twe Ephraim Bogardus en Petrus Bogardus sullen vorder uyt de gantscht Staat groot gebracht werden tot dat sy tot har en Mondigen daagen Komen (A. B. and E. B. and P. B. shall comply with my bequests (or wishes), that E. B. and P. B. shall be well brought up until they reach their majority) "sonder dat Jemant van myn kind of kinderen hier in sullen tegen Seggen met plyten of Regten (none of my children shall go to law against the rest, or overreach each other) "maar sullen alle myn negen kinderen Eenveel hebben (but all my nine children shall divide equally) except het boven genoemde landt (except the above mentioned land), van Jacob Salamonse ende van Volckert & Jan Tomasse Sullen Antony Bogardus ende Ephraim Bogardus ende Petrus Bogardus Elck in haar part het haare geniete gelyck boven genoent is datse het selve Landt voor uyt sullen hebben (of J. S. and V. and J. T., which A. B. and E. B. and P. B. shall divide equally, as above mentioned, and to have said land in advance) ende dan met de andere kinderen in de Rest Egaal sullen dylen (and then divide the rest with the other children) begeere dat het selve tot syn Effect sal koomen alwaart Schoon Soo dat Eenige Solemnityten naar Regten ofter Style Vereyscht hier imme niet volkommen weesen geobserveert versoerkende het uyterste benifitie te moogen genieten (and wishes that these requests shall be fulfilled, even if legal forms or precepts have not been strictly observed).

Signed by the testator, but not witnessed. On Sept. 20, 1703 before *Henricus Beekman*, Esq., Judge of ye Court of Common Pleas, Mr. *Evert Wynkoop*, Esq., Major *Johannis Wynkoop*, Justices of the Peace, appeared *John Gasherie, Cornelis Bogardus, Lysbet Heermans*, wife of *Jan Heermans, Madleen Slegt*, wife of *Mattys Slegt*, and *Maria Hooghtyling*, widow, proving the will.

(This will appears on record in N. Y. Sur. Office, Liber 8, p. 29. The widow, Wyntje Bogardus, dying without taking out letters of administration, they were granted, May 8, 1714, to his son, Evert Bogardus.

Dom. *Everardus Bogardus*, b. *Woerden*, near *Utrecht*, 1607, ordained by the Classis of Amsterdam, June 14, 1632, arrived with Governor *Van Twiller*, in April, 1633, accompanied by *Adam Roelandsen*, a schoolmaster, and became the second minister at New Amsterdam in 1633, resigning in 1647, on July 22, sailing for Holland Aug. 16th on "*The Princess,*" but was drowned on Sept. 27, 1647. He was a widower, when he arrived, and married in 1638, 2., *Anneke Jans,* widow of *Roeloff Jans*, of Rensselaerwyck. Her first husband had received a valuable grant of land near Red Hook, and from Van Twiller a grant of 62 acres of Manhattan Island, which afterwards passed to his widow, and upon her marriage with Bogardus became known as the dominis's bouwerie. On Nov. 15, 1705, the farm, then called the King's farm, was given by patent to Trinity Church. Anneke Jans had with her first husband four children: *Sarah* m. *John Kiersted*, and afterwards *Cornelius Van Borsum; Catherine*, m. *John Van Brough; Fytie*, m. *Peter Hartgers*, and *Jan*, m. *Annetje Peters.*

Evert Bogardus and Anneke Jans had issue: i. *Willem*, m. Aug. 29, 1659, *Wyntje Sybrends*, and 2., a dau. of *Nicasius de Sille;* ii. *Cornelis*, b. 1640, m. *Rachel de Witt;* iii. *Jonas*, b. 1643, d. unm.; iv. *Peter.*

Mr. *George H. Lewis*, of *Poughkepsie*, N. Y. has Dom. Everardus Bogardus, bible, dated 1543.—For further accounts about E. B., see Minutes of the Classis of Amsterdam, vols. iv, 22, 23; Minutes of the Synod of North Holland, Doc. Hist. N. Y., iii, p. 367; Amsterdam Correspondence, 1632-1650; Col. Hist. N. Y., i. pps. 206, 299, 345, 417, ii. p. 144; Church Intelligencer, July 20, 1833; Poughkepsie Press; etc.

Pieter Bogardus, bt. Apr. 2, 1645 in N. Y., settled in Albany, was a magistrate there 1673 (Albany Co. Rec., Nov. 2, 1673), removed to Kingston, m. *Wyntje Cornelis Bosh*, dau. of *Cornelis Teunise B.* and *Maritie Thomas Mingael,* and had issue: i. *Evert* (see Evert Bogardus); ii. *Shibboleth;* iii. *Hannah*, b. Jan. 22, 1679, m. *Pieter Bronck;* iv. *Maria* (m. *Johannes Van Vechten* of *Schagticoke*); v. *Anthony;* vi. *Rachel*, bt. Febr. 13, 1684; vii. *Ephraim*, bt. Aug. 14, 1687, went to *North Carolina;* viii. *Cornelis,* who made his will, May 2, 1711, in which he says "about to go with his brother Ephraim to North Carolina, leaves everything to brother-in-law, Johannes van Vechten of Renselaerwyck Manor (Clerk of Court of Appeal's Office, Albany, wills, B. p. 8); ix. *Petrus,* bt. Apr. 30, 1691. (For desc., see *Pearson's* "First Settlers of Albany, p. 21).

Peter Bogardus and Jonas Bogardus, on July 17, 1667, for themselves, and as attorneys for *Pieter Hartgers, Mr. Johannes Van Brugh, Sara Roeloffse,* widow of the late Mr. *Hans Kierstede,* chirurgeon, *Jan Roeloffse, William Bogardus,* and on the part of the widow of the late *Cornelius Bogardus,* all children and heirs of their mother, *Annetje Bogardus* (Anneke Jans), grant to *Dirck Wesselse* (Ten Broeck), Annetie Bogardus' house and lot in Albany, occupied by said Dirck Wesselse (Albany Co. Rec.).

Page 296.—DE WITT, LUYCAS,

Will dated Febr. 15, 1702/3, and written in Dutch.

"Myn oudste sooon *Jan* sal vooruyt genieten voor syn voorreght als oudste Soon als hy tot syn Mondige Jaren is uyt de geheele Staat de somme van vyf pont aan gelt."

"Myn vrouw *Antie* sal hebben d' geregte helft van alles wat overigh sal blyven te Weten van huys, Erf, Roerende en onroerende goederen En oock van t' geene my gemaakt is van myn vader, t'welck syn Testament sal uyt wysen."

"Myn kinderen te Weten myn Soon Jan, En myn doghter *Jannetje*, En t'geen myn vrouw Antie nu swanger van is, sullen de andere helft hebben te Weten van huys, Erf, Roerende en onroende goederen en oock van t' geen my gemaakt is van myn vader t'welck syn testement sal uytwysen te Wetten Elck syn part de eene niet meer als de andere."

'Indien myn vrouw Antie Comt weder te hertrouwen Sal gehouden syn" "twe voogden te Stellen over de onmondige kinderen" and to "leveren" to them "de geregte halve staat te Weten de kinders haar part."

"Indien myn vrouw Weduwe of Ongetrout blyft so sall sy in t'volle besitt van de Geheele Staat blyven."

(My eldest son Jan shall have, in advance, as his birth right, being my eldest son, when he reaches majority, out of the whole estate the sum of

£5.—My wife, Antie, shall have the just half of the residue in house, land, real and personal property, as well as all that is coming to me from my father, as his testament will show.—My children, i. e., my son Jan and my daughter Jannetje, and my wife, Antie, who is at present with child, shall have the other half (as before).—If my wife should remarry, she is to appoint guardians over the minors, and to deliver to them one half part of the estate. If she remains unmarried, she is to possess everything.)

Signed by the testator.

TEUNIS ELISSEN (his mark)	(Cornelius Bogardus, Teunis Tappen,
TEUNIS TAPPEN	& Jan Heermans Junior, appeared be-
JAN HEERMANS JUER	fore the Court, March 9/10, 1703/4,
C. BOGARDUS	proving the will).

(Luycas De Witt, son of *Tjerck Claessen De Witt* (q. v.), m. Dec. 22, 1695, *Annatje Delva*, d. of *Anthony D.* and *Jannetie Hillebrants*, and had issue: i. *Jannetje*, bt. March 7, 1697, m. July 19, 1717, *Cornelis Langendyk* (bt. N. Y., July 10, 1689, s. of *Pieter Janse L.* and *Geertie Comelis*); ii. *Barbara*, bt. Nov. 12, 1699, m. March 25, 1715, *Johannes Van Leuven*, who m., 2., May 22, 1725, *Hilligond Roosa*; iii. *Jan*, bt. Dec. 8, 1700, m. after Sept. 26, 1731, *Ariantje Osterhoudt* (bt. March 9, 1712, d. of *Gysbert O.* and *Maritje Bogardus*, res. *Katskill*); iv. *Luycas*, bt. Sept. 16, 1703, m. Jan. 17, 1729, *Catherine Roosa* (bt. Febr. 16, 1709, b. *Hurley*, d. of *Evert R.* and *Tietje Van Etten*).—Antje, the widow of Luycas De Witt, m. 2., March 31, 1706, *Gerrit Van Bunschoten*, and m. 3., Oct. 26, 1721, *Hendrick Rosekrans*, widower of *Antje Vredenberg*.—Luycas De Witt was a commander and joint owner with his father of a sloop called St. Barbara.)

Page 319.—TEN BROECK, WESSEL, Senior, of Foxhall.

Will dated Febr. 14, 1695/6, and written in Dutch.

Long religious preamble.

"Myn will En begeerte, dat het houwelyck voorwaarde met myn huysvrouw *Laurentja Kellenaar* gemaakt volkomentlyck sal opgevolkt werden."

"Aan myn ouste Soon *Wessel ten Broeck*" "vier morgen Landt uyt myn Bouw Landt" "de geregte vierde part van myn gantsche Bouwery En dat het myn Bouwery in vier parcelen by morgen getal sal werden gelyt" "myn voors. soon" "sal" "betalen aan myn Andere drie soons wat de voors. gedeelte meerder in Waardy by onpartydige besworen Sal gewardeert Werden, als Wanneer myn soons: sullen tot Mondigen dage gekomen syn, vorders Soo geeve ick aan myn voors. soon Wessel ten Broeck" "de geregte agste part van myn huysing En gront in *Kingstowne*, En de regte agste part van al myn Roerende Staat. Myn voors. soon sal vrijstaan te mogen na sigh in Eijgendom te nemen Een Neger de keur van myn Negers, En daar voor te alloweren in de Erfenisse van de Roerende Staat de Somme van Ses en Dartigh pondt."

"Insgelyck ordonnere ick dat Niemant van myn Erfgenamen sullen mogen verhinderen of soecken te verhinderen t' Dammen tot preservatje van Water en de gront noodight tot het Dammen te Laten gebruyken En de Loop van het Water tot het gebruyck voor myn voors. soons Molen." "Myn voors. soon of syn ordre of Erfgenamen sullen gehouden syn te betalen de quantityt van Een Duysent Schepels tarw aan myn vier Dogters" "met namen *Maria, Elsie, Geertruy,* en *Sara*, jeder de geregte vierde part van voors. somme in den tyt van vier Jaren."

"Aan myn soon *Coenraat ten Broeck*" "de geregte vierde part van my gantsche Bouivery, Except wat hier voren, voor uyt gemaakt is aan myn Soon Wessel ten Broeck," "ende de aghste part van myn huysing en grondt in Kingstowne En de Aghste part van myn gantsche Roerende Staat En gehouden te betalen de quantityt van Een Duysen Schepels tarw aan myn vier dogters."

"Aan myn soon *Johannis ten Broeck*' "de geregte part van myn gentsche Bouivery, Except wat hier vooren voor uyt gemaakt is aan myn soon Wessel ten Broeck" also "de aghste part van myn huysing En grondt in Kingstown, En de aghste part van myn gantsche Roerende Staat, En betalen de quantityt van Een Duysent Schepels tarw, aan myn vier Dogters" (as before).

"Aan myn soon *Jacob ten Broeck*" "de geregte vierte part van myn gantsche Bouivery, Except wat hier vooren, voor uyt gemaakt is Aan myn Soon Wessel ten Broeck" also "de Aghste part van myn huysing En grondt In Kingstowne" (on condition as before).

"Aan myn vier Dogters met namen Maria huysvrouw van *Charles Brodhead,* Elsie huysvrouw van *Cornelis Decker,* Geertruy En Sara ten Broeck" "om Egalyck onder haar gedeelt Werden" "Een hondert & twe Ackers Landt" "gelegen ontrent t' Landt van *Gerrit Aartse* volgens grontbrief myn toe behoorende als mede de geregte helft van myn huysing En gront in het Dorp Kingstowne, En de geregte helft van myn gantsche Roerende Staat als mede de quantityt van vier Duysent Schepels tarw te Ontfangen van myn soons in sodanige terme als voren geordonn'rt is."

"Geen myn voors. soons Sullen vermogen haar portie in myn Bouivery to verkopen, Except t' selve door haar broeder of broeders gecogt Wert, En dat myn drie Jongste soons portie van voors. Bouiwery niet Ten Enemaal sal gedeelt werden voor dat de Jongste soon tot Mondigen daagen sal gekomen syn."

"Myn soon Wessel ten Broeck sal gehouden syn myn onmodige soons te alimenteren En optevoeden en te Laten Leeren lesen & schruyven, En Elck int besonder bequame kunst of handtwerck te Laten leeren waar best haar genegnthyt toe sal strecken En bequamhyt hebben."

"Indien" "dat Eenige van myn onmondige soons" mogte Comen te overlyden" t' portie van de overleden sal Egaalyck onder myn andere soons gedeelt werden, mits gehouden uyttekeeren en te betalen aan myn voors. Dogters de Somme dewelcke de overleden verobligeert waren."

"Myn ongetroude Dogters met namen Geertruy en Sara sullen hebben uyt myn Staat alswanner deselve mogten Comen in den houelycken Staat te treden sodanige uytsetting van bedding kleeding Etc. als myn andere getroude dogters genoten hebben."

(My will and desire is that the marriage contract with my wife Laurentja Kellenaar shall be fulfilled.—To my eldest son, Wessel Ten Broeck, four morgen land of my farm land, the just fourth part of my whole farm, my farm to be divided in four parcels of morgens, my son to pay to my three other sons the value of the said land, as appraised by uninterested witnesses. When my sons reach the age of majority, my son Wessel is to have ⅛ of my house and ground in Kingston, and ⅛ of all my personal estate, and my said son shall be permitted to take the choice of one of my negroes, and to allow therefore a sum of £36 in personal property.—I order that none of my heirs shall prevent or try to prevent the running of the water needed for my sons' grounds and mills. My said son to pay to my four daughters (named), 1000 schepels of wheat, each one quarter, payable in four years.—To my son Coenraat Ten Broeck the just fourth part of my whole farm, except what has been devised to my son Wessel. Also one eight part of my house and ground in Kingston, and one eight part of my whole personal estate, and to pay the quantity of 1000 schepels of wheat to my four daughters (as above).—Similar bequest to son Johannis.—Similar bequest to son Jacob.—To my four daughters. Maria, wife of Charles Broadhead, Elsie, wife of Cornelis Decker, Geertruy and Sara, 102 acres of land, to be equally divided between them, situated near the land of Gerrit Aartse, according to deed, and one half of my whole personal estate, as well as 4000 schepels of wheat to be received from my sons, on terms already stated.—My sons are not to sell their portions of my farm, except between themselves, and my three youngest sons' shares shall not be disposed of until the youngest one has reached the age of majority.—My son Wessel shall be bound to educate, maintain and teach my younger sons to read and write, and to let them acquire some profession or trade, which will be best for them.—If any of the minors should die, his portion to be divided among the other sons, they to pay to the daughters such sums as the deceased may be indebted to them.—My unmarried daughters, Geertruy and Sara are to have, when they marry, an outfit of beds and what thereto belongs, as well as clothing, similar to what my other married daughters received.)

Son Wessel ten Broeck appointed executor, with "schoonsoons Charles Brodhead, En Cornelis Decker."

Signed by the testator.

JAN LATHAER (his mark)
ABRAM TIETSOO
W. D. MEYER

(On Jan. 6, 1704/5 appeared before the Court Wm. De Meyer and Liftenant Jan Lathair, proving the will.)

(See his will, *supra*).

Page 326.—KETTLE, JEREMY, Senior, of Marbletown.

Will dated Jan. 20, 1703/4.

"Unto my deare and welbeloved wife *Elizabeth Kettle* my house & home lott where I now live during ye time of her naturall life and after her decease to my three youngest Children *Richard Susan,* and *Elizabeth*" also to wife "the Just fifth part of all my Estate and also all my household goods."

"Unto my Eldest Soon *Jeremy Kettle* the Just fifth part of all my

Estate Except of my house & home lott and house hold goods with this Condition that he pays out of his part of said Estate unto *William Annis* the summe or quantity of thirty schepples of good Winter Wheat."

"Unto my sonn *Richard* ye Just fifth part of all my Estate Except of my house & home lott Whereof I give him the third part upon this condition that out of his part of said Estate he pays unto William Annis the summe or quantity of thirty scipples of good Winter Wheat."

"Unto my Eldest daughter Susan ye Just fifth part of all my Estate (except as above and on condition as above).

"Unto my Joungest daughter Elizabeth (same share on condition as above).

"Unto William Annis ye Just & full Summe of one hundred and twenty Schepples of Wheat to be payd unto him by my Children (as provided).

In case of death, the survivors to divide the share. "My trusty & Welbeloved friends & Neighbours Mr. *John Cook* and Capt. *Charles Brodhead*" appointed executors.

Signed by the testator.

JOHN COOK
CHARLES BRODHEAD (On Sept. 7, 1704 appeared before the Court
JOHN NOBLE Mr. William Nottingham and Capt. Richard
RICHARD BRODHEAD Brodhead, proving the will.).
WM. NOTTINGHAM

(Jeremy Kettel m. 1., *Catharina Guderis*, and had: i. *Jeremy*, bt. prob. Apr. 24, 1675, m. 2., *Elisabeth Claessen*, and had: ii. *Rutsjert* (*Richard*), bt. July 4, 1697, iii. *Susanna*, bt. July 14, 1700, iv. *Elisabeth*, bt. Oct. 25, 1702.)

Page 360.—LOURENS, JAN, of Kingstown.

Will dated March 21, 1702/3, an written in Dutch.

"Myn huysvrouw *Jannecke Lourens* sal hebben & genieten de vrugte & profyte van myn geheele Staat gedurende haar Leven mits dat myn voors. huysvrouw gehouden is myn twe kinderen met name *Lourens* & *Blandina* te alimenteren En op te voeden En van behoorlycke nootdruft te versorgen."

"Aan myn twe kinderen Lourens En Blandina myn gantsche Staat om na het overlyden van myn huysvrow te possideren om Egalyck onder haar gedeelt te Werden, alleenlyck dat myn soon Lourens voor of saal trecken En genieten Dartien Schellinge, als mede dart myn voors. kinderen sullen gehouden syn of die geene die haar Erfdeel mogte Comen te vercrijgen om uyt te keeren & betalen aan myn voors. huysvrouw voorkinderen met namen *Johannis* vyftigh Schellinge aan *Mettje* vyf pondt, En aan *Johanna* vyftigh Schellinge."

(My wife, Jannecke Lourens shall have & enjoy the income and profits of my entire estate during her life, on condition that she maintains and educates my two children (named).—To said children (named above), my entire estate, to be possessed by wife until her decease,

Laurens to have, in advance, 30 shillings. My said children shall be bound, when they obtain their inheritance, to pay to my wife's children by her former marriage, Johannis and Johanna, 50 schillings each and to Mettje £5.

Wife appointed guardian over the minors.

In case of death, the survivors to divide the share.

"Tot voogdesse over myn onmondige kinderen myn huysvrow." Wife appointed executrix.

JAN LOURENS (his mark)

THO. NOXON
JOHN DAVENPORT
W. D. MEYER

(Sept. 6, 1705, Thomas Noxon & Wm. D' Meyer appeared before the Court and proved the will).

(*Jan Laurenssen* m. *Jannetjje Schouten*, and had: i. *Laurens*, bt. Dec. 25, 1696, ii. *Blandina*, bt. Aug. 20, 1699.)

Page 368.—HERMANS, JAN, Junior, of Kingstown.

Will dated July 18, 1705, and written in Dutch.

"Myn huysvrouw *Antie Heermans* Sal in het besit blyven van myn gantsche Staat" "gedurende den tijt van haar Weduwschap" (my wife to remain in possession of my entire estate during her widowhood). She to sell what is neecessary to maintain herself and the children during her widowhood, but "het Wijlandt myn toebehorende sal overkogt blyven" (the pasture land shall remain unsold) until the children reach the age of majority, when they are to divide it. Should the widow marry again, she is to have the profits of the estate until the children become of age, to maintain and educate them, they then to have one half of the property.

"Indien myn vrouws Broeder *Evert van Wageninge* quam t' Schoemakers Ambugt op te Setten (As my wife's brother (named), has gone into the shoemaker's trade) dat hy alsdann vry heeft om Een sesde van de gront to gebruycken voor hem in Eijgendom, door myn gecogt van de trustees van Kingstowne, gelegen by t' *Molen Killetje* tot Een Loijerij als mede t' Sesde gebruyck van de Steen tot malen van syn Runn (he is to have free one sixth of the ground to till, which I bought from the trustees of Kingston, situated at the Mill Kill, at a tannery, as well as a sixth part in the use of the stone to grind his tan).

"Aan myn kindered met namen *Jacob, Engeltie* en *Jan* (to my children, named), "alle Sodannige portie van myn Staat als hier vooren geschreven is in her vierde Artyckel Wegens myn huysvrouw" (all such portions of my estate as have been described in the fourth article (first paragraph); survivors to divide share of deceased children.

"Tot voogden over myn onmondige kinderen (as guardians over my children, who are under age) myn Vader (my father) *Jan Heermans,* myn Schoonvader (my father in law) *Jacob Aartse,* myn broeder (my brother), *Aart van Wageninge."* Wife appointed executrix. Signed by the testator.

THO: NOXON
JOHN ROELAND
D'MEYER, Clarke

(All the witnesses appeared, Jan. 2, 1705/6, before the Court, proving the will).

(Son of *Jan Heermans, Sr.* (q. v.). Jan Hermans, Jr. m. *Annatje*, dau. of *Jacob Aartse (Van Wagenen)* (q. v.), and had issue: i. *Engeltje*, bt. Sept. 11, 1698, d. Sept. 22, 1788, m. Dec. 16, 1720, *Cornelis*, s. of *Conrad Elmendorf* and *Aeriantje Gerritse (Van den Berg)*; ii. *Jacob*, bt. Febr. 2, 1701, m. 1., Apr. 28, 1725, *Maritje*, bt. March 15, 1725, dau. of *Jan Crispel* and *Geertie Roosa*, m. 2., July 24, 1730, a dau. of *Dirck Van Vliet* and *Annatje Adrianse;* iii. *Jan*, bt. Aug. 8, 1703, m. Apr. 24, 1731, *Jacomyntje* bt. March 23, 1701, dau, of *Adam Swart* and *Metje Van Slyck*.)

Page 425.—CRESPEL, ANTOIN, of Kingston.

Will dated Nov. 6, 1707, and written in Dutch.

(Long religious preamble.)

"Soo bekenne ick dat ick getransporteert hebbe aan de kindere van Wijlen *Pieter Crespel* myn Outste soon te weeten *Antojn Johannis* en *Aryaentie Crespel* al dat Seeker parceel lants gelegen op *Horly* of in desselfs Limieten beginninde van een gemerkte boom ontrent de waage weg tot een Seker fontyn genoemt de *groote fontyn* die in de *groote kill* uytwatert als mede ses ackers bos Landt aan de andere Syde van het padt en ook de derde part van myn lant en de geregtigh't gelegen in de Limieten va het pettent van het dorp van de *Niewe Paltz* als ook een lott in de vly van *Horly* leggende tusschen lott van de Erfgenamen van *Jan Elting* en het lott van *Pieter Pieterson* alles volgens de transport dragende dato den Seven en twintigste dag van december Een duysent Seven hondert en vyf.

"Als dat myn Soon *Jan Crespel* van myn gecogt heeft myn land op *Horley* (Except wat hier boven bekent is) voor de somme ofte quantityt van een duysent Schepels tarw, welke Somme ten deele betaalt is, als mede 't geen hem Competerende was *Van Walrand die Mont* wegens syn Ervenisse van *Mattys Blanchan* heeft die voors. Jan Crespel Insgelyck geordonn'rt om door myn te ontfangen in part van betaling ook heeft de voors. Jan Crespel Een neger van myn gehadt met naame *Ffredrik*" "myn voors. Soon Jan Crespel sal hebbe ende genieten" "alles wat myn is Competerende van het gecogte landt en de neeger."

"Aan myn dogter *Maria Magdeleen* huysvrouw van *Mattys Slegt*" "een negerintie met naame *Margriet* als mede dat ick aan haar getransporteert hebbe de derde part (volgens verslag by myn gemaakt) van myn landt gelegen in de Limieten van 't pattent ven het dorp van de *Niewe Paltz* als meede soo geeve ick aan myn voors. dogter" "voor Recompens van verschyde Jaaren kostgelt en de groote dienste aan myn gedaan (gelyck sy nu noch aan myn dagelyck dort) all het gelt truyn is toe komende volgens hiboteek van *Moyse Le Cont,* En el het gelt myn toe komende van *Stephanus Gacherie* volgens hypoteek."

"Soo bekenne ick getransporteert te hebbe aan myn dogter *Jannetie* huysvrouw van *Nicolas Hofman* al het huys en Erf door myn van *Jan Gachérie* gecogt waar een hiboteek op is waar op nog drie en twintig pondt" "aan myn voor. Dogter Jannetie" "de geregte dèrde part van myn geheale Staat Except wat bove vermarkt is."

"Aan myn dogter *Elizabeth* huysvrouw van *Elias Uin* getransporteert te hebbe de derde part (volgens overslag by myn gemakt) van myn Landt en geregtighyt gelegen in de Limiten van t' pattent van de *Niewe Paltz*" "aan myn voors. dogter Elizabeth" "de derde part van myn geheele Staat Except wat bove vergaven is."

"Myn Schoonsoon *Huybert Suylandt* van myn gecogt heeft myn bogaert en gront gelegen in het dorp van *Horly* volgens transport aan hem gepasseert voor het welke hy noyt meeder als een hondert Schepels tarw betaalt heeft als mede hebbe verschyde Somme aan hem verschoten en voor hem betaalt als ook hebbe aan hem betaalt 't geen Syn Vrouw *Sara* myn dogter was Competerende wegens haar Ervenisse van *Mattys Blanchan*," "myn voors. dogter Sal hebben en de genieten" "all 't geene myn is Competerende wegens bogaert en gront ende mede myn verschote gelt verder" "aan dogter Sara" "der derde part van myn geheele Staat Except wat bove vermaakt is."

"Schoonsoons Mattys Slegt ende Nicholas Hofman" appointed executors.

Signed by the testator.

JOHANNIES WESTBROECK
JACOBUS ELMENDORP
PAIRE GUIMARD
WM. NOTTINGHAM

(William Nottingham, Mr. Jacobus Elmendorp, and Mr. Pieter Gimair appeared, Jan. 10, 1707/8 before the Court, proving the will).

(I declare that I have conveyed to the children of Pieter Crespel, deceased, my eldest son, named Antojn, Johannis and Aryaentie Crespel, all that parcel of land, situated in Hurly, beginning at a tree near the wagon-road to a certain spring called the Great Spring, which flows into the Great Kill, as well as six acres of wood land (or turf land) on the other side of the road, as also a third part of my land in the patent of the village of New Paltz, also a lot on the way to Hurly, near the lot of the heirs of Jan Elting and the lot of Pieter Pieterson, all according to deeds, dated Dec. 20, 1705.—As my son Jan Crespel has bought of me my land at Hurly (except what has been mentioned above) for 1000 schepels of wheat, of which ten parts have been paid, as also there was due him from Walrand die Mont, as heir of Mattys Blanchan, the said Jan Crespel has arranged for me to receive in payment a negro by the name Ffredrik, now my said son Jan Crespel shall have and enjoy all that is due me for that land and the negro.

To my daughter Maria M., wife of Mattys Slegt, a negro woman, Margriet, and as I have conveyed to her the third part of my land in New Paltz, I now give to her, for several years board, and in recognition of her great services to me, all the money which is due me from a mortgage of Moyse Le Cont and Stephanus Gacherie.

I declare that I have conveyed to my daughter Jannetie, wife of Nicolas Hofman, all that house and ground, purchased of Jan Gacherie, whereon there is yet a mortgage of £23. Also a third part of the entire estate.

To daughter Elizabeth, wife of Elias Uin, a third part of my land in New Paltz, and the third part of my entire estate.—My son in law, Huybert Suylandt has purchased of me my orchard (boomgard) and ground in Hurly, for which he has not paid more than 100 schepels wheat, and as I have advanced him and have paid to his wife, Sara, my daughter, what was due her as heir of Mattys Blanchan, therefore said daughter shall have and enjoy all that is due me for this orchard and ground, and money advanced. To my daughter Sara one third part of my whole estate, except what has been devised above).

(*Anthony Krypel* (*Crispel, Crespel*) came with his wife, *Marie*, daughter of *Matthys Blanchan* (q. v.) from *Artois, France*, in the "*Gilded Otter,*" April 27, 1660, and had by her: i. *Mary Magdalena*, bt. Febr. 12, 1662, m. *Mattys Sleght*, s. of *Cornelis Barentsen Slecht* and *Tryntje Tysen Bos* (q. v.); ii. *Pieter*, bt. Dec. 21, 1664, m. *Neeltje Gerritse Newkirk*, dau. of *Gerrit Cornelissen N.* and *Hendrikje Paulus* (the widow m. 2., Febr. 18, 1697, *Johannes Schepmoes*, bt. Apr. 7, 1672, s. of *Dirck Janse S.* and *Maria Willems*); iii. *Lysbet*, bt. Oct. 3, 1666, d. y.; iv. *Lysbet*, bt. Oct. 15, 1668, m. *Elias Ean*; v. *Sara*, bt. June 18, 1671, m. *Huybert Suylandt*; vi. *John*, bt. July 21, 1674, m., May 25, 1701, *Geertje Janse Roosa*.
Anthony Crispel m., 2., *Petronella Demon*, and had issue: vii. *Jannetje*, bt. June 4, 1682, d. y.; viii. *Jean*, bt. Oct. 12, 1684, d. y.; ix. *Jannetie*, bt. Febr. 7, 1686, m., Dec. 3, 1704, *Nicholas Hoffman*, s. of *Martinus H.* and *Emmerentje De Witt* (see Nicholas Hoofman).

Page 429.—LOW, PIETER CORNELISSE, of Kingstown, Yeoman.

Will dated Dec. 20, 1690.

"My deare beloved wife *Elizabeth* shall possess and Injoy all my Estate of lands Chattles, and Implements of household goods and tenements" "during her widdo ship" "but if my said wife shall Come to Remarry again yt shee shall deliver to my Children ye Right halfe of all my Estate" "and yt she shall have ye other halfe" "and yt the other halfe of my Estate to be Rented out or uppon use untill ye Youngest of my Children be Come to their age and then what is Left of that halfe to bee Equally Devided among them all and noot before, also I will yt my wife Shall w'th in one Yere after my death deliver or Cause to be delivered to my Eldest Sonn *Cornelis Pieterse Low* one horse."

WILLIAM HAYNES
JOHN PETERSE (his mark)
HUMPHREY DAVENPORT

PIETER CORNELISSE LOW (the mark of, sett by his own hand)
(Humphrey Davenport appeared, March 4, 1707/8, before the Court, proving the will).

(See his former will, *supra*.)

Page 431.—SWART, CORNELISSE, THEUNIS and VAN DER LIN= DEN, Elizabeth,

Will dated July 21, 1677, and written in Dutch.

"Naar de middagh ontrent 7 uren voor my *Lodevicus Cobes* Secrets: van *Schanegtede* ende voor de naargenoemde getuygen gecompareert ende Verschenen zyn, den Eersamen Theunis Cornelisse Swart, ende Elizabeth vander Linden Echte beyden my Secretario wel bekent" knowing the shortness of the human life, etc., the longest liver to have "actien en Crediten, gelt, gout, zilver, gemunt en ongemunt, Juweelen, Kleederen, linnen, woolen, huysraat en de anders" and if the longest liver were to marry "de helft eene Schifinge en de Deelinge gemaakt Sal worden voor haare Elf kinderen te Samen geproucureert ende in 't leven zynde Insgelyke Soo sy byde testateuren mogten komen te overlyden sonder in eenander heuwelyk te treden, is haar begeeren dat de minder jaarige kinderen uyt de Effecten Sullen groot gemaakt worden."

(Near noon about 7 o'clock (!) before me, Lodevicus Cobes, Secretary of Schenectady and for the undersigned witnesses, appeared the worthy Theunis Cornelisse Swart and Elizabeth van der Linden, his wife,—the longest liver to have bonds, book-debts, money, gold, silver, coined and uncoined, jewels, clothing, linnen, woolen, household-goods. "If the survivor should marry, one half to go to their" children, begotten by them, and if so should happen that both the testators should die without having married again, the minors shall be brought up from the proceeds of the estate.)

THEUNIS CORNELISSE (het mark)
LEYSEBETH VAN DER LENDEN

SWEER THONISSEN (het merk)
DOMINE AUKES

MY PRESENT

Lodevicus Cobes Secrets:

(T. C. S. and *Elizabeth Lendt (Van de Linde)* had issue: i. *Cornelis*, b. 1652; ii. *Esais*, b. 1653; iii. *Teunis;* iv. *Frederic;* v. *Adam;* vi. *Marytje* (m. *Claas Lourense Van de Volgen*); vii. *Jacomyntje* (m. 1., *Pieter Viele*, m. 2., *Bennony Arentse Van Hoeck* and 3, *Cornelis Vynhout*). For their descendants, see: *Pearson's* First Settlers of *Schenectady*, pps. 180-184, and Pearson's First Settlers of *Albany*, p. 107.—T. C. S. on June 16, 1664 had a patent of "the double bouwery No. 10," in Schenectady Patent (Schen. Patents, 309).—Elizabeth, his widow, then wife of *Jacob Meese Vrooman*, of Albany, on Febr. 20, 1685-6, conveyed to her son, *Jesias Swart* 8 acres on the south end of this farm (Schen. Deeds, iii, p. 310).—Jacob Meese Vrooman, carpenter, and surveyor of *Beverwyck*, in his will, July 20, 1691, proved Sept. 22, 1691, mentions no children, the wife to occupy "my house by the bridge formerly Dom. Schaets."—Elizabeth, the widow, m. 3., Oct. 14, 1691, *Wouter Uythoff*, of Albany, and on Apr. 26, 1692, he and his wife, Elizabeth, for 540 beavers conveyed the whole farm to *Claas Laurense Van Purmerend (van der Volgen*) (Schen. Deeds, iv.. p. 34).

Page 442.—ROOSA, HYMAN, of Hurly.

Will dated Aug. 23, 1708, and written in Dutch.

(Long religious preamble.)

"Myn drie Soonen met namen *Allert Nicolas* en de *Gysbert* Sall hebben" "gelyk" "myn geheele vaste en onroende staat" "op Conditie dat sy daar voor betalen" "aan myn vier dogters met naamen *Jannetie* huysvrouw van *Philip Hooghtyling Wyntie* huysvrouw van *Willem Crom, Ragel* ende *Lea* de Somme van Een hondert vyftigh pondt." (My three sons, A. N. and G., to have my whole real and personal estate, on condition that they pay to my four daughters, J., wife of P. H., W., wife of W. C., R. and L., the sum of £150).

"Aan myn vier voors. dogters de bovege melde Somma van Een honder en vyftigh pondt" "in twe Jaaren na myn overlyden" (to my four daughters said sum of £150, to be paid within four years after my decease).

"Myn twe Jongste dogters Ragel en Lea Sal drie Jaaren na myn overlyden" "of myn staat Wel gekleet en de gereet Werden na behooren" (my youngest daughters, R. and L., shall be well clothed for three years after my decease).

"Aan myn Oudste Soon Allert voor uyt van myn Losse en Roerende Staat Een paart of een koe de keur van myn stat (my oldest son, A., shall have the choice of a horse or a cow in advance out of my estate).

Sons Allert Rosa, Nicolaes Rosa and Gysbert Rosa appointed executors. Signed by the testator.

JAN ROOSA
MATTYS LOUW
JACOBUS VAN NETTEN
WM. NOTTINGHAM

(Mr. William Nottingham and Jacobus Van Etten, on Sept. 9, 1708, appeared before the Court: Mr. William Legg, Esq., Judge, Capt. Dirck Schepmoes, Mr. John Cock and Capt. Charles Brodhead, Esq., Justices, proving the will.)

(*Albert Heymans*, farmer, came from *Herwynen, Gelderland*, April 15, 1660 in the "*Spotted Cow*," with his wife, *Wyntje Ariens* (*Weilke de Jonge*), and 8 children, aged resp. 17, 15, 14, 9, 8, 7, 4, and 2 years, settled in *Esopus*, and assumed the name of *ROOSA*.—Albert Hymans Roosa received on Aug. 19, 1664, a patent of land in *Wyldwyck*. He died Febr. 27, 1679. Of his children: *Heyman* was b. 1643, *Arien*, b. 1645, *Jan*, b. 1651, m. *Hillegondt Willems, Ilke*, m. *Roelof Kierstede, Mary*, m. *Laurens Jansen*,* *Neeltie*, m. after Nov. 3, 1676, *Henry Pawling, Jannetie*, m. in *Hurley*, Nov. 16, 1679, *Matthys Ten Eyck* of N. Y., *Guert*, bt. June 15, 1663. "Hic filius obijt ante baptismum" (this son died after baptism). (Albert Heymans, Arent Albertsen, his son, et al, were "convicted upon oath and affirmance for taking of arms in a riotous and illegal manner upon the 16th of Febr., 1666, to awe, terrify and supress his Majesty's English Garrison established at Esopus." They "deserved to be put to death" but the Governor, "inclining to mercy" sentences Albert Hymans to be bannished out of this Government, during life, and he is to have 48 hours to transport his estate, and that a fine of 100 bushels of wheat or value thereof be levied on his estate in the Esopus for charges of Court, and Arent Albertsen, his son, is sentenced to be banished for one whole year and a day, and he is to have 40 days to remain in the Esopus for the disposal of his and his father's affairs." One half of the time was remitted by the Governor, upon petition of A. H., and "he may remain in any part of the Government except Esopus, New York and Albany, and his son may remain till his corn is husked, threshed and disposed of."

Heyman Alderse Roosa m. *Ann Margriet Rosevelt*, and had issue: i. *Aldert*, bt. March 2, 1679, b. in Hurley, m. June 21, 1696, *Petronella Van Etten;* ii. *Claes* (*Nicholaes*), bt. Apr. 27, 1684, m. Dec. 18, 1720, *Zara Rutsz;* iii. *Gysbert*, bt. Oct. 17, 1686; iv. *Neeltie*, bt. Oct. 13, 1689; v. *Rachel*, bt. Apr. 19, 1696, m., Dec. 9, 1715, *Johannes Ten Broeck* (q. v.); *Jannetie*, m. Nov. 30, 1702, *Philip Hoogteeling; Wyntje*, m. Nov. 12, 1699, *Willem Crom*, of *Marbletown; Lea;* (Jannetie and Wyntje were born, prob., before Rachel and Lea). (See also Doc. Hist. N. Y., iii, p. 36, iv., p. 39; Doc. rel. to Col. Hist. of N. Y., xiii, Hist. of Kingston, p. 22, 28-29; N. Y. Gen. Reg. 1000 pps. 163·; Hist. of the State of N. Y., by Broadhead, p. 690; Reg. of New Netherland, by O'Callaghan, p. 71, 158).

Page 452.—HENDRIX, GRITIE, "weduwe van Wijlen" (widow of deceased) Dirck Hendrikse, of Foxhall.

Will dated Sept. 26, 1708, and written in Dutch.

"Myn neger man met naame *Pieter* Sal vry syn van Slaverny Sonder

---

(*Laurens Jansen Low*, b. in *Holland*, 1651, brother of *Cornelis Jansen Kortright*, d. in 1727. They were sons of *Jan Bastiaesen*, who came over in 1663 with his two sons. C. J. Kortright m., 1665, *Metje*, dau. of *Bastiaen Elyessen* (*Metje Cornelis*).

dat Jemant mynent Wegen of op Eenige andere manier de voors. neger tot een Slaaf Sal mogen gebruyken of aanvenden, Insgelyck Soo geeve ik aan myn voors. neger de geregte Derde van myn huys en gront in Kingstown, alsmede een vaars van drie Jaren out, twaalf en een vierde Stuk van Agten voor syn Wek te goet bij *Abram Chambers,* twe en veertigh guldens te goet bij *Mattys Slegt* voor Speck, alle myn Bijlen & Wiggen, al myn Slaap geet, te Weter, Bed, peulen, kussen, & Deekens, als mede de geregte derde van all myne overige Roerende Staat, Except wat hiernader particulier uytgedrukt is (my negro by the name P. shall be free from slavery, and nobody shall use him for my sake or for any other reason; I also give him one third of my house and land in K., a bullock three years old, 12¼ pieces of eight, for his work due him from A. C., 42 guldens from M. S. for pork, all my hatches and wedges, all my 'sleeping goods', that is, bed, pillows, cushions and coverlets, as well as a third of all my personal estate, except what I have disposed of here below).

"Aan de Doacony van de duyste gereformeerde Kerk van Kingstown" "in der tyt de geregte Derde van myn huys & gront in Kingstowne als mede all t' geene my Deugdelyk is Competerende van *Jan van Vliet* (to the deaconry of the Dutch Reformed Church of K. one third of my house and land in K., as well as all what is virtually due me from J. van V.).

"Aan Mr. *William Legg*" "Een hondert ackers op Landt myn tobehoerende gelegen in de Corporatie Kingstowne volgens transport van de trustees van voors: Corporatie (to Mr. W. L. 100 acres of land in the Corporation of K., conveyed to me by the Trustees thereof).

"Aan *Bastyaen de Witt* van Kingstowne" "de geregte Derde van myn huys en gront in Kingstowne als mede een geregte derde van myn Roerende Staat" (to B. de W. of K. one third of my house and land in K., as well as one third of my personal estate).

"Aan *Willem Traphagen*" "all 't geene my Deugdelyk is Competerende van *Huybert Aarts* volgens bont aan my gepasseert, als mede een geregte derde van myn Roerende Staat" "mits dat de voors: Willem Traphagen gehouden is de onkoste van myn begraven te betalen" (to W. T. all what is virtually due me from H. A., according to a bond, as well as one third of my personal estate" "provided said W. T. pays for the costs of my burial).

"Aan *Geertie Maston* dogter van *Cornelis Maston* Een koe genaemt Blaar" (to G. M., daughter of C. M., a cow called B.).

Mr. William Legg and William Traphagen appointed executors.

GRITIE HENDRIX (her mark)

Witnessed by *Abraham Lamaitre, Cornelis Maston,* and *D. Meyer,* who all appeared before the Court, Jan. 17, 1708/9, proving the will.

The following wills of *Hugh Frere* in the possession of Mr. *Ralph Lefevre*, of *New Paltz*, are not on record in *Kingston*, *Albany* or *New York*.

I. FRERE, HUGUE, of The Paltz, laborer.

Will dated Sept. 4, 1697/8, and written in French.

Nostre aide soit au nom de Dieu qui a fait le ciel et la terre. Amen.

Par devant *Abraham Hasbroucq*, Justicier de paix au palle Comtes de Ulster et *Louis Beviere* et *Jean Cottin* demeurant au dit *Palle* comparu *Hugue Frere,* labourer, demeurant aussi au palle de sa pure et franche volonte estant tres saint d'esprit et d'entendement, sachant quel'heure de la mort est incogneue a tous les hommes desirant qu'apres son trepas tous ses enfants vivent en bonne union et concorde nous a declare sa volonte pour son testament pour a qui regarde tous ses biens, meuble et immeuble, premierement a dit que *hugue Frere* son fils aisnes aura dix pieces de huit pour son droit d'aisnes aussi a dit que trois de ses plus jeune enfans *Jacob, Jean* et *Sara* apres son trespas ils jouiront de toutes les terres et sa maison et tous ses parterre en fin de tous les immeujusques a ce que la dite fille Sara soit parvenue a l'age de seize ans sans payer aucune louage a leur autres frere et soeurs et apres que la dite fille Sara aura seize ans ils pourront partager tous ensemble tous les meuble et immeuble egalement apres quil auront payer toutes les dettes la reserve que sa fille Sara aura un lit de plume et un traver et deux couver et une vache et elle aura cecy hors de part et par dessus les autres et son fils Jacob aura en cheval a choisir dans son escurie. Il aura le dit cheval hors de part et par desu les autres, et son fils Jean prendra aussy un cheval a choisir et ils aura aussy le dit cheval hors de part et par dessus les autres pareillement a leur autres freres et soeurs que ont pris cy devant chacun un cheval et *Marie Frere* une vache.

La dit hugue Frere, testateur, establie et suplie son fils huge Frere de maintenir le bon droit et interest de ses freres et soeurs jusque a ce quils seront en age, les dit enfans Jacob, Jean et Sara jouiront aussi bien des meubles que des immeubles jusque specifie cy dessus.

Le dit testateur recommande tous ses enfans a la sainte protection du bon Dieu et qu'il le benis de ses benedictions, temporel et spirituel.

Fait au palle le quatrieme jour de Januie mil six cens nonnante sept. 1697/8.

JEAN COTTIN, temoin;
ABRAHAM HASBROUCK, temoin;   Marq X HUGUE FRERE.
LOUYS BAYVYR, temoin.

May our help be in the name of God who made the heaven and the earth. Amen.

Before Abraham Hasbrouck justice of the peace at the Paltz, county of Ulster, and Louis Bevier and Jean Cottin living at the Paltz appeared Hugo Frere, laborer, living also at the Paltz, of his (own) pure and free will, being of sound mind, and understanding that the hour of death is unknown to all men, desiring that after his death all his children may live in good unity and concord has declared to us his desire for his testament in regard to his properties, moveable and immovable.

First, to wit, that Hugo Frere his eldest son shall have ten pieces of eight as his birthright; also to wit that three of the younger children, Jacob, John and Sara after his death shall have all the lands and his house and all the garden plat, in a word all the real property, until said daughter Sara attains the age of 16 years, without paying any rent whatever to their other brothers and sisters, and after the said daughter Sara is sixteen years old they may divide equally among themselves all the household stock and the real property, after they have paid all the debts; with the reservation that the daughter Sara shall have one feather bed, one bolster, and two covers (blankets) and one cow, and she shall have these over and above the others; and the son Jacob shall choose from his stable a horse and he shall have the said horse, over and above the others; and his son Jean shall also choose a horse which shall be over and above the others, similarly to their other brothers and sisters who have taken each a horse, and Marie Frere a cow.

The aforesaid Hugo Frere, testator, appoints and entreats his son Hugo Frere to maintain the good rights and interests of his brothers and sisters until they are of age. The said children Jacob, Jean and Sarah shall have the household things and the real property until the time specified above.

The testator commends all his children to the divine protection of the good God and asks the blessing of his benificence, temporal and spiritual.

Made at the Paltz the fourth day of January, one thousand six hundred ninety-seven. (1697/8.)

(Hughe Freer, a deacon of the church at New Paltz, Jan. 22, 1683-Dec. 8, 1693, m. 1, Maria Haye, m. 2, Janneke Wibau. "The wife of H. F. died in the Lord." Issue: i. *Hugue*, b. 1668, m. June 7, 1690, *Maria Anna Le Roy;* ii. *Abraham*, b. 1670, m. Apr. 28, 1694, *Aeche Willem Titsoort;* iii. *Isaac*, bt. 1672, d. Aug. 9, 1690; by 2d wife: iv. *Jacob*, bt. June 9, 1679, m., 1705, *Antje Van Weyen;* v. *Joseph;* vi. *Jean*, bt. Apr. 16, 1682 at *Marmur*, m. ab. 1704, *Rebecca Van Wagenen*, d. of *Jacob Aartsen* (q. v.), and *Sarah Pels;* vii. *Mary*, bt. 1686 at *Hurley*, m. *Louis Velle* of *Schenectady;* (See N. Y. Gen. Reg., 1902, p. 31 et seq. for an account).

II. FRERE, HUGH, New Paltz.

Will dated Febr. 12, 1706/7 (only pps. 1-2 remains, the rest are missing).

(Long religious preamble.)

"Myn huysvrouw *Marie Anne* sall blyven in volle possessie van myn geheele stadt" "gedurende haer weduwschap" (my wife to remain in full possession of my whole estate during her widowhood) "en Indien sy sal koomen te hertrouwen sall sy gehoude syn om twee derde van myn voors. staet aan myn eerfgenamen" "uyt te keeren ende opte Leevere" (and if she should happen to marry, she shall be bound to deliver one third of said estate to my heirs) "Ende na haer overlyden sall de andere derde van myn voors. staet ock an myn Erfgenemen koomen" (and after her death said third part to go to the heirs).

"Aen myn outste soon *Huge* voor uyt de somma van £5 voor syn Reght van Eerste geboorene" (to my eldest son, H., £5 for his right of primogeniture).

"Tot Erfgenamen myn kinders By namen Huge, *Isaac, Simon, Marie, Sara, Hester, Cattrina, Blandina, Johannes,* and *Benjamin.* (As heirs, children named). "Ende voort de kinders die Ick en myn voors. huysvrouw uyt ons staende hywelyck moghte coome te procurere om myn geheele voors. staet Egaalyck" (and the children which I and my said wife may have shall divide equally with my other children).

(See his later will.)

BOOK OF DEEDS II. (BB), MARKED 1710.

Page 39.—LEGG, WILLIAM, of Kingstown.

Will dated June 5, 1710.

"Unto my dear wife *Susana Legg* my whole Estate dureing her Widdowhood but if she hapen to Contract Mariage that then Shee Shall but injoy one third of the same & the other two thirds to be to the only proper use benefit & behoofe of my Children hereafter Exprest dureing her natural Life and then to Returne to my Children as followeth."

"Unto my Well beloved Son *William Legg*" "the Sixth part of all my Stock & moveables Except three Milk Cows bequeathed hereafter with all my land that I dwell upon by name *Jacob's Hook* and the Iland with the orchard house and barne" "after his mothers decease provided that it shall be vallued by three men upon Oath & in Convenient time after his mothers decease and that the one halfe of the mony that it shall be vallued at the said William shall be bound to pay to my other Children under Expressed in three yeare" (to each a third).

"Unto my well beloved Son *John Legg*" "the Just sixth part of my Stock & moveables Except three milk Cows hereafter bequeathed With the Just fifth part of my Reale Estate Excepting the which I have above bequeathed to my son Wm. Legg."

"Unto my Loveing Son in Law *Jacobis De Boy*" "the sixth part of all my Stock and Moveables Except three Milk Cows" "& the Just fifth part of all my Reale Estate Except the Land and premises bequeathed to my son William."

"Unto my Loveing Son in Law *John Davenport*" "the Just Sixth part of all my Stock and Moveables & one Milk Cow of the three above Excepted. And Likewise the Just fifth part of my Reale Estate Except what is above bequeathed to my Son William."

"Unto my Loveing Son In law *Johannis Borhans*" "the Just Sixth part of all my Stock & moveables and one Milk Cow one of the three above Excepted with the fifth part of all my Reale Estate Except what is above bequeathed to my Son William."

"Unto my beloved daughter *Sarah Legg*" "the Just sixth part of all my Stock & moveables and one Cow the Last of the three above Excepted and the fifth part of all my Reale Estate Except what is above bequeathed to my Son William."

"Friends and neighbours *James Whitaker* and *Edward Whitaker*" appointed executors. Signed by the testator.

   KRYN OSTERHOUDT   (Witnesses appeared before the
   HENDERIK BURHANS   Court, Aug. 28, 1710, proving
   PIETER OSTERHOUT (his mark). the will).

(W. L. m. *Susanna Maret* (*Marrid*), and had issue: i. *William*, m. *Geesje Ploeg*, dau. of *Henric P.* (see his will); ii. *Susanna*, bt. Sept. 22, 1678, m. March 26, 1699, *Jan* (*Jacobus*) *Du Bois*, b. *Leyden, Holland;* iii. *Maria*, bt. Apr. 9, 1682, m., after Nov. 15, 1707, *John Devenport;* in the baptismal records, her parents name are given as *Wm. Lucasz* and Susanna *Marrid;* iv. *Margriet*, bt. Jan. 27, 1684 (dau. of Willem *Luyck* and Susanna Marrid), m. 1. *Johannes Borhans*, m. 2., Apr. 7, 1726, *Barent Van Benthuysen*, widower of *Jannetjen Van Wageningen;* v. *Sara*, bt. June 6, 1686, m., 1711, *Jacob Kool;* vi. *Samuel*, bt. March 25, 1688; and *John Legg*, b. *Kingston*, m., Apr. 21, 1701, *Annetje Fynhout*).

Page 192.—SCHOONMAKER, HENDRICK, of Kingstown.

Will dated Jan. 12, 1711/12.

"Unto my well beloved and dear wife *Geertruy* my whole Estate both Real and personall dureing her widdowhood but If She Should Contract Marige that then two thirds of my whole Estate both real and personall to be to" "my Children" "and only one third to my wife during her naturall life and then to Return to my said Children."

"To my beloved son *Hendrick Schoonmaker*" "negro boy named Tom and With the eleventh part of my whole Estate both real and personall."

"To my well beloved Son *Johanis Schoonmaker*" "the Just Eleventh part of my whole Estate both real and personall Excepting a negro boy Tom."

"To my well beloved son *Tyrk Schoonmaker*" "the Just Eleaventh part of my whole Estate real and personall Excepting a negro boy."

"To my Beloved Son *Jacobus Schoonmaker*" "the Just Eleaventh part of my whole Estate both real and personall Excepting a negro boy."

"To my beloved Son *Heskiah Schoonmaker*" "the just Eleaventh part of my whole Estate" "Excepting a negro boy."

"To my well beloved daughter *Barbarae Schoonmaker*" "the Just Eleventh part of my whole Estate" "Excepting The negor boy Tom."

"To my beloved daughter *Else Schoonmaker*" the Eleventh part.— "To beloved daughter *Janitie Schoonmaker*" "the Eleaventh part."—"To beloved daughter *Sarae Schoonmaker*" the eleventh part. To daughter *Catriena Schoonmaker* the eleventh part.—To daughter *Mariae Schoonmaker* the eleventh part.

If any of the children should die "under age", the survivors to divide that share. "Broder *Egbert Schoonmaker* and my friend and neighbour Edward Whittaker" appointed executors. Signed by the testator.

JAMES WHITTAKER
CORNELES VERNOY
PETER OSTERHOUT (his mark).

(Mr. James Whittaker, Mr. Corneles Vernoy Jun'r. & Mr. Peter Osterhout appeared before the Court, Apr. 12, 1712, proving the will).

HENR. BEEKMAN
ARIEN GERRITSEN
EVERT WYNKOOP

A true Coppy WM. NOTTINGHAM, Clark.

Hendrick Hendrixen Schoonmaker, s. of *Hendrick Jochemse S.* and *Elsie Janse* (see *Jochem S.*), m., March 24, 1688, *Geertruy de Witt,* dau. of *Tjerck Claessen De Witt* (q. v.), and had issue: i. *Elsie,* bt. Apr. 14, 1689, d. y.; ii. *Heskia,* bt. Apr. 14, 1689; iii. *Barbara,* bt. May 26, 1691, m., Oct. 30, 1719, *Wihelmus Ploeg*; iv. *Elsie,* bt. Apr. 17, 1692, m., June 13, 1713, *Nicholas De Meyer* (bt. Oct. 14, 1683, s. of *Wilhelmus De Meyer* and *Catherine Bayard* (q. v.); v. *Hendrick,* bt. June 3, 1694, m., Oct. 16, 1724, *Tryntje Oosterhoudt;* vi. *Jannetje,* bt. Aug. 18, 1695, d. y.; vii. *Johannes,* bt. July 4, 1697, m., May 15, 1729, *Ariaentje Hoogteling* (see *Johannes S.*); viii. *Tjerck,* bt. Jan. 22, 1699, m., Nov. 21, 1729, *Theodosia Whittaker,* bt. May 7, 1719, d. March 6, 1791, dau. of *Edward W.* and *Hillitje Burhans* (see *Tyrrick S.*); ix. *Jacob,* bt. Nov. 3, 1700; x. *Jannetje,* bt. Oct. 4, 1702, m., Sept. 30, 1720, *Hendrick Oosterhoudt;* xi. *Sarah,* bt. March 2, 1707, d. y.; xii. *Catrina,* bt. Febr. 11, 1709, m., Jan. 14, 1731, *Abraham Person;* xiii. *Sarah,* bt. Oct. 12, 1710, m., Aug. 19, 1726, *Cornelis Macklin*).

Page 196.—MASTON, CORNELIS, of Kingstown.

Will dated Jan. 30, 1712, and written in Dutch.

(Long religious preamble.)

"Aan myn outste soon *Johanis Masten* Een schiet roer tegenwoordig In zyn possessie." "Myn beminde huysvrouw *Elizabeth* sall blyve in Volle possessie van myn geheele Staat gedurende de tyt Van haar Weduweschap en Indien sy Comt te hertrouwen sall zy gehouden zyn om de gerechtige helleft van voors. Staat aan myn kinders uyt te keren ende na haar Doot sall de andere helft ook aan myn kinders Coomen."

(To my eldest son, J. M., a gun, now in his possession. My said wife Elisabeth shall remain in full possession of my whole estate during her widowhood, and if she should happen to marry, she shall be bound to convey one half of my estate to my children, and at her death the other half shall also go to my children.)

"Aan myn vyf Kinders mett naamen Johannis Maston *Aart Masten,* die vertie huysvrouw van *Gysbert Van den Bergh* (named *Diewertje* (*Deborah*), as will be seen later), *Antie Maston* en *Geertie* huysvrouw van *Arien Vliet*" "myn gehele Staat" (to my five children, by name J. M., A. M., the worthy wife of G. V. d. B., A. M., and G., wife of A. V., my entire estate).

Wife appointed executrix. Signed by the testator, and witnessed by *Abraham Lametter, Willem Schepmoes, Aart Van Wagenen,* and *Wm. Nottingham,* who all appeared before the Court: *Henry Beekman, Jacob Rutsen, Dirck Schepmoes,* on March 6, 1711/12, proving the will.

(Cornelius Masten, (s. of *John Masten,* or *Marston,* an Englishman, who settled at *Flushing* previous to 1644, and m. *Dievertje Jans,* Oct. 27, 1650, and who in his will, dated Febr. 14, 1670 (N. Y. Sur. Office, Liber I., p. 116) mentions "my two sons, *John* and *Cornelius,* under age, daughter *Elisabeth* and *Katherine*) m. ab. 1676, *Elisabeth Aartse* (*Van Wagenen*), dau. of *Aart Jacobsen* (*Van Wagenen*) and *Annetje Gerrits* (q. v.), and had issue: i. *Johannes,* bt. March 31, 1678, m. l., Oct. 19, 1701, *Marytje Swart,* m. 2., Jan. 25, 1712, *Maria Wells* (see *Ezekiel Masten*); ii. *Diewertje* (*Deborah*), m. Oct. 20, 1700, *Gysbert Van den Burgh;* iii. *Aart,* bt. Sept. 22, 1682, m., Sept. 9, 1704, *Pieternella Viele;* iv. *Antie,* bt. Aug. 18, 1684, m., May 1, 1712, *Mattys Janse,* s. of *Jan Matthysen* and *Magdalena Blanshan* (q. v.); v. *Geertie* (*Grietjen*), bt. Nov. 6, 1687, m., Febr. 11, 1711, *Arie,* bt. July 12, 1686, s. of *Dirck Van Vliet* and *Anna Andriesen*).

Page 205.—MOURITZ, FREDRICK PIETERSEN, of Marbletown.

Will dated May 30, 1709, and written in Dutch.

(Long religious preamble.)

"Myn huysvrouw *Engeltie* sall besitten En blyven in volle possestie van myn gehele Staat om geduerende haar Leven" "met Conditie zy ongeuwt blyeft maar Indien zy Comt te hertrouwen sall zy myn **geheele voors.** staat dat alsdan inweesen sall aan myn Erfgenamen hier onder beschreeven."

"Myn outse Soon *Pieter*" "dertigh schepels goede winter tarw voor Reght van Eerst geboorene."

"Aan myn seven kinders mett naamen Pieter *Jannetie Mourits Engeltie Oeyke Geertruy* ende *Elizabeth*" "myn geheele Staat om **Egaalyck** onder haar alle gedeelt te werden uytegenomen de dertigh schepele taruw aan Pieter."

(My wife E. shall possess and remain in possession of my whole estate during her life, on condition that if she should happen to marry, it shall go to my heirs named below. My eldest son, P., 30 schepels of winter wheat, his right of primogenitur. To my seven children, P., J., M., E., O., G., and E., my entire estate, to be equally divided among them with the exception of the 30 schepels of wheat given to P.)

Wife appointed executrix. Signed by the testator.

HENDRICK BOGART (his mark)

JANS MIDDAGH
JORIS MIDDAGH
WM. NOTTINGHAM.

(Mr. Hendrick Bogart, Capt. Joris Middagh, & Wm. Nottingham, appeared before the Court, May 30, 1709, proving the will).

(*Frederick Pietersen* (*Mouritz*) m. *Engeltje Hendrick*, and had issue: i. *Pieter*, bt. Oct. 16, 1667, m. after May 17, 1707, *Marya Haal*, widow of *Jan Bix*; ii. *Jannetie*, bt. June 18, 1671, m. before Nov. 13, 1692, *Isaac Davids*; iii. *Hendrick*, bt. prob. Apr. 24, 1675; iv. *Engel*, bt. Febr. 9, 1679; v. *Geertruid*, bt. July 28, 1684, m. (as *Geertruy Mouritse*), *Joseph Stevense*; vi. *Elysabeth*, bt. Dec. 5, 1686; vii. *Oeyke*, m. Aug. 29, 1703, *Joris* (*George*) *Hale* (her name is also spelled *Oeycke Mauritste, Outie Mouritse, Oetje Mauris*).

Page 323.—COTTIN, CATHERINE, of Kingston.

Will dated July 23, 1712, and written in French.

"Nostre Aid soit au nom de Dieu qui a fait le ciel et Laterre Amen Moy *Catherine Cottin* estant tres sain desprit et detendement Et ayant poir mon mary *Jean Cottin* Merchand demeurant a *Kingston* dans La County de Ulster province de nouvel York et Considerant que Lheur de la Mort Est Incognue a toutes Creature humaine apres avoir Recommande mon ame a Mon Creatur tous puissans dieu et mon Saveur & Redempteur et par Le merite de son fils Jesus Christ Je croy Estre sauvez et avoir Remission de mes pechez et Espere a La Resurection de Juste par la Vertur esticace de la passion de Nostre Seigneur Jesus Christ posseder Le Royaume du Ciel preparez a ses Eleu." (In the name of God, who has made the heaven and the earth, I, C. C., of good mind and memory, and being wife of Jean Cottin, merchant, living in K., in the county of U., New York, considering that the hour of death is unknown to all human creatures, I recommend my soul to my Creator, almighty God, and my

Saviour and Redeemer, hoping, by the merit of his son, Jesus Christ, that I shall find remission for all my sins, and at the resurrection of the righteous, by the virtue and passion of Our Lord, Jesus Christ, to possess the Kingdom of Heaven, prepared for his elect). "Dont il paroist par L'inventaire que Jay ffait aves mon dit Mary Jean Cottin" "Je doit avoir Le troisieme part du profitt que dieu nous a donnez par ces bontez ensemble—avec mondit Mary Jean Cottin de puis L'heur de nostre Mariage Jusques a Mon trespas premierement" (As it appears from an inventory, which I made with my said husband, J. C., that I should have one third of all the profits which God, in his grace, has given unto us, from the hour of my marriage with said husband, J. C., until I passes away) "Je veux" "que la franchise dattez du vingt deuxieme jour de septembre mil sept Cens Et deux que Je donne a *Rachel* quest son nom apres avoir Estez baptisez *Sera*" "et prandra apre ma mort dans masus de huit et Les autres chose qui sont dite dans Les dit affranchissement et elle Le prendra devant que mes Enfans puissent partir ma Troisieme part des dit profitt." (I will that the freedom, dated Sept. 22, 1702, which I have given to Rachel, as her name is now after having been baptized Sera, shall remain in force, and that she shall have 30 pieces of eight from said third part of the profits, and other things, as appears in said manumission, and she shall have it before my children divide their shares of my third interest in said profits)." "Et Aussy Je veux" "que la ffranchissement datez du dix septieme jour daouust mil sept Cens et neuf que Jay doonez a nostre negresse *Dina* sera observez et gardez en la pline force vertue." (I will that the letter of manumission, dated Aug. 17, 1709, which I have given to our negress, Dina, shall remain in force, and be properly observed). "Et Aussy Je veux" "qua La donations dattez du dixieme Jour de Mars mil six Cens nonans Sept Que Jay fait a ma fille *Sara* pour tous mes huit habit et une bagne dor sera observe." (I also wish that the donation, dated March 2, 1697, which I have made to my daughter, Sara, of all my new clothing and a gold ring, shall be properly observed.) "Aussy Je donnez a leglize flamend icy de Kingston Vingt piece de huit quel prendra apres ma mort dans ma susdit troisieme part de profitt et ce pour aider a Subvenier a les pauvres." (I give to the Dutch Church here in Kingston 20 pieces of eight, to be taken after my death from my third part of the profits, to be used for the benefit of the poor). "Et pour ce qui Concerne le Reste de ma sus dit troisieme part de profit" "a *Abraham Du Bois* et *Jacob Du Bois* et *David Du Bois* Et *Mathieu Du Bois* et les deux fils de dessunt Isaac Du Bois a eux Cinq Ensemble Je Leur donne quil prendrant aprez ma mort dans ma susdit troisieme part de profitt une quatrieme part et a *Salomon Du Bois* et a *Louis Du Bois* aeux Ensemble Je leur donne quil prendront apres ma mort dans ma susdit troisieme part de profit une quatrieme part et a Sara ma fille Je luy donne quel prendra apres ma morte les autres quatrieme part de ma susdit troisieme part de profit pour elle seul et pour leur effet de ma susdit Troisieme part de profitt eux tous mes enfans prendrons argens merchandise bonne et monnais dette Chacun a proportion de leur part." (And so far as the rest of said third part of the profits is concerned, I give to A. du B., J. du B., D. du B., M. du B. and to the two sons of Isaac Du Bois's, deceased, one quarter interest in said third part of the profits, to be divided equally between these five, another fourth part, I give to S. du B. and L. du B., and the two remaining four parths, I give to my daughter Sara, and for the performance hereof, each one of my children is to take according to his or her share, silver, merchandise, and good or bad debts).

"Mon Mary" (my husband) Jean Cottin, appointed executor. Signed by the testatrix, and witnessed by *Cornelis Swart, Mattys Pears,* and *Carol Barweer,* who appeared before the Court, Dec. 10, 1713, proving the will. (The provisions of this will are, however, practically annulled by an Indenture, for which see "Ulster Co. Deeds.").

(See *Jean Cottin*).

Page 333.—DU MONT, WALRANDT, Sen'r., of Kingston.

Will dated March 15, 1701, and written in Dutch.

(Long religious preamble).

"Myn Huysvrouw *Gryetie Du Mondt* sal hebben En genieten gedurende haar Leven de baate en profyte van myn geheele Staat om daar over te disponeren na Welgevallen En Ingevallen myn Schulden quamen betalt te syn alvoren myn voors. huysvrouw quam te overlyden als dan na het overlyden van myn voors. huysvrouw de Roerende Staat alsdann in Wesen sal syn ten behoeve van myn Erfgenamen hier onder ges: om Egaalick onder haar gedeelt te werden dogh de Neger sal syn ten behoeve van myn soon *Jan Babtista Du Mont,* mits betalen de voor voors: Neger tot sodanige prys als twe Eerlycke Lieden sullen oordelen voors: Neger Wardigh te syn na het overlyden van myn voors: huysvrouw dat het selfe uyt voors: Roerende staat sal moeten betaalt werden En 't overige alsdann te deelen als vooren." (My wife G., shall have and enjoy during her life the income and profits out of my entire estate, to dispose of at her pleasure, my debts to be paid before she dies, and then the personal estate shall be equally divided among my heirs, but the negro shall go to my son J. B. du M., he to pay for said negro such price as two honorable appraisers may decide upon).

"Aan myn drie soons met namen *Weibrandt Jan Baptist En Pieter*" "myn huys Tuyn En Boom gaert Beginninde van het Killitie ontrent myn huys" (to my three sons, W. J. B., and P., my house, garden, and orchard, beginning at the little kill near my house).

"Aan myn outste soon Walrandt du Mont" "en morgen Landt uyt myn bouwerij voor het Regt van Eerst geboorte." "Insgelyck soo geeve ick" "de geregte Derde van myn Bouwery t' Bovenstaande morgen Eerst ofgetrocken Welck Bouwery in Drien sal gedeelt werden der Lott in gelyke grote Ente Lopen van het Killtie tot op de grote Kill En dat myn voor: soon de Keur der selven sal hebben en het morgen als boven gegeven" on condition that he pays to "myn drye dogters hier na beschreven Een hondert pont" "in twe Jaren na het overlie den van myn voors: huysvrouw Jeder de geregte helft." (To my eldest son, W. du M. one morgen of land from my farm, his right of primogeniture. Also one third of my farm, which farm shall be divided in three equal parts from the little kill to the great kill, the above mentioned morgen first to be withdrawn, on condition that he pays to my three daughters £100 in two years after my wife's decease, one half yearly; he also to have the choice of the lots).

"Aan myn soon Jan Baptista du Mont" "de derde part van myn Bouwery Except t' Morgen Landt voor afgegeven aan myn soon Walrandt syn portie gekosen heft voorde andere twe parte met syn Broeder Pieter du Mont" "myn voors: soon" is te betalen" "aan myn drie dogters" "Een hondert pont" "in twe Jaren." (to my son J. B. du M. one third of my farm, except the morgen given to Waalrandt, he also to pay my daughters £100 in two years).

"Aan myn soon Pieter du Mondt" "derde van myn Bouwery" except what has already been devised," and on condition that he pays to "myn drie dogters" one hundred pounds "oock soo hebbe ick aan myn soon Pieter vercogt Een stuckje grondt in myn Wijbepalt aan *Ffredrick Klute* Walrand du Mondt het Killitie en de wegh van myn huys tot het Konings padt voor de Somme van Een hondert Stuck van agten waarop door myn ontfangen twintygh soo dat Resteert Taghgentigh stuck van aghten, welcke somme myn voors: soon gehouden is in twe Jaren te betalen na het overlyden van myn voors: huysvrouw Jeder Jaar de gerechte helft aan myn vrouws voor doghter *Antie Kip*." (To son Pieter a third. I have sold to him a piece of land in my pasture at Ffredrick Klute Walrandt du Mondt, the little kill and the road from my house to the King's Road for a sum of 100 pieces of eight, of which I received 20 pieces, so there remains 80 pieces of eight, which sum my said son is bound to pay in two years after my wife's decease to my wife's daughter by a previous marriage, Antie Kip).

"Aan myn Doghter *Margriet* huysvrouw van *William Loverige*" "Een hondert pondt" "haar Broeders te betalen in Manieren als voors:"

"Aan myn dogter *Jannetie* huysvrouw van *Mychiel Dirk*" "Een hondert pont," to be paid by her brothers.

"Aan myn Dogter *Ffrancyntie* huysvrouw van *Fredrick Cloete*" "Een hondert pondt" to be paid by her brothers.

"Aan myn vrouws voor Dogter Antie Kip" "vier & twyntigh pont" to be paid by "myn soon Pieter du Mont."

BOOK OF DEEDS, Liber II. 87

(To my daughters Margriet, wife of William Loverige £100; to Jannetie, wife of Michiel Dirk £100; to Ffrancyntie, wife of Fredrick Cloete £100; and to my wife's daughter Antie Kip £25).
Wife appointed executor. Signed by the testator.

JAKOBUS DU BOIS (his mark)

JAN LA CHAIR

W. D. MEYER

(All witnesses, except W. D. Meyer appeared, Sept. 3, 1713, before the Court: Coll. *Henry Beekman, Capt. Dirck Schepmoes,* Esq., Judges, and Mr. *Arien Gerritsen,* Coll. *Abrah. Gaasbeek Chambers,* Capt. *Egbert Schoonmaker,* Justices, and Major *Johannis Hardenbergh,* Esq., High Sheriffe, proving the will, "Coll. Wm de Meyer deceased.")

(Codicil.)

Page 337.—DU MONT, WALRANDT, Sen'r, of Kingston.

Dated June 25, 1713, and written in Dutch.

The previous will, dated March 15, 1701 shall "opgevolght werden".

"Unde door dien Ick int voornoemt Testament niet gedisponeert heboven myn huys schure boomgaart Tuyn en hofste zynde groot als nu in heyning Leyt en de grondt van myn soon *Jan Baptist du Mondt* du van ses morgen bos Landt dyen Ick gecoght heb van de Trustees van de Corporatie *Kingston* waar over Ick disponere en geeven als volght."

"Myn outste soon *Wallerand* sall van myn voor: huys schure boomgaart Truyn an hofste voor uyt hebben voor hem zyn order ofte Erfgename de waardy van hondert schepels Taruwe."

"Aan myn ses Kinderen Mett Namen *Wallerand: Jan Baptist: Pieter: Margaret: Jannetie* en *Ffrancyntie*" "myn voors: huys schuez boomgaart Truyn en Hofste (Except de wardy van voors: hondert schepels taruw bove an Wallerand vooruyt gemackt)."

"Aan myn soon Wallerand en Jan Baptist ses morgen bos Landt gelege aan de suyt syde van de hoge wegh tuschen het bos Land van de Erfgenamen van *Tierck Claasen De Witt* en het bos landt van Capt. *Mattys Mattysen* Wallrandt sall syn drie morget hebben naast het Landt van Capt. Mattys Mattysen Jan Baptist sall zyn drie morgen nast het bos Landt van de Erfgenamen van Tjerck Clasen De Witt hebbe" "uyt Consideratie dat zy het aan de Trustees betaalt hebben."

"So is myn Will en begerten dat myn geheele Bouwery by myn voornoemde Testament aan myn drie soone gemaeckt noyt aan vreemden vercogt ofte verallineert sal werden ten sy aan die de naame van Du Mont dragen so dat het voors: bouwery Ewugh aan di van de naam van Du Mont zyn."

(As I did not dispose of my house, barn, garden, and yards, and my son Jan Baptist du Mondt's 6 morgen wood-land, which I bought of the Trustees of the Corporation of Kingston, I dispose of these possessions as follows. To my eldest son W. in advance the value of 100 schepels of wheat out of said house, barn, garden and yards. To my six children named W., J. B., P., M., J., and F., said barn, garden, and yard, except the value of the 100 schepels of wheat given to W. To my sons W. and J. B. six morgens wood-land on the south side of the highway, adjoining the woodland, belonging to the heirs of T. C. de W., and the woodland belonging to Capt. M. M., Wallrandt shall have the three morgens next to Capt. M. M's land, and J. B. shall have the three morgens next to the land belonging to the heirs of T. C. de W., on condition that they have paid for it to the Trustees. My will is that my whole farm shall go to my three sons, not to be sold to strangers, or alienated, but retain the name of Du Mont for all time).

"Myn huysvrouw Grietie" appointed executrix.

(Mark of) WALLRAND DU MONT.

CORNELIS ELTINGE
TJERCK DE WITT
WM. NOTTINGHAM

(Att a Court of Common Pleas held at Kingston this 3d Sept. 1713.

"The same persons appeared as at the probation of the will."

(*Wallarand Du Mont*, b. in *Coomen, Flanders*, came to this country in 1657 from *Amsterdam*, served as a cadet in the Hon. West India Company, m. at *Esopus*, Jan. 13, 1664, *Margaret* (*Greytie*) *Hendricks*, of *Wie*, near *Swol*, widow of *Jan Arentsen*. Wallarand's sister, *Margaret*, was wife of *Pierre Noue*, a Walloon, who emigrated in 1673. W. du M. and M. H. had issue: i. *Margaret*, bt. Dec. 28, 1664, m. *Wm. Loveridge*; ii. *Walran*, bt. Nov. 13, 1667, m., March 24, 1688, *Catrina Ter Bosch*; iii. *Jan Baptist*, m. *Neeltje Cornelis Van Veghten*; iv. *Jannetje*, m. *Michel Dirk Van Veghten*; v. *Francyntie*, bt. July 21, 1674, m. *Fred. Clute*; vi. *Peter*, bt. Apr. 20, 1679, m. 1., Dec. 25, 1700, *Femmetje Teunise van Middle Swart*, dau. of *Jan Teunissen*, m. 2., Febr. 23, 1707, *Catelyntje*, dau. of *Jeronimus Jorise Rapalie*, m. 3., Nov. 16, 1711, *Jannetje*, dau. of *Hendrick Claessen Vechten*.

Michel Dirk Van Vechten was s. of *Derick Teunissen*, b. 1634 at *Vechten*, dio. of *Utrecht*, who came with his father, *Teunis Derricksen* to Albany.

William Loverige came from *Wool, Dorsetshire, England*, and died at Perth Amboy, N. J., 1703.

Pieter Du Mont settled on the *Raritan River, N. J.*

Page 375.—HASBROUCK, JEAN, of New Paltz.

Will dated Aug. 26, 1712, and written in Dutch.

(Long religious preamble).

"Aan myn soon *Jacob Hasbrouck*" "all myn Land gelegen onder de Lemitten van 't Pattent van de *Neiuw Paltz*" "met huys schuer Ende alle andere myn Timerage en daar op zynde Ende Haande oock myn Wagons ploegen Eggen & Alles wat daar aan is behoorende Ende ook myn twee Negers mett namen *Gerrit* & *James* als ook al hett geweer en wat ddar aan hoort Ende de Cleederen van myn overleeden soon *Isaac Hasbrouck* Ende all myn boecken Except drie hier onder aaan myn Doghter *Elizabeth* vermacht Ende ook de gerechtige helft van de Rest van myn geheele Losse ofte Roerende staat Except van wat hier onder aan myn Dochter *Mary* ende Elizabeth vermacht is waar hy sall uyt keerenende betalen als hier na in dese tegen woordige is geordeonert mett Conditie dat zyn outste soon het stuck Landt Leggende tuschen het Land van *Abraham Du Bois* En myn Dochter *Mary* Langes de *Paltze Kill* ten suyde der selve Enten hoorde van t' Paltz Dorp sall voor hem syn order ofte Erfgenamen vooruyt hebben."

"Indien myn soon *Abraham Hasbrouck* (die van dese Proventie verstrocken is) mocht in't Leven zyn En hier weder Coomen so sall myn voors soon Jacob aan hem Leveren Een goet part voor hett Recht van Eerst geboorten & ook aan hem op Leveren voor hem zyn ordere ofte Erfgenamen de gerechtige helft van myn geheele vaste staat so als boven aan myn voors soon Abraham Itwes meer van myn staat sall hebben ofte Predendereeren."

"Aan my Dochter Mary" "de Somme van seven en vyftig pont Corrant gelt van *Niew York* myn toekomende van *Abraham Rutan* volgens obligatie twee en veertigh pont en van *Pieter Du Bois* volgens obligatie vyftien pont Ook geeve Ick aan haar all wat zy voordeesen van myn heeft genooten."

"Aan *Pieter Guymard* Eenigste Soon van myn overleedene Doghter *Hester* de Somme van vyftien pondt" "t' welck myn voors soon Jacob aan voors Pieter Guymard sall betaalen als hy komt te trouwen of tot de ouderdom van Een en twintigh Jaaren maar so hy Comt te overlyden Eeer hy trouwt of Een en twintig Jaaren si soo Sal myn soon Jacob vry zyn om voors som van vyftien pont te betalen."

"Aan myn doghter Elizabeth" "Sestigh pont" "ook myn Negerin met naame *Molly* en ook drie boecken Een testament de oeffening der godtsaligheyt en Een predecatie boeck van *Pieter Du Mollin* gemaackt in het fransse gedruckt Ende ook de gerechtige helft van myn geheele Losse ofte Roerende staat Except van t' geen boven vermackt is met Conditie dat Indien de negerin Molly Kinders kryght sall Jacob de Erste dogter daar van hebben maar moet by de moeder blyve tot dat hett een Jaar out is."

"Indien myn soon Jacob will te overlyden sonder kint ofte kinders wettigh by hem geprocureert dat all het geen aan hem gemackt by dese als dan aan myn twee voors. doghters Mary ende Elizabeth en haar orddre ofte Erfgenamen all Coomen om onder haar twee gedeelt te werden als volgt dat is Elizabeth sall dan vooruyt hebben myn huys schuer en Erf en boomgaart aghter de Schuer en hett wyland gelegen tusschen de wyjen van Abraham Du Bois en myn voors. Doghter Mary Ende all de Rest sullen sy Mary Ende Elizabeth Egaal Deelen."

"Indien myn voors Doghter Elizabeth quam te overleyden sonder Kint ofte Kinders dat dan het geene by dese aan haar gemackt sall Coomen aan myn soon Jacob en Doghter Mary."

"Indien myn soon Jacob en myn dogter Elizabeth quamen beyden te overleyden sonder Kint ofte Kinders so sal al hett geene by dese aan haar gemacht Coomen aan de twee soonen van myn voors. doghter Mary mett namen *Daniel* & *Phillip*."

Son Jacob Hasbrouck & "Myn Cousyns *Andre Lefevre* ende Louys Du Bois" appointed executors.

JEAN HASBROUCK (his mark)

ABRAHAM HASBROUCK
ROELOFF ELTINGE
ABRAHAM DOYO
WM. NOTTINGHAM

(Capt. Abraham Hasbrouck, Mr. Roeloff Eltinge & William Nottingham appeared, Aug. 14, 1714, before the Court in presence of Mr. *Arien Gerritsen* and Capt. *Joris Middagh*, Esq., Justices, proving the will).

(To my son, Jacob Hasbrouck" "all my land, lying within the boundaries of the patent of New Paltz" "with house, barn, and all my other buildings thereon being and standing, also my wagons, ploughs, harrows and everything thereto belonging and also my two negroes named Gerrit and James; further the gun and what belongs to it and the clothing of my deceased son Isaac Hasbrouck and all my books excepting three hereafter bequeathed to my daughter Elizabeth, also one just half of the balance of my whole personal or movable estate, excepting what hereafter is bequeathed to my daughters Mary and Elizabeth" he to pay as hereafter is directed, on condition that his oldest son shall first have "the piece of land lying between the land of Abraham Dubois and my daughter Mary along the Paltz Kill on the south thereof, and north of the Paltz village."

"If my son Abraham, who removed from this Province, should be alive and return here, then my son Jacob shall deliver to him a good horse for his birth-right, and also the just half of my whole real estate" Abraham not to have any further claim on the estate.

"To my daughter Mary £57, due from Abraham Rutan, according to a bond of £42, and from Pieter Du Bois, according to a bond £15" she to have no further claim on the estate.

"To Pieter Guymard, only son of my deceased daughter Hester £15, which sum Jacob shall pay to Pieter Guymard, when he marries or at age of 21." Should he die before that age, Jacob is to be relieved from paying said sum.

"To my daughter Elizabeth £60, also my negress Molly, three books, one Testament, the Practice of Devotion, and a book of sermons by Pieter Du Mollin, printed in French; also the just half of my whole personal estate, excepting what hereabove has been bequeathed, on condition that if the negress Molly should bear children, Jacob shall have the first daughter, but she is to remain with her mother until she is one year old."

"If my son Jacob should die without child or children lawfully begotten by him, all that is given to him shall go to Mary and Elizabeth, the latter to have the house, barn, lot and orchard behind the barn, and the pasture land, lying between the pasture of Abraham Dubois and my daughter Mary, and all the rest to go to said Mary and Elizabeth, to be equally divided.

If Elizabeth should die without lawful issue, her share to go to Jacob and Mary equally.—If Jacob and Elizabeth both should die without issue, their shares to go to Mary's two sons, Daniel and Phillip.

(Jean Hasbrouck came from *Calais, France*, 1673, with wife, *Anna Doyan* (*Deyo*). His brother, *Abraham Hasbrouck*, came in Apr. 1675 to *Boston*, m., Nov. 27, 1675, Maria, dau. of *Christian Doyon*, and had five children: *Rachel, Joseph, Solomon, Daniel* and *Benjamin*. (See Abraham Hasbrouck). Jean Hasbrouck and Anna Deyo had issue: i. *Maria*, bt. at *Manheim, Germany*, m. at *Kingston*, June 1, 1683, *Isaac Dubois*, s. of *Louis Du Bois* and *Cath. Blanshan* (q. v.); ii. *Hester*, b. *Manheim*, m. *Kingston*, Apr. 18, 1692, *Pierre Guimard*, b. at *Moise, Saintonge, France*, s. of *Pierre Guimard* and *Anne Damour* (see P. G.'s will); iii. *Abraham*, bt. Kingston, March 31, 1678; iv. *Elizabeth*, bt. *New Paltz*, Apr. 4, 1685, m. K., June 2, 1713, *Louis Bevier*; v. *Jacob*, bt. N. P. Apr. 15, 1688, m. K., Dec. 14, 1717, Esther Bevier).

Page 414.—SWARTWOUT, ROELOFF,

Will dated March 30, 1714, and written in Dutch.

(Long religious preamble).

"Aan myn outste Soon *Thomas*" "vyf en twentigh pont" "voor syn Recht van Eerst geboorten."

"Aan myn voornoemde soon Thomas en aan myn soon *Barnardus* my geheele vaste" "staat myn tobehoorende in de County van Ulster" on condition that he pays the other heirs a sum of £325 in two years, if he cannot pay in two years then he may have four years to pay in "om de Selve te betalen mits dat sy vyften hondert betalen aan myn andere Erfgenamen voor interest."

"Aan myn dogter *Hendricke* huysvrouw van *Huybert Lambertsen*" a sum of £65.

"Aan de kinders van myn soon *Anthony*" a sum of £65.

"Aan de Kinders van myn dochter *Cornelia overlyden*" a sum of of £65.

"Aan myn dogter *Ragel* huysvrouw van Jacob Kip" the sum of £65.—"Aan myn Dochter *Eva* huysvrouw van *Jacob Dingman*" a sum of £65.

"Alle myne Clederen" "aan myn soons Thomas en Barnardus."

As executors appointed "myn soons Thomas Swartwout Barnardus Swartwout & *Jacob Kyp*."

Signed by the testator.

HANS KIERSTEDE
PIETER OSTRANDER
WM. NOTTINGHAM

(Witnesses appeared, May 14, 1715, before the Court, Dirck Schepmoes, Esq., Judge, Arien Gerritsen and Cornelis Cool, Justices, proving the will."

(To my eldest son Thomas £25, his right as being the first-born.—Also to Thomas and to my son Barnardus my entire estate in Co. Ulster, on condition (as above) the £1500 to my other heirs.—To my daughter, Hendricke, wife of Huybert Lambertsen £65. To children of my son Anthony £65. To children of my daughter Cornelia, deceased, £65. To my daughter Ragel, wife of Jacob Kip £65. To my daughter Eva, wife of Jacob Dingman £65. All my clothing to my sons Thomas and Barnardus).

(*Roeloff Swartwout*, bt. in the Oude-Kerk, *Amsterdam, Holland*, June 1, 1634 (s. of *Thomas Swartwout*) of *Groningen*, later of *New Amsterdam*, and *Adrientje Symons* (m. Feb. 4, 1630), on Aug. 13, 1657, in the presence of his father, *Thomas Swartwout*, covenanted a marriage contract with *Eva Albertsen*, widow of the late *Anthony de Hooges*, in presence of her father, *Albert Andriessen Bratt*, they to bring together all their property, according to the custom of *Holland*, except that the bride reserves for her children with her former husband, *Marichen Anneken, Catrina, Johannes* and *Eleonora De Hooges*, 100 gulden for each of them. *Barent Albertse Bratt* and *Teunis Slingsland*, brother and brother-in-law of said Eva Albertse, shall be guardians of said children. (Albany Co. Records).—He m. 2., at New York, Oct. 8, 1691, *Francyntje Andries*, widow of *Abraham Lubbertsen*. With his first wife, he had issue: i. *Thomas*, m. before Feb. 4, 1683, *Lysbeth Gordenier* (*Lysbeth Jacobse Hovenier*); ii. *Hendricke*, m., as of Albany, in Kingston, March 16, 1679, *Huybert Lambertsen;* iii. *Antoni*, bt. Jan. 8, 1662 (when *Toomes Swartwout* was a witness); iv. *Antoni*, bt. May 11, 1663, m. *Jannetje Jacobus* (*Coobes*), and had: a. *Roelof*, bt. June 9, 1695, b. *Jacobus*, bt. March 29, 1696; v. *Cornelia*, bt. March 13, 1667, m. before Apr. 28, 1689, *Hendrick Klaesen Schoonhoven* (see *Henderick Claesse*(*n*)); vi. *Rachel*, m. *Jacob Kip* before Febr. 9, 1696; vii. *Eva*, b. in *Hurley*, m., Oct. 9, 1698, *Jacob Dingmans*, b. *Kinderhook;* viii. *Barnardus*, bt. Apr. 26, 1673 (*Rudolfus Swartwout* and *Jacomeyna Swartwout*, witnesses), res. *Hurley*, m. May 19, 1700, *Rachel Schepmoes*).

R. S. on Aug. 15, 1659 conveyed to *Philip Pieterse Schuyler* a garden in *Beverwyck*, granted originally to *Antony De Hooges*, deceased (Albany Co. Rec.)—R. S. was appointed the first Sheriff of Wiltwyck, at Esopus, 1660, at which appointment Gov. Stuyvesant expressed "great surprise," on the ground that R. S. was a 'minor and incompetent for the office' (See *O'Callaghan*, New Netherland, ii., p. 431).—R. S. was appointed justice and collector of the grand excise of Ulster Co., 1689-90.—On Jan. 23, 1664-67, Gov. *Lovelace* issued a deed of confirmation to R. S. for land at Wiltwyck, at Esopus (N. Y. Land Papers, I., p. 22).—On or about June 1670 Mr. R. S., dwelling in Esopus, conveys to *Ryckie Dareth*, widow of *Jan Dareth*, of Albany, a lot east of the house of *Volckert Janse* (Douw) (Ibid.).—On May 28, 1686, a survey was taken of 47 acres land, part of Hurley great piece, on the north side of Esopus Kill, also of a house lot in Hurley, and of two lots at Hurley fly, or meadow ground, Nos. 11, 13, laid out for R. S. by *Philipps Welles*, surveyor (N. Y. Land Papers, i. p. 187).—On Nov. 12, 1697, R. S. petitioned for 200 acres land in Ulster Co., part of land called *Waghgashkenck*). See also "The Swartwout Chronicle by A. J. Wells."

Page 435.—BOGART, HENDRICK, of Marbletown.

Will dated Dec. 12, 1707, and written in Dutch.

(Long religious preamble.)

"Soo is myn Wil En begeerten dat het heuwlycke Contract tuschen myn en myn tegen woordige huysvrouw *Ruth Waldron* gemackt sall in waarde gehouden zyn."

"Aan myn twe soons met namen *Cornelis* en *Marten*" the sum of £75, Cornelis £38 and Marten £37, Cornelis being the first born."

"Myn kinders die on getrouwt sullen zun ten tyt van myn overleyde sullen hebben Ende voor uyt genieten behoorlyke uyt sett soo als myn kinders die alsdan getrout syn gehadt hebben."

"Aan myn aght kinders mett namen *Cornelis Mayke* huysvrouw van *Thomas Jansen Marten Aaltie Sarah Neeltie Rebecca* Ends *Rachell*" "En gereghtig aghtste part van myn geheele staat."

"Indien Eenige van myn voors. kinders moghte Coomen te overlyden in haar onmondige Jaaren dat des selfs portie ofte porties alsdan Egaallyk on de Rest van haar gedeelt sall werden."

As executors appointed sons Cornelius and Marten and "myn Schoon soon Thomas Janse Ends myn swager Capt. *Joris Middagh*."

HENDRICK BOGART (his mark).

(My will is that the marriage contract entered into between me and my worthy wife, Ruth Waldron, shall be fulfilled. To my two sons, Cornelis and Marten £75. My children who are unmarried at my death an outfit similar to my married children's. To my eight children, named, ⅛ part of my entire estate. If any of my children should happen to die during their minority, their portions shall be divided among the survivors.)

CLAES KEATOR (his mark)

JNO RUTSEN

ABRAHAM LAMETTERE JUNR. (his mark)

WM. NOTTINGHAM.

(Capt. Jno. Rutsen, Claes Keator & Wm. Nottingham appeared before the Court, May 9, 1716, proving the will of Hendrick Bogart "late of Marbletown deceased.")

(Hendrik Bogaart m., Aug. 17, 1703, in New York, *Rutthje Waldron*, widow of *Jan de la Maistre*, whom she had m. in N. Y., Aug. 11, 1678 (see *Abraham Delamater*). (She was prob. dau. of Samuel Waldron and Niesje Bloetgoet).
They had issue:—*Mayke*, m. Nov. 22, 1702, *Thomas Janssen*; *Aaltjen*, m. Apr. 27, 1711, *Adriaan Nieuwkerk*; *Sarah*, m., Jan. 19, 1711, *Abraham de Lameetere* ("They are the first that I, Domine *Petrus Vas*, have married."); *Neeltje*, m., Nov. 1, 1715, *Anthony Slegt*; *Rachel*, b. *Albany*, m., March 14, 1716, *Benjamin de Mes*, b. in *Vrenkryk* (*France*); *Cornelis*, b. Marbletown, m., May 27, 1704, *Cornelia de la Mettre*, b. *New Harlem*; *Marthen*, m., May 7, 1713, *Tanneken de Lamecter*, both of Marbletown. The children's names were spelled: *Bogard, Bogaard, Bogaart, Boogaard, Bogart, Bogardus*.—Capt. Joris Middagh, b. at *Hycoop in Holland*, m., Apr. 22, 1696, *Marritje Martissen*.).

Page 471.—AARTSEN, JACOB, of Wagendal.

Will dated Oct. 5, 1714, and written in Dutch.

"Myn beminde huysvrouw *Sara* sal blyve in 't volle besitt En possessie van myn geheele staat" "Indien myn voors. huysvrouw Quam te hertrouwen soo sal zy allenlyk hebben de derde van de baten en profytten van myn voors geheele staat."

"Aan myn outsten soon *Aart*" "myn groote Bybel Ende Een Catechizatie boeck geschreven door *Petrum De Witte* Ende myn scheit Roer mett zyn tobehooren sonder dat hy Jtwes meerder dies weegen sal hebben ofte predendeeren 't welck hy sall hebben Ende ontfangen aanstondts na myn overlyden Ende na myn voors. soons overleyden sal het silve aan syn outste soon *Jacob* koomen."

"Aan myn Jongsten soon *Isaac*" "myn grote Kist die Ick van myn vader geerft heb en ook all myn Clederen die aan myn Lyf behooren sonder hy Jtwes voor de Selve aan myn andere Erfgenamen sal uyt keeren ofte betaalen."

"Myn Jongste doghter *Sara* sal aanstondts na haar moeders overleyden hebben" "al haar moeders Clederen die aan haar lyf behooren Ende Ook Een neuive Cleere Kas En Een nieuve Tafell die *Thomas Beekman* gemackt heeft En Een tinne Kom twee Isere potten Een groote En Een Klyne Ende myn huys spiegel die wy nu gebruyken Ende ook twee melck Koys En Een nieuw sondaghs Kleet 't welck Ick aan myn voors dogter Sara maak voor haar uytsett."

"*Sara Kool* doghter van *Symon Kool* sal hebben" "Een Bedt mett zyn toebehooren En Een sondaghs nieuw Kleet En Een melck Kou."

"Aan myn Doghter *Rebecca* huysvrouw van *Jan Ffrere*" "Een seekere stuck bouw-landt belendende ten noortwesten en ten noortoosten aan hett Bosslandt voor dese door myn aan voors. Jan Ffrer getransporteert Ende Ten suytoosten aan de *Ronduyts Kill* van daar Loopen met Een Rechte Lyn tot aan andere steen in de grondt gerett in hett bouwlandt na by Een klyn slootie En van daar tot aan Een Schemmelbast Eyk Boomtie gemerckt staande by Een kiletie dat de suytwestelyke lemiten is vant voors. boslandt aan voors. Jan Frere getransporteert Dan Langert het solve bos. landt m't Ronde tot aan de Ronduytskill dan Langst de selve tot de Eerste steen Ende ook Een stuck Landt geleegen aan de suytoosten zyvande Ronduyts kill Loopende van Een seekere Sloptie dat van de bergh in de kill Loopt noortoostelyck tuschen de kill en hett Landt van *William West* Langest deselve totaan hett land van Coll. *Henricus Beekman*" "Ende ook vrye previlegie om hout en steen te haalen En gebruyken uyt het bos landt" "aan myn voors. Doghter" "de gerechtige twalfde part van myn geheele" "staat Except van't geen dat boven vermaackt is."

"Aan myn Ellest andere kinderen mett namen *Aart Evert, Symon, Jacob, Benjamin, Abraham, Isaac, Annetie Geertie* huysvrouw van *Jacob Decker, Jannetie* huysvrouw van *Johannis Turck,* Ende *Sara*" "myn geheele staat."

In case of death, the survivors to divide the property, except the property devised to the youngest son Isaac, which in case of his death shall go to his other brothers equally, and except the property devised to the youngest daughter Sara, which shall go to the other sisters.

"Myn drie soons Aart Evert ende Symon" appointed executors. Signed by the testator.

(My beloved wife Sara to remain in full possession of my entire estate, and if she should happen to marry, she shall have one third of the income and profit of my entire estate. To my eldest son Aart my great bible and a confirmation-book with the name of Petrum de Witte, and my gun; if he should die, then all to go to his eldest son Jacob. To my youngest son Isaac my great chest which I inherited from my father and all my clothing of my body. My youngest daughter Sara shall immediately after her mother's death have her mother's clothing, a new clothing chest, and a new table which Thomas Beekman made, and a tin-comb, two iron-potts, a large one and a small one, and my house-mirror which we now use, and two milk-cows, and a new Sunday dress, which I give for my daughter Sara's marriage-outfit. Sara Kool, daughter of Symon Kool, shall have a bed with belongings and a new Sunday dress, and a milk-cow.—To my daughter Rebecca, wife of Jan Ffrere, a certain piece of land, situated to the northwest and northeast of the wood-land, conveyed to Jan Ffrer and southwest to Ronduyts Kill, from there running with a straight line to a stone in the ground in said farmland near a little moat (or ditch), and from there to a small marked oak tree (*),

---

(*) Schemmelbast, i. e. with mouldy bark.

standing at a little kill, which is the boundary of said wood-land, round the Ronduyts kill, then along the same to the first mentioned stone. Also a piece of land, situated on the southeast side of Ronduyts Kill, running from a certain little outlet, which runs from the mountain to the kill in a north-eastern direction, adjoining the kill and the land of William West and the land of Coll. Henricus Beekman, to have the free privilege to cut wood and haul stone. Also to said daughter 1/12 part of my entire estate, except what has been previously devised. To my other children (named above, of which Geertie was wife of Jacob Decker, Jannetie wife of Johannis Turck), my entire estate.)

J. HARDENBERGH
TJERCK MATTYSEN
CORNELIS D. LAMETTER
PITTRE WAMBOMEZ

(Major Johannis Hardenbergh, Tjerck Mattysen & Cornelis De La Matter appeared before the Court on March 7, 1716/7, proving the will of "Major Jacob Aertsen, late of the Corporation Kingston deceased.")

(*Jacob Aertsen* (*Van Wagenen*), s. of *Aert Jacobsen* (*Van Wagonen*), (see *Gerrit Aartse*), b. Febr. 14, 1652, m., Febr. 25, 1677, *Sara*, dau. of *Evart Pels*, b. July 3, 1659, and had issue: i. *Annatje*, bt. Sept. 15, 1678, m. *Jan Heermans* (q. v.); ii. *Aart*, bt. Oct. 26, 1679, d. June 10, 1740, m. Oct. 14, 1705, *Marytje*, bt. Jan. 1, 1686, d. June 20, 1733, dau. of *Pieter Low* and *Lysbet Blanchan*; iii. *Evert*, bt. Apr. 24, 1681, m. ab. 1709, *Hillegond*, bt. N. Y., Nov. 14, 1686, dau. of *Claes Jansen Van Heyningen* and *Janneken Kiersen*; removed to near *Poughkeepsie, Dutchess Co.*, N. Y.; iv. *Gerrit*, bt. Nov. 12, 1682, d. y.; v. *Rebecca*, bt. Apr. 12, 1685, m. *Jan Freer*; vi. *Geertje*, bt. Sept. 5, 1686, m., Sept. 17, 1709, *Jacob Gerritse Decker*, bt. Febr. 24, 1684, s. of *Gerrit Janse D.* and *Magdalena Schut*; vii. *Jannetje*, bt. Apr. 8, 1688, d. y.; viii. *Jannetje*, bt. Apr. 14, 1689, m., Oct. 7, 1711, *Johannis Turk*, bt. May 16, 1687, s. of *Jacobus T.* and *Catryntje Van Benthuysen*; ix. *Gerrit*, bt. May 26, 1691, d. Nov. 17, 1709; x. *Symon*, bt. Apr. 23, 1693, m., Nov. 17, 1720, *Sara*, bt. Dec. 23, 1699, d. Jan. 27, 1759, dau. of *Solomon Du Bois* and *Tryntje Gerritse*; xi. *Jacob Aartse*, bt. at *Albany*, Febr. 20, 1695; xii. *Benjamin*, bt. Jan. 1, 1697, m., May 28, 1726, *Elisabeth*, dau. of *Gysbert van den Berg* and *Diewertje Masten* (q. v.); xiii. *Abraham*, bt. Febr. 12, 1699, m., Febr. 26, 1726, *Hilligard Crispel*, b. Apr. 17, 1704, d. Febr. 22, 1774. He died June 7, 1787 (see his will); xiv. *Sara*, bt. Dec. 21, 1701, m., Apr. 7, 1721, *Solomon*, b. at *New Paltz*, Oct. 17, 1686, s. of *Abraham Hasbrouck* and *Maria Deyo* (q. v.); xv. *Isaac*, bt. Aug. 22, 1703, m., March 10, 1723, *Catrina Freer*).

Page 507.—TENHOUT, SEVERYN, of Shawankonk, Lantman.

Will dated Febr. 5, 1708/9, and written in Dutch.

"In't sevende Jaar van de regering van onse Souveraigne vrouw Anna Koninginne van groot Britantie &c."

(Long religious preamble.)

"Myn huysvrouw *Geertruy Tenhout* sall hebben en possidereeren myn gantsche vaste" "staat."

"Aan myn vrouws soon *Jacobus Bruyn* myn gantsche vaste" "staat benestens negers paarden & beesten En wat vorders aan myn staat is dependeerende om in Eygendom aanstondts na hett overlyden van myn voors. huysvrouw aan te vaarden En te possideeren geduren de zyn Leven En dat na de voors. Jacobus Bruyns overlyden de voors. Staat sal zyn ten behoeve van voors. Jacobus Bruyns soon met name *Severyn* ten voor hem en zyn ordre of Erfgenamen voor Eewigh dogh Indien de voors. Severyn Tenhout tot syn mondigen quam voor het overlyden van syn vader Jacobus Bruyn dat als dan de voors. Jacobus Bruyn aan syn soon Severyn tenhout sal uyt keeren En betalen Een hondert pondt" "En dat na doot van voors. Jacobus Bruyn, En de voors. Severyn tenhout desself soon in possessie syn de van myn voors. staat, de voors. Severyn tenhout sal gehouden syn om uyt te keeren en betalen aan de twede soon van voors. Jacobus Bruyn of syn ordre of Erfgenamen de suyvere en nette somme van Een hondert pont."

Wife and Jacobus Bruyn appointed executors.

Signed by the testator.

(In the 7th year of the reign of our Sovereign lady Anne, Queen of Great Britain, etc.—My wife, G. T., shall have and possess my whole real estate.—To my wife's son, J. B., my whole real estate, besides negroes, horses and cattle, and whatever belongs to (depending upon) my estate, immediately after my wife's decease for his life, and after his death to his son, S.—If said S. T. should reach his majority before the death of his father, J. B., then said J. B. shall pay to his son, S., £100, and after the death of said J. B., and when the said S. T. is in possession of said estate, he shall be bound to pay to the second son of said J. B., or his heirs, the net sum of £100.)

JACOB RUTSEN
J. HARDENBERGH
JOHANIS SCHEPMOES
D. MEYER
JOHANNIS TEN BROECK

(Coll. Jacob Rutsen, Major Johannis Hardenbergh & Capt. Johannis Schepmoes and Johannis Tenbroeck appeared on March 6, 1717/8 before the Court Coll. Jacob Rutsen, Mr. Arien Gerretsen and Coll. Gaasbeek Chambers Judges, and Capt. Egbert Schoonmaker, Capt. Edward Whittaker and Mr. Cornelis Cool, Justices, proving the will of Severyn Tenhout "late of Shawangunk, deceased.)

(*Severyn Tenhout* m. *Geertruit Ysselstein* (dau. of *Jan Willemse Esselstein* and *Willemtje Jans*), widow of *Jacobus Bruyn* (q. v.), m. before Oct. 6, 1678, who had a son, *Jacobus Bruyn*, who m. after Nov. 18, 1704, *Tryntje Schoonmaker* (see Jacobus Bruyn).

BOOK OF DEEDS III. (CC), MARKED 1718—1728.

Page 40.—HOOGENBOOM, ANNETIE, "Weduve van Cornelis Hogenboom Van Wylen, van Kingston, overleden."

Will dated May 4, 1719, and written in Dutch.

(Long religious preamble.)

"Aan myn suster *Jacomyntie's* dogter *Hilletje* huysvrouw van Capt. *Gerrit Wynkoop* alle myn Cleeragie Ende Linne aan my left behoorende."

"Aan *Annetje Wynkoop* Doghter van voors. Gerrit Wynkoop en *Hilletie* zyn huysvrouw myn bed Ende bedding met zyn toebehooren."

"Aan *Roeloft Eltinge* Ende *Cornelis Eltinge* soonen van myn voors. suster Jacomyntie," "al myn geheele staat" "Om Egalyk onder haar tweeje gedeelt te werden uytgenomen het geene boven vermaakt is dat is te seggen aan Roeloft Eltinge" "de gerechtige helft van myn voors. staat En aan Cornelis Eltinge" "de andere gerechtige helft van myn voors. staat."

(To my sister J.'s daughter, H., wife of Capt. G. W., all my clothing and linen. To A. W., daughter of said G. W. and to his wife, H., my bed with what thereto belongs.—To R. E. and C. E., sons of my said sister J., my whole estate, to be divided equally between them, excepting what I have previously disposed of, that is to say, to R. E. half of my said estate, and to C. E. the other half thereof.)

Roeloft and Cornelis Eltinge appointed executors. Signed by the testatrix, and witnessed by *Jno. Rutsen, Nicolas Dupuis, Wm. Harris* (his mark), and *Wm. Nottingham,* who all appeared before the Court, Sept. 17, 1719, proving the will.

(See Cornelis Hoogeboom's will.)

Page 111.—BEVIERE, LOUIS, Senr., of Nieuw Paltz.

Will dated May 2, 1720, and written in Dutch.

(Long religious preamble.)

"Aan myn outste soon *Jean Bevier*" "de somma van Een pont."

"Item door dien myn soon *Andre Bevier* van God den heer besoght is dat hy niet (Compus mente ofte) well by syn sinne is daarom niet bequaam om syn portie van myn staat aan te werden en te Rogeeren Soo is myn will en Begeertten En ick ordonneere & belaste myn andere Kinderen, als sy het selve voor Gods Oordeel sullen verant woorden dat sy alle wegen well op haar broeder Andre sullen passen En goede acht namen en hem well onder houden van all nodrift van Cleeragie en wat anders jy sonde kunne ofte mogen outbreken gedurende syn naturlyke Leven en na syn overleyden hem Eerlyk te begraven Naar soo God in genaden hem wederom syn voorige kennisse en verstant sall gelieve te geven dat als dan hy myn voors. soon Andre sall hebben en genieten voor hem" "de gerechtige vyfde part van myn geheele vaste" "staat" "ende Wardy van de sesde part van myn losse of roerenden staat. Dogh vermagh de vaste staat niet verkoopen alsraan syn broeder ofte broeders Item soo is myn will en begeerten dat Indien myn voors. soon in dese Onoselle staat blyft syn vyfde part van myn vaste staat; en sesde part van myn losse staat of te wardy daar van sall blyve in handen van myn Executors, om voor syn best en Oudhout verhuert en uyt gedaan te werden En na syn overleyden sall selve Egalyck onder myn vier andere soonen en Doghter" "gedeelt werden."

"Aan myn voors. soon Jean Bevier" "de gerechtige vyfde part van myn geheele vasten en onroerende staat als mde de gerechtige sesde part van myn Losse en Roerende staat En ook de bovegeschreven Recht in de portie of part van myn soon Andre waar voor hy sal betalen En uyt Keeren aan myn doghter *Hester* huysvrouw van *Jacob Hasbrouck* als hier onder vermaakt is aan haar."

"Aan myn soon *Abraham Bevier*" "de gerechtige vyfde part van myn geheele vaste staat als mede de gerechtige sesde part van myn geheele Losse staat Ook de bove geschreven Recht in de portie ofte part van myn soon Andre; Waarvoor hy sall betalen en uytkeren aan myn doghter Hester als hier onderaan haar vermackt is."

"Aan myn soon *Samuel Bevier*" the fifth part of the real estate and the sixth part of the personal property, on same condition as before.

"Aan myn soon *Louis Bevier Junr.*" the fifth part of the real estate and the sixth part of the personal property, on same condition as before.

"Aan myn doghter Hester als hier order aan haar vermaakt is."— "Myn soon Samuel sall de preferentie of Keur van de vyf parten hebbe uyt Reden dat hy verhuyst is en by myn in kome woonen."

All the real property to be appraised and divided in five parts among the four sons and the daughter Hester, who also is to receive the sixth part of the personal property," "also myn bed en bedding met syn toe behooren."

The four sons and "myn schoon soon Jacob Hasbrouck" appointed executors. Signed by the testator.

HANS KIERSTEDEN
ANDRE LEFEVRE
JOSEPH HASBROUCK
WM. NOTTINGHAM

(Doctor Hans Kiersteden, Joseph Hasbrouck & Wm. Nottingham appeared before the Court July 4, 1720, proving the will).

(To my eldest son, Jean Bevier, the sum of one pound.

And as my son Andre Bevier has been inflicted by the Lord God, and is not in his right mind, on which account he cannot well care for his share of my estate, my will is, and I command my other children, as they themselves are accountable to God's judgment, to take good care of their brother Andre, to preserve him from all want during his natural life, and to bury him honorably. If God, in his grace, should restore him to mind and memory, my son Andre shall have 1/5 part of my real estate, and the value of a sixth part of the personal property, but he must not sell the real estate except to his sisters or brothers. If my son remains in this unresponsible (innocent, silly) condition, his fifth part is to be retained by the estate; the sixth part of my personal property is then to remain in the hands of my executors, to be leased for him and for his old age. At death, his property or share to be divided equally between my four other sons and my daughter.

To my said son Jean Bevier, the 1/5 part of my real estate, and the sixth part of my personal property, my son to pay to my daughter Hester, wife of Jacob Hasbrouck, as here below is provided for.

To my son Abraham Bevier the 1/5 part of the real estate, and the sixth part of the personal property, on the same condition.

Other fifth parts of the real estate and sixth part of the personal property to go to sons Samuel and Louis, Jr., and to daughter Hester. Son Samuel to have the first choice of the five parts, the reason being that he has removed to my house to live.

Son in law Jacob Hasbrouck and the four sons appointed executors.

(Louis Beviere, Sr., was born at *Lille* about 1648, removed previous to 1675 to *Frankenthal*, as appears from a certificate from the Pastor there, H. *Lucasse*, dated March 5, 1675, witnessed by *Andre Le Blanc*, came to New York 1675/6, went to *England* 1710, where he procured denization papers, returned to New Paltz. He m. 1673, *Maria Le Blanc*, and had issue: i. *Maria*, b. July 9, 1674; ii. *Jean*, b. Jan. 2, 1676, m., Apr. 14, 1712, *Catherine Montaign*, b. Rochester; iii. *Abraham*, b. Jan. 20, and bt. March 31, 1678 (s. of *Louies Bevery* and *Maria Blan*), m., after Febr. 8, 1707, *Racheltie Vernooy*, b. Kingston; iv. *Samuel*, b. Jan. 21, 1680, m. *Magdalena Blanshan*; v. *Andries*, b. July 12, bt. Sept, 24, 1682, d. unm., 1768; vi. *Louis*, b. Pals, Nov. 6, 1684, m. June 2, 1713, *Lysbeth Haasbrouck*, dau of *Jacob H.* (see will of his son, *Louis B.'s* widow, *Esther*); vii. *Esther*, b. Nov. 16, 1686, m. Dec. 7, 1714, *Jacob Hasbrouck*, s. of *Jan H.*); viii. *Solomon*, b. July 12, 1689, d. inf.—See History of New Paltz, pps. 225—et seq. for further data).

Page 128.—COCK, JOHN, of Marbletown.

Will dated July 20, 1710.

"My well beloved wife *Magdelen* shall be and Remain in the full possession of my whole Estate Real and Personal dureing the term of her widdow hood," "without to be accountable to my heirs hereafter named for the same," but if she should marry agains then she is only to have the thirds of the uses & profits of my sd Estate and no more."

"First Out of my Estate unto my two sons and two Daughters, *William Samuel Alice* & *Margaret* Each two working horses or mares & Each two Cows & to Wm. & Samuel Each a gun & hanger that they now use and to Alice and Margaret Each three sheep this being in Consideration of what I already have given unto my sons, *John* & *Thomas*."

"Unto my Eldest son John one Creature ye Choice of my whole stock after the above given Creatures are taken Out, be it horse or mares Cow or Ox In Consideration of being my first Borne, and I have taken up thirty pounds" "for my said son John Which promised me to pay again and if he do not pay the same according to his promises" "the said thirty pounds shall be deducted of his portion of my Estate" "and also the

Interest of six per Cent per anhum from the month of May one thousand seven hundred and seaven till such time that my Estate shall be devided among my Children."

"Whereas I became security for my son Thomas" "all what my Estate shold Come to be Charged or Incumbered by being security as aforesaid shall be deducted out of his portion of my said Estate."

"Unto my six Children by name John Thomas William Samuel Alice & Margaret" "my whole Estate as of Lands Houses orchards pastures goods Chattells & all what belongs to the same to be Equally devided amongst them."

"If any of my said children should depart this life before they are of age or Married theire portion shall be Equally devided amongst the Rest of my Children."

All the children appointed joint executors.

Signed by the testator.

THO: GARTON
RICH'D BRODHEAD
ANNE GARTON JUNR.
WM. NOTTINGHAM

(Mrs. Anne Garton Junr. & Wm. Nottingham appeared before the Court: Mr. *Jacob Rutsen,* Judge, and Mr. *Arien Gerritsen* & Mr. *Vincent Mathews,* Justices, proving the will, and stating that Thomas Garton & Rich Brodhead "signed with them as witnesses."

(Jan Cock came from *Out Engelant (Old England),* m., July 27, 1679, *Maddeleen Wood,* from England, both res. *Marbletown,* and had: i. *John;* ii. *Thomas,* bt. Jan. 5, 1682; iii. *William,* bt. at M., Jan. 20, 1684, m., June 8, 1716, *Catrina Esfort;* iv. *Elsje,* bt. Jan. 1, 1687; v. *Elsje,* bt. June 3, 1694; vi. *Samuel,* bt. May 24, 1696, m., July 5, 1722, *Bregjen Middagh;* vii. *Margit,* bt. Apr. 27, 1701).

Page 132.—BEATTY, JOHN, of Marbletown.

Will dated April 26, 1720, "according to the Computation of the Church of England."

"Very sick & Weak in body."

"Unto *Zusanna* my truly and well beloved wife all my Low land on the fifth stick or piece between the Land of *Thomas Cock* & *Hendrick Claese* and the woodland Meddowes & Swomps thereto adjoyning along the bounds of Thomas Cock together with my house barne orchards pastures goods Debts & Moueable affects for the Terme of her Natural Life & after her decease to be parted in Equall shares amongst all my Children upon Condition that my said wife shall pay all my Lawful Debts."

"Unto my Eldest son *Robert* upon Consideration of my first born son one milch Cow Likewise that Certain piece of land he now Lives on or so much as shall fall to his share when all the woodland is devided Beginning at a pine tree neare to the East end of a small swamp in the pine woods then along my bounds to *Rochester* highway as my bounds Runs To the bounds of Thomas Cock & farther so as my bounds Runs to the bounds *Daniel Brodhead* then along his bounds to an old marked pine tree

& from thence with a straight Line to the first station and if said Robert has too much for his part or share with the Rest of my Children he shall Loose it at the south west End or if he have to little he shall have it In the pine woods at the northwest end where the bounds of said Daniel Brodhead and the swamp where he first began at the same breadth to make it a Complement with the Rest."

"Unto my son *John* all my third part in the mill Likewise twenty acres of Land near by which was promised to be Conveyed to me by *Matthias Blanchan* before the Trustees of *Marbletown* but afterwards said Matthias Blanchan sold me that all there was above one hundred acres I might take for he would take no more as to pay one shilling Quitt and when I surveyed it I found it to be twenty three acres above his hundred, but his mother is to have said part of the Mill so long as the Debts Is paid unless she Chance to Marry in the mean while then is it to be delivered up to my said son John & he is to have it and no more for his part or share of my Estate except his part of the moueables."

"To my Daughter *Agness* ten pounds for her dutiful Care of my family when my Children were small and Tender."

"Unto my poor afflicted & distressed brother *Thomas Beatty* in *Ireland* who hath through great sickness another visitation from almighty God is become blind & is now maintained by the Charity of his half sister fifteen pounds Current silver money of *New York* with al possible speed it should be taken up at Interest Hopeing it will be taken from my hands and all the Rest of my family as an acceptable offering from allmighty God."

"All the rest of my wood land lying within the Limmitts of *Marbletown* & Rochester I give unto the Rest of my Children, vizt: *William Charles Thomas Edward James* and *Henry* and to my two Daughters Aggness & *Martha*" to be divided equally "or Else In quantity according to quallity as they shall think fitt & to take two honest neighbors upon Oath and to view said lott to the best of their knowledge and to Lay so much money upon the best as they shall think fitt to be paid unto them that Receives the worst lots & then said Eight Children to draw lots for said land."

Signed by the testator.

THO: COCK
WM. COCK
JORIS MIDDAGH
ELLEANOR COCK

(Witnesses appeared before the Court March 9, 1720/1, proving the will).

(*John Beaty* m. *Susanna Ashfordby*, and had issue: i. *Robert Batty* (*Bettis*), m., after May 17, 1719, *Bata Middagh;* ii. *William*, bt. June 9, 1695; iii. *Charles*, bt. Jan. 9, 1698 (see his will); iv. *Agnes*, bt. Oct 29, 1699 (dau. *Jan Betti* & S. A.); v. *Jan*, bt. March 2, 1701 (m., Sept. 10, 1743, *Merry Brink*); vi. *Thomas*, bt. March 14, 1703, m. Oct. 23, 1729, *Maria Jansz;* vii. *Marta*, bt. Apr. 20, 1707, "Bina Membra Ecclesiae Anglicanae" (member of the English Church), m. Nov. 24, 1728, Johannes Middagh).

Page 169.—SCHUTT, WILLEM JANSEN, of Shawangunk.

Will dated May 6, 1706, and written in Dutch.

(Long religious preamble).

"Myn huysvrouw *Grietie* sall blyve in volle possessie van myn geheele Staet."

"Aan de Kinders van myn outste soon *Jan Schutt* 100 guldens," to be paid in one year by the widow.

"Aan myn soon *Myndert Schutt* 100 gulden in two years."—"Aan myn soon Salomon Schutt 100 gulden in three years."—"Aan myn dochter *Magdaleen*" 100 gulden in four years."—"Aan myn dochter *Neyltie*" 100 gulden in five years."—"Aan myn dochter *Marytie*" 100 gulden in six years."

"Aan myn soon *Abraham Schutt* myn Land gelegen *op Shawongonck*" "in Consideratie dat hy by myn blyft in myn hooge kouderdom Endemyn groote dienst godaen heeft en noch dost, voor welck landt myn voors. soon Abraham sall betalen en uyt Keeren de bove vermackte ses hondert guldens."

Wife and son Abraham appointed executors.

Signed by the testator.

JACOBUS BRUN
BENYAMEN SMEDES
NICOLAS HOFMAN
WM. NOTTINGHAM

(Capt. Nicolas Hofman and the other witnesses appeared, June 4, 1722, before the Court, proving the will).

(My wife G. is to remain in full possession of my whole estate. 100 guldens to be paid by the widow to the children of my eldest son, J. S.—To sons, M., S., and daughters M., N., and M., 100 guldens each.—To my son, A. S., my land at S., in consideration that he remains on my farm and in my service, and that he pays 600 guldens for said land).

(*Willem Jans* (*Schut*), m. *Gritie Jacobs*, and had issue: i. *Jan Willem*, m. before Sept. 18, 1692, *Marytje Ter Bos*; ii. *Solomon*, bt. June 18, 1671 (s. of *Willem Jansen* and G. J.), m., before Jan. 29, 1699, *Jannetje Tysens* (*Sesums*), m. 2., Sept. 1, 1712, *Marytjen Mone*, widow of *Paulus Mone*, b. in Hog-duysland (*Germany*); iii. *Magdalena*, b. *Albany*, m. 1., after Apr. 2, 1684, *Gerrit Decker*, m., 2., Apr. 22, 1696, *Joris Middagh*, b. *Hycoop, Holland*; iv. *Marytie*; v. *Abraham*, b. *Marbletown*, m. 1., after Nov. 9, 1709, *Heyltjen Dekkers*, m., 2., Apr. 25, 1714, *Geerthen Kortregt*; vi. *Meindert*, m. before Nov. 16, 1694, *Sara Jansen*; vii. *Neeltie*, bt. Oct. 8, 1682; viii. *Menasses*, bt. Dec. 30, 1683, and ix. *Ephraim*, bt. same day).

Page 198.—AARTSE, GERRIT, of Kingston, " Landtman."

Will dated Dec. 17, 1715, and written in Dutch.

Long religious preamble.

"Myn waarde huysvrouw *Claartie Aartse* de gerechte derde van de profyte van myn gantsche staat gedurende haar Leven, En dat myn voors. huysvrouwe Sall vry heydt hebbe om in het huys tegenwoordrigh door myn bewoont In te blyve woone geduerende haar Leven."

"Myn Jongste Soon *Simen van Wageninge* Sall hebben En genieten

In ware en vrye Eigendom" "all myn Landt gelegent noorderlyke van de *Esopus Kill* soo als 't selve myn aengekomen is van de Erfegenise van myn vader *Aart Jacobse*, en oock volgens transpoort van *Sweer Teunissen* alse mede myn wy En Bouwlandt gelegen suydelyke van voors. Kill, beneffens huys En Schuer, heyninge Etz.: mits dat myn voors. Soon oft syn ordr of Erfgenamen gehouden sullen syn voor het selve te betaalen aan myn Erfgenamen hier onder geschreven waer van hy Een is, te betalen de somme van Ses hondred pondt" "In vyfve Jaaren te betaalen jeder jaar de gerichte vyfde part."

"So stel Ick tot Erfgenamen over myn gantsche Staat myn aght kinderen Wettelyke geproureert met myn voors huysvrouw met namen *Evert van Wageninge, Barent van Wageninge, Goosen van Wageninge, Jacob van Wageninge, Simen van Wageninge, Jannetie* huysvrouw van *Barent van Benthuysen, Annetie* huysvrouw van *Henricus Heermans*, En *Neeltie van Wageningen* En oosk *Gerrit van Wageninge* Soon van myn oudste Soon Wylen *Aart van Wageningen*" equally "doch dat voors. Gerret van Wageninge" "sall trucke En geniete alvorens de deeling van myn Staat geschieden sall de Somme van vyftigh pondt."

(To my worthy wife, C. A., one third of the income from my whole estate for life, she to have the right to live in the house I now occupy.— My youngest son, S. v. W., shall have all my land north of E. K., as the same was inherited by me from my father, A. J., as well as conveyed to me by S. T.—He shall also have my pasture land and farm south of said Kill with house and barn, he and his heirs to be bound to pay for the same to my other heirs the sum of £600 in five years, one fifth each year.—As heirs to my whole estate, I appoint my eight children, begotten by my said wife, by name E. v. W., B. v. W., G. v. W., J. v. W., S. v. W., J., wife of B. v. B., A., wife of H. H., and N. v. W., as well as G. v. W., son of my oldest son, A. v. W., deceased. G. v. W. shall have, in advance, a sum of £50).

(*Aert Jacobsen* (*Van Wagonen*) was an early resident of *Albany*, who on Sept 17, 1660, purchased 47 morgens 215 rods of land at *Esopus* from *Johanna De Laet*, wife of *Jeronimus Ebbinck*. He had five children: i. *Gerrit Aertse* (s. of Aert Jacobsen and *Annetje Gerrits*), m. *Clara*, bt. N. Y. Sept. 10, 1651, dau. of *Evert Pels* and *Jannetje Symens*, and had issue: a. *Aert*, m., Oct. 20, 1695, *Aaltje Elting*, (see *Elting Roelofsen*); b. *Evert*, bt. Apr. 18, 1675, m., June 1, 1701, *Marytje Van Heyningen*; c. *Barent*, bt. Apr. 18, 1675, m., Sept. 28, 1703, *Lea Schepmoes*; d. *Goosen Van Wagenen*, m. June 15, 1715, *Gertruyd Swart*; e. *Jannetje*, bt. June 25, 1682, m. Apr. 21, 1701, *Barent Van Benthuysen*; f. *Anntje*, bt. Sept. 7, 1684, m. *Hendricus Heermans*; g. *Jacob*, bt. Oct. 3, 1686; h. *Simon*, bt. Apr. 7, 1689, m. May 26, 1720, *Maria Schepmoes*; i. *Neeltje*, bt. Apr. 17, 1692, m. *Andries Focken*; j. *Rebecca*, bt. Nov. 11, 1694;—ii. *Neeltje Aartsen*, m., June 6, 1667, *Cornelis Tynhout* (q. v.); iii. *Jacobus*, m., Febr. 25, 1677, *Sarah*, dau. of *Evert Pells* (q. v.); iv. *Grietje Aartsen*, m., Jan. 28, 1668, *Jacobus C. Elmendorf*; v. *Elizabeth*, m. ab. 1676, *Cornelius Masten* (q. v.).

Page 219.—MATTYSEN, JAN, of Kingston.

Will dated Oct. 7, 1719, and written in Dutch.

(Long religious preamble).

"Myn huysvrouw *Maddeleen Mattysen* Sal hebben en blyve in hett besit van myn gantsche Staatt Gedurende haar weduwlycke Staat Sonder dat sy gehouden sal syn Reeckenschap te geven aan Eenige van myn

Kinderen Dogh Indien myn voors. huysvrouw wederom quam te her trouwen Dat als dan myn voors. huysvrouw gehouden is de geregte helft van myn voor. staat uyt te keeren Ente betalen aan myn Erfgenamen hier onder ges. En de andere helft van voor. Staat sall myn voors. huysvrouw on de benifitie van Inventaries de bate En Profyten des selve genieten geduren de Leven En na haar overlyden dat Sulex Insgelyex soll syn ten Behoeve van myn Erfgenamen hier onder geschreven."

"Aan myn outste Soon *Mattys Jansen*" "Een paart de keyr van myn Stall voort Reght van Eerst geboorten."

"Aan myn kinderen mett namen Mattys, *Thomas, Jan, Hendrick, David, Margrieta* Huysvrouw van *Barent Burhans Catrina* huysvrouw van *John Croke Junr, Daniell Brodhead* Soon van my overleden Doghter Magdalena in haar leven huysvrouw van *Richard Brodhead* En aan de drie kinderen van myn overleden doghter *Sara* in haar leven huysvrouw van *Elias Bunshoten* met namen *Teunis, Johannis* En *Gerretie*" "myn gantsche Staat."

"(Door dien myn Soon *Jan* naar *Engelandt* vertrocken is en wy van gedaghten zyn dat hy overleden is) dat myn andere Erfgenamen Syn portie van myn voors. Staat sal Deelen aan Stondts na myn En myn voors. huysvrouw, overlyden, mits dat Een Jeder van haar sal gehouden Syn om golde borgh te geven aan myn Executors hier onder genoemt dat Indien myn voors. Soon Jan moght weder on in dese provintie arriveeren if syn twettige kint ofte kinderen sy als dan kem ofte syn kinders syn part ofte portie van myn voors. Staat dat Sy onder haar hebben wederom sal oplevere Ende betalen."

"Myn Soon *Thomas Jansen*" shall have "de Bouwery met syn Dependentie myn tobehoerende de welche gecoght heb van *John Ward* En gelegen onder *Marbletown;* En nue in huere gebruyckt dooe myn voors. soon Thomas mits dat hy sal uyt keeren En betalen of Doen betalen ten behoeve van myn Erfgenamen" "£300" En Een Duysent negen hondert En Vyftigh Schepels Taruw of de Samen vyf hondert twe en t' negentigh pondt En sien Schellinge tot haar van voors. Thomas Jansen."

(My wife, M. M., shall remain in possession of my whole estate, as long as she remains my widow, and not be obliged to render an account to any one of my children, but if she should happen to marry, then she shall be bound to turn over one half of the estate to my heirs, and out of the other half she shall have the income and profit during her natural life, and then to go to my heirs. To my eldest son, M. J., the choice of a horse from my stable, his right of primogeniture. To my other children, by name M., T., J., H., D., M., wife of B. B., C., wife of J. C., Jr., D. B., son of my daughter M., deceased, in her lifetime wife of R. B., and to the three children of my daughter, S., deceased, in her lifetime wife of E. B., by name T., J., and G., my whole estate.—My son, J., having departed for England, and there is supposed to have died, it is my will that my other heirs shall divide his share after my own and my wife's decease, but each one shall be bound to give gold bonds to my executors, to provide for the case that his portion of my said estate may be paid to him or his children, should he, my said son Jan, return to this province.—My son T. J. shall have the farm with what thereto belongs, which I purchased from J. W., situated at M., and now in the possession of my said son T., for which he shall pay to my other heirs £300, and 1950 schepels of wheat or the sum of £592.10).

The four sons, Mattys Jansen, Thomas Jansen, Hendrick Jansen and David Jansen appointed executors. The youngest son David to have "Een Negers Jonge of the vertigh pont Courant gelt."

Signed by the testator.

W. Ten Broeck
A: Gaasbeck Chambers
Johannis ten Broeck
Wm. Nottingham.
(See Jan Tysen).

(Witnesses appeared before the Court, Nov. 24, 1724, proving the will.—Recorded and examined by Gil: Livingston, Clerk.)

Page 230.—HEERMANS, JAN, Senr., of Kingston.

Will dated Oct. 20, 1723, and written in Dutch.

(Long religious preamble).

"Aan myn Eenigste doghter *Margarieta*" "myn Neiuwe Cleere Kist met all haar linne dar daar in is, als mede haar bedste en bedding met syn toebehooren, voorugt myn Staat en verder dat myn voors doghter sal het gebruyck van myn kamer hebben, om in te woonen gedurende de tyt wan haar Natuerlycke Leven (te weten) de kamer van myn tegenwoodige woon huys."

"Aan de drie kinderen van myn overleden Soon *Jan Heermans* met namen *Jacob, Jan* En *Engeltie* huysvrouw van *Cornelis Elmendorf*" "de gerechte vierde part van myn geheele Staat."

(To my only daughter Margarieta my new linen-chest with all the linen therein, bed and bedding, and to have the use of my chamber for her life, that is the chamber in the house where I now live.

To the three children of my deceased son Jan Heermans, named Jacob, Jan, and Engeltie, wife of Cornelis Elmendorf, the fourth part of my estate).

"Aan myn Soon *Henricus Heermans*" the fourth part of the entire estate.—To son *Andreis Heermans* a fourth part of the estate.—To daughter *Margarieta* one fourth part of the estate, if she dies, her share to be divided among the "kinderen van" Jan, Henricus, and Andries.

Sons Henricus and Andries appointed executors.

Jan Heermanssen (his mark)

Tobias Van Beuren
Barent Nukerck
William Swart
W. Nottingham

(Witnesses appeared before the Court, March 5, 1724/5,—"This to Certifie that I Jacob Rutsen, Esq. Judge of the Inferior Court of Common pleas for said County of Ulster have carefully examined the within will and testament and find no Razors nor Interliniations, In the same and here by allow the same to be Entered on said County Records." Jacob Rutsen.

Vera Copia—Gil Livingston, Clerk).

(*Jan Focken* (*Heermans*) came from *Ruynen*, Prov. *Drenthe, Holland*, m. in N. Y. Aug. 23, 1676, *Engeltie Bresteede*, bt. Nov. 29, 1654, dau. of *Jan Jansen Breestede* and *Marritje Andries*, m. 2., ab. 1692, *Elisabeth Blanchan*, dau. of *Matthew B.* and widow of *Pieter Cornelis Low*. Had with first wife: i. *Jan*, bt. N. Y., Nov. 3, 1677, m. ab. 1697, *Annatje*, dau. *Jacob Aartse* (*Van Wagenen*) and *Sara Pels* (q. v.); ii. *Focke*, bt. July 20, 1679; iii. *Hendrick*, bt. Sept. 3, 1681, m. ab. 1708, *Annatie*, bt. Sept. 7, 1684, dau. of *Gerrit Aartsen* (*Van Wagenen*) and *Clara Pels;* iv. *Grietje*, bt. Apr. 6, 1683; v. *Andries*, bt. Apr. 12, 1685, m. *Neeltje*, b. Apr. 17, 1692, dau. of *Gerrit Aartsen* (*Van Wagenen*) and *Clara Pels*. Res. *Rhinebeck, Dutchess Co.*, N. Y.; vi. *Philippus*, bt. Jan. 1, 1687; vii. *Pieter*, bt. Dec. 30, 1688. By 2d wife: viii. *Wilhelmus*, bt. N. Y., May 7, 1693; ix. *Grietje*, bt. *Kingston*, Aug. 30, 1696, m., Apr. 21, 1727, *Jan Maklin*, b. March 7, 1703, s. of *Jan Maklin* and *Marritje De Witt*).

Page 233.—RUTSEN, JOHN.

Will dated March 5, 1724/5.

"My Beloved wife, *Cathrine* have and Enjoy all my Estate Real and personal of what kind so Ever During her natural Life, Except She maryeth & if in Case she marrieth then to keep and Enjoy the one halfe of my estate" "and the other halfe of my Estate to be Equally Divided amongst my Children."

"Unto my son *Jacob*, besides his part as is shall happen the Sume of one hundred pounds."

"After my wife Decease, all my Estate to be Equally Divided between my natural Children, and in Case my Children dye without issue then my said Estate after my wifes decease to be divided, the one halfe or moety to my wifes brother *Henry Beeckman* and his sister *Cornelia* the wife of *Gilbert Livingston*" "and the other halfe or moiety to my brother, and Sisters" (not named).

"I Impower my beloved wife Cathrin to sell and Dispose of all my Estate both Reall and personall."

Wife appointed executrix. Signed by the testator, "in my dwelling house at *Knightfield*."

JOHANNIS WESTBROCK
JOSEPH WHEALER
JOHANNIS SCHOONMAKER

(Witnesses appeared before the Court, Jacob Rutsen, Judge, Abr. Gaasbeck Chambers, Lodewyk Hornbeck, Justices, May 11, 1725.

(J. R., m., Dec. 4, 1712, *Catryntjen Beekman*, b. Sept. 16, 1683, dau. of *William B.*, and widow of *Cornelis Exveen*. She m., 3., *Albert Pawling*, of *Dutchess Co.*—J. R. and C. B. had issue: i. *Johanna*, bt. Apr. 11, 1714; ii. *Jacob*, bt. Apr. 29, 1716 (*Jacob Ruts*, Sr., and *Marytjen Hansen*, witn.); iii. *Henderikus*, bt. March 9, 1718, m., Nov. 24, 1737, *Allada Livingston;* iv. *Catrina*, bt. May 24, 1719, m. June 13, 1740, *Dirk Wesselse Ten Broeck*, res. *Albany*).

Page 268.—SHEPMOES, DIRCK, of Kingston.

Will dated Febr. 15, 1723/24, and written in Dutch.

Long religious preamble.

"Myn huysvrouw *Maragrietie Schepmoes* of *Tappen* (wife M. S. or Tappen) £40 and a "negerin met naame genaamt *Jenney* met all haar kindere" (negress by name Jenny with all her children). Wife also to have "het Goudt en sulver gemunt en ongemunt beding goldere en huys Raadt an all dat sy by myn gebrogt heeft" "twe paarde twee kouye twee shaapen en waage met strange touwe dar toie behooren de voor haer twe Doghters genaamt *Anna* & *Areyaantue* Schepmoes" (gold and silver, coined and uncoined, bedding, household goods, and all she had brought unto me, two horses, two cows, two sheep, a wagon, with string and cord belonging to it (harness), for her two daughters named A. & A. S.) also "helleft van het Raat Dot wy gecoght en laate maake hebben terwyl dat wy getrowt geweest syn" (half of the household-goods which we bought and had made when we married). "Myn huysvouw" "en haer twe dogters" "Jeder Elick Een Bedt met syn toiebehooren" (my wife and her two daughters a bed each with what belongs thereto).

The wife also to have a third part of "het wolle en Linne gaare of Linne Vlass geweeve of ongeweevn Sount en Smeer kerse slip vlys spek meet voor Broot en voorts alles watt Eat baare syn dat in myn huys of in de tuyn groeyt (the woolen, linen-thread or linen-flax, woven or not, and tallow candle, bacon, bread and all eatables in my house, or growing in the garden), en indien ick quam te sterve Dat het kooren noch in de Schuer te dorse was so sall myn voor syde huysvrouw Maragritie vier en twintigh Schepel tarrew twaalfe Scheepell maies Dartigh Scheepel have Een hallef beest en Een vet varrike dat dat gemest is hebben" (and if at my death the grain should yet be in the barn to be thrashed, my wife shall have 24 schepels of wheat, 12 schepels corn, 30 schepels oats, half a cattle, and a fat pig).

"Myn voorsyde vrouw" "in myn huys sal woome so Langh als sy ongetrouwt blyft en dat sy sall hebben tot haar wooningh de kelder kueken en op kaamer en up Solder en haar geryf in de kelder de haleve tuyn by het huys" (my said wife shall live in my house, so long as she is unmarried, and shall have for her occupancy the cellar, kitchen, and an upper room, and an upper garret, and her accommodation in the cellar, and half of the garden at the house) "ende derde part van de Boogaert van de appele en alle Boonvrughte die oft myn Landt in het bos grocien" (and the third part of the apple-orchard, and all the fruit from the trees, which grow on my land or in the woods). Also "de darde hok of Garref van omtrent tien morgen bowlandt dat door *Willem Schepmoes*" "sal behouwt werde maer myn voor boiemde Soon Willem sall gehouwden Syn het voornoiemde Landt te bequaamer tydt te sayen met winter en soomer kooren ock sall hy alle Iaaren Een halfe Schepel vlaas saat op be quam Landt te Sayen voor myn syde huysvrouw" "op haer tien morgen en Willem Schepmoes sall van het soomer kooren soo veel weer hebben als het vlas lant gegroit is" (the third part of the sheaves of about 10 morgen arable land, which W. S. shall be bound to seed with winter and summer grain, and to sow yearly sufficient for half a bushel of flax for my said wife, but he shall have as much grain therefrom as is grown on said flax-land) "de tien morgen voor myn vrouw Sall weesen de voorste houck in de lange Streek" (my wife's 10 morgen shall be at the first corner in the long row) "ock so sullen tween kouye twee kalvers en twee schaapen Loopen of te wyen daar syn vie Loopt en wydt" (and two cows, two calves, and two sheep may pasture where the son's cattle is grazing) "ock sall my huysvrouw" "de helfte van het hoy landt dat op haar Landt dat is de Lange street groot vry hebbe En myn soon W. S. sall het magen voor de helleft So hy will, oeck en Sal my huysvrouw voor het wyie van haer niet betalen" (my wife shall also have half of the hay land which is on her land on the long row, and my son, W. S., may cut the hay from this half if he so wishes, and my wife shall not pay anything for this land) "oock Sall myn huysvrouw" "den morge Schoon Bosslandt hebben waar zy will (my wife is also to have a morgen cleared woodland, whereever she wishes) en haer geryt van de Schuer en bergen hofstede haerkomen en vel In te bergen ente dorsen (and to have all her carting to the barn and on the farm, and her cattle brought in) : en soo myn voorsyde huysvrouw van het landt Een morgen Landt tot Een wey will maake Sal het moogen Doren all het voor sude Landt is myn voor Syde huysvrouw" "te hebbe Soo Langh als sy Leeft of ongetrowt blyft" (and if my wife wishes to make a pasture of her morgen land, she may do so, and she is to have said land as long as she lives or is unmarried) : en Een Spaa on Een greep Een byll: En scap en Een wan : en Spueel Slee ock Sall sy hebben de potte Bank en Eettens half en Leedekant Daar wy In Slaagen" "met het bedde goet dat in "en de twee brandt Isers hebbe en de bybell die wy gebruyckt hebben" (She is also to have a shovel, a dungfork, a small ax, a wooden shovel, a grain cleaner, a pleasure sleigh, the pott-bench (to place potts on), and corner closet (Eettens, i. e., a small three-cornered closet), a bedstead, where we sleep in (the testator wrote, by mistake, 'slaagen,' instead of 'slaapen,' i. e., 'where we fought in instead of where we slept in), with the bedding belonging thereto, the two iron stamps (marking irons), and the Bible, which we have used).

"Anna en Areyantie Schepmoes sall ock Een Beybel hebben Beneffense sall myn huysvrouw haer twe Doghters genaemt A. en E. S. Elleck vyftien Elle hollans Bettyk nevens het I gegeweeve : en ock het fyne Linne dat new geweve is of geweeve wort dat sy selleft gesponne hebben" (A. and A. S. shall also have a bible each, and my wife is to give said daughters each 15 yards Holland bedcloth which I have woven, and also the fine linen, which was woven, or which will be woven, which she has spun herself).

"Myn Soon Willem Schepmoes sal hebbe myn huys dat aghter is en Schuer en hofstee Boogaert en leegh Bowlandt dat ick nu behowen" (my son, W. S., shall have my house which is behind, and barn, and farm, and orchard, and low plough land which at present belongs to me) "het Landt dat ick new Sayie en ploiege en maey tot Sestien morge toie maer de voorste" (and the land which I am now sowing and plowing, and the 60 morgen low land) "sal van de *kisketamer* boom beginnin en de lange streek aan de sloot of het brugetie en dan met Een Reghte byn op de Sloot op Scepere Boomtie dat by de Sloot Staet en dan met Een Reghte byn op *Jan Roos* Boss landt en al dat Boss landt dat aen Deese seyde ban Leyn is Die Mr. *John Cook* gemeetenheeft dat sall Willem Schepmoes hebbe tot aen *Dierck Dewitt* syn Leyn voor welleke voornoiemde Landt huysen

Schuyr Boogaert:" "En ock myn neeger genaamt Will en Een wagen en ploiegh" (shall begin at the "chestnut-tree" at the long row on the creek at the bridge, and then with a straight line up the creek to the 'Scepere' tree, which stands on the creek, and then with a straight line to Jan Roos's woodland, and also all the woodland which is on this side of the line, which Mr. John Cook has marked, shall belong to Willem Schepmoes to Dierck Dewitt's line, for which said land, houses, barn, orchard and also my negro, by name Will and a wagon, a plow, he shall pay £400. He is also to receive "all myn Pocke ende Schrifte obligatsie en alle oblegaatsie Redderen" (all my books, writing-books and bonds, and to pay all my debts).

If the widow should re-marry, she is to give an account not later than four years after the testator's death, and money not paid by William Schepmoes on the £400 debt shall then be remitted.

"Aan myn klyn Soon *Dirck Willemse Schepmoes* myn vleg by het binnenwaeter leggende en myn Singenet ofte waapen Rinck Rottingh en Schiet Roier sall hebben" (to my little son, D. W. S., my row-boat on the lake, and my signet-ring (or ring with coat of arms) my walking-stick and gun).

"Myn soon *Johannes Schepmoes* sal hebben de tuyn die naest syn grondt an Leydt met en Reghte Leyn op het koonigs padt en dat Landt dat buyten De Schoongemaekt is" "syn Eerste geboorte Reght" (my son, J. S., shall have the garden, which adjoins his land, with a straight line from the King's Way, and the land which is beyond the cleared land, his right of primogeniture).

All the 60 morgen land now occupied and plowed by Willem Schepmoes to be equally divided among the children "en het Boss Landt dat Tusen Willem an Johannes Schepmoes Leydt volgens de Leyn die John Crook geloopen heeft" (and the woodland which lies between W. and J. S.'s land, and follows the line which J. C. marked) is to be divided among the children "myn doghters *Sara;* en *Dirckye: Ragell* en Leea: Willem en Rebeeka Anna en Areyantie Schepmoes." "Willem Schepmoes sall van dat Bowlandt niet hebben als syn part van het gelt soo daar overschiet soo sal Willem daer syn par van hebe vande vaste staet Dat Landt dat myn Sueeve kindere sullen deelen dat moet kosten Drie hondert ponden (W. S. shall not receive of this woodland more than his share of the money which remains due, he is also to have his share of the real estate; the land which my seven children are to divide, may cost £300).

"Maer So daer geldt of meel of kooren is dat Sall myn vrouw en myn Soon Willem hebbe om myn doost Schult daer mede te betaalen en de Rest dot dar moghte overigh weesen om myn andere Schulden te betalen en Sullen gehowden Syn Ses maan dan nae myn doot Reekeningk te doien aen de administratuers van myn nagebatene Staat. Ock Soo will Ick dat hy dat Landt Dat hey new In huer heeft, nock Een Jaer sall Bouwe mitten daer van de Derde hok of geris moist gedoe en als daer Soo veel Reet geldt niet gevonden wordt soo sall het uyt de naaste krop Betaalt weerden door myn Soon Willam Schepmoes Dat is te segge myn Doot Schulde Die aen myn begrafnis behooren en gedaan Sullen werden die moielen alle betaalt werden en niet naagelaten."

(Any money, flour or corn, which may be found, shall go to my wife and to my son William for the payment of my funeral expenses, and what remains shall be used to pay my other debts with. They are to be bound to give an account to my executors, six months after my death, of their expenses on that account. It is also my will that he (William) shall for one year more cultivate the land which he now has in rent, with barley, and if there should not be ready money enough, payment will have to be deferred to the proceeds of the next crop, as paid by my son William. The funeral expenses must, however, be paid promptly.)

Anna and Areyantie to have also "Een negerin" a negress each "als sy komen te trouwen" (when they marry). If necessary, Anna is to have the first choice of Jenny's children, (van Jinny haer kinderen) Areyantie shall have two of Jenny's children. My two daughters, Anna and Areyantie, shall have "Ellek harre Ige kist met het geene daar in is te weeten (each her own trunk with what is therein, that is) linen and woolen goods, silver, coined and uncoined, and all the small pictures and all the stoneware that belongs to her, a Hollandish copper kettle (Een hollandse Coopre kaetell), a little teapot, six chairs, two iron potts, a clock, a warming pan (huegel): "affchop en tangh" (coalshuttle and tongs), six spoons, six pewter plates, a cup, a pewter dish (schuttel), a copper smoothing iron, a good spinning wheel. As guardian (vooghde) over my wife and my two children, Anna and Aryantie, both under age, I appoint, *Johannis Hardenberg, Pieter Tappen,* and *Hendrik Pruyn.* As executors I appoint *Jhuenes Tappen, Barnardus Swartwout, Barent van Waagenen, Aldert Roosa, Johannis Hardenbergh, Pieter Tappen* and *Hendrik Pruyn.*

Signed by the testator, and witnessed by *Gil: Livingston, Jno. Rutsen, Salomon Davis,* and *Jacobus Van Dyck.*

On Sept. 20, 1725, Gilbert Livingston, Solomon Davis, and Jacobus Van Dyck appeared before the Court, *Arian Gerretsen,* Esq., Judge, Capt. *Lambert Cool,* and Capt. *Coenraedt Elmendorp,* Esqrs., Justices, proving the will, and the signatures of the other witnesses.

(See his former will, *supra.*)

Page 293.—DOYO, ABRAHAM, of New Paltz.

Will dated Sept. 20, 1724, and written in French.

"Nostre Commancemant Soit au non de dieu" "en sentant malade au lit." (In the name of God, and sick in bed).

(Long religious preamble.)

"Item Cette ausy mon vouloir et Volonte que pres mon deces ma famme *Elche* demeura en la plaine posesion De tous me bien pour en youir paisiblement durant son vesuage san quel soit oublige de rendre

Conte a mon fit *Abraham."* (My wife Elsie to remain in full possession of my whole estate, without being obliged to render any account to my son Abraham.) "Mais sy elle ces venoit a se Remarier alor elle sera oblige de rendre sout a mon fils Abraham a souoir le taire du vilage et meson et grange et tous me neigre et Cheval es betacorne et meuble et jnmeuble orre argant." (But if she should marry again, she is to give an account to my son, A., for the land, house, all my negroes, horses, horned cattle, furniture and money) "Comme ausy tous le graint le graint quy seron vair ous saique et ausy tous ce qui mapartien an dite *nu pale* jtaime je daune plaint pouvoir a ma fame elche de savoir vandre et transporter ceste dit toire que deseus A *France* qui a quy ellse bons luy Semblere pour paier le frest des Ceste dite terre desus le france quil jtaime je daune et radonne amon fils Abraham tous le taire que je dans la patente du nu palle apre la mor de ma femme sil elle ne se reviene a marier Comme il est sy de seux." (Also all the grain, green or dry, as well as all what belongs to me in said New Paltz, besides full power to my wife Elsie to sell or dispose of all what may be in France at such price she may wish; I give to my son A. all the land which I have in the Patent of New Paltz, after my wife's death, if she does not remarry, as is provided for farther on). I give "tous me outien de Charon et Cotille atiere et tous ce quil apartien a Cotille a Abraham mon fils," (to Abraham, my son, all my wagons and what belongs thereto) "et en suite je baille tous me Livre amon fil Abraham et je reserve pour *Mari* ma fille le bible flament en un testament fancoij et on livre de sermon en un Livr a Saume et quatre pour *Wintie* a Savoir le vieux bible francoij et un testament francoij et le pratique de piete et un Livr de priere flament," (and I give my books to my son A., except four for Marie, my daughter, i. e. the Dutch Bible, a French Testament, a Book of Sermons, and a Psalm-Book, and four for Wintie, i. e., the old French Bible, a French Testament, The Practice of Piety, and a Dutch Prayer-Book).

To my son Abraham also "deux Chelin pour le droy darnaise Sent quil puis pleus rien a pretandre pour ce Senge." (two ropes for the right harness, with which he is to be satisfied, without any change). "J taime je hardonne que mon fils Abraham apre la mor de ma fame il faudra balier a ses deux seure so sente pistol de largant de *nouuel jorque* pour Leur par deritage a savoir frante pistolle pour Mary et Frante pistol pour Wintie apre troii aan apre la mor de ma fame." (I will that my son A., after my wife's death, shall give to his two sisters 60 Pistoles, (*) New York money, for their inheritance, that is 30 pistoles for Marie and 30 pistoles for Wintie) "Et ausy jordonne que ma fame elche ou mon fils Abraham seront oblige de donez a Wyntie Comme je balie a marie ma fille en mariage quan elle aura vinte aen." (Which is to be given to my daughter Marie on her marriage or when 20 years of age, by my wife or my son Abraham.)

(*) A pistole was a Spanish coin, worth ca. 60 cents.

"Maij sil plait a dieu de retirez de me enfent il Retournera a me enfent et il partiront egalement et sil vinne a mourir tous sent eritier il Retournera a la enfant de me deux frere a sovoir *Critiane* et *Henri Doyo.*" (When it shall please God to take me away from my children, it shall return to my children, to be divided equally, and if they should die without having inherited, it (the property) shall go to the children of my two brothers, Christian and Henry Doyo.)

Jacob Hasbrouck, Daniel Hasbrouck and the wife appointed executors. Signed by the testator, and witnessed by Jacob Hasbrouck, *Daniel Du Bois,* and Daniel Hasbrouck. Daniel and Jacob Hasbrouck appeared before the Court, Oct. 7, 1725, proving the will, and stating that they saw Daniel Du Bois sign the same as a witness.

(Abraham Doyo m. *Elsie Clearwater* in 1702.)

Page 313.—FALSETT, GERRET, of the Pals Creek, Labourer.

Will dated April 13, 1726.

"Being very sick and weake In body."
"To *Johannes Wine Cope* Senier of *Kingston*" £5.
"To well beloved Handly *Onomary Newkirk* of the Pals Creek" £5.—
"To my handlady Daughter In law *Geertry Newkirk* £5.
"To Loving frinds *Hendrieck Newkirk* & *Jahanas Newkirk* whome I likewise Constitute my Executors" "all my Estate of moneys Bonds Goods now belonging to me."

GARRET FALSETT (his mark).

JNO. HAYWOOD
HENDRYCK SCHOONMAKER
MATHISE SLIMER

(John Haywood & Mathis Slymer appeared before the Court, May 5, 1726, stating that they saw Hendrick Schoonmaker sign the will as a witness).

Page 342.—LAMBERTSE, CORNELIUS (or BRINK).

Will dated March 8, 1725/6, and written in Dutch.

"Aan myn Huysvrouw (to my wife) *Marritie Meyderse* the whole estate.—"An myn outste Soon (to my oldest son) *Eghbert* Brinck" de keur van alle de peerde (his choice of all the horses).—"Al myn vaste staet van lant en huys so in corporatie van Kingston als op Hurly ofte Elders aenders aen myn vier soons (all my real estate in K., and H., or elsewhere to my four sons) *Eghbert, Lambert, Henderick* En *Jacob* equally, they to pay the debts, and to their three sisters £50: *Ragel* De Huysvrouw (wife of) *Arent Ploegh; Jenneke* wife of *Samuel Burhans* and *Elisabeth* wife of *Jan Oosterhout,* to be paid within three years.— To said daughters also "all Myn Linne Schutels Borde En Comme" (linen, dishes, plates, and cups (or bowls). All the rest of the estate, as slaves, horses, and cattle to be divided among said children.—"Aan myn outste Soon" (to my eldest son) Eghbert" "In myn plaets te ackte als tetentier Int Patent. Nevens *Cornelis Cool* (to act in my place as holder in the Patent besides Cornelis Cool). Sons Eghbert and Lambert appointed executors. Signed by the testator, and witnessed by *Arien Gerretsen, Gerrit Newkirck, Timothy Low,* and *Cornelius Newkirck,* who all appeared before the Court, Nov. 21, 1726, proving the will.

(Cornelis Lambertz, born at sea, son of *Lambert Huibertsen* (q. v.), m., Apr. 27, 1685, *Maretie Egbertz* (*Meyndertsen*), of *New York,* and had issue: i. *Eghbert* (see *Cornelis Brink*); ii. *Lambert;* iii. *Hendricje,* bt. Apr. 19, 1686; iv. *Henderik,* bt. Jan. 28, 1692; v. *Jacob* and vi. *Rachel,* twins, bt. June 3, 1693; vii. *Jacob,* bt. Jan. 5, 1696; viii. *Mynert,* bt. May 1, 1698; ix. *Janneke,* bt. May 7, 1699, m. 1., Dec. 16, 1720, *Samuel Burhans,* m. 2., Oct. 5, 1734, *Walran Dumont;* x. *Lysbet,* bt. March 23, 1701, m. *Jan Oosterhout;* xi. *Annatie,* bt. March 24, 1706.— The widow m., Oct. 5, 1734, *Walran Dumond*).

The following wills, in possession of Mr. *Ralph Le Fevre,* of New Paltz, are not on record in Kingston, Albany or New York.

FRERE, HUGH, New Paltz.

Will dated Jan. 15, 1727/8, and written in Dutch.

"Aen myn Oudste soon *Hugo*" "voor het Recht van syn Eerste geboorte geve ick hem Een paart de keur van myn Stat" (to my eldest son, H., the choice of a horse, for his right of primogeniture).

"Aen myn Soon *Isaac*" "myn weves getouw en syn toebehooren en twee rieten en oock Een voste merry paardt, die van myn broeder *Jan Frere* gehooren is, voruyt voor syn getrouw Diensten aen myn gedaan" (to my son, I., my weaver's loom with what thereto belongs, as well as two reeds, and a sorrel mare, in advance of division, for his faithful service).

"Myn Jongste Kinderen sullen onderhouden en opgevedt werden naar vermoogen en ter Schoolen laaten gaan" (my youngest children shall be provided for, and brought up as well as possible, and permitted to attend school).

"Aan myn Derteen kinderen met namen Hugo, Isaac, *Simon, Jonas, Marya, Sarah, Hester, Chatharina, Blandina, Rachel, Jannetie, Rebecca,* en *Elizabeth*" "myn geheele staet" (my thirteen children, named, to equavally divide the property) "mets gevende aen de Vleeschlycke Vreught Van *Tryntie Van Cleck,* Dochter van *Johannes Van Kleck* die sy nu draagt so het leeft tot de mondige Jaaren ofte tot Een Twentigh Jaaren" "een even geluck part en portie met myn boven gen. kinderen" (to the 'fruit of the flesh' of Tryntie Van Cleck, daughter of Johannes Van Kleck, which she now goes with, it shall receive, if it lives to majority, or to the age of 20, an equal share of the estate with my said children) "En by aldien het vreught ofte kint quam onmondigh te overleyden" (and if any of the children should die before the age of majority) the survivors are to divide the share of deceased.

"Myn ongetrouwde kinderen als sy Comen te trouwen en huwelycken sullen dan haaren Uytsett hebben als myn anderen kinderen gehedt hebben doe se trouwden" (when the minors marry, they are to have an outfit, similar to those, which my married children received, when they married).

"Aan myn Dochter, *Rachel,* £5" (to my daughter, R., £5), to daughter, *Jannetie,* £6, to daughter, *Rebecca,* £7, and to daughter, *Elisabeth,* £8, as well as my "silver Tuymelaar" (silver tumbler).

The children to give their brothers and sisters preference, if they wish to sell their shares.

Executors: sons Hugo, Isaac, Simon. Guardians: "my drie broeders" (my three brothers), *Abraham Freer, Jacob Freer,* and *Jan Freer,* and "myn Vrindt" (my friend), *Aart Van Wagenen.*

HUGH FREER (his mark).

Witnessed by *Ande le feure, Samuel Beuier,* and *Daniel Hasbroucq.*

DUBOIS, DANIEL.

Will dated Aug. 16, 1729, and written in French.

"Soit Notoire a tous Eeux qu'il appartiendra qu' aujourdhuy le Siexieme Jour du mois D' aoust de L'an Mille sept Cent et vingt Neuf moy soubsine Daniel Dubois hebitant du Nieu Paltz en la Conte de Ulster en la Province de Nieu York dans L'Amerique Estant en sante de corps et d'Esprit Dieu en soit Loue; Feu que le jour et L'heure de la mort nous est Incertaine Dieu nous ayant Cache le Temps et le Moment qu'il s'est reserve a sou Adorable Providence; c'est pourquoy aussy J'ay voulu jcy declarer par les presentes ma derniere volonte et Testament en la forme et en la maniere Comme L'ensuit." (Be it known to all whom it may concern, that to-day, Aug. 16th, 1729, I, Daniel Dubois, resident of N. P., Ulster County, Province of New York in America, being well in body and mind, for which God be praised; knowing that the day and hour of death is uncertain to us, God having hidden from us the time and the moment which he has reserved in his adorable providence; therefore, I have wished to declare by these presents my last will and testament in manner and form as follows.)

"Je Casse je Reuoque J'annule et met a neant tout autre Testament que j'ay fait ou passe soit de parolle ou par Eseuit: il serront nul et de nulle valleur." (I dissolve, revoke, annul and make void every other testament, which I have made by word or writing: it shall be void, and null, and of no effect.) "Mais Celluy cy est et sera ma demiere volonte et Testament et non autre." (But this is and shall be my last will and testament.) "Et Ainsy je Recommende mon ame a Dieu mon Creatur a Jesus Christ mon Sauueur Et au Sainct Espt. mon Consolateur et Sanctificateur. Et mon Corps a la Terre d'ou il a Este pris Jusques a ce qu'il plaise a Dieu au Jour qu'il a destermine en son Conseil Esternel de Ressusciter nos Corps pour les reunir a nos Ames, afin que tous ensemble de jouir a jamais de la vie Eternelle et bien heureuse que Jesus Christ son fils nostre Seigneur nous a acquire par son sang qu'il a promis de donner a tous Eux quy luy seront fidelle jusqu'a la mort."

(And thus I recommend my soul to God, my creator, to Jesus Christ my saviour, and to the Holy Ghost, my consoler and sanctifier, and my body to the earth from which it was taken, until it shall please God, on the day which he has determined in his eternal counsel, to raise our bodies, to reunite them to our souls so as together to enjoy forever life eternal, and most blessed, which Jesus Christ, his son, our Lord, had secured for us by his blood, which he has promised to give to all those who are faithful unto death.)

"Pour ce quy est de mes biens temporels qu'il a pleu a Dieu de me donner beaucoup plus que je n'ay merritte: Comme Terres, Maisons, Granges, frutiers, pastures, et heritage; Cheweaus, Bestes a Corne et autres Bestial; or, argent, monnoye ou autrement, Estains, Euyores, fers & ferrement, et tout autres Utencilles quy appartient a mon bien Je donne et ordonne Comme il Lenssuit." (As for my temporal goods which it has pleased God to give me, much more than I deserve: as lands, houses, barns, orchards, pastures, and heritage, horses, cattle, gold, silver, coined or uncoined, cooking-utensils, iron tools, and all other utensils, I give and bequeath as follows).

"Premierement S'est mon Voloir et volonte que toutes mes Ligitures Debts Soit Payee en temps Conunabl par mes Executeurs ycy apres nommes." (First, it is my will and desire that all my debts be paid by my executors, hereafter named, immediately after my death.)

"2e. Cest aussy mon voulier et volonte Expresse que ma femme *Marie* demeurera en la pleine possession et Jouissance de tous mes biens mouuable et jonmouvables apres mon desces pour en jouir paisiblement durant son veufage sans quelle soit obligee den rendre Conte a mes Enfans ny a personne quy que ce soit, mais sy en cas quelle Vin Sent a se remarier, elle aura nu tiers dans les reuenus de toutes mes terres aussy elle aura une negresse trois ou quatre vaches trois Cheueaus et tous les meubles de ma maison pour sa vie durant et apres son desces ils reuiendront Et Seront a tous mes Enfans en general pour estre esgallement divise et partage parmy Eux et eutre eux; Ses pourquoy il faudra faire une jnventaire." (My wife, Marie, to remain in full, undisturbed possession of all my estate, during her widowhood, without being obliged to render an account to my children, or anyone else; if she should happen to remarry, she is to have one third of the profits from all my lands, one negress, three or four cows, three horses, all the furniture in my house, for life, and after her death, all to go to the children to be divided equally. An inventory will, therefore, be necessary.)

"3e. Mon fils aine *Benjamin* aura pour son desit d'ainesse tout ma monture de Cavallerie Excepte le Cheuel sans pretendre pour Cette raison rien autres Choses." (My eldest son, B., for his birthright, my cavalry equipment, except the horse; he not to pretend to chose something else, on that account.)

"4e. Tous mes biens meubles et jnmeubles mouvables et jnmouvables a mes six Enfants *Elisabeth, Benjamin, Marie, Simon, Rachel,* et *Isaac,* a Eux" "une juste part." ((To my children, named, one sixth part each of the whole estate.)

"5e. Mais Sy en cas ma famme procree ou ait d'autres Enfants durant mon vie, ils diviseront" "une just part." (If my wife should have other children during my life, they are to inherit equally with the rest.)

"6e. S'il arriuoit que ma famme fut Enceinte a mon Desces et accouchat de fils ou fille legitimement procree de moy alons ce fruit la doit partage dans tous l'heritage." (If my wife should be enciente at my death, and a legitimate son or daughter be born, such child shall inherit with the rest.)

The children to give preference to each other, if they wish to sell their shares.

"Mon frere *Philipe Dubois* mon uncle *Jacob Hasbrouck* et mon frere Pierre Cantin" (my brother, P. D., my uncle, J. H., and my brother, P. C.) appointed executors.

Witnessed by *Jean Theuenin, Samuel Beuier,* and *Stephen Gasherie.*

Page 353.—JANSEN, MATTYS, of Kingston, Cordwainer.

Will dated Aug. 21, 1727.

"Eldest son *Johannis* shall have for his birth right £30."

"My daughter *Magdalena* to be paid at the day of her marriage £20."

"My daughter *Ragel* to be paid at the day of her marriage £20."

"My son *Thomas* £30 to be paid when he arrives at the age of 21 years."

"My son *Cornelis* £35 to be paid when he arrives at the age of 21 years."

"My son *Jacobus* £35 to be paid when he arrives at the age of 21 years."

"My sons Cornelis and Jacobus shall have three silver Cups and twelve silver spoons which I had by their mother, and the said Cornelis and Jacobus shall have the preference of the Lott of Ground, lying in *Kingston* between the house and Lott of *Jan Heermans* deceased and they house and Lott of *William Swart,* if sold or divided they Giving as mauch for the same as one of the other Children will give."

"An inventory be taken of all my Goods and Chattels and that my family keep and Remaine in my now dwelling house untill next Spring and then my Goods and Chattels to be sold by my Executors and the money ther from arising to be put out at Interest, and out of the Interest my Children that are under age to be maintained."

"After payment of debts all real and personal property to be divided among the children: Johannis, Thomas, Cornelis, Jacobus, *Grietie* now wife of *Lewis de Bois, Marritie* now wife of *Johannis Decker, Magdalena* and *Ragel.*" In case of death under the age of 21, the share to be divided among the survivors.

"My son Johannis full power" "to sell" "such lands and estate which I have had by my father *Jan Mathysen* deceased which is yett undivided."

"Eldest son Johannis, my Brother *Thomas Jansen* and Brother *John Crooke Junr."* appointed guardians "untill my youngest Child shall be of the age of 21 years" and then "my four sons, Johannis, Thomas, Cornelis and Jacob" to be executors. Signed by the testator.

PETRUS VAS
HENDRICK JANSEN
GIL LIVINGSTON

(Witnesses appeared before the Court Oct. 5, first year of George II.)

(Codicil.)

"My eldest son Johannis Jansen full power" "to release and confirm the divisions made with the heirs of my father *Jan Mathysen* deceased." Aug. 21, 1727. Same witnesses. Entered Oct. 5, first year of George II. (1727).

(M. J., s. of *Jan Mattysen*, (q. v.), m. 1., June 7, 1675, *Anna Elmendorp*, m .2., June 13, 1703, *Rachel Popinga*, b. N. Y., res. *Kingston*, m. 3., May 1, 1712, *Annatjen Masten*. Issue with 1st wife: i. *Johannes*, bt. Nov. 15, 1696, m., July 8, 1725, *Anna Schepmoes;* ii. *Margrietje*, bt. June 4, 1699, m., June 21, 1720, *Lowies Du Bois*. With 2d wife: iii. *Marytje*, bt. Sept. 3, 1704, m., May 17, 1726, *Johannes Decker;* iv. *Magdalena*, bt. March 17, 1706, m., Oct. 26, 1733, *Daniel Schoonmaker* (q. v.); v. *Tomas*, bt. June 20, 1708; vi. *Rachel*, bt. May 7, 1710, m., May 15, 1729, *Benjamin Smedes*, (q. v.); by 3d wife: vii. *Cornelis*, bt. March 1, 1713, m., Oct. 8, 1748, *Catharina Swart;* viii. *Jacobus*, bt. Dec. 19, 1714; ix. *David*, bt. Jan. 20, 1717; x. *Elisabeth*, bt. Febr. 22, 1719).

BOOK OF DEEDS IV. (DD), MARKED 1728—1745.

Page 251.—De WITT, JAN, of Mombacckus (Rochester).

Will dated Oct. 29, 1700, and written in Dutch.

"Van Lychaam kranck de Betten Leggende" (sick and lying in bed).—"Aan myn huysvrouw *Wyntje De Witt* (to wife W. de W.) one half of the estate, the other half to "myn vier kindere by Name (my four children by name) *Barber De Wyt, Eycken De Wyt, Blandine De Wyt, Ragel De Wyt*" of "huys Landt paerde Beeste Gelt" (land, horses, cattle, money).—"Eenigen van myn kinderen in haren Onmondige Jaren Mochte Come Te Sterve" (if any of my children should die during their minority) share of deceased shall be divided among the survivors.— "Myn Broeder (my brother) *Anderis De Witt & Cornelis Swyf*" appointed executors.

JAN DE WYT (his mark).

Witnessed by *Anderes De Wiedt, Cornelis Swyt,* and *Jacob De Wyt.*

Mr. *Moses Du Puis* and Mr. Cornelis Switts appeared before the Court, April 12, 1715, proving the will.

(Son of *Tjerck Claessen De Witt,* q. v. Had issue: i. *Barbara,* bt. April 17, 1692, m., *Jan Gerritse Decker,* bt. July 28, 1688, s. of *Gerrit Janse D.* and *Magdalena;* ii. *Ikee,* bt. June 3, 1694; iii. *Blandina,* bt. Apr. 12, 1696, m., Oct. 24, 1719, *Jurian Westphael,* bt. Sept. 27, 1698, s. of *Simon W.* and *Neeltje Quackenbos;* iv. *Rachel,* bt. Aug. 23, 1698, m., Apr. 15, 1723, *Isaac Van Aken;* v. *Jannetje,* bt. July 13, 1701, m. Abraham Van Aken).

Page 276.—COOL, CORNELIS, of Hurley, Yeoman.

Will dated Jan. 10, 1732/3.

"Being in Tolerable health."

"My dear wife *Janneke Cool*" "yearly and every year during her Naturall Life the Just Sixth Schepell of all the Winter Wheat and Rye as shall be raised on my land and Twelve Schepell Indian Corne and the Use of my Chamber Next the Barn and Seller and Loft Room with the priviledges as I Now Enjoy, in the House Where I Now Live which I hereby give to my son *Lambert,* and my Negro Man Called *Carlyn* One Negro Woman Calles *Susannah* and the Two Milk Cows and fodder in the Winter and pasturage on the farm of my son Lambert."

"The children of my Daughter *Antie: Jannike* wife of *Gerardus Hardenbergh* and *Margritta* wife of *Thomas Gaasbeek*" £750 "and the fourth part of all my Goods and Chattes to be Divided between them in the manner following: After myn and wifes Decease My Executors shall pay to them" "all the Moneys that arise of the Debts Due to me by Bond or Bonds Which Money so payed shall goe towards the Discharging said £750, always Provided that the said Janneke & Margritta or their assignes shall first Deduct ¼ part of such sum as part of their fourth of the Goods and Chattels, and whereas the said Gerardus Hardenbergh is Indebted to me by Bond" out of Janneke's part is to be deducted the principal and interest.

"And whereas I have Lent the said Margritta £50" said money to be deducted out of her share. Son Lambert and daughters Hendricke and Gertie to pay "what shall be vanting in three years after myn and wifes decease."

"To my son Lambert Cool" "all my land on the south side of the *Esopus Kill* in the bounds of Hurley Between the Land of *Jannetie Newkerk* and the Land of *Aldert Kiersteden* Together with Housen Barns Barghs Buildings Ochards Pastures Gardens fences with all and singular the appurtenances as also a certain tract of Land lying on the North Side of the aforesaid Esopus Kill being part of a piece of land knove by the name of the *New farm* or *Neve Bovery*" "bounded north easterly by the Land of *Jacob Du Bois* north westerly by the land of *Jannetie Newkerck* south westerly by the Old Kill and Easterly by the aforesaid Esopus Kill and also a certain Tract of Land known by the Name of *Jan Joostens* Land being bounded according to the Conveyance thereof to me made Appears the said Lambert paying yearly and Every year to Jannike my said wife or her assignes During her Naturall Life the Sixth Schepell of Winter Wheat and Rye which he Raiseth on said Land and four Schepell Indian Corn and to allow to my said wife the Priviledges in the House as Abovesaid and Pasturage and fodder for Two Milk Cows on said farm and paying within three years after myn and wifes Decease to the said Jannike and Margritta" "the third part of the Residue of the Seven Hundred and fifty pounds after the Dedactions made as aforesaid."

"Unto my son Lambert my Bible."

"All the yearly Rents Income and Profitts of that Certain Tract or parcell of Land Scituate Lying and being on the North side of the said Esopus Kill between the Land of Jacob Du Bois and the land of *Arie Gerretse* so as the same is conveyed to me by *Barnardus Swartwoudt* Together with Housen Barns, Barghs, Buildings, fences, Orchards, Pastures, Gardens" with appurtenances to be paid during the life of "my daughter *Hendricke Low* wife of *Timothy Low* of *Hurley*, Esq." After her decease said land to "my Grand Children of the Body of my said Daughter" if alive; if dead under the age of 21, the share to be divided among the survivors.

"To my wife" "during her Naturall Life the sixth Schepell of Winter Wheat and Rye, which shall be Raised on said Land and four Schepell of Indian Corn" and within three years after decease of testator and wife, the third part of the residue of the £750, after deductions made, to go to Jannike and Margritta or survivor.

"To daughter Geertie wife of Mr. *Derrick Wynkoop*" tract of land on Hurleys Great Peice, bounded north east by land of *Cornelis Lambertse,* southwest by land of *Arie Gerretse* with Housen, Barns, and Bargh fences, pastures, Orchards, Gardens, with appurtenances. Also Eight Morgan or sixteen acres of wood land upon the hill northwest of the last mentioned land, paying yearly to wife the sixth Schepel of winter wheat and rye which shall be raised on said land and also four schepell Indian corn.

"Whereas I have an undevided Ninth part of a certain Tract of Land on the north side of Esopus Creek conveyed by *Johannis Hardenbergh and Company* to myself and Company" "to my son Lambert Cool In fee Tail after his Decease to his eldest son and from Eldest son to Eldest son for Ever provided alvays that the Tennents in possession for the time being of the Land" "shall for ever have free Commage and feeding of all Commonable Beasts and Catle and Liberty to Cut Break and Carry avay all sorts of wood and timber and stone."

"After death of testator and wife, the property to be divided, ¼ to son Lambert, to the executors ¼ "to the use of my daughter Hendrickie," to daughter Geertie ¼, and ¼ to Jannike and Margritta besides the £750 before given them."

"Beloved son Lambert Cool and my beloved son-in-law Dirick Wynkoop" appointed executors. The will "being writt on Two Sheats of Common paper Consisting of Eight pages."

CORNELIS COOL (his mark).

HANS KIERSTEDE
DERCK VAN VLIET
GIL: LIVINGSTON
HENRY LIVINGSTON

(Witnesses appeared before the Court Sept. 7, 1736, proving the will.

A. GAASBECK CHAMBERS
CHRISTOEFFEL TAPPEN
JOHANNIS JANSEN.

(*Cornelis Teunisen Cool* was son of *Teunis Bartiansen Cool,* who came to this country with his son in the ship "The Spotted Cow," 1663. C. T. C. m., *Jannetje Lamberts,* dau. of *Lambert Huybertsen* (q. v.), and had issue: i. *Teunis,* bt. Jan. 22, 1683, m., Dec. 23, 1720, *Zara Biks;* ii. *Lambert,* bt. Dec. 7, 1684; iii. *Anna,* bt. Aug. 28, 1687; iv. *Annatje,* bt. Apr. 14, 1689, m., after Oct. 9, 1706, *Jacobus Elmendorff,* q. v.; v. *Henderikje,* bt. Nov. 6, 1692; vi. *Hendrickje,* bt. Nov. 19, 1699, m., Sept. 4, 1719, *Timothy (Tomotius) Low;* vii. *Geertje,* bt. Apr. 25, 1703, m., July 3, 1725, *Derick Wynkoop.*—C. C., on Oct. 24, 1704, for and on the behalf of the inhabitants and freeholders of Hurley, petitioned for a warrant for the surveyor to lay out and ascertain the limits and bounds of a tract of land, between the north bounds of Kingston and the great mountain, called the *Blue Hills* (N. Y. Land Papers, iv., p. 26).—Petitioned also on March 18, 1708, with *Adrian Geritse* for a patent of land (Ibid., p. 115).—And on Oct. 12, 1708, for land, adjoining the bounds of *New Paltz* (Ibid., p. 157).—And in 1710 with *Jacob Rutsen* for a warrant to run the division line between Hurley and *Marbletown* (Ibid., v., p. 76, vii., p. 47).

Page 336.—SWYTS, CORNELUS, of Rochester, Lantman.

Will dated April 13, 1735, and written in Dutch.

(Long religious preamble.)

"Myn waade huysvrouw *Jannetie Swits*" all the land in Rochester "an de suydt sy van de *RonduytsKyl*" "all myn Slaven, Negers, Negerinnen, Negers kinders, paerde in besten Schapen Zweyne hoendert." (My worthy wife, J. S., land on the south side of R. K., all my slaves, negroes, negresses, negro-children, horses, cattle, sheep, hogs, poultry.)

Wife appointed executrix.

CORNELIUS SWYTS (his mark).

LODEWYK HORNBEEK
JOHN SCHOONMAKER
CORNELIUS HORNBECK

(Lodewyck and Cornelis Hornbeck appeared before the Court, May 2, 1738, proving the will, and stating that they saw John Schoonmaker sign the same as a witness.)

(*Claes Cornelissen Swits*, a "Duytsman", i.e. a German, (and probably a Swiss, from the Island of *Schouwen*, thence from *Amsterdam* to *New Netherland*), on May 18, 1638 had a lease of the *Otter-Spoor* farm there from Jonkheer *Van Curler*.—Claes "Rademaker" (wheelmaker), as he was called, was killed by the Indians. His son, *Cornelius Claeszen* (*Switzer, Switz, Switzart*), m. *Ariantje Comelis Trommels*, who m., 2., in N. Y., Nov. 18, 1656, *Albert Leonards*, of *Amsterdam*. They had issue: i. *Claes*, b. 1640 (*Claes Cornelissen van Schoonhoven*), m., July 28, 1670, *Catalyn Jans;* ii. *Apolonitje*, bt. Febr. 17, 1641; iii. *Jacob*, bt. Oct. 5, 1642 ,twin with iv. *Isaac*, bt. same day, "klyne Isaac," who went to *Schenectady*, and m. *Susanna*, dau. of *Simon Groot;* v. *Jacob*, bt. Febr. 5, 1645, m. *Aeltie Fredrix;* vi. *Abraham*, bt. March 10, 1647; vii. *Apollonia*, bt. Oct. 25, 1648, m. before Apr. 17, 1680, *Jans Thomasen Aken;* vii. *CORNELIS*, bt. July 9, 1651, came to Kingston 1678, m. *Jannetje*, bt. Febr. 12, 1662, dau. of *Tjerck Claessen De Witt* (q. v.). She made her will Febr. 21, 1737/8, q. v.; ix. *Pieter*, bt. Oct. 12, 1653; x. *Cornelia*, bt. Oct. 31, 1655 (dau. of Cornelius Claeszen, Rademaecker).

BOOK OF DEEDS V. (EE).

Page 1.—LEGG, WILLIAM, Junr.

Will dated March 8, 1743/4.

"Unto *Marytie* my Dear Wife the use of my Whole Estate both Reall and Personall as Long as she Remains my Widow, and that she shall Take Care for the Educating and Instructing of my Children and Honestly Maintaining, according to the Capacity of my Estate, untill my said Children arive to the age of Twenty one years or Come to Marry "but if my said wife Happen to Marry" then the estate to return to the children.

"To my eldest son *William Legg*" all my whole Estate Where I Now Dwell named *Jacobs Hook* and the *Island* with House, Barn Barricks Orchards and Pasture Ground and all the appurtenances" "when he shall arrive at the age of 21 years if his mother then be Married or Deceast, and not otherwise. In consideration of the Same, he shall pay unto my Three Other Children Namely *Samuel Legg Barent Legg* and *Margret Legg*" £120 "sixty pounds as they shall arrive to the age of 21 years to each of them one year afterwards. If William happens to receive the estate before the other children come of age, he shall be obliged" to maintain my other Three children, and give them Learning Untill they arrive at the age of 21 years or happen to marry, and to put my two youngest sons Samuel and Barent To such Trades as they shall be Willing to Learn."

"Unto my Three Sons William Samuel and Barent all my Close."

Executors empowered to sell "the land I have Lying at the flat bush Within the Limits" "of Kingston it being one Quarter part of the Land my father bought of *Arent Ploegh*" "the money to be used for discharge of debts.

"To son Samuel Legg £120 to be paid by my son William."—"To son Barent £120 to be paid by William."—"To daughter Margaret £120 to be paid by William."

Survivors to divide share of deceased heir. Brothers-in-law *Wilhelmus Burhans, Richard Davenport,* and *Philip Viele Junr.,* and "my friend and Neighbour *Edward James Whitaker*" appointed executors. Signed by the testator.

HENDR. HENDR. SCHOONMAKER
JOHN WHITAKER
TOBIAS WYNKOOP

(John Whitaker and Tobias Wynkoop appeared before the Court May 29, 1745, proving the will, and confirming the signature of Hendrick Hendrickse Schoonmaker.)

(Codicil.)

"My son William shall not be obliged to pay the said Legacies (of £120 to the other children) during the time my wife shall enjoy my Estate but when my said Estate shall fall Legaly into my said sons hands" then he is commanded to pay the legacies as ordered. Executors given full power to sell all interest in the estate of "my Grandfather *Hendrick Ploogh* deceased, which was given and bequeathed unto me by the last will and testament of my mother *Gessie* deceased and also all the right and title made unto me by the last will of my uncle *Abraham Ploogh*" and by the will of "my aunt *Geertje* deceased."

WILLIAM LEGG JUNIOR.

JAN PYETERSEN OSTERHOUT
JOHN WHITKER
JACOB BURHANS

(Witnesses appeared before the Court May 30, 1745, proving the will of the late William Legg Jr. of Kingston, deceased.)

(*William Legg*, bt. Nov. 1, 1713, son of *William Legg* and *Geesje Ploeg*, q. v., m., Dec. 7, 1733, *Mareitje Burhans*, b. Brabant, and had issue: i. *Geesje*, bt. Sept. 8, 1734; ii. *Willem*, bt. Oct. 19, 1735; iii. *Margerit*, bt. Aug. 14, 1737, m. June 11, 1761, *Henricus Post*, of *Albany;* iv. *Zamuel*, bt. Aug. 5, 1739, m. 1., Aug. 16, 1760, *Sara Du Bois*, and 2., Jan. 23, 1773, *Marya Osterhoudt;* v. *Barent*, bt. Dec. 25, 1740; vi. *Jan*, bt. June 12, 1743).

Page 6.—DU BOIS, JACOB, of Hurley, Landtman.

Will dated April 3, 1739, and written in Dutch.

"Aan myn Huysvrouw *Gerretje Du Bois* de Inkomste ofte Huer van myn Bouwery op Hurley (welke ick aen myn soon Johannis verhuert Hoof Goduerende myn en myn Vrouws Leven) so Lange als zy leeft."— To wife also "de Huer welke myn vier soons *Barent, Lewis, Isaac* en *Gerret* Verplecht zyn te betalen Voor het Landt op *Salem* in *Niew Jersey*" "Ende ook het Gebruycj van alle Myn losse off personeele Staat."

"Myn vyf kinders *Magdalena, Catharina, Rebecca, Sarah* Ende *Neeltje*" £110 each "aen Landt van myn Landt over aen de Noordoste noord Weste zyde Van de *Esopuse Kill* En Myn soon Johannis" £120 "van het zelfde Landt Ende ook myn Vrouws Dochter *Jacomyntje* £50 het welk Landt ick Schatt ofte Waarder op £1200."

(To my wife Gerretje Du Bois, for life, income from the rent from my farm at Hurley (which I have leased to my son Johannis during my and my wife's lives).—To wife also rent which my four sons, named, have agreed to pay for the land in Salem, New Jersey, as well as the use of all my personal estate.

My five children, named, £110 each and land from my land on the nordeast and nordwest side of Esopus Kill, and to my son Johannis £120 of same land, and to my wife's daughter, Jacomyntie, £50 from the same land, which I value at £1200).

After wife's death, all other property to be divided among the children: Barent Lewis Isaac Gerret *Johannis* Magdalena Catherina Rebecca Sarah "en Neeltje en myn huysvrouws Dochter Jacomyntie."

Property devised to daughter Magdalena to be sold by the executors and the interest given her yearly until her death, when the entire amount is to be divided among her children.

Wife and sons appointed executors.

Signed by the testator.

JOHANNIS HARDENBERGH
CATHATRENNA KOOL
JOHN CROOKE JUNR.

(Major Johannis Hardenbergh and John Crooke appeared before the Court, June 7, 1745, proving the will.)

(Jacob Du Bois, (son of *Louis Du Bois*, q. v.), b. Oct. —, 1661, settled at *Hurley*, m. *Gerretje Gerretsen*, bt. March 12, 1669, dau. of *Gerrit Cornelisen*, and had issue: i. *Magdalena*, bt. May 25, 1690; ii. *Barent*, b. Hurley; iii. *Louis*, bt. June 9, 1695; iv. *Gieltje*, bt. May 13, 1697; v. *Gerrit*, bt. March 29, 1700; vi. *Isaac*, bt. Febr. 1, 1702, m. *Neeltje Roosa;* vii. *Gerrit*, bt. Febr. 13, 1704, m., July 18, 1731, *Margrietje Elmendorff;* viii. *Cathareyntie*, bt. March 24, 1706, m., Febr. 12, 1725, *Petrus Smedes;* ix. *Rebecca*, bt. Oct. 31, 1708, m. *Petrus Bogardus;* x. *Johannes*, bt. Nov. 10, 1710, m., Dec. 11, 1736, *Judikje Wynkoop*, dau. of *Cornelius W.;* xi. *Zara*, bt. Dec. 20, 1713, m., June 21, 1734, *Conrad Elmendorf;* xii. *Neeltjen*, bt. May 27, 1716, m., Sept. 9, 1737, *Cornelius Nieuwkerk*).

Page 8.—BRUYN, JACOBUS, of Bruynswick.

Will dated June 20, 1744.

To eldest son *Jacobus* farm whereon I now live at Shawangonk, containing 410 acres, granted by letter patent to *Thomas Lloyd,* also land granted by letter patent to *Gertie Brown* between the first mentioned tract and the land granted to *Jan Kamp* and Company, also woodland (adjoining Thomas Lloyd's land) on northwest side of *Shawangunk Kill* of 300 acres, part of land granted by letter patent to *John Rutsen* and myself, and conveyed to me by John Rutsen, also all my part of a tract of land purchased by me from the Trustees of *Rochester* on south side of Shawangunk Mountains together with all buildings Barns Baraiks Gristmill Bolting Mill Skreen Orchard Gardens and appurtenances. The son to pay yearly "to my well beloved wife *Tryntie*" £25 for her naturall life and to allow her the use of Three Rooms in my house and liberty of the Seller as she shall have occasion for it for her own use" "my son Jacobus shall pasture and fodder or Keep in Winter "for said wife" two horses four Milck Cows and five Sheep and to sow for her half a Shepple of flaxseed yearly," all this to wife in liew of her Dower.

Said Son Jacobus within one year after decease of wife to pay to "my three other sons: *Cornelis Severyn* and *Johannis* £500, or £166.13.4 each."

To son Cornelius land in Ulster County called *Pakanasink* on the North side of Shawangunk Creek or River, containing 500 acres, granted to me by letter patent, Nov. 26, 1719; also land on the south east side of Shawangunk River opposet te Packanasink, my 1/7 part of 2000 acres (part of a tract of 2500 acres granted to myself and *Henry Wileman* by letter patent, April 20, 1722, with appurtenances)."

To son Cornelius also £200 to be paid out of the money I have at interest.

To son Severin all my lands called the *five Thousand Acres* in Ulster County on both sides of the *Paltz River,* granted by letter patent to *Francis Harrison,* Esq. and Company, July 7, 1720, together with rents and arrears of rent due. To Severyn also £250.

To son Johannis all my land within a tract of 2000 acres, granted by letter patent to *Peter Matthews* and Company, on both sides of the Paltz River, of 335 acres; also 100 acres (adjoining the northwest side of the land granted to Peter Matthews), conveyed to me by *Johannis Rutsen;* also a Marsch and Woodland thereunto adjoining called the *Gebrande Vley* or the Burned Meadows, of 200 acres on the southeast side of Shawangunk Creek, granted to me by letter patent, Nov. 26, 1719. Together with liberty to cart, hew down and carry away all sorts of wood trees and timber for the use of the said lands Given to him only within any part of my land by mee purchased of the Trustees of Rochester, on the south east side of Shawangunk Mountains.—To Johannis also £50.

To daughter *Peternella* wife of *Jacob Hardenbergh* land on southeast side of the Paltz River of 667 acres by mee purchased of the executors of Captain *Lancaster Syms* Deceased, part of tract of 3500 acres, granted to *David Provoost Kip van Dam* and *Company*."

To my daughter *Catharin* the wife of *Abraham Hasbrouck* undevided half part of dwelling house at *Newburgh* upon *Hudson River* whereof I am seized jointly with *Cadwallader Colden,* Esq., and my moiety or halfe of the two lotts number 9 and 17 thereunto belonging, and also my right to the store house there built and the lott of ground belonging to it; also those several lotts No. 4, 12, 20, 29, 32, and No. 39 at Newburgh, conveyed to me by Cadwallader Colden; also messuage or tenement and lott of ground conveyed to me by two conveyances from *John Harris, John Haywood* and *Thomas Haywood,* scituated in *New York* city upon the Dock near to *Pearl* Street."

To my daughters *Peternella, Catharina, Mary* and *Hanna* and to my two grandchildren: *Lewis Du Bois* and *Rachel Du Bois* the children of my Daughter *Gertruy* deceased the late wife of *Nathaniel Du Bois* 4/15 part of land called *The Eight Thousand Acres,* granted by letters patent, July 7, 1720 to *Philip Schuyler* and Company; also land in *Rochester,* conveyed to me by *Joseph Gee* and *Anthony Hill.*

Also to my daughters Mary and Hannah £150 each. To each of them one feather Bed Beding and furniture Thereunto Belonging in order to make them equal with my other Daughters they having had an Equivalent thereto in my Life time.

After payments of all debts, to my three granddaughters and two grandchildren, to Peternella £60, to Mary £264, to Hanna £264, to grandchildren £264 equally to be divided between them. If there should not be sufficient outstanding at interest, to pay these legacies, the daughters and grandchildren to lose 1/5 part of what my said Cash and money at Interest shall fall short of.

To son Severyn my Silver Tankard, and to my son Jacobus my Beamscales and Weights which I use in my Grist mill. To each of them also one of my Saddles and a good horse and a good mare, the choice to be taken by them before any division be made of my stock.

To my four sons also all my Law Books and History books. To sons Cornelius, Severyn and Johannis all my wearing apparell belonging to my body as also all the Residue and Remainder of my money out at Interest upon mortgages Bonds Bills Notes or other Securities. Debts to be paid first out of the money in hand arising from my last years crop.

Executors to put my son Johannis to School as soon as they can conveniently; £1500 given them to be applied towards his education, said sum to be raised out of my crop of Wheate and other grain now in the ground.

To daughter Peternella £10 to be paid her out of my crop of wheat and flower now in my house and Mill.

To son Cornelius my mill stones now lying at the mill.

To said daughters and grandchildren all household goods, furniture, pictures, Books and Plates, 1/5 to the daughters and grandchildren, all household goods used by wife excepted during her life.

To said four sons all my slaves Stock of Horses black Cattles Sheep Hoggs and also my book Debts Crop of Corn now on the Lands Wagons sleds Ploughs Harrows and other farming utinsells and all other Reall and Personall Estate. Jacobus to have the use of Severyn and Johannis shares until they come of age, or marry, my son Jacobus maintaining and Cloathing the said Negroes and Wintering the said Cattle and Horses.

To wife during her life one Negro man and a negro wench her Choice out of all my Slaves and Two horses and four milck Cows and five Sheep and also the use of Two Bedds and furniture for them and all such Household Goods furniture Pictures and Plates as she shall have occasion for dureing her life. Also one good fat steer and five hoggs to Kill for her first Winters Provisions. Wife to deliver a true Schedule of all personal property, within six months after my decease.

In case any of the grandchildren should die the survivor to have the share. If both grandchildren or any of my children should die before they come of age, without lawful issue, the shares to be divided among my three youngest sons and daughters.

Sons Jacobus and Cornelius and son-in-law Abraham Hasbrouck appointed executors, and to discharge the debts out of money made by sale of crop of wheate and flower in the house and mill or at the Land-ing place (my family having first taken their bread out of the same) Executors empowered and instructed to pay out and provide for payments of legacies. Signed by the testator.

JACOB HASBROUCK
ZACHARIAS HOFMAN
CHAS CLINTON

(Charles Clinton and Zaghrya Hofman appeared before the Court, June 11, 1745, proving the will, as well as the signature of Jacob Hasbrouck.

Johannes Hardenburgh, Judge, Cornelis De Lamater, Justice, Moses Depuy Junr. Justice).

(Jacobus Bruyn, Sr. came from *Norway* ab. 1660, m. *Gertrude Ysselstein (Esselstein)*, bt. May 22, 1650, dau. of *Jan Willemse E.* and *Willemtje Jans*. She m., 2., *Severyn Ten Hout* (q. v.). Issue: i. *Jan*, bt. Oct. 6, 1678; ii. *Jacobus, Jr.*, b. Nov. 30, 1680, d. Nov. 21, 1744, m. after Nov. 18, 1704, *Tryntje*, bt. Nov. 22, 1684, d. Aug. 27, 1763, dau. of *Jochem Hendrickse Schoonmaker* and *Petronella Sleght*, q. v., and had issue: a. *Severyn Tenhout*, bt. March 24, 1706, d. y.; b. *Jacobus Bruyn*, bt. Jan. 5, 1707, d. Apr. 26, 1781, m. *Jeannie Graham;* c. *Geertruy*, bt. Febr. 18, 1709, m. May 13, 1726, *Nathaniel Dubois*, bt. June 6, 1703, s. of *Louis D.* and *Rachel Hasbrouck; d. Cornelis*, bt. Jan. 7, 1711, m. Oct. 12, 1743, *Ida Hoffman*, bt. Dec. 24, 1721, dau. of *Zachariah H.*, and *Hester Bruyn;* C. B. died Dec. 21, 1777; e. *Johannes*, bt. Aug. 10, 1712, (d. Jan. 31, 1755), m., June 21, 1750, *Maria Schoonmaker*, bt. Febr. 12, 1727, dau. of *Benjamin S.* and *Catharina Dupuy;* f. *Josias*, bt. Oct. 23, 1713, d. y.; g. *Pieternella*, bt. June 5, 1715, d. inf.; h. *Tryntjen*, bt. Febr. 10, 1717, d. inf.; i. *Picternelletjen*, bt. Oct. 19, 1718, m., Oct. 7, 1737, *Jacob Hardenburg*, bt. March 10, 1717, d. Febr. 27, 1773, s. of *Johannes H.* and *Catharina Rutsen;* j. *Catryna*, bt. Aug. 21, 1720 (d. Aug. 10, 1793), m., Jan. 5, 1739, *Abraham Hasbrouck*, bt. Aug. 21, 1707, d. Nov. 10, 1791, s. of *Joseph H.* and *Elsie Schoonmaker;* k. *Hanna*, bt. Dec. 25, 1721, d. inf.; l. *Maria*, bt. June 23, 1723, (d. Oct. 8, 1776), m., Aug. 30, 1745, *Isaac Hasbrouck*, bt. March 11, 1722, s. of Jacob H. and *Esther Bevier;* m. *Hannah*, bt. Dec. 27, 1724, m., Nov. 2, 1749, *Solomon Van Wagenen*, bt. May 6, 1722, s. of *Simon Van W.*, and *Sara Dubois;* n. *Severyn Ten Hout Bruyn*, bt. May 25, 1726, (d. Aug. 19, 1759), m. Jan. 13, 1750, *Catharina Ten Broeck*, bt. June 11, 1757, d. Nov. 1, 1802, dau. of *Johannes T. B.*, and *Rachel Roosa;* the widow m., 1765, Col. *Jonathan Elmendorf*).

Page 47.—SWYTS, JANNETJE, "Wedevrouw' van Cornelis Swyts van het Dorp Rochester."

Will dated Febr. 21, 1737/8, and written in Dutch.
"Synde Swack Van lichaem."
(Long religious preamble).
"Aan myn overlede mans suster *Aplonica Aken* myn Eene koey met het bonte behanxel met de toe behoore in thien pondt an Gelt."
"Aan myn suster *Rachel Bogardus* myn andere Koey met het rootachtye behanxel met de toebehore in thien pondt an Gelt."
"Aan myn nieght *Jenneke Wynkoop* myn Grote Spiegel in myn Grote tafel."—"Aan nieght *Cathariena de Duytser* myn klook in myn Swarte repper in Een kaper in de helft van de Mutse die ik op myn hooft draag."
—"Aan myn nieght *Margriet Oosterhout* Een Swarte Schort in Een Stoffe Schort in Een kaper in Een gekwytte Schort in de Andere helft van myn Mutse die Ik op myn hooft draag."—"Aan myn Vrindin *Arientje Hoornbeck* myn Grote Kast."—"Aan myn Nieght *Barber Tapper* myn Beddepan." Residue to be sold to pay debts. "Cosyn Egbert Dewitt ende myn Nieght Barber Tapper" appointed executors.

MARIA HOORNBECK
ANNETJE HOORNBECK
CORNELUS HOORNBECK

JANNETJE SWYTS (her mark)

(Weak in body.—To my deceased husband's sister Aplonica Aken my cow with the spotted hide and £10 in money.—To my sister, R. B., my other cow with the reddish hide and £10 in money.—To my niece, J. W., my large mirror and my large table.—To my niece, C. de D., my cloak, my black top-coat and cap, and half of the bonnet which I wear on my head.—To my niece, M. O., a black apron, and a knitted apron, and the other half of the bonnet, which I wear on my head.—To my friend, A. H., my large cupboard. To my niece, B. T., my warming-pan).

(Codicil)

Dated May 29, 1739, and written in Dutch.

"Overschot" (remainder) of the estate to go to the niece, Janneke Wynkoop, who is also appointed an executrix.

Witnessed by *Cornelus Hoornbeck, Maria Hoornbeck, Willem C. Kool*, who all appeared before the Court, June 3, 1746, proving the will. John Crooke, Clerk.

(See will of *Cornelis Swits*, supra).

Page 57.—LIVINGSTON, GILBERT, of Kingston.

Will dated Dec. 12, 1745.

"Whereas there is to be raised out of the Land Given by my father in Law Coll. *Henry Beekman* Deceased to my beloved Espouse *Cornelia Livingston* Deceased £3000 in money or land for my ten Younger Children: my sons, *Henry, Gilbert, Phillip, James, Samuel,* and *Cornelius Livingston,* my Daughters *Alida* Wife of Capt. *Jacob Rutsen, Joanna, Catharina* and *Margrieta Livingston* in such proportion as I shall think fitt and direct, and my will is that the said £3000 shall be eqally divided amongst them. "In case of death before the age of 21, the survivors to divide the share of deceased.

"Whereas there is £1000 in money or land to be raised out of the lands aforesaid for me" "I give said £1000 and all my lands tenements and Hereditaments" "unto my Children: to eldest son *Robert Livingston,* and my ten children above named."

Sons Robert and Henry, son in law Capt. Jacob Rutsen and "my beloved Couzin Robert Livingston son of my Brother Robert Livingston" appointed executors. Signed by the testator.

THOS. BEEKMAN	(Witnesses appeared before John Crooke,
JOHANNIS DE LAMETTER	Surrogate, July 31, 1746, proving the
JOHN VIELE	will).

(*Robert Livingston*, the first Lord of the Manor of L., born at *Ancrum, Scotland*, Dec. 13, 1654, m. July 9, 1679, *Alida Schuyler*, widow of Rev. *Nicholaus Van Rensselaer*, and died at *Linlithgo*, 1728. They had issue: i. *Philip*, ii. *Robert*, iii. *Gilbert*, of whom presently; iv. *Margaret*; v. *Joanna*.—R. L. on July 12, 1683, purchased from the Indians 2000 acres land on the *Hudson River* and *Roeloff Jansen's Kill*, which he partly sold, Oct. 26, 1694, to *Derrick Wessel Ten Broeck*.

Gilbert Livingston (*Gysbert Lievestont*), of *Roelof Jans Kil, Columbia Co.,* m., Dec. 22, 1711, at *Kingston, Cornelia Beekman*, dau. of Col. *Henry B.,* and had: i. *Robert*, bt. Jan. 11, 1713;

ii. *Hendricus*, bt. N. Y., Aug. 29, 1714; iii. *Joanna*, bt. Sept. 9, 1722; iv. *Wilhelmus*, bt. Aug. 23, 1724; v. *Philippus*, bt. June 26, 1726; vi. *Jacobus*, bt. Apr. 7, 1728; vii. *Zamuel*, bt. Febr. 1, 1730; viii. *Cornelis*, bt. Apr. 30, 1732; ix. *Catrina*, bt. July 21, 1734; x. *Margrieta*, bt. June 23, 1738; and *Alida*, m., Nov. 24, 1737, Capt. Jacob Rutsen, Jr).

Page 109.—OOSTERHOUT, TEUNIS, of Rochester, Yeoman.

Will dated June 14, 1739.

"Unto my Eldest Son *Jan Oosterhout*" "Lott of Low land called the *Long Streek*" "on the north side of *Mombacus Kill* or Creek, purchased by me of *Hendrick Decker* now in his occupation, also the woodland by me purchased of said Hendrick Decker adjoining, and also the wood land by me purchased of *Jan Gerritse Decker* likewise in the occupation of my son Jan, bounded easterly by the outway of *Philip Dubois*, southerly by the brow of the hill next to the low land west by the brow of the Hill running along the east side of a run of water called Het *Lange Stucks Killitie* and northerly by the Commons of *Rochester* together with the house barn and other Buildings thereon now in his possession; he to pay for the same £25 to my two grandchildren, the sons of my son *Aldert Oosterhout* Deceased: *Jacobus Oosterhout* and *Aldert Oosterhout*, £12. 10 each, when they arrive to age of 21.

"Lot of low land on the south side of Mombaccus Kill, purchased of Hendrick Decker, between the land of Philip Dubois and the land of the late *Jochim Schoonmaker* Deceased" "to my son *Petrus Oosterhout*", he to pay my daughter *Engeltje* the wife of *Nicholas Keeter* £50, within two years after my decease.

"My Lands Tenements Meadows Pastures Dwelling houses Brewhouse Barn Stables Grist Mill Saw Mill the fall and Stream of water thereunto belonging orchards Gardens fences" "in Rochester on the north side of the Mombaccus Kill" "now in my possession or occupation unto my youngest son *Hendricus Oosterhout*" he to pay to my Daughter Marytie the wife of *Mathews Tirwillegen* £50 within two years of my decease.

"To son Hendricus Oosterhout also my large Dutch Bible now being in my possession."

"To daughter Engeltje the wife of Nicholas Keter" "tract of land now in his possession on the east side of the Waggon Path Runing to Dominies Creple Bush bounded south by the land herein before given to my son Henricus east and north by a small run west by said waggon Path together with the house and all other Buildings thereon Standing."

"To daughter *Annatje* the wife of *Cornelius Hoornbeek* my 1/12 part of land, conveyed by the Trustees of Rochester to said Cornelius Hoornbeek, Jan. 6, 1728/9, for which he gave a bond to convey to me the said 1/12 part.

"To Eldest son Jan Oosterhout 6 Shillings for his Birth right as being my Eldest Son and heir at law. Residue of estate to be divided among "my Ten Children and Two Grand Children" equally: to son Jan 1/11 part, son *Kryn* 1/11 part, two grandchildren Jacobus Oosterhout and

Aldert Oosterhout 1/11 part, my son Johannes 1/11 part, son Petrus 1/11 part, son Hendricus 1/11 part, daughter Annatje the wife of Cornelius Hoornbeek 1/11 part, my daughter Marytje the wife of Methews Terwillegen 1/11 part, my daughter *Ariaentje* the wife of *Harmon Rosenkrans* 1/11 part, my daughter Engeltje wife of Nicholas Keeter 1/11 part. "I have in my life time assisted some of my children in their Trades and others I have given land by Deed or Gift and others of my said children I have paid Considerable Sums of Money."

Sons Jan, Kryn and Henricus appointed executors.

Signed by the testator.

JACOB DEWITT (his mark)
JOHN SCHOONMAKER
J. BRUYN JUNR.

(Jacob Dewitt and John Schoonmaker appeared before John Crooke, Surrogate, Febr. 2, 1747/8, proving the will, and signature of Jacobus Bruyn as witness).

(*Jan Janszen van Oosterhout* (Brabant), m. *Anna Hendricks*, and had several children. *Teunis Oosterhout* m. *Ariaantje Roose*, and had issue: i. *Jan.* bt. June 3, 1694; ii. *Ari* (*Ariaan*), bt. Apr. 26, 1696, m. 1., Nov. 8, 1728, *Appolonia Roosekrans*, m. 2., March 17, 1734, *Geesjen van der Merken*; iii. *Annetje*, bt. May 1, 1698, m., Apr. 5, 1717, *Cornelis Hoornbeek*; iv. *Marytje*, bt. Dec. 31, 1699; v. *Kryn*, bt. March 16, 1701 (*Cryn Oosterhout* and *Rebecca Roosa*, witn.), m. Jan. 22, 1723, *Geertjen Dekker*; vi. *Allert*, bt. Jan. 3, 1703, m., Febr. 26, 1725, *Helena Roosekrans*; vii. *Maria*, bt. Apr. 15, 1705, m., May 3, 1723, *Matheus Terwilliger*, b. Shawangunk; viii. *Aryaantie*, bt. Sept. 29, 1706, m., Apr. 29, 1725, *Herman Rosenkrans*; ix. *Johannes*, bt. June 20, 1708, m., May 21, 1728, *Johanna Hoorenbeek*; x. *Engeltje*, bt. May 7, 1710, m., March 12, 1729, *Nicholas Keeter, Jr.*, b. Marbletown; xi. *Petrus*, bt. Dec. 2, 1711, m., Oct. 5, 1739, *Lisbeth Burhans*; xii. *Hendricus*, bt. Febr. 5, 1716, m. after Febr. 20, 1743, Pieternella Bosch).

Page 138.—ROOSA, EVERT, of Hurly.

Will dated March 5, 1726/7, and written in Dutch.

"Tot myn huys op Horrely in de Corporatie Van Kingstown" "Seer Sieck En Swack."

(Long religious preamble).

"Aan myn HuysVrouw *Tietje van Ette* myn Geheele Staet" "Geduerende haer Leven."—"En So het De Heere Geliefde uyt Dese Wearelt te Haele Voor En aller myn Yongste Kint tot Syn of haer mondige Jaaren Syn So sall myn soon *Jacobus* myn Staet besitten mits Dat hy myn Kinders Daer yaerlicks En alle Jaere De Huer van betaelt tot dat het youngste Kint Monditgh is en dan Eengaal onder hein De Voor noende Jacobus *Abraham* En *Aldert* myn Drie Jongste Soons Gedeelt te werde mits Sy aen Eyder van myn Doghters uytkeere de som van £20." "Voor het huys Schuer *Jacob Aertsens* Lant Cremakers Lant en Wassemakers Lant Geheeten Dit voornoende Lant Moet onder de voorseyde drie soons Engaal Gedeelt werde als het Youngste Kint mondigh als Voore En dan aen haer susters Eyder Twintigh als voor seyt is Geve Vizt an *Antje Marytje Catharine Sara Lea* En *Ragell* Samme Een hondert En Twintigh Pont En" "het Heere Geliefde Jacobus uyt Dese Waerelt te haele sonder wettelicke Erfgename So sall syn part vervalle aen syn two Jongste Broeders als Abraham En Aldert En als Abraham Sterft als voore sydt is van

Jacobus so sall syn part vervalle an Aldert en als Aldert ook sterft sonder Erfgename so sulle myn Doghters voornoemt alle Eengall deele nevens haer Broeder *Arrie*.

"Aan myn oudste soon Arrie twe Darde van myn Lant over de Revier in *Dutches County* En gekent als part van het Lant dat *Gerrit Aertsen Arien Roosa Jan Eltinge Henderick* En *Jacob Kip* Patent En het is het Lott No. 4" "als het jongste kint mondigh is de somme van £40" "om onder syn voorhoende susters Vizt. Antje Marytje Catharine Sarra Lea en Ragell gedeelt te werde, En·als dat Arie van stonde aen vry sonder huer of Molistastie het selfde magh besitten En voor syn Eerste geboorten Reght En Hengst Vuele als sy tot deeling Comen."

"Aen myn Doghter Marytje De huysvrouw van *Jacob Oosterhaude* de andere Darde part van voornoemde Lott No. 4 moet naest *Hendericus Heermanse* syn."

"An alle myn Kinders nae de Doodt van myn Huysvrouw alle myn Losse Staet, als paerde, Beeste En ander Goot."

"Myn Broeder *Aldert Roosa* En Timothy Low" appointed executors. Signed by the testator.

> ARIEN GERRITSEN
> GERRIT NEWKERCKE
> TIMOTHY LOW

"Kennelick Syen" "Dat de meeningh van my Evert Roosa is dat all het ik heir Boven Vermaakt heb aen myn Kindere" "is" "voor Eewigh En om Dat het gedoght Wert Dat de Getuygen Heir nevens of voore Geteykent niet Suffisant waare So So hebbe meede heir andere versoght met de Verklaeringh heir voore of heir nevens in Kennisse waer van Heb ik myn hant En Seegel heir nevens Geset." March 8, 1726/7.

(At my house in H. in the corporation of K.—To my wife, T. v. E. my whole estate for life. And if the beloved Lord should call her from this world before all my youngest children are of age, my son Jacob shall then have the estate, he to pay yearly rent until my children are of age, and then the estate to be equally divided among the said J., A., and A., my three youngest sons; and to an outfit for each one of my daughters, the sum of £20. The house, barn, Jacob Aertsen's land, Cremaker's land and Wassemaker's land shall be equally divided among said three sons, when the youngest child is of age, and then to each one of their sisters £20, as before provided for. I give to A., M., C., S., L., and R., the sum of £120, and if the beloved Lord should take Jacobus out of this world without leaving him any heirs, born in wedlock, his part shall then go to his two youngest brothers, A. and A., and if Abraham should died before J., his part shall then go to Aldert, and if he should die without issue, my daughters shall then divide equally with their brother Arrie.

To my oldest son A. two thirds of my land over the river in D. Co., known as the land of G. A., A. R., J. E., H. and J. K.'s patent, that is lot No. 4, and when the youngest child is of age the sum of £40 shall be divided among his said sisters, A., M., C., S., L., and R. Arie shall be free from paying rent, and also to receive, as his right of primogeniture, a stallion.—To my daughter M., wife of J. O., the other part of said lot No. 4, next to H. H.—After my wife's death my personal estate is to go to all my children, as well as horses, cattle, and other articles. Brother A. R. appointed executor. (In note: Be it known that my meaning is that all what I have here devised to my children is for all time).

ALERT ROOSA
SALOMON TERWELGE
HARMANIS OSTRANDER
TIMOTHY LOW

(Alert Roosa, Salomon Terwillege and Harmanus Oostrander, on May 3, 1749, appeared before the Court, Abraham Gaasbeek Chambers, Judge, Cornelius Hoornbeek, Johannis De Lametter, Cornelius De Lametter, Cornelis Dupuy, assistant justices, proving the will, and signature of Timothy Low, Deceased, as a witness.)

(Evert Roosa m., May 10, 1702, *Tiletje (Tit, Tietje) Van Etten,* b. Marbletown and had issue: i. *Arie,* bt. Jan. 31, 1703, m., Feb. 9, 1722, *Geesjen Oostrander;* ii. *Marytie,* bt. Sept. 8, 1706, m., Nov. 11, 1726, *Jacob Oostrander* (as it appears in the Kingston Church Records, or *Oosterhoude,* as per will); iii. *Catharina,* bt. Sept. 16, 1700, m., Jan. 17, 1729, *Luycas De Wit;* iv. *Jacobus,* bt. Apr. 22, 1711, m., after Febr. 24, 1751, *Catharina Zynders,* res. *Churchland (Saugerties);* v. *Zara,* bt. Apr. 24, 1715, m., Dec. 10, 1746, *Jan Louw;* vi. *Lea,* bt. Febr. 9, 1718; vii. *Rachel,* bt. Nov. 29, 1719; viii. *Abraham,* bt. Nov. 5, 1721, m., after June 17, 1744, *Elisabeth Rutz,* b. Rosendale, res. at a place where *Joh. Hardenberg* has lived; ix. *Aldert,* bt. Febr. 26, 1727; *Antje).*

Page 344.—BOMSCHOTEN, SALOMON, Senior, of Kingston.

Will dated Nov. 14, 1737, and written in Dutch.

(Long religious preamble.)

"Myn huysvrouw *Elsiee Bomschoten*" "myn Geheele Staat" "Geduringe haar Weduweschap."

"Tot erfgenamen "Myn Aeght Kinders" "*Tunis Bunscho Aenneca Bunschoten Maria Bunschoten Elsie Bunschoten Gerretje Bunschoten Sara Bunschoten* en *Johannis Bunschoten*"

"Aen myn twe sone Tunis en Johannis Bunschoten" "myn Geheele Staat" "Lant huyse Schuren Bogert "negers Negerinne en paerde," "na de doot van myn en myn Vrouw" "mits Conditie" "Schulden sullen betalen" "die daer syn sullen na myn en mun Vrouws doodt" "en met Conditie" "sullen betalen aan myn" "ses doghters: Elizabeth Bunschoten £70" "aen myn" "doghter Aeneca Bunschoten" "£70," aen myn Dochter Maria" "£70" aen myn doghter Elsie Bumschoten" "£70" aen myn Doghter Gerritie" "£70" aen myn Doghter Sara" "£70."

"Myn ses doghters" "Boven het geen ik haer all rede Gemack hebbe" "Except myn Boeken."

"Aen myn" "son Tunis Bumschoten" "voor Eerste gebortie reght myn Grotie Schietrore."—"Aen myn son Johannis Bumshoten" "myn klynne Rorer."—

"Myn twe" "sone" "sullen betalen" "aen myn doghters" "en Jeder £70" "in drie Jaare" "Jeder Jaer de Gerechtige derden."

"Als het mooght komen te happen" "dat een van myn Sone moghtie komen te sterven in haar Onmondige Jaare" "de Langhtslevended ofte syn Erfgenamen" shall divide his share. If both should die, the daughters to divide the property.—Similar provisions made in case of death of the daughters "in haar Onmondige Jaren."

(My wife Elsie Bomschoten my entire estate during her widowhood. As heirs I appoint my eight children (named).—To my two sons, named, my entire estate of land, houses, barns, orchard, negroes, negresses and horses, after my wife's death, on condition that they pay debts which may exist after my wife's death, and on condition that they pay to my six daughters £70 each. My six daughters all personal property except my books. To my son Tunis, as his right being my first born my large gun. To my son Johannis my little gun. My two sons are to pay my six daughters £70 each in three years, each year one third. If any of my children should happen to die during minority, the survivors are to divide his or her share.)

Son Tunis Bumschoten, and *Johannis Dumon* appointed executors.

SALOMON VAN BUNTSCHOTEN.

HENDR. HENDR. SCHOONMAKER
JOHANNIS SCHOONMAKER
SARA VAN HOOGHTEGLINGH

(June 7, 1754, *Sarah Van Buren*, wife of *Cornelis Van Buren*, formerly Sarah Van Hooghtyling the only surviving witness, appeared before the Court, proving the will.)

Zalomon Van Buntschooten, van Buytschooten, Bomshoten. van Ben-Schoten (prob. s. of *Teunis van Bomschoten* and *Gerritje Gerrits*), m., Dec. 17, 1715, *Elsjen Schoonmaker*, dau. of *Egbert Hendricksen S.* and *Annetje Berry* (see *Jochem S.*), and had issue: i. *Teunis*, bt. July 15, 1716, m., before Apr. 18, 1742, *Anna Slegt*; ii. *Egbert Hendriks*, bt. July 21, 1717; iii. *Elisabeth*, bt. Aug. 24, 1718; iv. *Anneken*, twin with E., bt. same day, m., Nov. 4, 1744, *Gerrit van Buren*; v. *Maria*, bt. Jan. 22, 1721; vi. *Catrina*, bt. Dec. 2, 1722; vii. *Elsje*, bt. July 11, 1725, m., May 24, 1747, *Cornelis Lammertsen Brink*; viii. *Gerritjen*, bt. Febr. 26, 1727; ix. *Zara*, bt. Sept. 22, 1728; and *Johannis*).

Page 348.—HOOFMAN, NICOLAS, of the County of Dutches.

Will dated Febr. 12, 1749.

"Unto my Loving Wife *Jannitie* all the Land which I bought of *Cornelis Knickerbacker* with the house barn Orchards Garden and all other Edefices Buildings and Improvements thereon and Also all the Land which I bought of *Johannis Shever* with the appurtenances Dureing her Widowhood, and also the use and occupation of all my Stock of Cattle horses & Sheep my Waggons Sleds plows harrows and all my farming Utensells Dure the time of her Widowhood of her Naturall Life also the Use of a Negro Wench to serve her Dureing her Naturall Life and the use and occupation of my beding furniture and household Goods Dureing her Widowhood." "If my wife should Deliver over the farm before the Expiration of her Life, then my said Wife Shall Receive the sum of £20" "yearly & Every Year Dureing her Naturall Life which money shall be rased & Levied out of my Estate: with the use of a Negro wench to Serve & Assist my said Wife Dureing her Naturall Life."

"Unto my Eldest son *Martin Hoofman* my negro man named *Fortune*" and "all that Tract or parcell of Land along the East Side of *Hudsens River* in Dutchess County" "from the house he now Dwelleth in to the Land I bought of Cornelis Knickerbacker and from thence along the road of said Knickerbacker to the Land of *Martinus Shoe* and from thence along the Road to the Land of *Hans Jacob Dings* & then along the fence of said Dinghs to a Valley which Streches to Hudsons River to a place on the north side of the *White Clay Kill* or brook and from thence along Hudsons River to the first Station includeing the Said Dwelling house barn and Barricks with the appurtenances" "and also my Grist mill on the East side of Hudsens River now in the Occupation of my said son with the Dam and Every thing thereunto belonging and the Land which Lueth between the fence of *Martinus Shew* & the mill Creek Containing about three acres & I do also Give unto my said Son Martin and my son *Petrus Hoofman* (to share equally) all the Land of Martinus Shoe & Hans Jacob Dings to the bounds of *Barent V Bentheysen*" "in consideration of which Martinus is to pay "unto my son Petrus" £50 "after my Decease in four Equal payments on the first day of May in Each year."—"My son Martinus" "shall pay unto my Loveing Wife Janetie" "£5 yearly & Every year Dureing the time that She Shall remain my Widow and free Grinding to lett her have & Boalting the wheat She shall raise on the Land" "and also her Bread Corn and Indian Corn meel Tole Free."

"My son *Anthony Hoofman*" "(not to reenter untill three Years after the Decease of my said wife) all the Land which I bought of Cornelis Knickerbacker with the houses barns Gardens Oarchards and all other Edifices Buildings & Improvements thereon and also all the Land I bought of *Johanis Shever* with the appertenances" "with all my Smiths tools with a Negro Wench called *Bishe*" "my son Anthony Shall pay unto my son Petrus Hoofman" "£50 after my Decease in four Equal payments on the first of may in Every year."

"Unto my son *Zacarias Hofman*' "the house of *Petrus Viele* with the barns Gardens Oarchards & all the Lotts of Land thereunto appertaining" "with a piece of Land or Swamp at or near the River of Hudson Lately in possession of *Robert Livingston* as also the Land & houses of *Christian Diederick*" "with the Land of *Jacob Best* that Runs to the River along the line of *Jan Vosburgh* that Leads to the River with the Land of William Sneyder" "with my Negro Wench *Pegge*."

"Unto my son Petrus Hoofman" "all the Land now or Late in possession of *Philip Loundert* and all the Land belonging to the two Lotts of Land the said Loundert now or Late did live on" "as also the one Equal half of the Land of Martinus Shoe and Hans Jacob Dings (in partner Ship with my Son Martin) to the bounds of Barent V Benthuysen with my two Negro Boys *Joe* & *Benjamin.*'

"Unto my Daughter *Marytie Hoofman*" "my Right & Title of the obligation Bonds of *Diederick Martestock* of £100, as also two Negro Wenches Named *Bette* & *Mary*, as also A Silver Teapott A Silver Salt box as also a Large Cubberd and Bedstead & bedding and all thereunto appertaining."

Survivors to divide share of deceased children.

"All My Land on the East Side of Hudsons River Shall Remain Coomon for my four sons" "for Cutting firewood, and" "if any of my Sons Should be Ejected or Sued for the Land I have Devised" "the rest shall Equally help and Contribute to Defend the Title and if any of them Should Loose the part or Share of Land them Respectively Given or be Invicted thereof or of part thereof the rest of my said Sons Shall make Good the Vallue of Such Land to him or them So Invicted."

"Unto my Grandson *Niccolas* son of my son Martin one Silver Spoon."

"Unto my Grandson *Niccolas* Son of my son Anthony one Silver Spoon."—"Unto my daughter *Maritye*" "all the Silver Spoons Excepting the two above mentioned."

All four sons appointed executors. Signed by the testator.

JACOBUS PERSEN
JOISG KLUN
JOHN WEST

(Febr. 1, 1752, before me *Theodorus Van Wyck*, Judge of the Court of Common Pleas for Dutchess County, *John Brinkerhoff* and *Arnout Viele*, Justices of the Peace, appeared Jacobus Persen and *George Clom* proving the will."—John Crooke, Clerk).

August 5, 1754.

(Niccolas Hoofman was son of *Martinus Hoffman* (*Marten Hermanse Hoofman*), of *Sweden*, who m. in Ref. Dutch Church, *Brooklyn*, Apr. 22, 1663, *Lysbeth Hermans*, and 2dly, May 16, 1664, *Emmerentje De Witt*, a sister of *Tjerck Claessen De Witt* (q. v.).—Nicholas, m., after Dec. 30, 1704, *Jannetje*, dau. of *Antony Crispel* (q. v.), and had issue: i. *Martin*, bt. March 17, 1706, settled in *Red Hook*, m. 1., 1733, *Tryntje*, dau. of *Robert Benson* and *Cornelia Roos*, and 2., *Alida*, dau. of *Philip Livingston*; ii. *Antje*, bt. Febr. 11, 1709; iii. *Anthony*, bt. March 18, 1711, settled in Kingston, m., Jan. 6, 1738, *Catharine*, dau. of *Abraham Gaasbeck Chambers* (q. v.); iv. *Zachariah*, bt. Dec. 6, 1713, lived at *Shawangunk* (q. v.); v. *Petrus*, bt. Dec. 22, 1716; vi. *Hendricus*, bt. June 7, 1719; vii. *Annetjen*, bt. Dec. 3, 1721; viii. Marytje, b. 1730).

Page 356.—ELMENDORPH, WILHELMUS, of Hurly.

Will dated March 7, 1754, and written in Dutch.

(Long religious preamble.)

"Het Lant welk ik Gekopt heb van *Gysbert Vandenbergh* En Ook het Lant Welck ik Gekoght heb van *Dirck* En *Abraham Rosa* dat Sal Verkogt werden op te profytelyste Maniere om myn Schult meede te betalen En So dat Selve niet genoeg mag weesen So Will ick dat So Vell van my Vee verkogt werde."

"Myn Waerde Huysvrouw *Jenneke*" "Gedurende haer Weduwschap alles het overige van myn Geheele" "Staat." "Maer als Sy wederom komt te Hertrouwen" "Sal alleenigte Vreede Moete Syn met de Dienst van myn Negerin (*Dien*) Genaemt En het Negertje (Herry) Genaemt Gedurende haer Leeven," and after her death to the children.

"Myn Soon *Koenraedt*" "myn Schietroer Twee Pistools en houwer En myn Ruyters Sadel En" "Een Geregte darde part van al het Overige van myn" "Staedt."

"Aen myn dogter *Hendrika*" "Een geregte darde part van all myn" "Staadt."—"Aan myn Dogter *Blandiena*" "Een Geregte darde part."

Survivors to divide share of deceased children.

"Myn Oom *Dirck Wynkoop* En Myn Broeder *Luykes Elmendorph*" appointed executors. Signed by the testator.

(The land which I purchased from Gysbert Vandenbergh as well as the land which I bought from Dirck and Abraham Rosa shall be sold to pay my debts, and if that should not be enough, my cattle are to be sold.— My worthy wife, Jenneke to have the residue of my entire estate during her widowhood. If she should happen to marry, she is to be satisfied with the service of my negress Dien and the negroboy Herry during her life. To my son Koenraedt my gun, two pistols, one broadsword, and my riding saddle, and one third part of the residue of my estate. My uncle Dirck Wynkoop, and my brother Luykes Elmendorph appointed executors.)

JAN VAN DUESEN
MARGRIETJE DUBOES
JAN ELTINGE

(On Dec. 16, 1754, Jan Van Deusen, Junr. and Jan Eltinge appeared before the Court, proving the will, and the signature of Margrietje Dubois as a witness.)

(W. E. was son of *Coenradt E.* and *Blandina Kierstede* (q. v.), and had issue: i. *Henrica*, bt. Oct. 8, 1749, m., Nov. 16, 1771, *Gerrit Elmendorf*, s. of *Gerrit E.* and *Jannetje Newkerk*; ii. *Conrad*, bt. Dec. 8, 1751, m., Aug. 18, 1776, *Annatje van Steenberg*, bt. June 9, 1754; iii. *Blandina*, bt. Jan. 20, 1754, m., Apr. 28, 1776, *Cornelis Eltinge*, s. of *Jonas E.* and *Magdalena Du Bois*).

The following will, in possession of Benj. M. Brink, Esq., of Kingston, is not recorded anywhere, so far as is known.

PERSEN, MATTHYS, of Kingston.

Will dated July 20, 1748, and written in Dutch.

(Long religious preamble.)

"Aen myn oudste Soon *Adam Persen*, voor syn Regt van Eerstgeboorte" "ses Schelling." (To my eldest son, for his birth-right, six schillings.)

"Aen myn drie Soons" "Adam, *Jan En Cornelus*" "Een geregte Derde part In myn twe Mans plaetse In Onse Kerk Hier in Kingstoun." (To my three sons (named), each a third interest in my two men's seats in our church here in Kingston.)

"Myn gesyde Soon Cornelis" "all myn kleerasie aen Myn Lichaem behoorende." (To my said son, Cornelis, all my clothing, belonging to my body.)

"Aen myn Waerde En beminde huysvrouw *Tanna Persen* Een geregte Drder part van al myn Roerende Staedt, En nog Desom van Dertigh pont" "En alle haer klerasie, En Linne Goet, Als Laken, En Sloopen" "De Rest van al myn Roerende En onroerende Staet gedurende haer Weduwschap." (To my worthy and beloved wife the just third part of all my personal estate, also £30, all her clothing, linnen-ware, as sheets, and pillow-cases, and all the rest of my real estate during her widowhood.)

"Aen myn Dogter *Sara*, En Aen de Drie Dogters van myn overlede Dogter *Annatje*, met name *Sara, Tanneke* En *Cattrina*, Alle myn Linne Goet van Lakens En Slopen han Docken En tafel Lakens (om te genieten na myn vrouws overlyde) En dat als dan de Drie Dogters van myn Dogter Annetje, In haer Moeders plaets, Met Myn Dogter Sare het selve Dele Eengael." (To my daughter Sara, and the three daughters of my daughter Annatje, deceased (named), all my linnen-ware of sheets and pillow-cases, towels, and table cloths (to enjoy after my wife's death) the three daughters of my daughter Annatje to take their mother's place in dividing with my daughter Sare.)

"To son Adam 1/5 of the entire estate, after his mother's death."— Son Jan 1/5, son Cornelis 1/5 part.

"De nege kinderen van myn overleden Dogter *Anna*, Met Name, *Hiskia, Mattheus, Jacobus, Davidt, Cornelis, Adam, Sara, Tanneke* En *Cattrina* (to the nine children of my daughter Anna, deceased) 1/5 part of the estate.

"Aen myn Dochter *Sara*, huysvrouw van *Tobias Van Steenberge*" (to my daughter Sara, wife of T. van S.) 1/5 part. Survivor to divide share of deceased, if without issue.

Wife, sons, "myn two Schoonsoons *Hiskia Dubois* En Tobias Van Steenbergen" (sons in law), appointed executors.

Signed by the testator.

JOHANNIS DE LAMETTER
JAN ELTINGE
WILLEM ELTINGE

(A seal of red sealing-wax, with an eagle displayed, as a device, attached hereto.)

(*Mattys Pars, Peers, Puis, Persen*, m. *Anna Winnen* (*Tanna Winne*), Dec. 7, 1701, and had issue: i. *Anna*, bt. Oct. 11, 1702, m., June 17, 1722, *Hiskia Dubois;* ii. *Adam*, bt. Jan. 13, 1706, in *Kinderhook* (m., June 25, 1736, *Catalyntje Swart*); iii. *Jan*, bt. Oct. 24, 1708, (m., Dec. 14, 1748, *Deborah van Bergen*); iv. *Sarah*, bt. Nov. 10, 1710, m. 1., March 4, 1732, *Abraham Elting*, m. 2., Oct. 8, 1737, *Tobias Van Steenberge;* v. *Cornelis*, bt. Oct. 26, 1712, m. 1., Aug. 31, 1734, *Catharin Dyrk* (*Turk*), and 2., Oct. 4, 1748, *Alida van Slyk* (see his will); vi. *Maria*, bt. Febr. 22, 1719).

BOOK OF DEEDS VI. (1760).

Page 235.—LEGG, JOHN, of Kingston.

Will dated Dec. 15, 1743.

"Unto my Oldest Son *William Legg*" "my Gun and Sword with my Farm or Peice of Low land Lying or Joining next to the Land of *Tyrick Schoonmaker* then runing along the Creek to the *Great Ditch* then runing along said Ditch to the Sothermost Corner thereof, from thence Westerly to a marked Stone and from thence Southerly with a Straight Line to another marked Stone with the Upland House, barn, Berke, Oarcherd, Garden and all thereunto Appertaining, with another Peice of Ground Known by the name of *Dudleys Plantation,* Lying above the Fall with the One Equal half of the Saw Mill with the Priviledges thereunto belonging then Runing from the Fall up the Ridge that Leads Southerly from said Fall to the Narrowest part of the Ridge, from thence Southwesterly to another marked Stone with the one Equal half of my Real Estate known by the name of *Peter Mours's Land,* with the one Equal half of my right in the great Fly with the one ffifth part of all my Moveables as also my Negro Man named *John,* you to pay the one Equal half of the rent of your Brother *John* Land bought of *Ed'd Wood*" "& paying unto my Daughter *Nieltie* wife of *Peter Luyck* the sum of £60" "£15 to be paid within three Months after my Decease & £15 to be paid in twelve months following," "and £15" "in the twelve Months following the Last"; also "paying unto my Daughter *Sara Legg*" "the sum of £34" (to be paid in a similar manner).

"To my Son John Legg" "that Piece of Ground which I bought of Edward Wood with four acres of Marsh Lying on the *Flatts* with the House, Barn, Berke, Orchard, Garden" "with a piece of Low & uplant" "between the two first pieces of Land above mentioned of my son William with one Equal half of the Saw Mill with the priviledges" "with the one Equal half of my Real Estate known by the name of Peter Mours's Land with the one Equal half of my right in the great Fley with the one fifth part of all my Moveables Except my Gun & Sword" "also my Negrou Man named *Cuffe,*" "paying unto my Daughter *Susanna Legg* the sum of £60 (in a similar manner as before indicated); also "paying unto my Daughter Sara Legg" £26 (in a similar manner).

"Unto my Daughter *Nieltie,* wife of *Peter Luyck* (the Just fifth part of all my Movables Except my Gun & Sword."—"Unto my Daughter Susanna Legg" "one fifth of the Moveables."—"Unto my daughter Sara Legg" "one fifth of the moveables."

Sons William and John Legg appointed executors with son in law Peter Luyck. Signed by the testator.

ANDRIES VAN LEUVAN	(Sept. 18, 1765, Peter Van Luven of
PETER VAN LEIVEN	Kingston appeared before George
JOHN WEST	Clinton, Surrogate, proving the will.)

(Jan (John) Legg, s. of *William Legg* and *Susanna Maret* (q. v.), m., Apr. 21, 1701, *Annetje Fynhout*, and had issue: i. *Neeltje*, bt. Nov. 29, 1702, m., after May 19, 1722, *Peter Luyck*, b. in *Germany*; ii. *Susanna*, bt. Sept. 3, 1704; iii. *Willem*, bt. Oct. 31, 1708, m., Oct. 20, 1738, *Helena Ploeg* (see his will); iv. *Samuel*, bt. Jan. 28, 1710; v. *Cornelis*, bt. Apr. 5, 1713; vi. *Jan*, bt. Febr. 19, 1716, m., June 19, 1741, *Beeletjen Kool*, b. *Dutchess Co.*; and *Sara*).

BOOK OF DEEDS VII. (GG), 1770—1780.

Page 490.—NEWKIRK, JOHANNIS, of the Wall Kill, yeoman.

Will dated October 5, 1771.

"In perfect Health."

"To well beloved son *Hendrick Newkirk*" "all that lott pice or parcel of Land situate in the Precinct of the Wall kill" "containing 200 acres, which I purchased of *George Harrison* and others whereon he the said Hendrick now lives 100 acres whereof I formerly conveyed to him with the Hereditaments and appurtenances," "in fee Simple Chargeable" "with the payment of £20" "to my second Daughter *Elezabeth* now married to *Jacob Bordine* being part of a legacy herein after bequeathed to her."

"To my well beloved Son *Adam Newkirk*" "all that Farm Lott pice or parcel of Land whereon he" "now lives which I purchased from the Heirs Executors or Devises of *Fredrick Philips* deceased," "in fee Simple" on "payment of £20" "unto my Daughter *Rachel* her being my Youngest Daughter now married unto *Stavannis Christ*" "part of a lagacy herein after bequeathed to her."

"To my well beloved Son *Jacob Newkirk*" "all that the Northwestermost full and Eaqual Moity or half part of the Farm or Lott of Land I did formerly live on being Lott Number fifteen of a Tract of Land" "in Walkill" "called the *Five Thousand Acres* which Lott I purchased of *William Sharps*, Esq., Deceased, being bounded Southerly by a line run Northeast and Southwest and Also the one full and Equal undivided Moiety or half part of fifty acres of Land in the same Tract called the undevided which I also purchased of the said William Sharps," "in fee Simple all which I have let unto him by a Lase, June 10, 1769."

"To my well beloved Son *Johnnis Newkirk*" "All that the Southermost Equal Moity or half Part of the Farm or Lott of Land I formerly lived on Situate in the Precinct of the Wallkill" "bounded Northwesterly by the line dividing the Part thereof" "devided to Jacob Newkirk" "and Also all the remaining Equal undevided Moity or half Part of the said 50 acres of Land called the undevided" "in fee simple" on "payment of £20 "to my daughter Rachel and my Daughter Elezebeth" "in Case that any of three Sons Refuses to pay the Money" "to my Daughters" "that they my two Daughters is to Possess their Lands."

"Unto my Daughter *Ann Mree* one Negro Winch named *Phill* which I have given *Yoest German* her Husband a Bill of Sale of July 27, 1771, which I gave him in her Portion."

Sons Hendrick and Johannis Newkirk appointed executors. Signed by the testator.

JAMES CONNELLER
BENYAMEN KONSTPEL
CHRISTOPHEL CONSTABLE

(Febr. 7, 1777, Benjamin and Christopher Constable, both of Hanover Precinct, yeomen, appeared before the Surrogate proving the will, and signature of James Connellen. Geo. Clinton, Surrogate. Christ. Tappen, Dep. Clerk.

(Johannes (Jan) Newkerk, son of *Cornelis Gerritse* (*Newkerk*), q. v., m. *Dorothea Douw* (*Douwe*), and had issue: i. *Adam;* ii. *Jacob;* iii. *Johannis;* iv. *Ann Mary*, m. *Joost German;* v. *Adrian*, bt. June 12, 1720; vi. *Hendericus*, bt. Nov. 12, 1721; vii. *Elizabeth*, bt. March 24, 1723, m. *Jacob Bodine;* viii. *Gerrit*, bt. Dec. 20, 1724; ix. *Meyndert*, bt. Apr. 17, 1726; x. *Neeltjen*, bt. Apr. 7, 1728; xi. *Rachel*, m. *Stavennus Christ.*

Page 564.—SMITH, JOHANNIS, of Marbletown.

Will dated Aug. 13, 1776.

"It is my Express Will and Command that all my Estate both Real and personal be sold and disposed of" "for the Benefitt of my Children."

"My Executors shall have power to Use for the Education of my Son *Abraham* so much of the money made out of my Estate" "for his further Education as they" "shall think fit and proper."

Of the remainder "one third part to my Daughter *Marrslye*" "as soon as she shall arrive to the Age of 18 years."

"Also one third part of said Money to my Daughter *Nelly* as soon as she shall arrive to the age of 18 Years."

The remaining third part "shall be paid to my Son Abraham as soon as he shall arrive at the years of 21."

"My two Brothers *Petrus* and *Fallen Smith* and my good frind *Matthew Cantine*" appointed executors, and Overseers. Signed by the testator.

WM. CANTINE
JOHN KEALET
JAMES CONES

(March 14, 1780, William Cantine appeared before the Court, *Dirck Wynkoop*, Judge, proving the will, and signatures of the other witnesses.)

(*Johannes* (*Jan*) *Smit* with wife *Margriet Schoonhoven* had: i. *Abraham*, bt. Aug. 1, 1725; ii. *Hendrik*, bt. Nov. 6, 1726; iii. *Daniel*, bt. Nov. 3, 1728).

BOOK OF DEEDS VIII. (HH), 1780--1785.

Page 14.—KRANS, JOHANNIS, of the Precinct of Hanover.

Will dated April 17, 1775.

"To my loving Wife *Christeen*, a Negro Girl named *Nancy*."

"To my sons *Hendricus Krans, Stofel Krans*, and *Petrus Krans* each" "£15" "one year after my decease And whereas I lent my son *Wilhelmus* the sum of £48.4.0" "he pay unto my Executors" "the sum of £33 and the remaining £15 to remain in his own hands And besides what I have already given unto my son *Jacobus*" "unto my said son Jacobus the sum of £5."

'To my daughters *Catherine* the wife of *John Williams* and to *Elizabeth* the wife of *Andries Trumper* the sum of £15" "one year after my decease."

"To my Daughters *Susannah Krans* and *Maria Krans* each the sum of £30" "as they arrive to the age of 21 years, or Day of marriage which may first happen. If Maria should die, her share to go to Susannah.

"To my gran Daughter *Elizabeth Krans* the sum of £30" "when she arrives at the age of 18 Years or Day of marriage" "provided she will discharge my Estate, and my son Petrus concerning an Inventory of her Fathers Effects, which was taken by my said son Petrus and disposed of by him."

"Unto my son *Adam* all the Farm and Messuage, whereon I now dwell, and all the Lands and Tenement that is in my possession at the Time of my Death including all my Estate real and personal whatsoever" "and I charge him with the payment of all the Legacies abovementioned."

"My said son Adam shall give my said wife a good suffecient maintenance so long as she shall remain my Widow."

Son Adam and "my brother in law *Jacob Milspaugh*" appointed executors. Signed by the testator.

JOHANNIS FELDEN
CHRISTOPHER MOULL
JAMES FULTON

(July 5, 1777, Johannis Felden & Christopher Moull of Hanover, yeomen, appeared before *Jacobus Bruyn*, Surrogate, proving the will, and signature of James Fulton as a witness.)

Page 24.—HARDENBERGH, LEONARD, of the Township of Marbletown.

Will dated June 12, 1766.

"Unto my Eldest Son *Gerradus*" "the Sum of 20 Shillings in Bann of what he can claim as my Heir at Law."

"Unto my Loving Wife *Rachel* all my Real and Personall Estate" "to use Occupy possess and Enjoy the same and have the income thereof during her natural Life or as long as she shall remain my Widow she making no Spoil Wast or Destruction thereupon and from and after her Decease or Remarriage which of the two may first happen."

"I Give Devise and Bequeath the same (that is all my said Real and Personale Estate) unto my Children" "Gerradus, *Philip, Leonard, Abraham, Cathrine & Margrieth.*"

If any of the children "should die before they come to the age of 21 years without lawful Issue of his her or their Body begotten" the share to be divided among the survivors.

Wife appointed executrix and "my Eldest Son Gerradus and my Brother *Johannis Hardenbergh* Executors."

Signed by the testator.

A DE WITT
NATHANIEL CANTIEN
WILLIAM PICK

"My will is that my Executrix and Executors" "shall in convenient Time after my Decease first pay all my Just Debts. June 12, 1766."
(May 8, 1782, Nathaniel Cantine appeared before the Court, proving the will and signatures of *Andries De Witt* and William Pick as witnesses.) Entered at the Request of Mr. Johannis L. Hardenbergh May 12, 1782.

(Leonard Hardenberg, son of Col. *Johannes H.*, q. v., m., Nov. 7, 1738, *Rachel Hoogteling*, and had issue: i. *Sara*, bt. May 21, 1739; ii. *Philippus*, bt. in *Marbletown*, Febr. 23, 1746; iii. *Leonardus*, bt. Apr. 15, 1750; iv. *Abraham*, bt. Sept. 5, 1756, besides *Gerrardus, Catherine* and *Margaret*.)

Page 72.—RAINEY, JAMES, of Hannover, Yeoman.

Will dated August 1, 1775.

"Unto my two Sons *Samuel* and *David*" "all that Lot of 549 acres of Land or thereabout and the Farm whereon I now live with the Appurtenances by me purchased of the *Widow Phillipse* and her children the one half to my said son Samuell on which he now lives on the Weast side of the Dwarse Kill" "and the other half thereof to my said Son David on the East side of the Dwarse Kill on which I now live" "the East Division of said lot shall include the said Creek but no farther from the North side of said Lot to the first falls in Cluding the falls and no farther."

"After Payment of my just Debts and funerall Charges I Give" "unto my Daughters *Hesia Mary Christian Esther*" £4 each."

"To my Daughters *Martha Ruth* and *Susen* all my Personal Estate to be Equally Divided."

"To my Beloved Wife *Sara* the full use and Benefit of my said Farme whereon I live as also of all my Personal Estate" "During the term of her Widowhood and no longer."

Wife Sara and *William Wilkin* and *John Wilkin* appointed executors. Signed by the testator.

JOHN WILKIN
JAMES STRAHAN
GAVIN MILLAR

(March 2, 1776, James Strahan, Cordwainer, appeared before George Clinton, Surrogate, proving the will, and signatures of the other witnesses.)

BOOK OF DEEDS IX. (II), 1785. (WRONGLY MARKED 10).

Page 13.—ELMENDORPH, PETRUS EDMUNDUS, of Kingston, Merchant.

Will dated May 17, 1763.

"Unto my Welbeloved Wife *Mary Elmendorph* All the income of all my whole Estate, Real and personal during all such Time as she shall remain my Widdow and not longer, But if in case she should merry again then my Estate shall be divided amongst my Children."

"Unto my Son *John* my best Horse, Saddle and Bridle for his Birth right."

"Unto my five Children: John, *Catharine, Blandina, Elizabeth* and *Sara*" "All my whole Estate Real and Personal to be divided between them soon after my Wifes Decease or after her Marriage again, Share and Share alike."

Wife, son John and "my Brother *Lucas Elmendorph*" appointed executors, "to have £25 each." Signed by the testator.

JOHANNES SCHOONMAKER
R. JOSIAS ELTINGE
JOHN D. WYNKOOP

(Sept. 27, 1765, John D. Wynkoop of Kingston appeared before *George Clinton,* Surrogate, proving the will, and signatures of the other witnesses.)

(P. E. E., son of Major *Coenradt E.* (q. v.) and *Blandina Kierstede,* for many years Sheriff of Ulster Co., and Surrogate at the time of his death, m., Apr. 29, 1743, *Mary,* dau. of *John Crook,* County Clerk, and had issue: i. *John,* bt. Febr. 3, 1745; ii. *Catherine,* bt. Febr. 1, 1747, m., Oct. 31, 1768, *Rutger Bleeker,* of *Albany;* iii. *John,* bt. March 24, 1749; iv. *William,* bt. May 12, 1751; v. *Blandina,* bt. Aug. 12, 1753; m. March 18, 1782, *Jacobus Bruyn,* bt. Oct. 27, 1751, s. of *Severyn B.* and *Catherine Ten Broeck;* vi. *William,* bt. June 22, 1755; vii. *Elisabeth,* bt. Jan. 30, 1757, m. *Cornelius Ray* of N. Y.; viii. *Sara,* bt. Apr. 8, 1759; ix. *Petrus Edmundus,* bt. Apr. 19, 1761; x. *Petrus Edmundus,* bt. Sept. 23, 1764, m. *Eliza Van Rensselaer.*

"In memory of Peter Edmundus Elmendorf, born the 27th day of August, 1715, and departed this life July 13th, 1765, aged 50 years. Mary Elmendorf, his wife, born the 15th Aug., 1721, and died the 15th of Aug., 1794, aged 73 years."—Inscription on tombstone in the First Dutch Ref. Church-yard at Kingston).

BOOK OF DEEDS X. (KK), 1787—1791. (WRONGLY MARKED 11).

Page 31.—VAN AALSTEYN, MARTINUS, of Skoherry Kill, Co. Albany.

Will dated July 15, 1784.

"Unto *Nicholas Gerleogh* a small piece of Land Adjoining to the Skoherry Kill Begining on the West Bank of said Kill whare the division fence between *Isaac Van Aalsteyn* and the said Martinus Van Aalsteyn joins upon the said Kill and so along said fence Westerly to the first brook or run of Water and then along the said run of Water down the Streem to where it empties into the Skoherry Kill and then along said Kill to the place of beginning Containing about 8 or 9 Acres be the same more or less."

"Unto my Cousin *Peter Laruah* now living with me all my Goods and Chattels and personal Estate to Gether with all my Substance whatsoever."—"Also all the rest of my Lands and Tenements lying at the Skoherry Kill in the County of Albany, and now in my possession, together with the House Barn and Orchard, and all the other Appurtenances thereto belonging."

"My true and trusty friend John Laruah and Isaac Van Aalsteyn" appointed executors.

MARTYNUS VAN AALSTEYN (his mark).

JEREMIAH ELIGH
PETER WEST
GEYSBERT DEDERICK

(Oct. 6, 1787, Jeremiah Eligh and Geysbert Dederick appeared before the Court of Common Pleas of Ulster County, Dirck Wynkoop, Judge, proving the will, and signature of Peter West as a witness.)

Page 208.—ELMENDORPH, COENRAET, of Kingston.

Will dated Sept. 2, 1749.

"If my beloved wife *Blandina Elmendorph* survives me" "she shall remain in full Possession of all my Real and Personall Estate During her Wedowhood; and in case shee Marry then shee is only to have out of my Estate the sum of £15" "yearly during her Natural life."

"To my Eldest son *Jacobus Elmendorph*" "over and above his share of my Estate my fowling piece Sword and belt and my Cane."—"Also" "five Morgen of Land" "on the North side of *Esopus Creek* after myn and my Wifes Decease and to take the same where he pleases in my said

Land (Provided he takes the same in one piece and to begin at one of the four corners of my said Land)" "and to "pay for the same at or before the Expiration of three Years after myn and wifes Decease to my Executors the sum of £180" "to be divided Among All my Children."

"Whereas My son *Coenraedt Elmendorph Junr.* has a Conveyance of me for my Land in the *Wassemakers Land* and has given me a Bond for the payment of the sum of £400" "within three years after myn and Wifes Decease, And he has Allso promised and agreed with mee to pay the sum of £20" "more In the same manner as the 400 My Will is that the said £420 shall be Divided in like manner Among all my Children."

"Whereas I have paid for my son *Gerrit Elmendorph* £180" "for five Morgan of Land which he had bought of *Simon Van Wagenen* My Will is that" "he pay the said sum to my Executors within three years after myn and Wifes Decease to be Divided among all my Children" "in Case" he "should happen to deny refuse neglect or Delay to pay the said sum" then "my said son Gerrit" "shall be Utterly Excluded and Debarred from having any Right or Benefit by or in this Will."

"Whereas I have conveyed to my son *Petrus Edmundus Elmendorph* five morgan of Land on the north side of the Esopus Creek my will is that my said son" "pay for the same £180" "within three years after my and Wifes Decease to be Divided among all my Children."

"Whereas I have conveyed unto my son *Luykes Elmendorph* five Morgan of Land My Will is that he" "pay for the same unto my Executors the sum of £180" within three years (as before).

If they deny or refuse, or neglect to pay, they are to be debarred from all benefits.

"To my son *Cornelus Elmendorph*" "five Morgan of Land on the north side of the Esopus Creek, he to pay £180 within three years."

"To my son *Wilhelmus Elmendorph*" "five Morgan of my land on the north side of the Esopus Creek" and to pay therefore £180.

"To my son *Jonathan Elmendorph*" "five Morgan of my Land on the north side of Esopus Creek" and to pay therefor £180.

"To my three sons" "each one third part of my Dwelling House where I now live in Together with barn, buildings orchards Gardens and pasters" "between the Esopus Creek and the Kingsroad and between the Land of my son Gerrit and ye Land of the *Widow Schepmoes*, And also my Bushland or pasture" "between the Land of Capt. *John Sleght* and the Heirs of *John Rosa* and between the Land of my son Petrus and my son Luykes" each to pay therefor £20 to be divided among the children.

"To my son Luykes all my Coopers tools and Utensils."—"To my son Wilhelmus All my weavers tuels and Utensils."—"To my son Jonathan all my Shoomakers tools with Leather and all utensils."—"My sons shall each take possession of the Lands" "given them" "as soon as my wife departs this life or at the day of her Marriage."

"After my wifes Decease or marriage all the Remainder of my Real & Personall Estate" "and the Priviledges I have in the woods on the south side of the Esopus Creek in *Hurly* (called *Cool and Company*), "As Allso all the money" "to be paid by my sons to my Executors shall be equally Devided among all my Children: Jacobus, Gerrit, Cornelis, Coenraedt, Petrus Etmundus, Luykes, Wilhelmus, Jonathan, *Jenneke* Widow of *Abraham Ten Eyck* Deceased *Margrieta* Wife of Mr. *Gerrit Dubois* and *Sarah Elmendorph*," "each 1/11 part."

Sons Jacobus, Petrus Etmundus, and Luykes appointed executors. Signed by the testator.

ALDERT KIERSTED
JAN ELTINGE
WILLEM ELTINGE

(Oct. 24, 1788, Jacomyntje Eltinge appeared and swore "that she was well acquainted with the handwriting of her Brother Jan Eltinge now deceased that she has frequently seen him write his name in his lifetime, that she has viewed the handwriting and Name of Jant Eltinge Subscribed hereunto as one of the Witnesses to the within Will, and veriely believes the same to be the handwriting of her said Brother."—"I therefore do allow the same to be Recorded." Dirck Wynkoop (first Judge of the Court of Common Pleas for Ulster Co.)

(C. E., son of Jacobus E. and Grietje van Wagenen (q. v.), had with first wife, *Arientje:* i. *Jacobus*, bt. June 3, 1694, m. Dec. 1, 1722, *Ariaantje Newkerk*, bt. Nov. 19, 1699, dau. of *Ariaan Gerritsen* and *Lysbeth Lammertje;* ii. *Gerrit*, bt. Jan. 26, 1696, m. Jan. 15, 1730, *Jannetjen Nieuwkerk*, bt. Oct. 12, 1712, dau. of *Gerrit Nieuwkerk* and *Grietje Ten Eyck;* iii. *Cornelis*, bt. Oct. 31, 1697, m. Dec. 16, 1720, *Engeltje Heermans*, bt. Sept. 11, 1698, dau. of *Jan. H.* and *Annatje Aartse (van Wagenen);* iv. *Margrietje*, bt. Jan. 1, 1701, d. y. By 2d wife: *v. Jenneke*, bt. Jan. 6, 1706, m. Dec. 18, 1726, *Abraham Ten Eyck*, bt. Nov. 5, 1699, s. of *Matthys T. E.* and *Janneke Rosa;* vi. *Margrietje*, bt. June 20, 1708, m. July 17, 1731, *Gerrit Du Bois*, bt. Febr. 13, 1704, s. of *Jacob Dubois* and *Gerritje Gerritsen;* vii. *Coenrad*, bt. Oct. 10, 1710, m. June 21, 1734, *Sarah Dubois*, bt. Dec. 20, 1713, dau. of *Jacob Dubois* and *Gerritje Gerritsen;* viii. *Sara*, bt. Jan. 25, 1713; ix. *Petrus Edmundus*, bt. Sept. 11, 1715, m. April 29, 1744, *Mary Crook*, bt. Aug. 20, 1721, dau. of *John C.* and *Catrina Janse*, (he died July 13, 1765); xi. *Wilhelmus*, bt. Febr. 19, 1721, m. June 17, 1748, *Janneke Low*, bt. Nov. 18, 1722, dau. of *Timotheus L.* and *Hendrikje Kool* (see his will); xii. *Jonathan*, bt. Dec. 26, 1723, m. 1., May 29, 1749, *Helena Smedes*, bt. Aug. 25, 1728, dau. of *Petrus S.* and *Catherine Dubois*, m. 2., Oct. 6, 1675, *Catherine Ten Broeck*, bt. June 11, 1727, dau. of *Johannes T. B.* and *Rachel Roosa*, and widow of *Severin Ten Hout;* xiii. *Tobyas*, bt. March 12, 1727.)

Page 274.—SNYDER, MARTINUS, of Kingston, Yeoman.

Will dated May 5, 1778.

"My Dear beloved Wife *Aantje* shall have the income of my whole Estate Real and Personall during her life."

"To my beloved Son *Zacheriah* for his birth right as my eldest Son my Gun or fuzee."

"My two Sons: *Martynis* and *Isaak* shall have my whole Estate Real and Personall" "provided they comply with my directions hereafter."

"My said two sons, Martinis and Isaak shall in lieu of the said State hereby given to them, shall after the decease of me and my Wife pay" "unto my Children: Zachariah, *Johannis, Jeremiah, Willem, Christian,*

Benjamin, Hendricus & *Abraham* the Sum of £300 (£40 to each).—They shall also pay "to my three Daughters £90" "to the Heirs of my Daughter *Aantje* the late Wife of *Johannis Hommel*" £30—"Unto my Daughter *Grietje* the wife of *Johannis Wolven*" £30—"Unto my Daughter *Cattrienna* the Wife of *Jacobus Rosa*" £30, "including £16 which she hath already received."

"Unto son Isaak my little Negro Boy named *Jack*."—If Martinus or Isaak should die without issue, their shares to be divided among the survivors.

"My beloved sons Benjamin and Martynis" appointed executors.

MARTYNUS SNYDER (his mark)

CORNEL BICKER
HENRY BICKER
JOH'S SNYDER

(On May 9, 1789, Johannis Snyder appeared before Dirck Wynkoop, Judge, proving the will, and signatures of the other witnesses).—The will allowed to be recorded.—A true Record entered at the request of Capt. Zacharias Snyder this 11th day of May 1789.

Christ Tappen, Dep. Clerk.)

(Martinus Snyder (*Martin Schneider*) was born at *Hackenberg, Germany*, June, 1698, and m. there *Annah Deamute Backer* (*Anna Demold Bakkerin, Becker*), b. in 1703. They emigrated to this country with son Henry, settling in *New Paltz*, and afterwards in *Kingston*, near a stream called *Mud Kill*. M. S. brought the following certificate: "I certify that Martin Snyder from *Kished*, his wife and two children, from the government of *Hackenberg*, in the church district of *Flounders*, felt desire to go to America, and the *Kirckenberg* enquired regarding his standing, which was found to be good, and that he was of good moral character. He therefore secured some assistance for his passage, and the Prima Kerckkberg granted him full permission to leave. Whereunto he has caused his seal to be affixed and signed his own handwriting in *Swenenberg*, 26 March, 1726. I. D. L. Griekholf" (Transl. for 'Olde Ulster,' Jan. 1905).

They had: i. *Henry*, bt. Aug. 10, 1723; ii. *Annah*, m. *Johannes Hommel;* iii *Margarit*, bt. Oct. 15, 1727, m. 1., *Peter Hommel*, and 2., *Johannes Wolfen;* iv. *Catherine*, bt. Sept. 14, 1729, m. *Jacobus Roosa;* v. *Zechariah*, m. *Margaret Fiero*, d. *New Jersey*, ae. 88; vi. *Johannes;* bt. Dec. 5, 1733, m. *Helena Osterhoudt*, and d. July 24, 1809; vii. *William*, bt. Febr. 12, 1725, m. *Mary Righmyer*, and d. May 25, 1823; viii. *Jeremiah*, bt. Oct. 22, 1738, m. *Catharine Holley*, and d. June 1828; ix. *Christian*, b. Apr. 21, 1740, m. *Elizabeth Backer*, and d. Apr. 22, 1822; x. *Benjamin*, b. Nov. 24, 1742, m. *Annah Brink*, and d. Sept. 12, 1831; xi. *Henry*, m. *Maria Hommel*, and d. Jan. 1, 1832; xii. *Martin*, b. Febr. 22, 1748, m. 1., *Trineke Newkerk*, m. 2., *Mary* (*Overbagh*) *Carn*, and d. Febr. 2, 1831; xiii. *Abraham*, b. Aug. 9, 1750, m. Nov. 30, 1775, *Maria Freelich* (*Freligh*), and d. May 11, 1830; xiv. *Isaac*, b. Aug. 9, 1750, m. *Susan Margaret Carn*, and d. Jan. 26, 1829.

End of wills recorded in the Deed Books.

Abstracts of Wills on File in the County Clerk's Office, City of Kingston, N. Y.

(Entered in a Thin Folio Volume, Marked ULSTER COMMON PLEAS, Record of Wills and Testaments 1790—1827).

Page 1.—DELAMATTER, DAVID, of Kingston.

Will dated Sept. 23, 1769.

"Unto my son *David Delametter* my large Dutch bible, shouting gun, Sword, Belt, and Cane in lue and sted of any thing he might Claim as being my Heir at Law."

"Unto my Daughter *Sara De Lamatter*" "one half of all my land and Tenements" "at or near the *Platte Kill* in *Newburrow* precinct in Ulster County as also all that lot of land or home Lott" "in Kingston" "between the Lotts of *Cornelius Swart, John Beekman* and *Sara Ten Brouck* as also two acres or one Morgen of land commonly called *Armboury* adjoyning the *Kings Highway* leeding from Kingston to the Strand between the Lotts of *Jan McLeen* and *Cornelius Masten* as also my Negro Whinch *Deian* and Negrow boay *Mingo* my large Cubbord, large looking Glass and my best Bed Bedsted and all the Bed Cloths" "with the Curtains-six of my best Chairs and large joiners Table and to have so much more of my household furniture as to make and outset to what my Daughter *Catharine* has had and also two Milch Cows one Ox and one Haffer as also the sum of £162.10."

"Unto my Daughter *Catharine* the wife of *Jacob Delamatter*" "one half" "of all my lands and Tenements" "at or near the Platte Kill in the Precinct of Nueburrow" "also my Negro Whinch named *Deen* and Negroe Man named *Tone* as also the sum of £162.10."

"Unto my son David De Lamatter" "my Dwelling House and Lott of Ground as also all my Lands and Tenements" "in Kingston/Excepting the Home Lott and two acres of Armboury given to my Daughter Sara/for which David shall pay to my daughters Sara and Catharine" £250 five years after my Decease" to daughter Sara £25 yearly for five years."

"Unto son David all my wearing Appearell and two of my best Horses my Waggon Slays Plows Harrows and all my farming Utensels of all kinds, as also my bed bolster and pillows & Rugg and Blanketts which is standing in my Oald Shop or Outleat—As also one Milch Cow one Ox and one Heffer my Negrows *Dick* and *Anna*."

"Unto my daughter Sara out of the House and Lott which I have herein above devised to my son David one room in my dwelling House to wit the Chamber and liberty of passing trough the Entry or Gangway and also to have as much room in the Celler and loft as she shall have Occasion for as long as she shall remain single or Unmerryed."

"Unto my two Daughters Sara and Catharine all the rest and Residue of my household Furniture."

"Unto son David half of all my Crop in the Barn and Barks as also half of the Crop now sowed and that he shall have the use of all my Slaves Negrows and Whinches until he has Gethered in the Crop now sowed and to make use of my Cretures for Killing and Viggetables Until that time."

"Unto my three Children David, Sara and Catharine" "all the rest and Residue of my Personal Estate."

Survivors to divide share of deceased children.

Son David Delamatter and son in Law Jacob Delamatter and friend Dirck Wynkoop Junr., appointed executors. Signed by the testator.

JACOBUS DE LAMETTER
JACOB SCHRIVER
D. WYNKOOP JUNR.

(Sept. 3d Tuesday, 1790, before Dirck Wynkoop, Esq. first Judge, Jacob De Lametter, Esq., one of the Judges and Johannis Snyder, Esq., one of the Assistant Justices, appeared Jacob Snyder, proving the will.— Whereupon it was ordered by the Court that the Clerk of the said Court Record the said Will and Testament together with the proof thereof agreeable to an Act of the Legislature of the State of New York passed the 4th day of April 1786).

(Arme bowerij., i. e. poor land.)
David Delamater was son of *Abraham De Lamater* (q. v.) and m. May 10, 1728, *Laurentia* (*Louwernsjen*) *Ten Broeck*. Issue: i. *Abraham*, bt. March 2, 1729, d. y.; ii. *Zara*, bt. Febr. 18, 1733, d. y.; iii. *Johannes*, bt. Apr. 20, 1735 (m. Oct. 20, 1764, *Catharina Van Vliet*); iv. *Cornelius*, bt. May 19, 1737; v. *Jacobus*, bt. Oct. 14, 1739; vi. *Zara*, bt. March 28, 1742; vii. *David*, bt. June 10, 1744 (m. Nov. 5, 1763, *Sarah Hoffman*, d. Oct. 30, 1815); viii. *Abraham*, bt. Febr. 22, 1747; ix. *Catherine*, bt. Nov. 27, 1748 (m. Apr. 14, 1768, *Jacob De Lamater*.)

Page 5.—VAN LEUVEN, JOHN, of Marbletown, yeoman.

Will dated Oct. 9, 1781.

"All my Just debts and Funeral Expenses be well and truly paid and discharged by my son *Daniel Van Leuven*."

"My well beloved wife *Meribah* shall be and remain in full and Ample possession of my whole Estate Real and Personal" "as long as she shall remain my Widdow or depart of this life."

"Unto my Eldest son *Petrus Van Leuven* One Shilling" "for his share and portion."

"Unto my sone Daniel and unto my three Daughters" "all my Real Estate which I now possess unto my said son Daniel the North and Northeast part thereof and unto my three Daughters *Maribah, Elisabeth & Rachel* the South and Southwestermost part thereof, of a certain Division to run Between them to begin at the Southwest side of a Gully by the Corner of a fence so as the same now stands and runs then along the fence as it now stands South Easterly to the extream bounds of my land."

"Unto my son Daniel all my farming Utensels such as now on my farme belongs."

"Unto my well beloved wife Meribah all my Household furniture such as is now in the House and likewise my Bees—And Also two Maris which she now owns."

Wife and daughter Meribah appointed executors. Signed by the testator.

HENDRICUS P. OSTERHOUDT
JACOBUS ROSEKRANS
GERRET DEVENPORT

(On the first Tuesday of Jan. 1791 before the Court, *Dirck Wynkoop,* Judge, *Cornelius E. Wynkoop, Andries Bevier* and *Nathaniel Dubois,* Assistant Justices, came Jacobus Rosekrans and Hendricus P. Osterhout, proving the will, and signature of Gerrit Devenport.—A true Record entered Jan. 7, 1791.)

(*John Van Leuven* m. *Margariet Wood,* and had issue: i. *Hanna,* bt. Sept. 21, 1701; ii. *Mary,* bt. June 6, 1703; iii. *John,* bt. March 14, 1708, m. *Meriba Herker* and had issue: a. *Petrus,* b. *Rachel,* bt. Jan. 5, 1745, c. *Daniel,* m. before Jan. 18, 1778, *Elisabeth Etkens,* d. *Maribah,* e. *Elisabeth;* iv. *Dina,* bt. Jan. 6, 1712; v. *Petrus,* bt. Jan. 31, 1714 (m. June 3, 1743, *Angenietjen Van Slyk*); vi. *Catrina,* bt. Sept. 15, 1723 (m. June 11, 1744, *Johannes Davids.*)

Page 8.—SMITH, WILLIAM, of Montgomery Precinct, Yeoman.

Will dated Aug. 14, 1784.

"To my loving Wife *Elizabeth Smith* one third of the Yearly Income of my real Estate" "in said Precinct" "with my room in my Dwelling House, that She may choose also two Milch Cows and keeping for the same Summer and Winter as long as she remains my Wedow."

"My Grand Daughter *Mary Bookstaver* £125" "payable in six Months after my Decease."

"My son *Henry Smith* all my lands and Tenements whatsoever, whereof I shall die seized."

"Residue of my Goods and Chattels and Personal Estate" "to my said son Henry Smith."

Son Henry and "my Goed Friend *Adam Beamer*" appointed executors. Signed by the testator.

MATTHEW HUNTER
WILLIAM JOHNSTON
JOHN MCKINSTRY

(On the first Tuesday (of Jan.) 1791 came John McKenstry, proving the will, and signatures of the other witnesses.)

Page 10.—LEFEVER, ANDRIES, of the New Paltz.

Will dated April 19, 1738.

(Long religious preamble).

"Unto my Dearly beloved Wife *Cornelae Lafeaver* all my whole Estate Rale and persenally during her widdow Ship or naturall If She never Marry es as also I do give unto my wife all the Income of all my Money During her Widow Ship." "Unto my beloved wife" "my negro men *Charles* And the Choise of my horses."

"Unto my Eldest Son *Simon Lefaver*" "first out of my Estate my pistles & houlsters In Consideration as being my Eldest son on which account he shall not Have or pretend to have any thing more by any ways or pretenses whatsoever."

"Unto my Daughter *Elezebet* wife of *Joneton Dubois*" "my negro Girle by name *Judy* for which" she is to pay "£12" to my five Daughters: *Sary Lefever, Mary Lefever, Catrine Lefever, Magdelen Lefever* and *Rachel Lefever*."

"Unto my Daughter *Margrete*" "my Negroe Girle *Suesan*."—"Unto my Seven Daughters" "my Two Negro by name *Tom* and *Seasar* that they shall be sold and the Money devided amongst my seven Daughters when the youngest is Eighteen years old."

"Unto my two sons Simon Lefever, *Mattys Lefever*" "my Land houses out house orchards Gardens Improvements Tenements" "within" "the New Paltz" on condition that they pay" to my seven Daughters" "the sums of money" "hereafter" "is given and bequeathed unto them."

"Unto my seven daughters (named) £400 to be paid by the sons four years after the decease of my wife.

"Unto my son Simon Lefevre" "my Tenpits with all Leader Shuemakers Tools Iron Stofe or Kaffel my Gun my begg french bible."

"Unto my son Mattys Lefevre" "all my wearing Close Shurths Stocken & Shoues Every thing belonging to body my brweing pott my Two bibles one Duch one french."

"Unto my two sons" "all my farmers Utensils as of plows harrows waggons Sleds and all other Tools and Gier that is or hath been used on my farme."

"Unto my seven Daughters (named) all my Cows and all my Money out att Intrust as all my house hold goods & moveables."

"Each Daughter Shall have £12 for an out Sett if they have had none out of my Estate or In Come of the Estate & In Come of the Money Two out setts Shall be paid in a year and for every Year the Sons pay Two out setts they shall have a Year Longer to pay the aforesaid four hundred pounds."

"In case any of my Seven Daughter Shall come to dye Leaving no Chid or Children of her Body" her share to be divided.

"Unto my two sons (named) all my Horses except one horse to my wife first the Choice out of all the horses."—Also "my Two negro by name *Jack* & *James* to be Equally devided Share and Share alike."

"Unto my Seven Daughters" "all my Shipe & hoogs."

Sons Simon and Mattys and "my Brother *Jan Lefevre*" appointed executors. Signed by the testator.

JACOB HASBROUCK

NAITHEN S. BEVIER

CHARLES BRODHEAD

(On the first Tuesday in May, 1793, *John Addison*, Esq., produced to the Court the last will of Andries Lefever, it appearing" "that all the subscribing witnesses" "were ded, Whereupon *Jacob Hasbrouck* of the New Paltz appeared" "and said that he was well Acquainted with the handwriting of Jacob Hasbrouck deceased his father" "and that the lands devised in the last will of Andries Lefever have been and now are to the best of his knowledge in the Actual possession of the Heirs" "of said Andries Lefever. And *John C. Dewitt* Esq. also appeared" "and said that he was well acquainted with the handwriting of Charles Broadhead deceased"—"Whereupon the will was admitted."

(*Simon Le Fevre* (*Le Februe*), the Patentee of *New Paltz*, m. *Elisabeth Deyo*, dau. of *Christian D.* She m. 2d *Moses Cantain* and had a son, *Peter Canteine*, bt. May 21, 1693. Simon Le Fevre and Lysbeth Deojou had issue: i. *Andries*, m. *Cornelia Blansian*, and had: a. *Simon*, bt. Sept. 11, 1709, m. June 24, 1725, *Petronella Hasbrouck* (see his will); b. *Matheus*, bt. Nov. 10, 1710, m. June 17, 1737, *Margaret Bevier*; c. *Elisabeth*, bt. Sept. 28, 1712, m. Dec. 23, 1732, *Jonathan Dubois*, of *Nescotack*; d. *Margrietjen*, bt. March 13, 1715, m. June 10, 1739, *Conraed Vernooy*; e. *Zara*, bt. Febr. 3, 1717, m. June 10, 1739, *Samuel Bevier*; f. *Marytjen*, bt. March 1, 1719, m. *Nathaniel Le Fevre*; g. *Catrina*, bt. Apr. 2, 1721, m. *Simon Du Bois*; h. *Magdalena*, bt. Oct. 11, 1724, m. Sept. 2, 1749, *Johannes Bevier*; i. *Rachel*, bt. June 23, 1728, m. Sept. 2, 1749, *Johannes Bevier*, of *Wawarsing*;—ii. *Abraham*, bt. May 11, 1679, d. y.; iii. *Isaac*, bt. at *New Paltz*, Oct. 28, 1683, m. 1., *Catrina Freer* (*Fire*), m. 2., May 16, 1718, *Marytjen Freer*, dau. of *Hugo F., Jr.*; iv. *Jean*, bt. Oct. 28, 1685, m. Nov. 20, 1712, *Catherine Blanshan*; v. *Maritje*, bt. Oct. 15, 1689, m. June 18, 1713, *Daniel Du Bois*.)

Page 16.—LOW, JACOBUS, of Kingston, Merchant.

Will dated Oct. 18, 1793.

"My loving Wife *Elizabeth Low* shall have the whole of my Estate both Real and Personal as long as She shall remain my Widow, or during her natural Life (in case she does not Intermarry) she making no spoil waste or destruction thereupon, but in the first place as my sole Executrix together with my Executors after named shall discharge my Funeral Expenses," etc.

"After an Intermarriage or the Decease of my said Wife" "I give the whole of my Estate both Real and Personal between my Eight Children *John Rachel Annatie Catharina Abraham Jennetie Elizabeth* and *Jacobus*" "my son John to be accountable for the sum of £133.6.8 with lawful Interest" "being so much advance for him for his one third Part of the Purchase Money Paid for the Sloop Sall—And the Share of my Daughter Rachel shall be considered to be given in trust to be equally divided between the Children already born or that may be born of her body, but in case she may become a Widow then she shall have the full use and Disposal of such her share for and towards the Support of her self and Children."

Survivors to divide share of deceased children "under age and without lawful Issue."

Wife and "loving Brothers *Abraham* and *Benjamin Low* and my trusty and good friend *Abraham B. Bancker* Esquire", appointed executors. Signed by the testator.

JNO ELMENDORF
ADAM J. DOLE
JACOBUS HASBROUCK JUNR.

(On the 10 day of Jan., 1794, Jacobus Hasbrouck Junr. and Adam J. Dole appeared before the Court, *Dirck Wynkoop*, Judge, *Moses Cantine Junr.* and *Philip D. Bevier*, Ass't Justices, proving the will, and signature of John Elmendorf as a witness. Entered at the request of Mrs. Elizabeth Low Jan. 11, 1794).

Page 20.—DAVIS, CHRISTOPHER, of Marbletown, Farmer.

Will dated June 12, 1778.

"Its my express Desire, and I hereby direct that whomsoever my Loving Wife *Elizabeth Davis* Shall please and think proper to live, my two sons *Isaac Davis* and *John Davis* shall Yearly each pay the half towards her Maintenance during her Natural Life, provided she remains my Widow, otherwise not."

"Unto my oldest Son *Richard Davis* my Own Gun and £5."—"Unto my Second Son Isaac Davis, all my Lands known by the Name of *Shocan* or *Kiskatama* with the Buildings thereon, and all my Horse Kind and Farmers Utensils thereunto appertaining."

"Unto my Third Son *John Davis* all my Lands" "in Marbletown on both sides of the *Esopus Kill* or River with the Buildings thereon, the Blacksmiths utensils & a Mare colt which he has now in Possession but the Cow which he has now, I do give" "to him and my Daughter *Anne Davis*, Each the Half, and Each the half of the cattle that may be raised from said Cow between them."

"If my son Davis should die, having no lawful issue" then "the said last mentioned Land with the Buildings and Blacksmiths utensils thereon, be equally divided among these seven of my Children, Namely Richard Davis, Anne Davis, *Esther* the wife of *Jacob Chambers*, *Wyntje Davis*, Isaac Davis, *Elizabeth Davis* and *Rachel Davis.*'

"Unto my Daughter Elizabeth Davis the cupboard which is in the house in which my son John Davis and Daughter Anne Davis now dwell."

"Unto my two Daughters Elisabeth Davis and Rachel Davis the two Beds, which are in the house, in which I now live namely at Shocan, Kiskatama, after my Decease And the Decease of my loving Wife Elizabeth, my Daughter Rachel to have the Choice thereof."

"In consideration of the Lands and Buildings" given them, the two sons, Isaac and John "shall give (six months after my Decease) unto my Third Daughter Esther" "Curtains for a bed, and Cupboard, each to pay there and there alike."—Said sons also to give (within six months) to Rachel "a cupboard" and to Elizabeth and Rachel" 50 pounds of good Feathers and Curtains."—Son John to give (twelve months after my Decease) to Anne Davis a cupboard one dosen Pewter Plates, one pair Tongs, one Shovel one Trammel and one pair Hand Irons," "and to Wyntje one pair tongs, one Shovel One Trammel, and one pair Hand Irons."

Residue devised to the four daughters.

Sons Richard, Isaac, and John appointed executors. Signed by the testator.

SAMUEL DAVIS
ALEX. CROOKSHANK
WILLIAM HUME

(On the third Tuesday in Sept., 1794, William Hume appeared. Entered at request of John C. Davis, Sept. 23, 1794).

(*Isaac Davids* (prob. b. in England) m. *Jannetje Maurits*, bt. June 18, 1671, dau. of *Frederick Pietersen Mourits* (q. v.) and *Engeltie Hendrick*, and had issue: i. *Marietje*, bt. Nov. 13, 1692; ii. *Engel*, bt. Nov. 16, 1694; iii. *Christoffer*, bt. May 30, 1697; iv. *Jannetje*, bt. Oct. 29, 1699; v. *Frederick*, bt. Sept. 21, 1701; vi. *Joris*, bt. Jan. 1, 1704; vii. *Samuel*, bt. March 17, 1706; viii. *Christoffel*, bt. Sept. 11, 1709; ix. *Isaak*, bt. Dec. 2, 1711.

Christoffel (*Stoffel*) *David* (*Davids*) m., Apr. 3, 1739, *Elizabeth Bradeth* (*Bradhead, Brodhead*), and had issue: i. *Mary*, bt. Sept. 30, 1739 (m., Febr. 20, 1761, *John Brodhead*); ii. *Isaak*, bt. Aug. 16, 1741; iii. *Ritsert*, bt. Oct. 2, 1743; iv. *En* (*Anna*), bt. Dec. 12, 1745; v. *Weyntjen*, bt. Aug. 19, 1750; vi. *Isaac*, bt. Dec. 31, 1752, and *John, Esther*, who m. *Jacob Chambers, Rachel*.

Page 24.—VAN STEENBERGH, THOMAS, of the West Camp, Yeoman.

Will dated Sept. 7, 1795.

"Unto my beloved Wife *Christina* my whole Estate both real and personal during the time that she shall Continue my Widow."

"To my three sons: *John Paul* and *Cornelius* all my Estate both Real and Personal" "Provided" "they pay out of my Estate" "£420" i. e. "to my son *Petrus* £60 and £60 to my son *Thomas* and £60 to my son *Abraham* and £60 to my Son *Mathew* and £60 to my son *Hendrick* and £60 to my Daughter *Margret* and also £60 to my Daughter *Helena*" "one year after the Death of my beloved Wife."

"My son Abraham Shall have one Milch Cow out of my stock of Cattle."—"My Daughter Helena shall have one Milch Cow and one Heifer out of my stock of Cattle."

"My beloved Wife Christina shall have my Negro Wench *Dina* and also the Bed & furniture thereunto belonging which is at present in Use—and also my largest lookingglass."

"My Daughter Helena shall have an Out Set so Called, out of my Estate after she Shall come to marry, which Out set shall be at the discretion of my said wife."

"My house Hold furniture shall be equally divided Between all my Children."

Son Paul and loving friends *Cornelius Persen* and *Benjamin Snyder* appointed executors. Signed by the testator.

PETRUS MYNDERSE
JOHANNIS SCHOONMAKER JUNR. (his mark)
JOHN HYSER

(On the first Tuesday in May, 1796 appeared Peter Mynderse before the Court, *Abraham B. Bancker, Philip D. Bevier*, Judges, *John Dumont, Abraham Van Gaasbeck*, Justices, proving the will, and signature of the other witnesses. Entered May 4, 1796).

(See next will).

Page 27.—VAN STEENBERGH, JOHN, of Kingston, farmer.

Will dated May 16, 1796.

"To my loving wife *Annatje Van Stenbergh* All the whole income of all my Estate Real and personal for her mentainance so long as" she "shall not marry again, but if" she "shall marry again, then to give up all my Estate to my Executors" "or to my Children" and then to have £50.

"Unto my two Children named *Thomas* and *Jane*" "all my Estate real and personal."

Wife "and my Brother in law, *Cornelis Burhans* and my friend *Benjamin Snyder*" appointed executors.

Signed by the testator.

CORNELIUS C. BRINCK (his mark)
ABRAHAM VAN STEENBERGHT
ELIZABETH VAN STEENBERGH

(On the third Tuesday in Sept., 1796, Cornelius C. Brinck appeared before the Court, *Abraham Bevier, Abraham B. Bancker,* Judges, *Abraham Van Gaasbeck, Junr., Johannis Miller* and *Moses Cantine Junior.*—Entered at request of Mr. *Benjamin Snyder,* Sept. 21, 1796).

(*Thomas Jansse (van Steenbergen) (Thomas Jansen, Thomas J. Steenberge*) m. after Febr. 3, 1683, *Maria Adams Metselaer* (*Salaeme, Zalome*) and had i. *Magriet,* bt. Febr. 24, 1684; ii. *Geerthruydt,* bt. March 5, 1688; iii. *Johannes,* bt. March 17, 1689; iv. *Catryn,* bt. Nov. 6, 1692; v. *Johannes,* bt. June 9, 1695; vi. *Abraam,* bt. Jan. 15, 1699; vii. *Henricus,* bt. Febr. 2, 1701.

vi. *Abraham van Steenbergen,* m. Apr. 14, 1728, Catrina Ploeg, and had issue; i. *Thomas,* bt. May 19, 1728; ii. *Alida,* bt. Sept. 24, 1732; iii. *Margrieta,* bt. Jan. 26, 1735.

Thomas van Steenbergen (s. of Abraham), called "*Jr.*", m. Oct. 6, 1750, *Christina (Christjen) Labonté*, and had issue: i. *Abraham*, bt. July 21, 1751, m. March 1, 1791, *Elizabeth Oosterhoudt;* ii. *Petrus*, bt. Dec. 2, 1753; iii. *Margaret*, bt. Jan. 4, 1756; iv. *Thomas*, bt. Oct. 30, 1757; v. *John*, bt. Dec. 26, 1761, m., Oct. 24, 1784, *Annatje Van Leuven; Cornelis; Matthew; Margaret; Helena.* (See his will *supra*).

John T. Van Steenbergen (s. of Thomas) and Annatje Van Leuwen had issue: i. Jannetje, bt. May 16, 1790; ii. Thomas, bt. Nov. 6, 1794. See his will above).

Page 30.—FREER, JOHANNIS, of the Town of New Paltz.

Will dated Sept. 1, 1796.

"Unto my Loving wife *Agetta* the use of my whole Estate Real and Personal and to receive the income and profits during her Natural Lifetime or as Long as she shall remain my wedow and no longer" if she "marry again" then "the sum of £10" yearly "during her natural life time Hoping and Trusting that she will be Satisfied with the same in Lue of her Dower."

"Unto *Agetta Freer* the Daughter of my nephew *Jonathan Freer*" "my whole Estate both Real and Personal" "in New Paltz or Elsewhere (the use thereof herein before given only Excepted), she to pay "unto *Margret Freer* the wife of my said Neppew Jonathan Freer £30" "within three months after the decease of my said Wife."

"My good friends *Peter Lefever Junr., Isaac Lefever* and *Johannis B. Doyo*" appointed executors. Signed by the testator.

JACOB DEYO
DANIEL SLUYTER
PETER LEFEVER JUNR.

(On Wednesday, July 15, 1797, all the witnesses appeared before the Court, *Abraham B. Bancker* and *Abraham Bevier*, Judges and *Justus Banks*, Esq., Ass't Justice.—Entered July 6, 1797).

(J. F., bt. Aug. 1, 1725, s. of *Hugo F.* (and *Bregjen Teerpenning*), s. of *Hugo F.* (and *Anna Maria Le Roy*) (see *Hugh Freer*), of *Bonticow*, m. May 5, 1749, *Agitta De Joo*, and had a son: Johannes, bt. July 1, 1750, d. y.

Agetta Freer, bt. Oct. 17, 1779, was dau. of *Jonathan Freer*, (bt. Aug. 1, 1754) (and *Margrietjen Doio*), s. of *Jacob F.* (bt. Sept. 1, 1723) (and *Zara Freer*, dau. of *Hugo*), s. of *Jacob Freer* (bt. June 9, 1679) (and *Antje Weyen*), s. of *Hugue F.* (see *Hugue Frere*). Agetta F. m. at Paltz, *Wilhelmus Hasbrouck.*)

Page 33.—DUBOIS, HENDRICUS, of New Paltz, Yeoman.

Will dated June 21, 1774.

"Unto my youngest Son *Methusalem*" "all that my Homestead being part of my farm whereon I now Dwell Containing Five acres of land which" "is to Begin at a stone set up on the south side of the *Kings Road* to the North East of my Dwelling House which said stone is marked M on the south side and is Distant 76 links on a south 1 Degree 45 Minutes west course from a Black Oak Tree standing on the North side of the Kings Road" "which Tree is marked with 3 Notches on two sides and was marked for the southermost corner of a lot by me conveyed to my son *Hendricus* and is to run from said stone south 1 Degree 45 minutes west 6 chains 24 links thence south 69 Degrees 45 minues west 8 chains thence north 40 degrees 15 minutes west 4 chains 39 links to the aforesaid Road thence along the same north 59 degrees East 10 Chains and North 77 Degrees 2 Chains to where it Began As Also 95 acres of land (being also part of my said farm) "on the North West side of said Road" "to begin at the aforesaid Black Oak Tree marked for the Southermost Corner of the aforesaid lot by me conveyed unto my son Hendricus and to Extend from thence South Westerly along the said Road to a lot by me heretofore Conveyed unto my son *Philip* in his life time and is to Extend Northwesterly from the said Road along" Hendrik's lot and lot conveyed to Philip "with the full Breadth between them untill it contains 95 acres Together with" "my Dwelling Houses out Houses Barn Barks Orchards Gardens and other Improvements" "in all containing 100 acres to son Methusalem" in Order to make him Equal with my other sons they having had an Equivalent thereto in my life time," he to pay after wife's decease "in consideration of the Improvements upon the same" £100 more than my son Hendricus shall pay towards my Grand Children's and my Daughter's Portions."

"Unto my son Hendricus and my said son Methusalem all the Residue" "of my Farm Lands Tenements" they to pay "to my two Daughters and Grand Children" £400 "Hendricus to pay" "£150" and Methusalem £100 in consideration of the Improvements" and also £150.

"To my two Daughters *Tryntie* the wife of *Matheus Dubois* and *Lea* the wife of *Christofel Kiersteden*" £100 each "and to my Grand Children the Children of my son Philip deceased £100 and to my Grand Children, the Children of my Daughter *Diena* deceased the late wife of *Abraham Eltinge*" "£100. To all the grandchildren and children "all my personall Estate."

"Unto said son Hendricus" "one Bench in the Church at the *Grootstuck* to have the choice of my Benches" and to Methusalem one Bench" in said Church. And all other seats which belong unto me in said Church and also in the Church at *Shawangunk*" "1/5 to the children of Philip, 1/5 to the children of Diena, 1/5 to Tryntie, 1/5 to Lea, and 1/5 to "my Daughter *Rachel* the wife of *Johannis A. Hardenbergh*." As I have already given my eldest son *Solomon* his full proportion in helping him to purchase an Estate after his Marriage I desire he may rest satisfyed therewith."—"My daughter Rachel shall not make any other demand out of my Estate other than her 1/5 part in the seats." My wife *Jannetie* shall remain in the full possession of my whole Estate" "during her lifetime."

Wife and sons Hendricus and Mathusalem appointed executors. Signed by the testator.

SEVERYN T. BRUYN
JACOBUS BRUYN JUNR.
JOH'S BRUYN

(June 4, 1782, Severyn T. Bruyn and Johannis Bruyn of Shawangunk, farmers, appeared before *Joseph Gasherie* Surrogate, proving the will, and signature of Jacobus Bruyn Junr. as a witness.—

On the same day the executors appeared and took "the oath of an Execut)r."

On Sept. 19, 1798, Johannis Bruyn of Shawangunk, Esq., appeared before the Court, Abraham Bevier, Abraham B. Bancker and Jonathan Hasbrouck, Judges, proving the will, and signatures of the other witnesses.—Entered at the request of Methusalem Dubois, Sept. 21, 1798.)

(Hendricus Dubois, s. of *Solomon Du Bois* and *Tryntje Gerritsen* (q. v.), b. *New Paltz*, Dec. 31, 1710, m., May 6, 1733, *Jannetjen Hoogteling*, and had issue: i. *Phillippus*, bt. Apr. 21, 1734, m., March 22, 1757, *Anne Hue*; ii. *Solomon*, bt. Febr. 15, 1736, m. Oct. 25, 1762, *Ariaantje Du Bois*; iii. *Dina*, bt. Febr. 12, 1738, m. Nov. 26, 1759, *Abraham Eltinge*; iv. *Treintje*, bt. in *Shawangunk*, Oct. 9, 1740, m. Matthew *Du Bois*; v. *Henricus*, bt. May 1, 1743, m. *Rebecca Van Wagenen*; vi. *Methusalem*, bt. June 30, 1745; vii. *Lea*, bt. June 28, 1747, m. *Christoffel Kierstede*; viii. *Rachel*, bt. Dec. 24, 1749, m. *Johannes A. Hardenbergh*; ix. *Methusalem*, bt. Oct. 27, 1751, m. i. *Gertrude Bruyn*, m. 2., *Catherine Bevier*).

On Oct. 15, 1762, Hendricus and Solomon Dubois petitioned for letters patent for 2000 acres of vacant land in Ulster Co., within the bounds of the line formerly granted to Capt. *John Evans*, south of Shawangunk mountain, and west of *Wall Kill*, also land without the bounds of said Patent, west of said mountain, N. W. and N. E. of the *Great Minnissinck Patent*. (N. Y. Land Papers, xvi, p. 125).

Page 39.—DUBOIS, CORNELIUS, of the New Paltz, Esq.,

Will dated Nov. 6, 1780.

"Unto my well beloved wife *Margaret*" "during her lifetime one Negro Slave named *Sime,* one Negro Wench named *Jane,* one Milch Cow, and also so much of my Household goods as she may Judge she shall have occasion for."

"Unto my son *Cornelius*" "during his natural lifetime All my whole Real Estate" "in New Paltz" "excepting such parts thereof as I shall hereafter order to be sold by my Executors" "together with all me buildings Houses Barns Orchards, Gardens" "after his decease" unto the Heirs of my said son Cornelius and to my Daughters *Tryntie, Jannetie, Jacominetie, Saretie,* and to my Grand Children *Nathaniel Dubois, Wilhelmus Dubois* and *Polly Dubois* the Children of my Daughter *Rachel* deceased and to my Grand children *Dirck Wynkoop* and *Lea Wynkoop* the Children of my daughter *Lea* deceased."

"Also to son Cornelius" "Eight horses the choice out of my stock" he to pay for the same "£80 in Gold or Silver at the rate of eight Shillings for a Spanish Dollar." Also "so many of my Slaves as he may think proper (to be taken before any division is made of my personal Estate) provided he" pays "for each Slave" £90 (at the same rate as before).

"Unto my said daughter Saretie" "one Negro Wench named *Rose*" to pay for the same £80 (at the same rate as before).

"Unto my said son Cornelius" "two seats I have in the Church at *Shawangunk.*"—To "my grandson *Cornelius Dubois Hasbrouck*" "one seat in the Church at *Marbletown.*"

"Residue of my whole personal Estate" "unto my said son, said Daughters and said grand Children." "Residue" "of my whole Real Estate" "in the County of Ulster" "or Else where" "and also the Liberty and previledge I have in the New Paltz patent of Hay stone and Timber" also to said children and grandchildren.

"In case any dispute should happen between my Heirs concerning this my last Will and Testament, It is my Will and desire that" they "shall leave it to an Arbitration."—Executors to sell "to the best advantage all that certain lot of land containing 66 acres" "in Co. Ulster" part of a certain tract of 1056 acres of land granted to me by Letters Patent" "July 2, 1739 so as the same is Surveyed by *Johannis Bruyn* as per his return of Survey dated May 16. And also that part of the land I have in the above recited patent, adjoining the abovesaid 66 acres" "on the southwest side of the *Platte Kill.*"

Son Cornelius, son in law Jacob Hasbrouck Junr. and my grand Sons Josia Hasbrouck, Nathaniel Dubois and Cornelius Hasbrouck appointed executors. Son in law *Cornelius D. Wynkoop* to be Guardian to the said Grand Children until they respectively come to age.

Signed by the testator.

DENIE D. RELYA (his mark)

JOSHUA DUBOIS

DAVID LOUW

(April 23, 1781, Denie Raleya of New Paltz, yeoman, and David Louw of same place, Blacksmith, appeared before *Joseph Gasherie,* Surrogate, proving the will, and signature of Joshua Dubois as a witness.

On the same day all the executors took the oath.

Sept. 19, 1798, Joshua Dubois, of Kingston, Tanner, appeared before the Court. *Methusalem Dubois* made oath that he had "given due notice to all present Heirs mentioned in the said Will" "of this intended application" "for the approbation of said Will.—Whereupon the Court" "ordered" the will to be recorded.

Entered Sept. 21, 1798.)

(*Cornelius Du Bois, Sr.,* s. of *Solomon Du Bois,* and *Tryntje Gerritsen,* m., Apr. 7, 1729, *Anna Margaret Hoogteling,* and had issue: i. *Tryntjen,* bt. March 29, 1730, m., Jan. 27, 1762, *Matthew Du Bois;* ii. *Jan(netie)* bt. 1732 (m. *Jacob Hasbrouck*); iii. *Wilhelmus,* bt. March 31, 1734; iv. *Josia,* bt. Oct. 21, 1736, in *Shawangunk* (see his will); v. *Rachel,* bt. Aug. 5, 1739, m. Col. *Lewis Du Bois,* of *Marlborough;* vi. *Lea,* bt. May 2, 1742, m., May 28, 1762, *Cornelius Wynkoop;* vii. *Jacomyntjen,* bt. Apr. 21, 1745, m. *Andries Bevier,* of *Wawarsing;* viii. *Sara,* bt. Oct. 4, 1747, m. *Jacob Hasbrouck,* of *Marbletown;* ix. *Cornelis,* bt. July 8, 1750, m. *Gertrude Bruyn.*

A much faded, and much worn copy of the original will is filed in the Estate Box No. 11, Surrogate's Office. To this has been attached a number of pertinent questions and answers by Peter W. Yates, dated Albany, May 9, 1781, pertaining to this will:

Ques. 1. Concerning the Crops of Wheat & Rye now in the Ground which were sown by the Testator and his only son in Partnership, whether the Moiety thereof, which should have belonged to the Testator, had he lived, shall go to the Executors or not?

Ques. 2. Whether the Widow of the Testator, in case she doth not comply with the Will, can recover her Thirds of the Personal Estate?

Ques. 3. In Case the Heirs of the Testator should make Division and Partition of the Real Estate of the Testator, in the Lifetime of his son Cornelius, whether it would be legal and stand in Law, and how is it to be made, as some of them are under Age?

Ques. 4. Whether the Testators Son may legally demise the Farm or Lands which were the Testators?

Ques. 5. If the Grand Children Dirk & Lea Wynkoop die under Age who is to have their Part?
Ques. 6. Whether any of the Devises can sell an undivided Part before the death of Cornelius?
I am of Opinion, as to the
Ques. I. That the Crop of Wheat and Rye will go to the Son and not to the Executors.
Ques. II. That the Testators Widow is by law entitled to no more of the Personal Estate than is given her by the Will. But that she is exclusive of the Will entitled to her Dowry. That is to say, the one third Part of all the Testators Lands and Tenements for and during her natural Life.
Ques. III. That no legal Division can be made until all the Parties to such Division are of lawful Age, unless it is done in Virtue of a Law of the Legislature passed the 8 Jan. 1762. But to avoid the Expenses of that Mode of Partition, it has been usual for some third Person to become Bound (in Behalf of the Minors interested in the Lands to be divided) that such Minors, when they arrive to Lawful Age, should agree to and confirm the Partition and execute Deeds for the Purpose.
Ques. IV. That the Testator's Son may demise or even sell for & during the Term of his natural Life the Real Estate devised to him by his Father's Will.
Ques. V. If one of the Testator's Grand Children Dirk & Lea Wynkoop should die under Age, the Part or share of the real Estate of the one so dying, will go to the Survivor of them. But if they should both die under Age, without lawful Issue, their whole Part will go to their Uncle, the Testators eldest Son, as Heir at Law.—But as to their Part of the Personal Estate Dirk may dispose of his at the Age of 14, and Lea at the age of 12 to whom they please, but not by Will, unless they previously make a Division between them of their Part.
Ques. VI. That any of the Devises may sell their undivided Part of the Real Estate before the Death of the Testators Son Cornelius.

(Signed) PETER W. YATES.

Albany 9. May 1781.

Page 44.—KLARWATER, ABRAHAM, of Marbletown.

Will dated April 23, 1776.

"To my son *Thomas* all my lands" "on the Southeest side of the *Kline Kill*" "of Marbletown."

"Al the rest" "of my lands together with my Dwelling House Barn, Barghs, Outhousen and all my Building together with all the appurtenances" "unto four of my sons namely *Fradrick, Isaac Danjel, Joseph*" "in consideration of the lands I have before given to my five sons herein before named they shall pay to my four Daughters and my son *Abraham* the sum of £90" i. e. "to my Daughter *Eve* £30" "in three equeel payment the first" "to be made one year after my decease" "to my Daughter *Wintje*" "£30 (in the same manner) to my daughter *Mary* wife of *Peter Vernoy*" £10 one year after my decease" "£10 to my Daughter *Esther* wife of *'Jacob Seale*" "£10 to my son Abraham."—To Abraham also "the Choice of al my Horses" "the choice of my Slays."

"To my daughter Wintje my Great Pot as also the choice of all my Heffers."

"All the remainder" "of my Householding Goods or furniture" "to my two Daughters Eve and Wintje as also my Bed, Bedsted and all the furniture thereunto belonging."

"All the remainder of my Estate Parsonal" "shall be devided amongst all my Children namely Abraham, Fradrick, Isaac, Danjel, *Jacob*, Thomas, Joseph, Eve, Mary, Esther, Wintje." "If any of my Children shud die leving no Issue" his or her share to be divided.

"My brother in law *Thomas Schoonmaker* and my son Fradrick" appointed executors.

ABRAHAM KLARWATER (his mark)

FREDERICK WOOD
THOMAS WOOD
MATTHEW CANTINE

(Sept. 19, 1798, Frederick Wood of Marbletown, farmer, appeared before the Court, *Abraham B. Bancker, Jonathan Hasbrouck,* Judges, *Abraham Van Gaasbeek* and *Peter Roggan,* Ass't Justices, proving the will, and signature of the other witnesses).

(*Theunis Jacobsen Klaarwater,* b. at *Baarn,* near *Rotterdam, Holland,* in 1624, had, in 1709, with son, *Jacobus,* brother-in-law, *Hendrick Vernooy, Abraham Doian, Rip Van Dam, Adolphus Phillipse,* Dr. *Gerardus Beekman,* and Col. *Wm. Peartree,* a patent of 4000 acres land (Seer. State, Albany, Office, Patents, vii, p. 54), situated in *Shauangunk,* bound east by the *Wallkill,* south by the *Dwaaskill,* and west by the *Shawangunk Kill.*—*Jacobus,* b. Holland, 1663, m. *Mary Deyo,* dau. of *Abraham.* Their son, *Abraham,* bt. July 2, 1699, at *New Paltz,* m., Oct. 20, 1738, *Lisabeth Schoonmaker,* and had—*Eva,* bt. July 13, 1740, *Abraham,* bt. Oct. 3, 1742, *Hester,* bt. Febr. 19, 1749, m. *Jacob Seale,* and *Frederick, Isaac, David, Joseph, Wyntje, Mary,* m. *Peter Vernooy, Jacob,* and *Thomas.*

A tablet to the memory of Theunis Jacobsen C. was erected in the Dutch Ref. Church, at Kingston, by his descendant, Judge *Alphonso Trumpbour Clearwater,* LL.D.")

Page 47.—LEFEVER, DANIEL, of New Paltz.

Will dated Sept. 4, 1784.

"Unto my beloved wife *Catharina Lefever* all that my whole Estate, Real and personal" "during her naturall life, or days of her my Widowship, and after her decease" "to my son *Peter Lefever* all that of my land & Tennements" "at the *Bontiekoe* in the New Paltz patent it being my Old Homested together with all the land I now own to the West of the *Grotiefly* or *big Meadow,* also my right of a Grandpears lot" "in the second Tier of the New Devision & runs through the Bidfly or Meadow to the East side thereof" "also" "my Negro man named *Jan,* also all my wearing Cloaths of all sorts."

"To my beloved wife" "my negro wench named *Bet* to be her own property."

"To my daughter *Elizabeth* the wife of *Mathew Lefever* & *Maria* the wife of *Jonathan Doyo* all that my lands and Tenements" "within the New Paltz patent at the *North River* No. 4, in the North Division, also all my right & title in the devision made at the *Platte Beni water*" "also my negro wench named *Margret.*"

"To my daughter *Maria*" "my Negro Wench named *Deyán.*"

"To my son *Peter Lefever* his choisc of three of my Horses" Residue to wife "or whenever she shall please to give the same up to her children" the property to be divided among them.

Wife, son Peter, and "my two son in Laws Mathew Lefever & Jonathan Doyo" appointed executors.

Signed by the testator.

JACOB LEFEVER
ISAAC LEFEVER JUNR.
JOH'S HARDENBERGH JUNR.

(May 7, 1800, Isaac Lefever of New Paltz, Surveyor, appeared before the Court, *James Oliver*, first Judge, and *Abraham Bevier* and *Abraham B. Bancker*, Judges, proving the will, and signature of the other witnesses).

(*Isaac Le Fevre*, bt. Oct. 28, 1683, s. of *Simon Le Fevre* (q. v.), m. 1. *Catrina Freer (Fire)*, and m. 2., May 16, 1718, *Marytje Freer*, dau. of *Hugo F., Jr.*, and had with 1st wife: i. *Philip*, bt. Apr. 1, 1711; with 2d wife: ii. *Ysaak*, bt. Dec. 25, 1718, d. unm.; iii. *Petrus*, bt. Febr. 19, 1721, m., Jan 2, 1760, *Elisabeth Vernoo;* iv. *Johannes*, bt. Nov. 18, 1722, m., May 29, 1752, *Sarah Vernooy*; v. *Daniel*, vi. *Simon*, bt. Nov. 10, 1728, d. y.; vii. *Mary*, bt. March 26, 1732, m. *Johannes Hardenbergh, Jr.;* viii. *Simon*, bt. Dec. 17, 1738, d. y.

DANIEL, bt. Dec. 12, 1725, m. *Catherine Cantein*, dau. of *Peter* (s. of *Moses C.* who m. *Elisabeth* (*Deyo*) *Le Fevre*, the grandfather of *Daniel Le Fevre*. Issue: i. *Simon*, bt. July 7, 1751, m., Oct 30, 1779, *Janneke Swart*; ii. *Maria*, bt. Apr. 11, 1756, m. *Jonathan Deyo;* iii. *Peter*, bt. Febr. 10, 1759; iv. *Moses*, bt. Jan. 24, 1762; v. *Elisabeth*, m. *Matthew Le Fevre*).

Page 50.—EEN, ABRAHAM, of New Paltz.

Will dated Nov. 30, 1805.

"Unto my beloved wife *Catrena* all the Household furniture she had from her father, also what her father bequeathed to her by his will, also £20 in money to be paid to her yearly" "during her natural life by my two sons *Elias* and *Petrus*" "also the choice of my Negro Wenches and a room to live in eitherly by Elias or Petrus where she shall chuse, and my two sons shall maintain her with meat and Drink, also one Bed with a Sett of Curtains of Callicoe furnished with what belongs to it, also one Bed with homespun Checkerd Curtains with all thereunto belonging, also my large Cupboard as it stands, also one Tea Table with Tea Cups and Saucers thereunto belonging, also two Iron pots and one Tremmel also six Chairs also the choice of all my Cows, also one Tea Kittle and my Negro *Jack* together with two Pails."

"Unto my son Elias one Horse or a Cow which he may chuse for his birth right, and also one Weavers Loom and the one half of my Reeds and Geers and all what belongs to the Loom."

"To my son Petrus the two best Horses, Waggon, Plough, Wood Sled, pleasure Slay, and the Weavers Loom, with the one half of the Reeds and Geers and all what belongs to the loom."

"To Elias all the Farm on which he now dwelleth—Except 15 acres of Bush right at the East end together with the buildings thereon containing 180 acres," "and a piece of land called the *Groote Buntecoe*."

"To my son Petrus the farm whereon I now dwell together with the buildings thereon—also a piece of land called the *Halfmoon* and 15 acres of the Bush right at the East end of the farm bequeathed to my son Elias."

If Petrus should die, Elias to have his share "but not to have possession until after the death or entermarriage of the wife of my said son Peter, she is to have the full enjoyment of the whole Estate during her Widowhood."

"Unto my two sons Elias and Petrus all my Bush right lying in the *New Paltz* patent, the one half to Elias and the other half to Petrus."

To sons "all the monies their shall be due to me by bond or Notes."

"Unto my three Daughters *Rachel Annatje* and *Catrena* "£40 each two years after my decease."—To said daughters also "all my Houshold furnature."

Residue to be divided among the five children. Son Elias Een, *Josiah Hasbrouck* and *Peter Lefever, Junr.* appointed executors.

ABRAHAM EIN

HENRY ELTING
HENRY JANSEN
CORN. TAPPEN

(Jan. 6, 1807, witnesses appeared before the Court, *Abraham Bevier* and *Jonathan Hasbrouck*, Judges, *John Van Steenbergh* and *Jacob Marius Groen*, Ass't Justices. Entered Jan. 6, 1807).

(*Elias Eign (In)*, of *New Paltz*, m. *Elizabeth*, dau. of *Anthony Crispel*, and had i. *Mary*, bt. Aug. 8, 1697; ii. *Jan*, bt. Febr. 18,1700; iii. *Mary Magdalena*, bt. Apr. 5, 1702; iv. *Sarah*, bt. Sept. 11, 1709, m., Febr. 16, 1739, *Isaack Walderon*, b. *New Castle, Del*. res. *Poughkepsie*.
JAN (above) m. Febr. 9, 1735, *Geesje Roosa*, and had: i. *Elizabeth*, bt. Febr. 15, 1736; ii. *Margaret*, bt. May 29, 1737; iii. *Elias*, bt. Apr. 1, 1739; iv. *Abraham*, bt. July 12, 1741; v. *Isaak*, bt. July 31, 1743.
ABRAHAM (above), m., Nov. 2, 1765, *Catharina Van Wagenen*, and had: i. *Elias*, bt. 1768, m. *Elisabeth Hasbrouck*; ii. *Annatje*, bt. Aug. 22, 1774, m. *Benjamin Hasbrouck*; iii. *Rachel*, m. *David Deyo*; iv. *Catharine*, m. *Jonathan Deyo*; v. *Peter*, b. 1781, m. *Maria Freer*).

Page 55.—DE WITT, ANDRIES, of Kingston.

Will dated March 17, 1800.

"Unto my beloved wife *Rachel*" "my Houses lands Tenements and Real Estate" "within the County of Ulster" also "all my personal Estate" "during her natural life time, or" "so long as she shall remain my Widow and no longer."

"Unto my Eldest son *Tjerck De Witt*" £50 "and my large Dutch Bible in lieu or stead of his birth right."

Upon death of wife to "my two sons Tjerck De Witt and *Isaac De Witt*" "my Houses lands and Tenements" "in the County of Ulster (except lot given hereinafter to my Daughter *Neltje*) in fee simple as Tenants in Common" "also all the rents and profits of "that certain tract or parcell of land formerly Demised by *Tjerck De Witt* deceased to *Gerrit Aartse* now in the possession of *Conradt G. Elmendorph*."

To son Tjerck "one of my Seat in the Dutch Church at Kingston, also my two Negro man Slaves named *Harry* and *Tom*." To son Isaac "one other of my Seats in the said Church" "also my two other Negro men Slaves named *James* and *Joe*."

To "my Daughter *Neeltje* wife of *Petrus Elmendorph* all that certain lot of Lowland" "on the North side of the *Esopus Creek* in the town of

Kingston" "containing about 10 acres so as the same hath lately been conveyed to me by the Heirs of *Cornelius Elmendorph* deceased." To her also "two Negro Wench Slaves both named *Bett,* now in her possession, and also £700" to be paid by the sons in three payments the first one year after my wife's decease or re-marriage.

"Unto my Grandchild *Andries* son of my Daughter Neeltje my Negro Boy named *Abram.*"

To sons "all my Cloathing and Wearing Appearel, and also all my Guns, Swords and other Warlike Weapons" "farmers Utensels as Plows Harrows Sleads slays Waggons Carts and every other implement of Husbandry, also my Canoes or Crafts usually kept for crossing the Creek, and also all the Stock of Horses and Coalts."

"Immediately after the death or re-marriage" of wife "the crop or crops of Hay, Grass, Grain or Corn lying standing or growing or otherwise Housed or in Barns or Barriks" to be equally divided among the two sons.

Residue to the two sons. Wife, sons and "my trusty friend Christopher Tappen" appointed executors. Signed by the testator.

LUKE KIERSTED
CORNELIUS DE WITT
GEO. TAPPEN

(Jan. 8, 1807, Cornelius De Witt of *New Burgh, Co. Orange,* Merchant, Luke Kiersted of Kingston, Physician, and George Tappen of same place, yeoman, appeared before the Court, *Abraham Bevier, Jonathan Hasbrouck* and *Johannis Bruyn,* Judges.—Will ordered to be recorded.)

(*Andries De Witt*, bt. March 3, 1728, s. of *Tjerck De Witt* and *Anne Pawling*, see *Henry De Witt*, m., Dec. 17, 1757, *Rachel Du Bois*, b. Jan. 5, 1737, (d. Aug. 24, 1823), dau. of *Isaac Du Bois* and *Neeltje Roosa*. He d. June 9, 1806. Issue: i. *Neeltje*, bt. June 24, 1759, m., Febr. 6, 1782, *Petrus Elmendorf*; ii. *Tjerck*, bt. May 23, 1762; iii. *Izaack*, bt. May 15, 1769).

Page 61.—HASBROUCK, JOHANNIS, of New Paltz.

Will dated Dec. 28, 1806.

"Executors athorized to sell all the personal estate as well as "all that lot of land being part of lot Number 5 in lot number 12 first tier south division, bounded southerly by land of the Heirs of *Petrus Lefever* deceased westerly by land of *Philip Schoonmaker* being part of said lot No. 5, and Northerly by a land between Lot No. 12 and lot No. 1, and Easterly by a lane between first and second tier of lots containing about 35 acres" "within the Town and Patent of the New Paltz."

"All the remainder of my land or Real Estate unto my four sons and two Daughters: *John E. Hasbrouck, William Hasbrouck Junr., Philip Hasbrouck, Andries Hasbrouck, Polly Hasbrouck* and *Rachel Hasbrouck*" —Also all the personal estate.

"My half brother *Philip Schoonmaker* and my good friends *Philip Eltinge* and *Elias Ean*" appointed executors, and Philip Schoonmaker Guardian "of the persons and Estates of all my said Children."

JOHANNIS HASBROUCK (his mark).

PETER LEFEVER
SAMUEL HASBROUCK
ELIAS BEVIER

(Jan. 8, 1807, all the witnesses appeared before the Court.—Entered at the request of Philip Schoonmaker, Jan. 8, 1807).

(*Johannes Hasbrouck* (s. of *Jan H.*, b. Febr. 1, 1739, m. Dec. 24, 1763, *Rachel Van Wagenen.* He was Son of *Solomon H.*, b. 1680, and *Sarah Van Wagenen*), m. a dau. of *Wm. McDonald.* Of their children (as above), *John E. H.*, m. Febr. 24, 1793, *Elisabeth Post*).

Page 66.—JENKENS, LAMBERT, of the Paltz Township.

Will dated 11th day of the 7th month 1799.

"To my beloved Wife (not named) a comfortable liveing out of my estate, whilst she remains my Widow & She to live with either of my Children that she shall choose & my sons shall all of them be equally at the expense of supporting her & if she should Marry she shall be deprived of the above priveleges & receive £50 or $125 in lieu of her Dower & All my sons shall pay share & share alike of said sum after my youngest Child shall be of age."

"My Estate shall remain undivided until my youngest Child shall be of Age & to be worked in company by my Family they enjoying the profits, equally amongst them except Building places for my Sons, "if they should Marry before the time appointed for said division" arbitrators and Executors to divide the property.

The whole estate to be divided among the "five sons: *John, James, William, Albert* & *Crines Jenkins.*"

"To my Six Daughters" "at the time of Marriage (each) two Cows per piece, with one Feather Bed & furniture per piece, with other necessary furniture for housekeeping" "and $250 per piece or £100" "after my Youngest Child shall become of Age to be paid by my five sons. My daughters Names are, *Margaret, Brijet, Catharine, Mary, Hannah* & *Elener.*"

"My Aged Father shall be comfortably & respectfully supported out of my estate—my five sons shall bear their equal expense thereof."

Survivors to divide share of deceased child "before they are Married or have lawful issue."

John Levever my near Neighbour & *Samuel Baldwin*" appointed executors. Signed by the testator.

JOHN DODGE
JAMES BRODHEAD
OLIVER BRODHEAD

(Sept. 17, 1807, James Brodhead appeared before the Court.—Entered Sept. 15, 1807.)

(*Crines Jenkins* m. *Rachel Hardenbergh*, dau. of *Jacob H.*, and *James Jenkins*, m. *Rachel Le Fevre*, dau. of *Johannes Le F.*)

Page 69.—DONALDSON, ABRAHAM, of New Paltz.

Will dated May 16, 1805.

"Unto my beloved wife *Catharine* a suitable sufficient and comfortable support from the farm I now live on and all the lands and premises" "during her life to be given her by my two sons *John* and *Samuel*" "if not supported" I give her full power and authority to ask" "1/3 of what my whole lands here or elsewhere may rent for or else to hold and take into her possession and for her own use 1/3 of my lands and premises for and during her natural life" also "my Negro Girl *Phillis* together with one cow five Sheep and the best bed with sufficient bedding and the curtains appertaining thereto and likewise so much household furniture as may enable her to keep house by herself if not supported by my said sons."

To sons equal shares of the lands they now live on, William on the south side and James on the north side of said lands. To son *Abraham* the house and lot of land he now lives on for his natural life at the end of which it shall return to my sons John and Samuel.

"Unto the children of my daughter *Magdalane* 1/5 part of my lott of land" "in New Paltz generally called the *Juoner* lott" "when they shall come to age."

"Unto the child of my daughter *Catharine* 1/5 part" should the child die, then Catharine is to dispose of this share "as she may think proper."

"Unto my other three daughters *Margaret Rachel* and *Esther* 1/5 each of said lott." "I have given" "unto my wife" "my negro Girl Phillis in lieu of her dower claim to said lott of land" "and therefore she is hereby excluded and cut of from in her dower right from said lott."

"Unto my son Abraham all my right" "to two certain lotts of land which are now possessed by *Titus* and *William Ketcham*." To sons John and Samuel personal property, they to pay all debts.

Jacob Coddington, John Donaldson my son and *Samuel Donaldson* my son appointed executors. Signed by the testator.

THOMAS G. SMITH
JOHN FURMAN
JOSEPH HOOD

(May 5, 1808, Rev. Thomas G. Smith of Kingston and Joseph Hood of same place, yeoman, appeared before the Court, *William A. Thompson*, first Judge, *Abraham Bevier, Jonathan Hasbrouck, Johannis Bruyn*, Judges, and *John Van Steenbergh*, Ass't Justice, proving the will, and signature of John Furman now also deceased.)

Page 73.—NEWKERK, COENRADT, of Hurley.

Will dated April 26, 1796.

"Unto my nine children to wit, *John, Charles, Coenradt, Andries, Margaret, Mary, Gerritie, Anne,* and *Blandina* all my lands which I own in the Great Patent lying in lot Number 3 which was by the last will of *Charles Brodhead* deceased devised unto my well beloved wife."

"Unto my four sons" "all my Horses and farmers utensils."—Residue of my personal Estate to the nine children.—Executors ordered and authorized to sell in fee simple "all my lands and Tenements lying in Hurley and *Kingston*" the money to be divided among the eight children: John Charles Andries Margaret Mary Gerretie Anne and Blandina "here I leve out my son Coenradt because of the expense I have had in Educating him" "executors" "to keep into their hands" daughter Mary's share, which they shall pay to her with interest" at such time as they shall judge necessary at their discretion."

No sale or division to be made "till after the decease of my well beloved wife, if she shall so long remain my Widow," she to remain in full possession thereof until then. After her death, son Andries and daughters Margaret and Anne to possess "the whole of my real Estate" "in Hurley and Kingston" "together with all the Moveables" "for three years" after decease of wife and no longer, the income thereof to be divided among them, Andries ½, and the two daughters ½.—The property after these three years to be sold and properly divided.—If the children should die before they arrive to full age, or without lawful issue, survivors to divide the share.

Wife and sons John, Coenradt and Andries appointed executors. Signed by the testator.

BENJAMIN NUKERK
MATTHEW TEN EYCK
GERRIT B. NEWKERK

(April 4, 1806, Gerret B. Newkerk of Hurley appeared before *Daniel Brodhead, Junior*, Surrogate, proving the will, and signatures of witnesses.

Before the Court, *Abraham Bevier* & *Jonathan Hasbrouck*, Judges, *John Van Steenbergh* and *Jacob M. Groen*, Ass't Justices, appeared Matthew Ten Eyck of Hurley, farmer, proving the will, and signature of Benjamin Newkerk and Garret B. Newkerk "since deceased."

Entered Jan. 4, 1809.)

(*Arie Gerrit van Newkirk* (s. of *Gerrit Cornelissen* and *Cheiltje Cornelis*, q. v.), b. in *Midwoud, Flatbush, L. I.*, m. *Lysbeth Lambertsen*, dau. of *Lambert Huybertsen*, and had: *Coenrad*, bt. May 14, 1722, m., May 13, 1749, *Anne De Witt*, sister of *Charles De Witt*, q. v., and had: i. *Johannes*, bt. Nov. 3, 1751, ii. *Charles*, bt. Apr. 22, 1753, iii. *Gerritje*, bt. March 5, 1758, iv. *Anne*, bt. Nov. 22, 1759, v. *Jannetje*, bt. June 20, 1762, vi. *Blandina*, bt. May 20, 1764, vii. *Coenrad*, bt. Jan 5, 1766, as well as *Andries* and *Margaret*).

Page 78.—HAUSBROUCK, JOSAPHAT, of New Paltz.

Will dated April 28, 1811.

"Unto my daughter *Wyntye* Wife of *Jonas Freer* £200."—"Unto my daughter *Rachel* Wife of *William Hausbrouck* £200," both legacies to be paid within 18 months of my decease.

"Unto my well beloved Wife *Cornelia* all my lands and Tenements as long as she remains my Widow." After her death "unto my Sons

Daniel I. Hausbrouck, Simon Hausbrouck, Zackariah Hausbrouck & Andries Hausbrouck." "To my son Andries my Sorrel Horse."

"Unto my three youngest Sons all my horned Cattle and Crop of Grain on the ground" "my Sons Daniel I. Hausbrouck, Simon Hausbrouck, Zachariah Hausbrouck & Andries Hausbrouck to maintain my Daughter *Catherine* and to provide for her all things that she may stand in need of during her natural life" "my son Daniel I. Hausbrouck to pay to my beloved Wife Cornelia the sum of £50 within one year after my decease."

Remainder of "my personal estate goods and chattels of what kind and nature soever" "unto all my children equally" "after the decease of my Wife."

Johannis and *John C. Brodhead* appointed sole executors. Signed by the testator.

JOHN ROE
CALEB CHURCH
HEZEKIAH SMITH

(Dec. 14, 1814, Caleb Church of New Paltz Yeoman, appeared before the Court, *William Bradley* and *William Soper,* Judges, and *John Beekman,* Ass't Justice, proving the will, and signatures of witnesses.)—Entered Apr. 1, 1815.

(*Josaphat Hasbrouck*, b. Apr. 29, 1739, (s. of *Daniel H.,* b. June 23, 1692, m. Apr. 2, 1734, *Wyntje Deyo,* dau. of *Abraham*) (s. of *Abr. Hasbrouck*), m. *Cornelia Du Bois,* dau. of *Simon,* and had: *Andries,* m. *Elisabeth Hasbrouck, Wyntje,* m. *Jonas Freer, Rachel,* m. *Wm. Hasbrouck*).

Page 80.—HASBROUCK, JACOB J., of Marbletown.

Will dated June 21, 1818.

"Unto my beloved wife *Sarah Hasbrouck* two beds, curtains, bolsters, pillows, sheets, blankets, coverlids, bedsteads, pillow cases (as many as she may chuse) a large cubbord, chest and trunk, two rooms in my dwellinghouse, as much household furniture as she may chuse, all the specie I may have at the time of my death."

"To my eldest son *Isaac* one silver hilted sword, also the bed with the bedding thereunto belonging and the bedstead he now make use of."

"To my son *Jacobus*" "a mortgage I have on the house, mill and lot of the *Greenkills* Also $750" "out of my personal property."

"To my son *Jacob J. Hasbrouck*" "$2500" "out of my bonds and notes."

"To sons *Josiah* and *Lewis*" "all that part of my real estate which was formerly conveyed to my father *Isaac Hasbrouck Junr.* deceased by *Daniel Brodhead Gerrit Brodhead* and others" "at Marbletown" they to pay to "my son Isaac yearly £100."—To Josiah also "one lot of wood land containing 30 acres" "at *the Peak.*" To son Lewis "one lot of wood land" which I purchased of *Frederick Merkle* containing 25 acres."

"To my daughter *Margaret*" "a lot of land "in Hurly at the Greenkills with the fulling mill" "also three other small lots of land with a dwelling house thereon conveyed by *John Blanshan* to my son Abraham."

Remainder "to my sons *Wilhelmus,* Jacobus, *Cornelius,* Jacob Josiah, Lewis and Abraham, and daughters Margaret and *Polly."*

Sons Josiah and Lewis appointed executors.

JACOBUS J. HASBROUCK (his mark).

PETER TAPPEN
CHAS. CANTINE
ISAAC S. HASBROUCK

(Aug. 14, 1818, Josiah Hasbrouck, Lewis Hasbrouck, by *Sudams & Ostrander,* their attorneys, inform the heirs of their intention to apply for probate, in accordance with the Act of March 5, 1813. Addressed to Isaac Hasbrouck, Jacobus Hasbrouck, Jacob J. Hasbrouck, *Mrs. Margaret Peters,* Wilhelmus Hasbrouck, Cornelius Hasbrouck, Polly Hasbrouck and Abraham J. Hasbrouck.

On Sept. 15, 1818, all the witnesses appeared before the Court, proving the will.—Recorded same day. *Chas. Tappen, Jun.* Clerk.)

Son of Isaac Hasbrouck (see letter of adm. after I. H.)

Page 87.—LOCKWOOD, HENRY, of Plattekill.

Will dated April 17, 1818.

"To my daughter *Sally* wife of *John Dunn"* £200. "To my granddaughter *Pheby* Dunn when she comes of age" £25. "To my son *Henry Lockwood Junr."* £150. "To my son *Jeremiah Lockwood"* £40. "To my grandchildren *Josiah Lockwood Gilbert Lockwood Samuel Lockwood* and *Robert Lockwood* £44 each." To *Patience* wife of *James Warring"* £25. "To my grandchildren *Uriah Lockwood Henry Lockwood Samuel Lockwood David Lockwood, Cornelius Lockwood* and *Sally Relyea* and *Abby Sellick* children of *David Lockwood* £25 each." "To my grandchildren *Jeremiah Dunn John Dunn* and *David Dunn Ann Godkins* £10 each, and to *Mary Philips* £30 and *Henry Decker* and *Sally Decker* £10 each children of my daughter *Amey Decker."* "To my grandchildren *David Brown Henry Brown Benjamin Brown Hannah Brown* £20.8 each and to *Anna Marven* £28 and *Mary Brown* £20.8 also my bed and bedding, children of my daughter *Rachel*—and to my son in law *Isaac Brown"* "all my wearing apparel." "To my grandson *Josiah Lockwood* £50, son of Henry Lockwood Junr.

"Remainder of my estate" "be apportioned according to all the different legacies except Sally Dunn wife of John Dunn and to her no more than £200."

"My trusty friends *John C. Brodhead, Cornelius Ostrander* and *John Shuart*" appointed executors. Signed by the testator.

HENRY PHILLIPS
WILHELMUS OSTRANDER
JOHN MACKEY 4

(John Shuart made oath that he had served on John Dunn and Sally, his wife, daughter of Henry Lockwood, deceased, and on Phebe Dunn, child of the said Sally, and on Gilbert Lockwood, Robert Lockwood and James Waring and Patience, his wife, said Gilbert, Robert and Patience being grandchildren of said Henry Lockwood and children of *Cornelius Lockwood* deceased, and on Uriah Lockwood, Henry, Samuel, David, Cornelius Lockwood *Lucas Relyea* & Sally his wife and *David Selleck* and Abby, his wife, said Uriah, Henry, Samuel, David, Cornelius, Sally, and Abby being children of *David Lockwood* deceased and grandchildren of said Henry Lockwood deceased and on David Dunn *Cornelius Phillips* and Mary, his wife and Henry Decker & Sally Decker, said David, Mary, Henry & Sally being children of Amy Decker deceased and grandchildren of said Henry Lockwood, and on David Brown, Henry Brown, Benjamin Brown, Hannah Brown and Mary Brown, children of Rachel Brown, and grandchildren of said Henry Lockwood copies of the annexed notice (to apply for probate) also copies of the annexed copy of the will" "the deponent being unable to find Samuel Lockwood, son of Cornelius Lockwood" "and been informed he is out of the State of New York, and also unable to find Josiah Dunn grandchild of Henry Lockwood, he also being out of the State" "deponent on June 18th fixed on the outside door of the house being the last place of abode of the said Henry Lockwood copies of annexed notice and will for these last mentioned Samuel Lockwood and Josiah Dunn."

On July 1, 1810, Cornelius Ostrander made oath that he was well acquainted with the deceased Henry Lockwood, that he has seven children (already named), that Sally, Henry and Jeremiah are still living, and that Cornelius, David, Anny and Rachel died before their father, that Cornelius had five children (already named), that David had seven children (already named), that Anny Decker had eight children: Jeremiah Dunn, Josiah Dunn, John Dunn, David Dunn, Anne, wife of *Frederick Godkins*, Mary Phillips, Henry Decker & Sally Decker. That Rachel wife of Isaac Brown had six children (already named, Anna being the wife of *Augustus Marvin*).

Jonathan Wood makes oath that he served Augustus & Anna Marvin with a copy of these papers.

Henry Phillips & John Mackey 4 make oath to having seen Henry Lockwood sign the will, and that Henry Lockwood was at the time "about 76 years old."

Will recorded by *Chas. Tappen, Junr.*, Clerk.)

Page 96.—FOWLER, STEPHEN, of Plattekill.

Will dated Sept. 17, 1807.

"Unto my son *Reuben* exclusive of what he has already received from me six acres of land joining his southerly bounds to run Parallal with his south line to the road then along the same northerly to his land."

"Unto my son *Stephen* besides what he has had from me $125 within one year." "To my daughter *Polly* the wife of *George Ronk* besides what she has already had and received from me in my lifetime $50 within nine months."—"Unto my loving wife *Caty* two milch Cows the choice of my cows and ten sheep the choice of my stock."

"Unto my two youngest sons: *Levi* and *David* the residue" "of my property both real and personal." "If either of them should happen to die before the age of 21 and without lawful issue, survivor to divide the share of deceased. If both should die (as above) the property to go to my three children: Reuben, Stephen and Polly."

Wife *Caty* to remain in full possession of all the property willed to the youngest sons until they are of age.

Sons Levi and David also my good friend *Levi Ostrander* and wife Caty appointed executors. Signed by the testator.

THOMAS FREER
ELIAS YORK
JOSIAH HASBROUCK

(Elias York makes oath that he well knew Stephen Fowler, and saw him and the witnesses sign it, and that Stephen Fowler was then above 21 years of age, to wit in advanced years, and that Thomas Freer & Josiah Hasbrouck have since departed this life.—April term of Court, 1822. *Jacob Snyder*, Clerk of Ulster County.

Francis Lynch, by *John Cole*, his attorney, on March 27, 1822, issues notice that he intends to apply for probate.

Levi Ostrander deposeth that he was well acquainted with the deceased, that he had five children (already named), and that Stephen Fowler has since died without children and without making a will.—*George W. Lynch* deposeth that his mother *Frances Lynch* has become the purchaser and owner of the 1/2 of a farm in Plattkill, of about 160 acres, devised by Stephen Fowler to his son, Levi, and that said Frances is interested in said will for the purpose of securing her title to said property.—March 28, 1822.

Will recorded, April term, 1822.)

Page 101.—TEN BROECK, WESSEL, of Kingston.

Will dated Sept. 27, 1820.

"To my nephew *Wessel Ten Broeck* the son of my deceased brother *Cornelius* all the personal property I may leave." Also "all that part of the farm now occupied by me together with the homestead thereon included within the following bounds viz. Beginning on the bounds of *Jacobus Van Gasbeck* at the swing Gate on the road leading from his house to Kingston thence running along said road as my fence stands southwardly to the bounds of the lands now in possession of *John* and *Henry Ten Broeck* thence along the fence the bounds of said land westwardly to the Vly or meadow to the big ditch and all along through the said ditch to the *Binnekill* at the new bridge then with a straight line to the large Elm tree on the opposite bank of the *Brunnekill* thence along the fence on the bank of said Binnekill untill a line drawn at right angles with the division fence between the lot of *Jacob Marieus Groen* and the lot known by the name of the *Great Piece* thence along such line to the fence on the bank of the *long wye Kill* thence long said fence and bank westwardly to the *Esopus Creek* then down all along said Creek to the bounds of Jacobus Van Gaasbeck and thence along his said bounds to the place of beginning."—"Also all that certain strip or parcel of land on the westwardly side of the Esopus Creek and opposite to the above devised land and the long wye commonly called the *Plaa* (Excepting thereout four acres to be located as follows) Beginning at the corner of *Thomas Van Gaasbeck's* land thence along his bounds and the bounds of Peter Marieus Groen to the East side of a small pond and thence with a southerly line to the said creek so as to contain four acres."—"Also all that certain piece or parcel of land lying on the Northerly side of said Creek being a part of what is called the *Rundale* Beginning at the South End thereof at a ditch formerly dug thence with a straight line to the division fence between me and Jacobus Van Gaasbeck and to include all the land lying south of said line as far as the creek."—"Also all those certain lots designated in the division of the *Commons of Kingston* as Lots Number 74 in the first class containing 39 acres and 6/10 and lot number 56 in the *Bennewater* class containing 32 acres and also my 10 acres lot in the *west Compensation* class."

Residue of my real estate unto my four Nephews, *John, Henry, Cornelius* and *Wessel Ten Broeck* the children of my deceased brother *Abraham.*"

"My nephew Wessel the son of my brother Cornelius" "shall pay all my just debts and that he shall support and maintain my nephew *John Delamater* during his life that he in like manner support and maintain my niece *Christia Delamater* or pay her annually $25 during her life at her option and that within one month after my decease he conveyt to my said nephews John, Henry, Cornelius and Wessel" "the house and land he inherited from his father Cornelius and which is now in possession of my nephew Cornelius Ten Broeck."—"In default" "all my Estate Real and Personal be equally divided among my said nephews (already named).

Wessel Ten Broeck, son of Cornelius, nephew John Ten Broeck, "and my friend Thomas Van Gaasbeck" appointed executors. Signed by the testator.

(Entered Sept. 7, 1824.

JOHN VAN GAASBECK
DAVID DELAMATER
PETER VAN GAASBECK

John Van Gaasbeck of Kingston, farmer, aged 68 years and upwards, David Delamater, of same place, farmer, aged 48 and upwards, and Peter Van Gaasbeck of same place, tailor, aged 56 years and upward, appear before the Court, Sept. 6, 1824, proving the will of Wessel Ten Broeck "of the age of 80 years or thereabout.")

(*Wessel Ten Broeck*, b. Nov. 15, bt. Nov. 19, 1738, d. unm., son of *Wessel Ten Broeck* and Blandina Gaasbeck Chambers (see his will).

Page 105.—CRAWFORD, HENRY, of Marlborough.

Will dated March 27, 1816.

"Unto my loving wife *Abagail* £1000 the use whereof she shall have while she remains my widow or does not marry any other man during her life she shall then have the entire Priveledge of desposing of the £1000 among her Connextion as she seet fit but if she Chuses or does Marry an other man then the £1000 shall be devided among her own Akin and among those whom my Executors may Judge will stand in the most real want of it of her akin" "and executors to see that it is not squandered but put to the best use. "Also the entire use of all my Property both personal and real as long as she remains my widow except $2000 (as bequeathed).

"Unto my nephew *Absalum Crawford* son of *Absalum Crawford* and *Phebe Crawford* $1000" "at age of 21 years and the interest of the same" "for bringing him up."—"Unto *Selah Tuthill Martin* $1000" "at age of 21" "and the interest" "for bringing him up he is a son of *James Martin* and *Phebe Martin.*"

"To my Nephew *Henry Crawford* son of *Charles Crawford* and *Lowis Crawford* $500."—"To my nephew *Henry Crawford* son of *Daniel Crawford* and *Nelly Crawford* $300" "and my $200 in the *Farmers turnpike* stock."—"To my nephew *Henry Crawford* son of *David Crawford* and *Jane Crawford* $500." "To my brother *John Crawford* $200" "six months after my decease."—"To *Henry C. Griggs* son of *Verdinant Griggs* and *Elizabeth Griggs* $500."—"To *Henry Fosdick* son of *Samuel Fosdick* and *Elizabeth Fosdick* $250.

"The above beginning (last paragraph) shall not be paid out to them except my brother John's untill my wife should marry or decease. Then those who are 21 years of age may have theirs, and the other when they are 21 years of age. Brothers and sisters of deceased to divide his share. "If Selah Tuthill Martin should decease before he comes into the possession of his then if his Mother be living" "the executors" "if they think best take charge of the same and for the relief of the Mother."

Residue of estate to be equally divided among "the heirs of all my brothers."

"I give my two blacks *Tom* and his wife *Yanna* free at my decease if they should Choose it if not to remain with my wife." "My two blacks if my place or farm should be sold shall be free and may and I do give and bequeath them and *James York* blackman against whose property I have a Mortgage of $3000 the use of which I give the three blacks" "during their lives and shall not be disturbed by the mortgage during their lives and after their decease my Executors to foreclose the mortgage," and divide it among the nephews.

Wife "and my trusty and well beloved friends Verdinent Griggs and *Nathaniel Chittenden*" appointed executors.

HENRY CRAWFORD (his mark).

NATHANIEL CHITTENDEN
WILLIAM BANKS
BENJAMIN GEE

(Nathaniel Chittenden made oath before the Court, Sept. 6, 1824, that he wrote the last will and Testament of Henry Crawford deceased, that he saw him sign the will, that the other witnesses signed their names, and that Benjamin Gee died some time within the year Past.

William Banks affirmed, at the same time the signature of testator and witnesses.

Entered at the Sept. term, 1824.

Page 109.—KETCH, DAVID, of New Paltz.

Will dated July 29, 1820.

"To my beloved wife *Phoebe* One Cow two beds and beding six Chairs knives & forks and all the other necessary furniture to keep house with for the accommodation of herself and Children" "in liew of her right of Dower."

"To my sons *William, Benjamin, Daniel, Peter, Henry & Stephen*" the residue subject to payments of Legacies, "equally between them Except William & Benjamin to one hundred each more than the rest to my Grand sons *Benjamin* and *Alexander* sons of my son William I will $25 to each." —"To my son John I will $50, to my son David $25, to my daughters *Aney, Phibe, Ruth, Abey, Maria, & Deby* $20 each and to my youngest son Stephen in addition to what is willed above my gun and with regard to my right in 15 acres of Land at the *South Brook Crom Elbow* now in possession of *John Howell* and I belive *William Roose* and *John Roose* or one of them" "to my children sons and daughters equally" "when of age, my sons at 21 and my daughters at 18 years.

My son William and my trusty friends *Barnabas Beuton* and *Wells Lake* appointed executors.

DEVD KEECH.

MARY ROSA	(Record entered Sept. term, 1824. Witnesses
WM GIDNEY	appeared, Sept. 6, 1824 before the Court, prov-
WM SOPER	ing the will).

Page 110.—FELTEN, PHILIP, of Kingston.

Will dated July 9, "in the year of our Lord Christ" (no year mentioned).

"To my son *Philip* my dwelling house & farm at the *Plattekill* Containing about 30 acres as he now occupies the same." Also "all my household furniture blacksmiths tools and all my stock of Cattle."

"To my son *Lawrence* Lot number 38 in the second class in the division of the late Commons of Kingston as he now occupies" "which said lot I make chargeable with the payment of $5 to each of my children *Johannis, Catherine* and *Elizabeth*."

"To my son Johannis and daughters Catharine and Elizabeth Lot number 59 (same location).

Residue to son Johannis and daughters (mentioned).
Sons Philip, Lawrence and Johannis appointed executors.

PHILIP FELTEN (his mark P F.)

WILLIAM J. STYLES
JAMES J. STYLES
GEO. TAPPEN

(Witnesses, all of full age, deposeth before the Court, that the saw Philip Felten the older of Kingston, deceased, sign his name, and that he was of full age that is above the age of 21. Sept. 5, 1825).

Philip Felten, through *H. & C. Tappen*, Counsel, issued notice of intention to apply for probate, Aug. 4, 1825, addressed to Lawrence Felten, Johannes Felten, *Mathew Carle* and *Elizabeth* his wife, *Beekman Thompson* and *Elizabeth*, his wife, *Lawrence Whittaker, Tjerck Whittaker, Caty Whittaker, Sawney Whittaker, Zazarias Whittaker, Peter S. Whittaker, Benjamin Whittaker, George Whittaker*.

Philip Felten deposeth that his father died about three years ago, leaving his heirs three sons, now living, deponent, Johannes and Lawrence, and two daughters, living, to wit, *Helena* the wife of *John A. Louw* & Elizabeth the wife of *Mathew Carle* and the following grandchildren being the issue of his daughter Catherine deceased to wit *Maria* the wife of *Samuel Van Aken, Elizabeth* the wife of Beekman Thompson also Tjerck & Lawrence & Caty & Sauney & *Philip* and also the following great grandchildren being the issue of *Philip Whittaker* the son of the said *Benjamin* Whittaker and *Catherine* his wife to wit Lazarus & Peters & George & Benjamin."

The deponent further says that notices have been sent to the above heirs "John A. Louw & Helena his wife" "living" "in the State of Ohio" "Lawrence Whittaker being absent from home" "Sanney Whittaker a young lad under age" "his sister Elizabeth with whom he lives & who acts as his mother, Sanney being an orphan" "and absent from home." "Benjamin Whittaker & his wife Catharine are both dead" "and Philip Whittaker the son of said Benjamin & Catharine is also dead."

Will recorded "by order of the Court" Sept. term, 1825.

(*Max*(*imilian*) *Velde* (*Velten*), b. in *Germany*, m., Aug. 12, 1732, *Margaret Hendrix*, and *Philip* (*Velten, Felten*), bt. Sept. 11, 1743, m. *Margrit Kohl* (*Cool*), who had: i. *Johannes*, bt. Oct. 22, 1769, m., Febr. 11, 1790, *Annatje Brink;* ii. *Catharina*, bt. Jan. 15, 1772, m. *Benjamin Whittaker;* iii. *Elisabeth*, bt. Aug. 27, 1776, m. *Mathew Carle;* iv. *Jacob*, bt. Dec. 26-28, 1779; v. *Laurens*, bt. Aug. 11, 1782; vi. *Lena*, bt. Febr. 28, 1785, m. *John A. Louw;* vii. *Mareitje*, bt. Jan. 10, 1788; viii. *Philip, Jr.*, m. *Maria Meijer*).

Page 114.—DUBOIS, JOSHUA, of Kingston.

Will dated Dec. 30, 1818.

"To my son *Joshua* my fowling piece as his birthright, Also two lots of land situate in Kingston" "the one at *Waghkonk* adjoining *Jacobus G. Van Etten's* land and containing 39 acres the other across the *Saghkill* & containing about 45 acres. Also a Lot of land at *Johannis Jansen's Wey* as the same is now in fence and possession of my said son Joshua Subject to the right of ditching across said last mentioned lot for the use and benefit of the owner of my adjoining hayland."

"To my three children Joshua, *Charles* and *Ann* as tenants in Common All my land at *Chaumant Bay* on *Lake Ontario* containing about 150 acres."

"All the rest and residue of my real estate" "to my son Charles."—"To my daughter Ann: $1200" "one year after my decease by my son Charles."

"All my Tanners Tools and every of the appurtenances to the Tannery to my said son Charles."—"To my daughter Ann" "her bed and bedding with the appurtenances and all her personal estate now in her use and possession."

Residue to the children ("first allowing to my wife her bed bedding and Clothing")."

"I charge the devises herein before granted to my son Charles and my daughter Ann with the decent and Comfortable support of my beloved wife, *Margaret,* during her natural life."

Sons Joshua and Charles appointed executors.

Signed by the testator.

TOBIAS HASBROUCK
CORNS. VAN BEUREN
CH. TAPPEN JUNR.

(Witnesses appear before the Court, Sept. 5, 1825, proving the will of Joshua Dubois the older.

Ch. Dubois, on Aug. 10, 1825, issued a notice of intention to apply for probate, addressed to Joshua Dubois & *Joseph Castle* & Ann his wife (this deponent's sister).

(*Joshua Dubois*, bt. Oct. 21, 1736 in *Shawangunk* (s. of *Cornelius Du Bois, Sr.* (q. v.), and *Anna Margaret Hooghteling*), m. 1., Apr. 15, 1769, *Catharina Schepmoes*, m. 2., Apr. 20, 1783, *Margrit Masten.* Issue by 1st wife: i. *Josua,* bt. March 6, 1770, by 2d wife: ii. *Annatje,* bt. March 14, 1784, m. *Joseph Castle,* iii. *Charles,* bt. Aug. 21, 1785.)

Page 120.—VAN OSTRANT, JOHN, of Hurley.

Will dated 17th of 1st month, 1822.

"My beloved wife *Anna Van Ostrant*" "all my property" "during her natural life or as long as she shall remain my widow." "After her decease or marriage:

"To my three sons *Lewis Van Ostrant, Frederick Van Ostrant* and *Elias Van Ostrant* all my real estate viz those my two farms they are lying in the town of Hurley the other in the town of *New Paltz* with the messuages and tenements" "except the saw mill," which is to "remain a Joint stock between my three sons."

"To my three daughters *Elizabeth Latting, Hannah Tilson* and *Dinah Van Ostrant* $150 each" "out of the real estate and also the Houshold furniture." "If Dinah should remain single untill after my decease" she is to have "an Outset equal to either of her sisters that are married over and above what is herein mentioned."

"Remainder of my property" "to my three sons."

Legacies to be paid within five years.

"My beloved friend *Daniel Geron"* wife and son Lewis appointed executors.

JOHN VAN VORSTRAND (his mark).

PETER J. CUNTANT
PAUL TILSON
PETER CUNTANT

(Will recorded "by order of the Court" June 14, 1827. Jacob Snyder, Clerk.

The sons issued notice, Febr. 5, 1827, to apply to *Jonathan D. Ostrander,* Surrogate, for probate, addressed to *John Latting* & Elizabeth, his wife, *Paul Tilson* & Hannah, his wife, and *Cornelius Delamater* & *Dinah,* his wife, and to the widow Ann Van Norstrand.

Albert Lester deposeth that he served a copy of this notice on John⁜ Latting and Elizabeth, his wife, of the County of Ontario, April 26th.

Peter J. Contant of Plattekill, Paul Tilson of Hurley, and Peter Coutant of Plattekill affirmed that the will, dated 17th of 1st month according to the Computation of the People called Quakers and in fact Jan. 17th, was signed by the testator.

Page 127.—PERSEN, CORNELIUS, of Saugerties.

Will dated June 27, 1814.

"To my beloved wife *Elizabeth* In lue of her Dowright" "$600" "and also the whole income or rent of my Farm at *Braubant* which is at Present in the Possession of *Henry Myer* with as many of my wood Lots lying in the town of Kingston as she shall detarm to keep and also as much Household furneture Beds & Bedding thereunto Belonging as she thinks proper to keep house with and also as much House Room and Stable Room as she may want and if my Daughter *Margret* should survive her mother then the above mentioned property shall remain in the hands of my executors" "for the mantainance of my daughter Margrit during her Lifetime."

Residue to "my Four children named *Catrina* the widow of *Isaac Post, Mary* the wife of Henry Myer *Elizabeth* the wife of *Cornelius Van Beuren, Annatie* the wife of *Andrew Brink."*

"My beloved wife Elizabeth," the daughters and their husbands appointed executors.

Signed by the testator.

Codicil.

SAMUEL POST
JEREMIAH SNYDER JUNR.
MATTHEW DUBOIS

Wife to have $800 out of my personal Estate which sum I give to her exclusive of what is given to her in my last will and Testament to dispose of as she think proper. Feb. 14, 1818. Cornelius Persen.

JOHN E. VAN AUKEN
PETER SCHOONMAKER
JURRY WM. DEDERICK

(*John Vant Buren* of *Kingston,* Counseller at Law, "deposeth that he is one of the grand children of Cornelius Persen, deceased, and well acquainted with the family. That Maria, wife of Henry Myer of Kingston, Elizabeth, wife of Cornelius Van Beuren of Kingston, Ann, wife of Andrew Brink of Saugerties, Catharine Post, widow of Isaac Post of Saugerties, and Margaret Persen of Saugerties are the children, that Cornelius Persen had no other children at the time of his decease or at any time since." That he departed this life in the month of Febr. 1827, and that Elizabeth Persen (the wife) died previous to her husband.—Dec. 26, 1828. *J. M. Newkerk,* Commissioner.

Henry Myer and Maria, his wife, through their attorneys, Romeyn & Van Buren, apply for probate, Nov. 27th.

Henry Van Buren makes oath to having served papers upon Andrew Brink.

Witnesses to the will and codicil make oath to the signature of the testator. Jan. Term, 1829.

Probated Jan. 13th, 1829.

(*Cornelis Paarsen (Perse, Persen)*, bt. Oct. 26, 1712 (s. of *Matthys Peers*, q. v.), m. 1., Aug. 31, 1734, *Catrina Dyrk (Turk)*, m. 2., Oct. 4, 1748, *Alida Van Slyk*. Issue with 1st wife: i. *Maria*, bt. July 20, 1735; ii. *Cornelis*, bt. Febr. 19, 1744; by 2d wife: iii. *Theunis*, bt. July 2, 1749.

Cornelis (above), m. *Elizabeth Masten*, and had: i. *Catharine*, bt. Aug. 19, 1771, m. *Isaac Post;* ii. *Cornelis*, bt. Dec. 1, 1776;—*Elisabeth*, m. *Cornelis Van Buren;*—*Annatie*, m., July 26, 1806, *Andrew Brink;*—*Margaret*).

End of wills recorded in said book.

Absrtacts of Original Wills, and Inventories, Not Recorded, Filed in the Estate Boxes, Surrogate's Office, Kingston, N. Y.

Box 3.—BURHANS, ABRAHAM, of "the Flattbush in Kingston."

Original will, dated October 3, 1763.

"Unto my son *Petrus Burhans* one derde of Land, Whare his Dwelling House Now Stands or Next adioyning thereto in Such Manner as he Has Cleered the Same as for his Birth Right. In Lue and Sted of any thing he Might Claim as being my Heir at Law."

"Unto my four Sons Named Petrus *Samuell Isaac* and *Abraham* all My Real Estate of House and Land Whereon I Now Dwell or Elsewhere Excepting one acre Herein before bequeathed" "to be Equally Devided amongst them" "providing that Said four Sons Shall pay My four Daughters the Sum of £300" "In Manner following To My Daughter *Helena* the Wife of *Johannes Van Steenbergen*" £75. "Unto My Daughter *Marritje*" £75. "Unto My Daughter *Sara*" £75. "Unto my Daughter *Jenneke* £75, "as Soon as My Said Sons enter Into the possession of My Said Real Estate."

"Unto my three Youngest Daughters Named Marritje Sara and Jenneke" "each of them and outsett Which shall be as Good and Equivelant To What My Daughter Helena has had as Neer as May be."

"Unto My Son Abraham" £25.—"Unto My Nephew *Abraham Osterhout* son of *Hendrecus Osterhout* one Nue Sute of Hollowday Cloth... one Nue Shouting Gun and one Good Gild..horse."—"All my personell Estate Not Herein before Given" "unto my Eight Children Named Petrus Helena Marritje Samuell Isaac Sara Jenneke and Abraham." "If any said Sons shall Happen to Dy Without Lawfull Issue then His Share Shall be Devided amongst the Surving Sons." (Similar provision regarding the daughters).—"Unto my Deer and Well beloved Wife *Annetje* During Her Naturall Life all My Real and personall Estate With all the profitts thereof and full power to sell and Dispose of any part of My personell Estate for paying my Just Debts or Her Needsery Support."

Wife, sons and "Brother In Law *Thunez Osterhout* and Trusty frind *Benjamin Tenbrook*" appointed executors.

Signed by the testator.

JAMES WITTEKER
PHILIP NOLAND
D: WYNKOOP, JUNR.

(Jacob Burhans, a soldier, on March 28, 1660, in the Netherlands service on the *Esopus*, schepen at *Wiltwyck*, 1666, had son *Jan*, who arrived, Apr. 16, 1663, in the "Spotted Cow," and who m. *Helena Traphagen*, dau. of William (q. v.). They had: i. *Janneke*, m. Oct. 12, 1697, *Pieter Du Bois;* ii. *Hillitje*, m. June 18, 1700, *Edward Whitaker;* iii. *Jacob*, bt. March 2, 1679, d. y.; iv. *Barent*, bt. Apr. 24, 1681, m. *Margriet Jans Matthysen*, dau. of *Jan Matthysen* (q. v.); v. *Johannes*, bt. Aug. 27, 1682, m. *Margriet Legg*, dau. of *William* (q. v.). She m., 2d., Apr. 7, 1726, *Barent Van Benthuysen*, widower of *Janneke Van Wagenen;* vi. *Elisabeth*, bt. July 7, 1684, m., *Jan Ploeg;* vii. *Willem*, bt. March 7, 1686, m. 1., June 22, 1731, *Grietjen Ten Eyck*, dau. of *Matthys;* m. 2., Sept. 20, 1749, *Catharine Kool*, widow of *Jacobus Van Etten;* viii. *Hendrick*, bt. Nov. 6, 1687 (q. v.); ix. ABRAHAM, bt. Nov. 28, 1690; x. *Isaac*, bt. Jan. 28, 1692, m., July 22, 1722, *Neeltje Westphael*, dau. of *Symon W.* and *Neeltje Quackenboss*. She m. 2., Oct. 25, 1737, at *Rhinebeck*, *Ary Roosa*, widower of *Johanna de Hoges;* xi. *Samuel*, bt. June 3, 1694, m. Dec. 16, 1720, *Janneke Brink*, dau. of *Cornelis Lammertse* and *Maritje Egberts*. She m. 2., Oct. 5, 1734, *Walrand Dumond;* xii. *David*, bt. Nov. 24; 1695, m., Nov. 12, 1731, *Debora Van Bommel*, dau. of *Pieter Van B.* and *Debora Davids*.

ABRAHAM (above), m., June 21, 1729, *Annetje Oosterhoudt* (bt. Jan. 19, 1701) dau. of *Pieter Jans O.* and *Heyltje Schut*, and had: i. *Petrus*, m. May 4, 1754, *Johanna Van Steenbergh*, dau. of *Benjamin v. S.* and *Rachel Suylandt;* ii. *Helena*, m., Oct. 19, 1752, *Johannes Van Steenbergen*, s. of *Aries v. S.* and *Baartjen Swart;* iii. *Maria*, bt. July 15, 1733, d. unm.; iv. *Zamuel*, bt. March 16, 1735, m. *Marytje Kip*, da. of *Jacob J. K.* and *Lea van Etten;* v. *Isaac*, bt. June 5, 1737, m., Nov. 19, 1765, *Susanna Foland*, dau. of *Philippus F.* and *Eva Switzler;* vi. *Zara*, bt. Apr. 8, 1739, m., Nov. 14, 1765, *Benjamin van Steenbergen*, s. of *Arie v. S.* and *Baartjen Swart;* vii. *Janneken*, bt. Apr. 19, 1741, m., Oct. 11, 1771, *Jan Osterhoudt*, s. of Lawrence O. and Helena Whitaker).

Box 11.—DEPUY, JACOBUS, of Rochester.

Original will, dated Dec. 15, 1778.

"To my Brother *Simon Depuy* my Negro *Jeck*," "In trust" he "paying for the same unto my Mother" "one Bond Due to her, Bearing Date June 3, 1777."—"Unto my Sister *Sara Depuy* the side saddle and Bridle."—"Unto my Brother Simon Dupuy all my Real Estate" "so as the same is Devised unto me By the Last will and Testament of My father *Jacobus Depuy*, Bearing Date Sept. 25, 1764," "In trust" he "to pay unto my Brothers & sister the sum of £450" "that is to say to my Brother *Moses*" £150 "unto my Brother *Jacob*" £150 "and unto my sister Sara" £150 "in four Quarterly Payments after my said Brother Simon shall have Received the Possession of my said Real Estate."—If Moses, Jacob or Sara should die before they "Come to Lawful age and Leave No Lawfull Issue Behind them" then the survivors to divide the share of deceased.—"Unto my Brother Jacob one Seat in the Pew No. 16."—"My Uncle *Cornelius Dupuy, Jacobus Van Wagenen*, and *Thomas Schoonmaker, Junr.*" appointed executors. Signed by the testator.

JOHN DEPUY
ANNATJE DEPUY
MOSES MILLER

(*Moses Depuy* (s. of *Nicholas*), m. 1., *Maria Wynkoop*, b. *Albany*, 1660, dau. of *Cornelis W.*, m. 2., Oct. 16, 1724, *Peterneltje De Pree*, widow of *Martinus Van Aken*, of *Rochester*, and had i. *Mareitje*, bt. Apr. 24, 1681; ii. *Nicolaes*, bt. Dec. 3, 1682, m., March 22, 1707, *Weyntjen Roosa;*. iii. *Catherina*, bt. Apr. 6, 1684; iv. *Magdalena*, bt. March 14, 1686; v. *Cornelis*, bt. Jan. 8, 1688, m., May 6, 1713, *Catrina Van Aken;* vi. *Catrina*, bt. May 25, 1690; vii. *Moses*, bt. Sept. 27, 1691, m., Febr. 14, 1716, *Margrietje Schoonmaker*, dau. of *Jochem H.;* viii. *Benjamin*, bt. Oct. 13, 1695, m. 1., Sept. 3, 1719, *Elisabeth Schoonmaker*, dau. *Jochem H.*, m. 2., Dec. 13, 1735, *Eiche De Witt;* ix. *Susanna*, bt. Jan. 9, 1698; x. *Catharina*, bt. Nov. 30, 1701, m., May 10, 1722, *Benjamin Schoonmaker*, s. of *Jochem H.;* xi. *Jacobus*, bt. Sept. 19, 1703, m., Aug. 26, 1725, *Sara Schoonmaker*, and had: a. *Jacobus*, bt. Nov. 6, 1726; b. *Maria*, bt. July 28, 1728; c. *Efraim*, bt. Febr. 8, 1730; d. *Elisabeth*, bt. Oct. 28, 1733; e. *Catrina*, bt. Febr. 13, 1737, f. *Zusanna*, bt. Nov. 12, 1738; g. *Daniel*, bt. June 8, 1746,—*Simon, Moses* and *Sara*).

Box 14.—FREER, CATHARINA, Widow and Relict of Jonas Freer, Deceased, late of New Paltz.

Original will, dated Sept. 22, 1781.

"Unto my only and well beloved Daughter *Maria* the Wife of *Gerrit Freer Junr.*" "All my Goods and Chattels of what kind or nature soever which I shall leave at the time of my Decease. And I do hereby make, nominate and appoint my trusty and well beloved friends *Jacob Hasbrouck Christoffel Deyo* and *Jacobus Hasbrouck Junr.*" my executors.

CATHARINA FREER (her mark).

ESTHER BEVIER
ELISABETH HASBROUCK
JOS: HASBROUCK

(*Jonas Freer*, b. ab. 1701, d. 1775 (s. of *Hugo F.* and *Maria Anne Le Roy*, see *Hugh F.*), m. *Catrina Stoker*, b. in *Germany*, and had: i. *Maria*, bt. Sept. 21, 1729, m. *Gerrit Freer*, bt. Apr. 30, 1727, s. of *Hugo F.* and *Bregje Terpenning*, s. of *Hugo F.* and *Maria Ann Le Roy*; ii. *Martinus*, bt. New Paltz, May 20, 1733; iii. *Johannes*, bt. Oct. 26, 1735, m., March 29, 1760, *Sara Bevier*, dau. of *Abraham*; iv. *Elias*, b. ab. 1740, m. *Martha Everitt*, dau. of *Robert E.* and *Esther*, of New Marlborough; v. *Jonas*, bt. 1737, m. *Magdalena Bevirs*, dau. of *Jacobus B.* and *Antje Freer*; vi. *Simon*, bt. Aug. 9, 1741, m., May 12, 1770, *Annatje Blanchan*, dau. of *Matthews B.* of *Hurley*; vii. *Petrus*, bt. Oct. 30, 1743; viii. *Lena*, bt. 1739, m. *Johannes Bevier*).

Box 22.—NUKERK, CORNELIS, of Hurley.

Original will, written in Dutch, and dated "tot mynen Huysen in Hurley" (at my house in Hurly) Sept. 15, 1787.

"In de name Van den Dreenigen godt, Vader, Soon En Hyligen geest Amen." (In the name of the Trinity, the Father, the Son and the Holy Ghost, Amen).

"Myn Sinne En Verstant Volkome magtigh, De Heere sy gelooft" (of perfect mind, the Lord be praised). (Long religious preamble).

"Myn Waarde Huysvrouw *Diena* Indien sy my overleft, van myn twee Soons soons *Philip* En *Cornelius*" "Sal hebben" £20 "Yaarlyk" "So lang sy leeft (my worthy wife Diena, if she lives after me, to have £20 yearly of my two sons (soons written twice, by mistake, as "klein-zoons" is grandsons). Also "De kuer van myn Negers En Negerinnen" "om haar te dienen so lang sy leeft (the choice of negroes and negresses, to serve her as long as she lives) "ook de kuer van de Ruymen Uyt Myn tegenwoordigh Huys (and the choice of the rooms in my house, where I now reside) "En ook twe kelkKoyen welke koeyen myn voornoemde Soons voor haar houde sullen Somer En Winter" (and two milk cows, which my said sons shall house during summer and winter).

"Myn soon Philip myn groote bybel sal hebben" (my son Philip to have my large bible).—"Myn twee voornoemende Soons sullen Uytkeeren of betaalen aan myn vier dogters, Namentlyk *Jannetye*, de Huysvrouw van *Benjamin Roosa, Lea* de Huysvrouw van *Gerrit Nukerk, Henderica* de Huysvrouw van *Cornelius du Mondt,* En *Aarieantye* de Huysvrouw van *Petrus du Boys*" £100 each (my said two sons shall pay to my four daughters, Jannetye, wife of Benjamin Roosa, Lea, wife of Gerrit Nukerk, Henderica, wife of Cornelius du Mont, and Aariaantye, the wife of Petrus du Bois, £100 each). Said sons also to pay £50 to "my soon *Arys* soon *Petrus*" (my son Ary's son Peter). Said sons to pay, thereof, £220 one year after testator's decease, and the other £225 two years after "myn doodt" (my death).

"Myn Reght In het partentees" (my right in the patent) to all the children and the grandchild, provided they reside in Hurly, otherwise not.—The personal estate to be divided among said children, and grandchild, to Cornelius and Philip the real estate, they to pay all the debts. Said sons appointed executors. Signed by the testator.

> HUYBERT OSTRANDER
> JOHANNIS SUYLAND
> JOH. V. DEUSEN

(*Arie Gerritsen van Neukerk* (s. of *Gerrit Cornelisze* and *Cheiltje Cornelis*), q. v., b. in *Midwoud, Flatbush, L. I.*, res. *Hurley*, m.. *Lysbeth Lambertsen*, dau. of *Lambert Huybertsen*, and had: i. *Ghilje*, bt. Jan. 29, 1688; ii. *Jan*, bt. Aug. 24, 1690; iii. *Henderikje*, bt. Nov. 11, 1692; iv. *Gerrit*, bt. May 30, 1697; v. *Ariaantje*, bt. Nov. 19, 1699; vi. *Lea*, bt. Aug. 9, 1702; vii. *Rachel*, bt. Apr. 9, 1704; viii. *Cornelis*, bt. Nov. 12, 1710, m. Oct. 29, 1731, *Diena* (*Dina*) *Hoogteling*, and had: a. *Elisabeth*, bt. Oct. 1, 1732; b. *Jannetye*, bt. Oct. 20, 1734, m. Nov. 18, 1759, *Benjamin Roosa*; c. *Ary*, bt. Sept. 11, 1737, d. y.; d. *Philippus*, bt. Apr. 3, 1740; e. *Ary*, bt. Oct. 3, 1742, m. Nov. 18, 1769, *Maria Crispel;* f. *Lea*, bt. Apr. 29, 1744, m. Dec. 8, 1764, *Gerrit Nukerk;* g. *Henderica*, bt. March 9, 1746, m. Oct. 30, 1785, *Cornelius du Mondt;* h. *Ariantje*, bt. Jan. 8, 1748, m. Dec. 23, 1779, *Petrus Du Bois;* i. *Cornelis*, bt. Oct. 15, 1752, m. June 12, 1779, *Sara Kiersteder;* see page 169 for another son of Arie Gerritsen: *Conrad*).

Box 24.—LEGG, WILLIAM, of Kingston, yeoman.

Original will, dated Oct. 8, 1780.

"My loving Wife *Sara* shall Remain and Injoy in full Possesion of my Whole Estate real and Personall During the time She Shall Continue my Widow and Shall have the Command of the Income of said Estate, Provided that my Daughter *Helena* who is Not able to Maintain herself, and my Two sons Named *William* and *Samuel* shall have their Maintainens with my said Wife out of the said Estate" they "shall be taught to Read, Write and Cypher at the Expense of my said wife the Mother of the said William and Samuel during the minority." "In case my "wife should merry again before my said sons should arrive to the age of 21 years" then "wife shall Give Up My Whole Estate Real and Personall to my Executors" and to be "debarred to Claim any Income or Dowry from the said Estate."—"To my son *Cornelis* for his Birth Right my Large Shooting Gun I have of My father."—My three sons (named) shall have my Real Estate where I now Dwell with the house, Barn & Barraks also my Estate called *Peter Mouries* Land that is to say the Souther part of said bowery" "as I now occupy and Use the same and Divided by me and brother John." Survivor to divide share of deceased. At death or remarriage of wife, the personal estate to be divided among said children, and "the Children of my Daughter *Annatje*, Deceased for her Mother 1/5." "Whereas I Received a Legacie of £100 by my first wife *Helena* Daughter of *Jan Ploegh,* Deceased, and as I think it just and Equitable that the Children begotten of the body of said Helena Should have the Benefitt of her Mothers Portion therefore" "said sum of £100 shall be paid out of my Real Estate as soon as my sons William & Samuel arrive at the age of 21 years" i. e. "to my son Cornelis" £30, and to children of "my daughter Annatje" £30, and "to my daughter Helena" £40." —"My son William my Shooting Gun and to my son Samuel my other small Gun before any Division shall be made."—If wife should continue "my widow after my sons William & Samuel arrive at the age of 21 years," then the wife is to receive yearly £12 for her maintainance during her life, to be paid by said sons.——"Loving son Cornelis and my son in (law?) *Tjerck Schoonmaker* and my friend *Edward Schoonmaker, Jr."* appointed executors. Signed by the testator.

   JOHN J. PERSEN
   MICHAEL PATTISON
   CHRISTOPHER MIDLER (his mark)

  (*William Legg,* bt. Oct. 31, 1708 (s. of *John Legg* and *Annatje Fynhout,* q. v.), m. 1., Oct. 20, 1738, *Helena Ploeg,* dau. of *John,* m. 2., March 11, 1762, *Sara Wulfin,* and had with 1st wife: i. *John,* bt. Oct. 14, 1739; ii. *John,* bt. Dec. 21, 1740; iii. *Anatje;* iv. *Elizabeth,* bt. Dec. 12, 1742; v. *Cornelis,* bt. Oct. 13, 1745, m., Febr. 28, 1787, *Maria Wolf;* vi. *John,* bt. Aug. 26, 1753; vii. *Helena,* bt. May 11, 1755; with 2d wife: viii. *William,* ix. *Samuel*).

Box 35.—SNYDER, JOHANNIS, of Kingston.

  Original will, dated June 5, 1771.

  "To my Loving Wife Named *Grietje* my Negro Wench Namĕd *Floor* During My said Wifes Life" also "one feather bed and straw bed" she also to "have the Use of My bedstead bedding and Every Thing belonging thereto During her Life And my house furniture Pots and Dishes During her Life, and also my Little Cobbert and Chist During her Life, and after her Decease the above house furniture (Excepting) the feather bed & straw bed shall be Divided among my Children."—"To my Daughter *Christinas* Son *Johannis* the sum of £65" "to be paid by his father *Christian Fiero* by virtue of an Obligation the said Christian Noes stands bound to Me and payable one Year after the Decease of Me and My Said Wife." "In case" "Johannis should Die before the said Money is Payable" then the "money shall be Divided among my Children Equel."—"To my Daughter Marya wife of *Cornelis Oosterhoudt* £10 being the residue of the above Obligation."—To "said Grandson Johannis my horse Saddle and Bridle" "and all my Cloathing belonging to my Body Whatsoever."—"All my Moveables (Excepting the Legacies above ordered) shall be Divided Between my two Children Named Christina" "and Marya."—"All the Moveables" "Brought to Me by Marriage Shall be Left to her (my wife)" she also to "have the Benefit and Recovery of her Entertainment by Virtue of two Oblagatory Instruments Signed one by Christian Fiero and the other by Cornelis Oosterhoudt During her Life" and if she "Should Not have Sufficient Entertainment by Sickness or other Exident" then the Executors shall "dispose of such of the Moveables Left to her Use as they shall think Necessary for her Support."—"My Nephew *Johannis Snyder,* Son of *Johannis Snyder Junr.* shall have one Cow."—"My said Negro Wench Floor after the Decease of my said Wife shall have her Choice to Live jther With my Daughter Christina or my Daughter Marya" "Provided the one half of her Value shall be paid by such as shall be Choset by her, to my other heir."

"My Loving frinds *Jurry Hommel* and *Jurry W: Rechtinger*" appointed executors. Signed by the testator.

CORNELIUS PERSEN
STEPHANUS FERO
JOH'S SNYDER, JUNR.

(*Johannes Snyder*, b. in *Germany*, m. March 1, 1724, *Antjen* (*Grietjen*) *Deunis* (*Theunis*), and had: i. *Christina*, bt. Febr. 14, 1725, m. *Christian Fierer*, Jr. (when her name is written '*Schneider*', and had: a. *Johannes Fierer*, bt. July 27, 1746 (witn. by *Johannes S.* and his wife, *Annatje Theungas*); b. *Christian Fierer*, bt. Aug. 2, 1747; ii. *Johannes*, bt. Jan. 23, 1726; iii. *Maria*, bt. Nov. 24, 1728, m. *Cornelis Osterhout*.

Johannes Snyder had a brother, *Jury* (*George*) *Snyder*, who m. 1., *Christina Thunjus*, m. 2., Dec. 5, 1724, *Johanna Swart,* and had issue: i. *Johannes*, bt. Jan. 24, 1720, m. *Rachel Swart;* ii. *Lea*, bt. Febr. 6, 1726; iii. *Ceeletjen*, bt. Apr. 30, 1727; iv. *Elisabeth*, bt. March 18, 1733, m. *Michel Devoe;* v. *Catrina*, bt. July 10, 1737; vi. *Maria*, bt. May 2, 1742; vii. *Johanna*, bt. Apr. 21, 1745.

Johannes Snyder and Rachel Swart had issue: i. *Christina*, bt. July 28, 1745; ii. *Petrus*, bt. Nov. 1, 1747; iii. *Johannes*, bt. Sept. 2, 1750 (mentioned above in the will of his grand-uncle); iv. *Seletje*, bt. May 27, 1753; v. *Rachel*, bt. July 11, 1756; vi. *Cornelia*, bt. Jan. 14, 1759; vii. *Elisabeth*, bt. May 31, 1761; viii. *Abraham*, bt. Apr. 20, 1764).

(*Inventarium* Oover het Losse Goed van den Overleeden Johannis Snyder Woonende aen de Beaverkill in de County van Ulster (Inventory of the personal estate of J. S., deceased, residing at Beaver Kill in Co. U.), Door ende met goede Vinden van de Gesteltc Executors *Jurgen Hommel* en *Jurgen W. Reghtmeyer* ook Erfgenaemen en agter Laatene Weduwe *Grietje Snydr Christ Fero* en *Cornelius Oosterhoudt* (and by the good friend, J. H., J. W. R. and heirs, and surviving widow G. S., C. F., and C. O.), dated July 16, 1771 (sic):

Neegers. Een Negerin met Een Jonge van Vyf Jaer Oudt (A negress with a boy five years old).

Beesten. Drie Melk Beesten en Een Jonge Vaarse (Three Milk Cows, and a young heifer).

Parden. Een Mear (a mare).

Schaapen. Neegen Stucks van Oud en Jong aen Schaapen (Nine young and old sheep).

Vaarkens. Twe Stucks aen Vaarkens (a couple of hogs).

Een Groote Caste met Inhoudend Goed, Seven stucks Laaken, Vier Kussen Sloopens, Een Bond Nehangsel, Een stuckje Linnen houdende 9¼ Ele 10 stucks hembden van Vaader, 5 Mutssen, 2 Neckjes, Een Seyde NeusDoeck, 2 Woole hoede Een Caster hoed (A great chest with contents, 7 sheets, 4 pillows, colored hangings, a piece of linnen of 9¼ yards, 10 of father's shirts, 5 caps, 3 scarfs, 1 silk handkerchief, 2 wool caps, and one beaver cap.

Geld. In all 21 schellinge meer 1 schellinge Vier koopers (21 schillings in all, with 1 schilling, four coppers).

Bande, Noten & andere Pampiers in Een Lessnaer geslooten (Books, (notes, and other papers in a locked desk). Een Musket, Een Deegen, haagel Sackje met 't kruythoorn, Twee schaape Scheeren, Een Slaapbanck, Een kist, Een key, Een Spiegel, Twee potte bancke, Een Casje, El paer Cousse van Vaader, nogh 1 paer meer van Vouse, 1 Camen mandje (a musket, a sword, shot-pouch with the powder-horn, two sheep-shears, a sleeping bench (bedstead in form of a chest), a chest, a flint (to strike fire on), a mirror, two cup-boards, a little box, a pair of father's stockings, one more pair of stock-ings, one comb basket).

Boekken. Een Groote Bybel, Een Predicate Boek, Twee gebedt Boekken, Twee Cate-chisms, 1 gebedt boeck van *Conr. Mell*, nogh 1 gesangh boeck in in Kerk met nogh Een boekje (a great bible, a book of sermons, two prayer-books, two confirmation books, one prayer book of Conr. Mell, also a hymn book in the church, as well as another book).

ABSTRACTS OF ORIGINAL WILLS AND INVENTORIES. 187

Tobac. Twee Rolletjes Tabac, 3 paer Wanden, nogh Een Muttss (2 rolls of tobacco, 3 pair of mittens, and one cap).

Kleederen. Twee groote Rokken, Vier sluyt Rokken Drie gevulte Camisools, vier hembder Rokken, Twee Linne broekken, nogh Een Linne broeck Drie Leeder broeks, Drie korte gestrepte broekke, Vier Eyge geweeve Camisools gestreept, Een Swart Camisool met broeck, Twee paer schoene met Een paer Gebsen, Een scheer mess met Een Oligsteen (two roomy coats (great coats probably), four narrow coats (i. e. close fitting), three double-lined waistcoats, four night shirts, two linnen breeches, also one pair of linnen breaches, three leather breeches, three short striped breeches, four striped, hand-made woven night-shirts, a black shirt (Guernsey) with breeches, two pair shoes with a pair of buckles, a razor with a hone).

Tinne Goed. Vier Tinne schuttels, 2 Tinne Comme nogh Een Tinne schuttel nogh Een Cometje, 14 Tinne Borde, 1 Trink Can, 19 Tinne lepel, 2 Tinne kopjes, Twee blikke Trechter, 2 Candelaers, 1 Tinne mutsjes, een hand blikje, 1 aerde en Een blikke Can Een vleesch vorkje 1 schuyn Spaen 4 aarde schuttels 1 pyp potje 1 blikke Commetje, Een Vlasche keller met 8 vlasche, Een vleschje met Soet Olie, nogh Een Vlessche (four pewter saucers, 2 pewter cups (or dishes), also one pewter saucer, and one small pewter cup, 14 pewter plates, 1 drinking can, 19 pewter spoons, 2 pewter cups, 2 tin funnels, 2 candlesticks, 1 pewter extinguisher, one earth and one tin can, one meat-fork, 1 skimming ladle, 4 earth saucers, a small coffee-pot, a small tin-cup, a bottle case with 8 bottles, a small bottle with sweet oil, and another little bottle).

Bed clothing. Een Veeder Bedt met kussens en Een Pelluwe Een bonde Roghe, Een Groene Roghe, Een Wilde Compaerss, Drie Eyge gemaekte Compaerse, Vier Bedde kleede, Een Sprie, Nogh Een Veeder Bedt bestaende in Drie kussen en Een Pelluwe ende Een Wilde Compaerse, nogh Een stroo bedt, Linne 24 Ell, Een stuckje Oover Leeder (a feather-bed with bolster and one pillow, and colored petticoat, a green petticoat, a natural quilt (probably made of skins of wild animals), three homemade quilts, four bed-covers, one counterpane, one more feather-bed with three bolsters, and one pillow, and one natural quilt, also a straw-bed, 24 yards of linnen, a piece of leather for covering).

Messe en Verkjes 10 Messe en Vyf Vorkjes nogh Een Vorkje (10 knives and 5 forks also one small fork).

Stoele. 6 Swarte stoele, 9 stucks Eyge gemaeckte stoele, Een groote stoel, 2 Tange, En Een aschschoop, Een paer brand.ysers, met Een rooster en Trefje, Twee heugels 1 paer stryk Eyser, Een paer Boots (6 black chairs, 9 homemade chairs, a big chair, 2 tongs, an ash-shovel, a pair of fire-blowers, a roaster, 2 pot-hooks, one pair of flat-iron, a pair of boots).

Gereedschapp. Een Saagh, Breedbyl ende haelmess, met een oud Vleysch, byl ende meer andere Saaken in Een gesloote kistje te samen gedaen, Een Zaadel met het gebitt ende Een paer Oude boots, (a saw, axe and drawing-knife with an old butchers-knife, and some other things, together with a little chest, a saddle with a bit and an old pair of boots).

Een Coye met stroobedt, Een Laake 1 Wilde Compaerse, 1 Eyge gemaekte Compaerse Twee kussens (a straw-bed, a sheet, a natural quilt, two bolsters).

Yzergoed. 7 stucks Potte aen kleen en groot 1 groote koopere, keetel Een Tee keetel, een hang Eyser met Comfoor, 2 panne 1 Trapje 1 Wolle Wiel Twee spinne Wiels 5 Emmers met henghsels Een blaasbalg Twee schappen Een Roy Dissel Een gleedje met all Toe behoorend goedje Een kleen Wagentje (7 pots, large and small, a large brass kettle, a tea-pot, a pot-hanger, with brazier, 2 frying pans, a step-ladder, a wool-winder, two spinning wheels, 5 buckets with handle, a pair of bellows, two shelves, a red shaft, a sledge with its belongings, a small cart).

KuyperGoed. Een Vleisch vat, Een Ancker vatje, 2 kleene Vatjes, Twee Oxhoofde, Een Loog Vat 2 barls, 2 Anckers, 3 Tobetjes, Een Emmer 3 Botter vatjes 3 aarde potte Een groote aarde Can Tween Barl Tobetjes 1 Oxhoofd Tobetje 1 Visch vat 1 Carn ende Een karnmelk vaatje Een baek Trokje 1 Verf Eymer Twee bakke 1 bottel met Traen 1 boomtje Vet 1 Coopere Craen 1 Quaste bakje 3 Tiene Mandjes. (a meat-barrel, a keg, 2 small barrels, 2 hogs-heads, 1 bucking-tub, 2 barrels, 2 kegs, 3 tubs, a bucket, 3 butter casks, 3 stone pots, one large jug, two small barrels, a small hogs-head, 1 fishtub, 1 churn, one buttermilk-barrel, a baking trough, 1 pail paint, 2 basins, 1 bottle with fish-oil, 1 tub grease, 1 brass tap, 1 small basin for brushes, 3 tin baskets).

Solder Goed. 4 Flolle Boome, Een Oxhooft, Een Meel Vat 1 Sappaen sieftje 26 kleen en groote Tiene an andere Mande 1 fijn Sieftje 1 back Troghje 2 quaste backjes 1 ander goede back 4 stucks kleeneschopjes nogh 2 kleene Schoppjes en 1 Werp Schopp 8 Sacksken Een Zeyde Oover Leeder met 3 stukke Sool Leeder 4 stuko voorers kleen en groot 3 kleene vaatjes 1 scheepel Een Wann nogh Een goed Schoppje 23½ vaem in Twee stukke goed Touw 5 knuyl Touw gaere 1 Trogh met Eyser hanghsels met deksel op Een schael,

7 lbs. Werke gaare 6½ lbs. Wolle gaere, 1 Merk Eyser 9 lbs. gewaschte Woll Een fyn Vlass heekell Een spyker heekele 2 lbs. geswonge Vlass 1 oudt Vat Een Spill voor Touwgaere te spinnin 1 stroo Mess, 1 steek mess, Een groote Trumm Saagh. (4 poles (to push forward a boat), a hogshead, a meal-tub, a straining cloth, 26 small and large, tin and other baskets, 1 thin sieve, 1 kneading-trough, 2 basins for brushes, 1 good basin, 4 shovels to clean, 2 other shovels to clean with, 1 spade, 8 bags, a cover of leather, and 3 covers of sole leather, 4 drills, large and small, 3 kegs, 1 bushel, 1 winnow and a good shovel, 23½ fathom good cord in two pieces, 5 balls of string, 1 trough, with iron hangings, and cover, a plate, 7 lbs. yarn, 6½ lbs. wool yarn, 1 branding iron, 9 lbs. washed wool, a thin flax reel, a cogged reel, 2 lbs. brooded flax, 1 old barrel, a spindle for the loom, a straw cutter, a pricking knife, a large trimming saw).

Leeder. 4 Zeyde of 2 gantsche huyde Leeder in de Loy Drogh met 2 Calver velle, 3 gehakte Drogge, Een Sleupsteen Een vierde part van Een Run Meule by *Petrus Lauw*, Een Sneuw Eyser om boomen te Sneuwen (4 parts of two hides in the tanpit with two calfskins, 3 wooden troughs, 1 grindstone, a fourth part of a tan mill, at Petrus Louw, a snow sledge for sledging trees).

Schulden (Debts). By *Pieter Scherp* staet nogt 19 sch., by Mr. *Cockburn* 3 sch., by *Benjamin Meyer* staet nogh mischien 26 sch. of wat meer, by *Pieter Winnen* Een Schaepe Lamm, by *Christ. Fiero Junr.* 12 sch. voor 1 foot vleesch, by *Steph. Fieoro* £3 voor Een Jong Vulletje, by *Daniel Lucas* voor Een koe £3.10 had Een Jaer Tyt te betaal by *Thom. Steenberg* 7 Ell Wolle Doppelsteen, En Een barl..........*Willem Freligh* voor Een harte vell 18 sch. (to P. S. yet 19s., to Mr. C. 3s., to B. M. 26s. or more, to P. W., a lamb, to C. F., Jr., 12s., to S. F. £3, for a colt, to D. L. £3.10 for a cow, a year to pay for it, to T. S. 7 yards wool die (means woven in die form), a barrel (blank space), W. F. for deer skin 18s.).

ADDENDA.

SECRETARY'S PAPERS, Liber D., page 13. (T. D. R., II., p. 351):
On Nov. 4, 1671 appeared before *Cornelis Barentsen Sleght* and *George Hall*, commissaries of the Hon. Court at Kingston in America,

AERDT MARTENSEN DOORN

husband and guardian of *Geertruy Andriesen*, widow of *Jacob Jansen Slicoten*, as well as the guardians of the latter's son, *Jan Jansen Slicoten*, the Heer *Willem Beecqman* and Roelof Swartwout, as the attorneys for said Geertruy Andriesen, who also appears. Said parties hereby grant full powers of attorney to Mr. *Nicolaes De Meyer*, merchant at *New York*, to enquire at *Amsterdam* for the last will of *Jan Jacobsen Slicoten*, grandfather of the said child, and also to learn what has been devised to *Willem Jansen Slicooten*, the uncle of said child, said uncle being killed here during the war with the indians, leaving no other heirs than the said child. And further to enquire after a will made by the great grandfather of Jacob Jansen Slicoten, who left something to the children of the son, which was expected by said Jacob Jansen Slicoten, and which would revert to the said child.

Said De Meyer to enquire diligently, and if necessary to bring suit. The parties humbly pray the Hon. Heeren Orphanmasters of the city of Amsterdam to assist the said Mr. De Meyer in securing the inheritance, which belongs to said child.

Said De Meyer to place any money secured at interest with the Orphan's Court, and to present a bond by the said Hon. Orphan-masters.

Wilh. Beeckman, Roelof Swartwout, Aert Maertsen Doorn, and Geertruyd Andresen (her mark).

Ibid., p. 18. (T. D. R., II., 353):

JACOB JANSEN VAN STOUTENBORGH

on Nov. 7, 1671 granted full power of attorney to Mr. *Nicolaes De Meyer*, merchant at *New York*, for the purpose of receiving his share in the property left by his father, *Jan Evertsen Maeter* and his mother, *Annetie Cornelis*. With him in this enquiry are associated his uncle, *Robberdt Evertsen* and *Saer Evertsen*, his guardians. Said inheritance is to be enquired for at Amersfordt, in the Secretary's office.

Signed by Jacob Jansen (his mark), in presence of *Jan Willemsen* and *Cornelis Barentsen Sleght*.

Ibid., Liber E., p. 43. (T. D. R., II., p. 400); written in English.

Sr Edmond Anders (about March 1676/7) appointed *Elisabet Hals* administratrix to the estate of *GORGE HALL,* latte of Kingston in Esopus, who had dyed Intestaet, leaving Elisabed his widdow.

Ibid., p. 58. (T. D. R., II., p. 404):

HENDRICK CORNELISEN SLEGHT.

Testamentary disposition, dated Nov. 15, 1677, and written in Dutch.

"He has three children, to whom his wife is to return half of the estate, in case she should happen to remarry. The whole estate to go to the children after her death. The oldest son to receive all of his father's clothing."

Signed *Hendrick Slecht,* and witnessed by *Jacobus Kip* and Gerrit Aertsen.

Ibid., p. 96. (T. D. R., II., p. 424):

AERDT AERDTSEN OTTERSPOOR.

Testamentary disposition, dated May 5, 1678, and written in Dutch.

"All his property, house, lot, Holland money, in *Holland* to go to *Cornelis Barensen* and his wife; a little closet excepted, which shall go to his daughter *Petronella.*

Aerdt Aerdsen Otterspoor (his mark); witnessed by *Pieter Cornelisen* (his mark), and *Barent Van Borsum.*

COURT RECORDS, Liber V., p. 170. (T. D. R., II., p. 569):

CAPT. THOOMAS CHAMBERS, widower of Margarietie Hendrix,

and *Louwerentia Kellenaer,* widow of Domine *Lourentius Van Gaesbeeck,* intend to enter the state of matrimony. The said widow grants to her children with said Gaesbecq, named *L. Jacomeyn, Maria,* and *Abraham Van Gaesbeeck,* 100 sch. of wheat each, when of age or married. The son Abraham is to receive of all his father's clothing.

Ibid., p. 186. (T. D. R., II., p. 574):

JOHANNA, widow of the deceased GEORGE DAVITS,

intends to enter the married state with *Hendericus Beecqman,* young man, therefore the said bride, *Johanna Lopers,* grants to her children with said Davits, named *Jacobus, Samuel,* and *Salomon* 500 sch. of winter wheat each, when of age. She will also give the children an honest and a Christian education, so far as she is able. As guardian over said children she appoints their uncle, *David Davits,* and *Dirck Jansen Schepmoes.*

As security, she mortgages her house and lot in Kingston.

Signed Joanna Loopers, and Henr. Beecqman; witnessed by *Wessel Ten Broeck,* and *W. D. Meyer.*

Ibid., Liber V., p. 239. (T. D. R., II., p. 595):

CORNELIS BARENTSEN SLEGHT, widower of the deceased Trynntie Tysen Bos,

bridegroom, and *Elsje Jans,* widow of *Hendrick Jochemsen,* bride, on Sept. 26, 1684, agreed to the following marriage contract: (usual beginning, then) the bridegroom donates to the bride as a dowry 200 sch. of wheat.

Signed by Cornelis Barentse Slecht, and Elsje Jans (her mark); witnessed by *Jan Eltinge* and........

Elsje Jans, having the greatest affection for her children, gives all her possessions, after her death, to *Jochem, Eghbert, Hendrick, Engeltie, Hendrix* and *Pieter Adriaens.*

Dated Oct. 8, 1684, and witnessed by *Yan Stol,* and *Jan Van Vliedt* (his mark).

Engeltie Hendrix, wife of *Nicolaes Anthony,* is to inherit her share, that is, her grandmother's small closet, 2 pewter saucers, and a cow.

Inventory of the estate of Cornelis Barentsen Sleght, A house and brewery, an orchard, hop-garden, 3 morgens of land across the Great Bridge, household furniture, described.

The money in Holland shall be inherited by the children.

The heirs of the deceased Tryntie Tysen Bos, in love and friendship with our father, Cornelis Barentsen Sleght have agreed to divide their mother's property in the following way: Cornelis Barentsen Slecht to retain the amount, 750 sch. of wheat, paying therefore 5% interest per annum, for which purpose he mortgages his real property, consisting of 3 morgens of land opposite the great bridge, house, orchard, brewery, and hop-garden. The entire property shall be inherited by *Hendrick, Jacomyntie, Mattys, Pietronella Slecht,* at his death, except the 200 sch. wheat to Elsje Jans, Cornelis Barentsen's second wife.

Signed *Cornelis Slecht,* and *Jan Elting;* witnessed by *Mattys Slecht* and *Jochem Hendricksen.*

Ibid., Liber VI., part A., p. 26. (T. D. R., II., p. 614):

HENDRICK JOCHEMSEN and Elsje Jochems, his wife.

Testamentary disposition, dated March 4, 1681/2, and written in Dutch.

"Survivor to possess everything, lands, money, goods, gold, silver, coined or uncoined;" should the survivor remarry, one half of the property is to be returned (to the other heirs).

The wife's children by a former marriage: *Jannetie* and *Sytie* shall have 150 gulders each, but as they both have died meanwhile, their children shall receive the said amounts.

As heirs are mentioned *Jochem Hendrix, Eghbert Hendrix, Engeltie Hendrix, Hendrick Hendrix,* and *Pieter Adriaensen.*

Hendrick Jochemsz, *Elsje Jansen,* wife of Hendrick Jochemsen (her mark); witnessed by *Wessel Ten Broeck* and *W. D. Meyer.*

Elsje Hendricks or *Elsje Jans,* wife of the deceased *Hendrick Jochemsen,* in full enjoyment of her senses, and considering how certain friends have exerted pressure and forced her, not leaving her any rest, to thoughtlessly sign certain illegal documents, dated in New Yorck before Notary *Bogardus,* on May 22, 1683, regarding the inheritance of the children of *Jacob Abrahamsen Santvoordt* and *Jan Barentsen Kunst,* now absolutely annuls said documents, as she has no desire to oppose her dead husband's wishes, as expressed by his will; God forbid that it shall ever again be broken.—Elsie Jans: witnessed by *Jan Van Vliet* and *Yan Stol.*

Ibid., part A., p. 56. (T. D. R., II., p. 635):

JAN BROERSEN and his wife Willemtie Jacobsz,

Testamentary disposition, dated June 1, 1682, at *Kingston,* and written in Dutch.

"Survivor to inherit everything, land, houses, money, moveables, etc.."—Both signed their marks. No witnesses.

Ibid. p. 57. (T. D. R., II., p. 635):

AERDT OTTERSPOOR

on July 25, 1682 annulled the will which he made in favor of Cornelis Barentsen's wife. The little closet, bequeathed to *Pieternel,* is not to be delivered to her.—Signed with a mark. No witnesses, except the Secretary, *Wm. Montagne.*

Ibid., Liber VI., part B., p. 235. (T. D. R., III., p. 184):

WILLEM BEECK.

Testamentary disposition, dated March 28, 1684.

"His wife shall share with the children the house and lot, one half to each of them. Whereas a woman indian has with the Governor's approval granted him a plot of land at *Waerwaersinck,* on condition that the said woman shall have a plantation there, the testator now orders that his wife shall have one half of said land, and the children the other half. Residue to wife. As guardians over the children: *Pieter Jacobsen Mouris, Jacob Abrahamsen, Isaack Van Vlerck,* and *Jan Willemsen Hooghteyling,*

Signed *W. P. Beeck,* and witnessed by *Roelof Kierstede* and *Arent Tuenessen.*

ADDITIONS AND CORRECTIONS.

PAGE

36—Last line should read: "See note, page 31."

53—5th line, read: "Van Wijlen," instead of "Van Wiljen."

77—Heading should read: "Will owned by *Ralph Lefevre, New Paltz.*"

79—Heading should read: "Will owned by *Ralph Lefevre, New Paltz.*"

93—22d line, read: *"Magdalena Schutt,"* instead of "Marritje Martissen."

102—9th line from bottom, add: "x. *Willem*, bt. Dec. 5, 1686."

113—13th line to be taken out entirely.

132—20th line, read: *"Znyder,"* instead of "Zynder."

177—5th line, read: "they saw," instead of "the saw."

181—1st line, read: "Abstracts," instead of "Absrtacts."

INDEX TO WILLS, TESTAMENTARY DISPOSITIONS, LETTERS OF ADMINISTRATION, ADMINISTRATION BONDS, POWER OF ATTORNEY, RENUNCIATIONS, MARRIAGE CONTRACTS, and INVENTORIES
ARRANGED ALPHABETICALLY.

ABBREVIATIONS USED: **A. B.** for Administration-Bonds; **Inv.** for Inventories; **L. A.** for Letters of Administration; **M. C.** for Marriage Contracts; **O. W.** for Original Wills; **P. A.** for Power of Attorney; **R.** for Renunciations; **T. D.** for Testamentary Dispositions; **W.** for Wills.

A

Name.	Residence.	Instrument.	Dated.	Filed or Probated.	Page.
AARTSE, GERRIT,	Kingston,	Will,	Dec. 17, 1715.	Mar. 9, 1720-1,	102
AARTSEN, JACOB, or *Van Wageningen*, or *Jacobse*. See also *Otterspoor*.	Wagendal,	Will,	Oct. 5, 1714,	Mar. 7, 1716-7,	93
ADREIJANSE, PETTER,	Kingston,	T.D.,	Feb. 30, 1686,		47
ADRYANSEN, JOOST, or *Joost Adriansen Vermeulen*.	Pynacker,	T.D.,	Sept. 2, 1665,		29
ANDRIESEN, GEERTRUY, and her husband, *Aert Martensen Doorn*.		P.A.,	Nov. 4, 1671,		189
ARYANCE, HENDRICK,		Will,	Sept. 11, 1690.	June 16, 1701,	58

B

Name.	Residence.	Instrument.	Dated.	Filed or Probated.	Page.
BARENTSEN, CORNELIS, or *Cornelis Barentse Slecht* and his wife, Tryntie Tysen Bosch.		T.D.,	Aug. 17, (?)		32
BEATTY, JOHN,	Marbletown.	W.,	Apr. 26, 1720,	Mar. 9, 1720,	100
BEECK, WILLEM,		T.D.,	Mar. 8, 1684,		191
BEECQMAN, HENDERICUS,		M.C.,			190
BEVIERE, LOUIS, SR.,	New Paltz,	Will,	May 2, 1720,	July 4, 1720,	97
BLANCHAN, MATTHES, and his wife, *Magdalen Joore*.		T.D.,	Aug. 22, 1671,	Apr. 30, 1688,	48
BLANCHAN, MATTHEUS,		T.D.,	Sept. 7-17, 1665,		30

NAME.	RESIDENCE.	INSTRU-MENT.	DATED.	FILED OR PROBATED.	PAGE.
BLANSJAN, CHATHARINA, and her husband, *Lowies Du Booys.*		T.D.,	Oct. 13, 1676,		34
BLANSJAN, ELISABETH, and her husband, *Peter Cornelissen (Low).*		T.D.,	Nov. 1, 1676,		35
BLANSJAN, MADELENA, and her husband, *Jan Tysen (Mattysen.)*		T.D.,	Sept. 25, 1676,		33
BOGARDIES, PIETER,	Kingston,	Will,	Feb. 3, 1701-2,	Sept. 20, 1703,	63
BOGART, HENDRICK,	Marbletown,	W.,	Dec. 12, 1707,	May 12, 1707,	92
BOMSCHOTEN, SALOMON, SR.,	Kingston,	W.,	Nov. 14, 1737,	June 7, 1754,	132
BOSCH, TRYNTIE TYSEN, or *Tryntie Barentsen,* and her husband, *Cornelis Barentsen* or *Cornelis Barentse Slecht.*		T.D.,	Aug. 17, (?)		32
BRINK, See *Lambert Huybertse,* and *Cornelius Lambertse.*					
BROERSON, JAN, and his wife, *Willemtje Jacobs (Jans).*		T.D.,	June 1, 1682,		192
BRUYN, JACOBUS,	Bruynswick,	W.,	June 20, 1744,	June 11, 1745,	124
BURHANS, ABRAHAM,	Kingston,	O.W..	Oct. 3, 1763,	Not recorded.	181

C

CHAMBERS, THOMAS,		M.C.,			190
CLAESSE(N), HENDERICK,		T.D.,	Nov. 12, 1688,		49
CLARWATER, ABRAHAM,	Marbletown,	W.,	Apr. 22, 1776,	Sept. 19, 1798,	162
COCK, JOHN,	Marbletown,	T.D.,	July 20, 1710,		99
COOL, CORNELIS,	Hurley,	Will,	Jan. 10, 1732,	Sept. 7, 1736,	118
CORNELIS, ANNETIE, and her husband, *Cornelis Vernooy.*		T.D.,	Feb. 23, 1682,		44
CORNELISE, MARTE, and his wife, *Mayke Cornelise.*	Claverak,	T.D.,	Aug. 13, 1685,	June 19, 1699,	53
CORNELISSE, THEUNIS, or *Theunis Cornelisse Swart,* and his wife, *Elizabeth Van der Linden,* or *Van der Lende.*		W.D.,	July 21, 1677,		73

NAME.	RESIDENCE.	INSTRUMENT.	DATED.	FILED OR PROBATED.	PAGE.
CORNELISSEN, PETER, or *Peter Cornelisen Low*, and his wife, *Elisabeth Blansjan*.		T.D.,	Nov. 1, 1676,		35
CORNELISSEN, PIETER, (LOW),	Kingston,	W.,	Dec. 20, 1690,	Mar. 4, 1707,	73
CORNELISON, GERRITT,	Hurley,	W.,	Feb. ?. 1686,	Mar. 4, 1695-6,	59
COTTIN, CATHERINE,	Kingston,	W.,	July 23, 1712,	Dec. 10, 1713,	83
CRANS, JOHANNIS,	Hanover,	W.,	Apr. 17, 1775,	July 5, 1777,	142
CRAWFORD, HENRY,	Marlborough,	W.,	Mar. 27, 1816,	Sept. 6, 1824,	174
CRESPEL, ANTOIN,	Kingston,	W.,	Nov. 6, 1707,	Jan. 10, 1707,	71

D

NAME.	RESIDENCE.	INSTRUMENT.	DATED.	FILED OR PROBATED.	PAGE.
DAVIS, CHRISTOPHER,	Marbletown,	W.,	June 12, 1778,	Sept. 23, 1794,	155
DAVITS, JOHANNA,		M.C.,			190
DEIJOU, CHRISTIAN,	New Paltz,	W.,	Febr. 1, 1687,	June 30, 1687.	47
DELAMATER, DAVID,	Kingston,	W.,	Sept. 23, 1769,	Sept. 3, 1790,	150
DEPUY, JACOBUS,	Rochester,	O.W.,	Dec. 15, 1778,	Not recorded.	182
DE WITT, ANDRIES,	Kingston,	W.,	Mar. 17, 1800,	Jan. 8, 1807,	165
DE WITT, BOUDEWYN, DR.,	Kingston,	W.,	June 24, 1703,	July 15, 1703,	62
DE WITT, DIRCK CLAES, see *Tjerck Claese De Witt*.					
DE WITT, JAN,	Mombacus,	W.,	Oct. 29, 1700,	Apr. 12, 1715,	118
DE WITT, JAN CLAETS,	Amsterdam,	W.,	Mar. 31, 1699,	June 26, 1699,	54
DE WITT, LUYCAS,		W.,	Feb. 15, 1702,	Mar. 9, 1703,	65
DE WITT, TJERCK CLAESE,	Kingston,	W.,	Mar. 4, 1687,	Mar. 6, 1700,	156
DONALDSON, ABRAHAM,	New Paltz,	W.,	May 16, 1805,	May 5, 1808,	168
DOORN, AERDT MARTENSEN, and his wife, *Geertruy Andriesen*.		P.A.,	Nov. 4, 1671,		189
DOYO, ABRAHAM,	New Paltz,	W.,	Sept. 20, 1724,	Oct. 7, 1725.	110
DUBOIS, CORNELIUS,	New Paltz,	W.,	Nov. 6, 1780,	Apr. 23, 1781,	160
DUBOIS, DANIEL,	New Paltz,	O.W.,	Aug. 16, 1729,		114
DUBOIS, HENDRICUS,	New Paltz,	W..	June 21, 1774,	June 4, 1782,	158
DUBOIS, JACOB,	Hurley,	W,	Apr. 3, 1739,	June 7, 1745,	123
DUBOIS, JOSHUA,	Kingston,	W.,	Dec. 30, 1818,	Sept. 5, 1825,	177
DUBOIS, LOUIS,	New Paltz,	W.,	Mar. 30, 1686,	May 5, 1686,	46
DUBOIS, LOWIES,	Kingston,	W..	Mar. 27, 1694,	June 23, 1696,	50
DUBOIS, LOWIES,	Kingston,	W.,	Feb. 22, 1695,	June 23, 1696,	51
DUBOIS, LOWIES, and his wife, *Chatharina Blansjan*.		T.D.,	Oct. 13, 1676,		34

Name.	Residence.	Instrument.	Dated.	Filed or Probated.	Page.
DU JOU, CHRISTIAN,	Hurley,	T.D.,	Aug. 10, 1676,		31
DU MONT, WALRANDT, SR.,	Kingston,	W.,	Mar. 15, 1701,	Sept. 3, 1713,	85

E

Name.	Residence.	Instrument.	Dated.	Filed or Probated.	Page.
EEN, ABRAHAM,	New Paltz,	W.,	Nov. 30, 1805,	Jan. 6, 1807,	164
ELMENDORPH, COENRAET,	Kingston,	W.,	Sept. 2, 1749,	Oct. 24, 1788,	146
ELMENDORPH, JACOBUS,	Kingston,	W.,	June 2, 1678,		37
ELMENDORPH, PETRUS EDMUNDUS,	Kingston,	W.,	May 17, 1763,	Sept. 27, 1765,	145
ELMENDORPH, WILHELMUS, See also under *Van Elmendorph*.	Hurley,	W.,	Mar. 7, 1754,	Dec. 16, 1754,	135
ELTYNGE, JAN, or *Eltinge Roelofsen*, and his wife, *Jacomyntie Slecht*.		T.D.,	Sept. 30, 1679,		39

F

Name.	Residence.	Instrument.	Dated.	Filed or Probated.	Page.
FALSETT, GERRET,	Fals Creek,	W.,	Apr. 13, 1726,	May 5, 1726,	112
FELTEN, PHILIP,	Kingston,	W.,	July 9, 182-,	Sept. 5, 1825,	176
FOCKEN, JAN, See *Jan Heermans, Sr.*		O.W.,	Jan. 15, 1727,	Not recorded.	113
FOWLER, STEPHEN,	Plattekill,	W.,	Sept. 17, 1807,	Mar. 26, 1822,	172
FRANCKFORD, ABRAHAM,	Kingston,	W.,	Sept. 28, 1689,		48
FREER, CATHARINA (wid. of *Jonas*).		O.W.,	Sept. 22, 1781,	Not recorded.	183
FREER, JOHANNIS,	New Paltz,	W.,	Sept. 1, 1796,	July 15, 1797,	158
FRERE, HUGUE,	Paltz,	O.W.,	Sept. 4, 1697,	Not recorded.	77
FRERE, HUGUE,	Paltz,	O.W.,	Feb. 12, 1706,	Not recorded.	78

G

Name.	Residence.	Instrument.	Dated.	Filed or Probated.	Page.
GERRETSEN, ALBERT,	Embderland,	T.D.,	Sept. 3, 1665,		30
GERRITSE, CORNELIS,	Hurley,	W.,	Feb. 7, 1665,	Mar. 4, 1695,	59

H

Name.	Residence.	Instrument.	Dated.	Filed or Probated.	Page.
HARDENBERGH, LEONARD,	Marbletown,	W.,	June 12, 1706,	May 8, 1766,	142
HARMILLE, TOMAS,		W.,	Mar. 12, 1689,	Apr. 21, 1690,	48
HASBROUCK, JACOB J.,		W.,	June 21, 1818,	Aug. 14, 1818,	170

NAME.	RESIDENCE.	INSTRUMENT.	DATED.	FILED OR PROBATED.	PAGE.
HASBROUCK, JEAN,	New Paltz,	W.,	Aug. 26, 1712,	Aug. 14, 1714,	88
HASBROUCK, JOHANNIS,	New Paltz,	W.,	Dec. 28, 1806,	Jan. 8, 1807,	166
HASBROUCK, JOSAPHAT,	New Paltz,	W.,	Apr. 28, 1811,	Dec. 14, 1814,	169
HEERMANS, JAN, SR.,	Kingston,	W.,	Oct. 20, 1723,	Mar. 5, 1724,	105
HENDRICKE, DIRCK,	Foxhall,	W.,	Jan. 8, 1699,	Sept. 9, 1703,	63
HENDRICKS, HENDRICK,	Kingston,	W.,	Dec. 30, 1686,		47
HENDRIX, GRITIE (wid. of Dirck),		W.,	Sept. 26, 1708,	Jan. 17, 1708,	75
HENDRIX, MARGARIETIE,		M.C.,			190
HENDRIX, MAYCKEN, and her husband, *Jan Joosten*.		T.D.,	Dec. 16, 1681,		41
HERMANS, JAN, JR.,	Kingston,	W.,	July 18, 1705,	Jan. 2, 1705,	70
HEYMANS, see *Roosa*.					
HILLEBRANT, PIETER,		M.C.,	Mar. 20, 1665,		29
HOOFMAN, NICHOLAS,	Co. Dutchess,	W.,	Feb. 12, 1749,	Feb. 1, 1752,	133
HOOGEBOOM, CORNELIS, and his wife, *Annetie Cornelisen Sleght*.		T.D.,	Aug. 17, 1676,		33
HOOGENBOOM, ANNETIE, (wid. of *Cornelis*).		W.,	May 4, 1719,	Sept. 17, 1719,	97
HOOGHTEYLINGH, JAN WILLEMSEN, or *Jan Willemsen*, and his wife, *Barbara Jans*.		T.D.,	Nov. 8, 1671,		36
HOOGHTEYLINGH, JAN WILLEMSEN,	Kingston,	W.,	Aug. 11, 1702,	Mar. 4, 1703,	61
HUYBERTSE, LAMBERT, or *Brink*.	Hurley,	W.,	Feb. 12, 1695,	Apr. 11, 1702,	60

J

JACOBS, WILLEMTJE,		T.D.,	June 1, 1682,		192
JACOBSE, see *Gerrit Aaertse*.					
JANS, BARBARA, or *Barbara Hooghteyling*, and her husband, *Jan Willemsen Hooghteyling* or *Jan Willemsen*.		T.D.,	Nov. 8, 1671,		36
JANS, ELSIE,		M.C.,	Oct. 8, 1684,		191
JANS, ELSIE,		T.D.,			192
JANS, GRITIE, or *Gritie Jansen*, widow of *Jan Lambertsen*.		T.D.,	June 27, 1684,		45

NAME.	RESIDENCE.	INSTRUMENT.	DATED.	FILED OR PROBATED.	PAGE.
JANSEN, JACOB, (van Stoutenborch),		P.A.,	Nov. 7, 1671,		189
JANSEN, MATTYS,	Kingston,	W.,	Aug. 21, 1727,	Oct. 5, 1727,	116
JANSEN, THOMAS, see Van Steenbergen.					
JENKENS, LAMBERT,	Paltz,	W.,	7mo., 11, 1799,	Sept. 17, 1807,	167
JOCHEMS, ELSJE, (JANS),		T.D.,	Mar. 4, 1681-2,		192
JOCHEMSEN, HENDRICK, and his wife, *Elsje Jochems (Jans)*.		T.D.,	Mar. 4, 1681-2,		192
JOORE, MAGDALEN, and her husband, *Matthes Blanchan*.		T.D.,	Aug. 22, 1671.	Apr. 30, 1688,	48
JOOSTEN, JACOB,		T.D.,	Aug. 1, 1680,		40
JOOSTEN, JAN, (VAN MEETEREN), and his wife, *Maycken Hendrix*.		T.D.,	Dec. 16, 1681,		41

K

KETCH, DAVID,	New Paltz,	W.,	July 29, 1820,	Sept. 6, 1824,	176
KETTLE, JEREMY, SR.,	Marbletown,	W.,	Jan. 20, 1703,	Sept. 7, 1704,	68
KLARWATER, ABRAHAM,	Marbletown,	W.,	Apr. 23, 1776,	Sept. 19, 1798,	162
KRANS, JOHANNIS,	Hanover,	W.,	Apr. 17, 1775,	July 5, 1777,	142

L

LAMBERTSE, CORNELIUS, or Brink,		W.,	Mar. 8, 1725,	Nov. 21, 1726,	112
LANSYNCK, AELTYE, and her husband, *Gerridt Van Slichtenhorst*.		T.D.,	Feb. 16, 1682		43
LAURENSEN, JAN, see *Jan Lourens*.					
LEFEVER, ANDRIES,	New Paltz,	W.,	Apr. 19, 1738,	May —, 1793,	153
LEFEVER, DANIEL,	New Paltz,	W.,	Sept. 4, 1784,	May 7, 1800,	163
LEGG, JOHN,	Kingston,	W.,	Dec. 15, 1743,	Sept. 18, 1765,	138
LEGG, WILLIAM,	Kingston,	W.,	June 5, 1710,	Aug. 28, 1710,	80
LEGG, WILLIAM,	Kingston,	O.W.,	Oct. 8, 1780,	Not recorded.	184
LEGG, WILLIAM, JR.,	Kingston,	W.,	Mar. 8, 1743,	May 29, 1745,	122
LIVINGSTON, GILBERT,	Kingston,	W.,	Dec. 12, 1745,	July 31, 1746,	128
LOCKWOOD, HENRY,	Plattekill,	W.,	Apr. 17, 1818,	July 1, 1819,	171
LOMMENDIEU, PETER,	Kingston,	W.,	Feb. 10, 1691,	Mar. 30, 1692,	49
LOOMAN, HENDRICK JANSEN,		Intestate.		Sept. 18, 1663,	21

Index to Instruments.

Name.	Residence.	Instrument.	Dated.	Filed or Probated.	Page.
LOURENS, JAN,	Kingston,	W.,	Mar. 21, 1702,	Sept. 6, 1705,	69
LOW, JACOBUS,	Kingston,	W.,	Oct. 18, 1793,	Jan. 10, 1794,	154
LOW, PIETER CORNE-LISSE,		W.,	Dec. 20, 1690,	Mar. 4, 1707,	73
LOW, see *Pieter Cornelisen.*					

M

Name.	Residence.	Instrument.	Dated.	Filed or Probated.	Page.
MASTON, CORNELIS,	Kingston,	W.,	Jan. 30, 1712,	Apr. 12, 1712,	82
MATTYSEN, JAN,		T.D.,	Sept. 25, 1676,		33
or *Jan Tysen*, and his wife, *Madelena Blansjan.*					
MATTYSEN, JAN,	Kingston,	W.,	Oct. 7, 1719,	Nov. 24, 1724,	103
MEYDERSEN, EGHBERT,		T.D.,	Apr. 9, 1684,		45
MOURITZ, FREDERICK PIETERSEN,		W.,	May 30, 1709,	May 30, 1709,	82

N

Name.	Residence.	Instrument.	Dated.	Filed or Probated.	Page.
NEWKERK, COENRADT,	Hurley.	W.,	Apr. 26, 1796,	Apr. 4, 1806.	168
NEWKERK, CORNELIS, see *Cornelis Gerritse.*					
NEWKIRK, JOHANNIS,	Wallkill.	W.,	Oct. 5, 1771,	Feb. 7, 1777,	140
NUKERK, CORNELIS,	Hurley,	O.W.,	Sept. 15, 1787,	Not recorded.	183

O

Name.	Residence.	Instrument.	Dated.	Filed or Probated.	Page.
OOSTERHOUT, TEUNIS,	Rochester,	W.,	June 14, 1739,	Feb. 2, 1747,	129
OTTERSPOOR, AERDT AERDTSEN,		T.D.,	May 5, 1678,		190
OTTERSPOOR, AERDT AERDTSEN,		Annullation,	July 25, 1682,		192

P

Name.	Residence.	Instrument.	Dated.	Filed or Probated.	Page.
PARYS, EVERDT,	Hurley,	W.,	Mar. 26, 1678,		37
PERSEN, CORNELIUS,	Saugerties.	W.,	June 27, 1814.	Jan. 12, 1829,	179
PERSEN, MATTHYS,	Kingston.	W.,	July 20, 1748,	Not recorded.	136
PIETERSEN, FREDERICK (MOURITZ),		W.,	May 30, 1709.	May 30, 1709.	82
POULSE, GOMMEN,	Kingston,	W.,	Apr. 6, 1699.	June 19, 1699,	53

R

Name.	Residence.	Instrument.	Dated.	Filed or Probated.	Page.
RAINEY, JAMES.	Hanover.	W.,	Aug. 1, 1775.	Mar. 2, 1776,	143
ROELOFSEN, ELTING,		T.D.,	Sept. 30, 1679.		39
or *Jan Eltinge* and his wife, *Jacomyntie Slecht.*					
ROOSA, ALBERT HYMAN,	Hurley,	W.,	Aug. 23, 1708.	Sept. 9, 1708,	74

Name.	Residence.	Instrument.	Dated.	Filed or Probated.	Page.
ROOSA, EVERT,	Hurley,	W.,	Mar. 5, 1726,	May 3, 1749,	130
ROOSA, HYMAN, see *Albert Hyman*.					
RUTSEN, JOHN,		W.,	Mar. 5, 1724,	May 11, 1725,	106

S

Name.	Residence.	Instrument.	Dated.	Filed or Probated.	Page.
SCHEPMOES, DIRCK JANSEN, and his wife, *Marya Willems*.		T.D.,	Nov. 1, 1682,		42
SCHEPMOES, DIRCK,	Kingston,	W.,	Feb. 15, 1723-4,	Sept. 20, 1725,	106
SCHOONHOVEN, HENDRICK CLAESEN,		T.D.,	Nov. 12, 1688,		49
SCHOONMAKER, HENDRICK,	Kingston,	W.,	Jan. 12, 1711,	Apr. 12, 1712,	81
SCHUTT, WM. JANSEN,	Shawangunk,	W.,	May 6, 1706,	June 4, 1752,	102
SEBA, WILLIM JANSEN,	Intestate.			Sept. 18, 1773,	21
SLECHT, CORNELIS BARENTSE, or *Cornelis Barentsen*, and his wife, *Tryntie Barentsen*, or *Tryntie Tysen Bosch*.		T.D.,	Aug. 17, 1676,		32
SLECHT, JACOMYNTIE, or *Jacomyntie Roelofsen*, wife of *Jan Eltinge*, or *Eltinge Roelofsen*.		T.D.,	Sept. 30, 1679,		39
SLECHT, ANNETIE CORNELISEN, wife of *Cornelis Hoogeboom*.		T.D.,	Aug. 17, 1676,		33
SLECHT, HENDRICK CORNELISEN,		T.D.,	Nov. 15, 1677,		190
SLEGHTENHORST, GERRIDT, or *G. V. Slichtenhorst*, and his wife, *Aeyltie Lansynck*.		T.D.,	Feb. 16, 1682,		43
SMITH, JOHANNIS,	Marbletown,	W.,	Aug. 13, 1776,	Mar. 14, 1780,	141
SMITH, WILLIAM,	Montgomery,	W.,	Aug. 15, 1784,	Jan. —, 1791,	152
SNYDER, JOHANNIS,	Kingston,	O.W.,	June 5, 1771,	Not recorded.	185
SNYDER, MARTINUS,	Kingston,	W.,	May 5, 1778,	May 9, 1789,	148
SWART, CORNELISE THEUNISE, or *Theunis Cornelisse*, and his wife, *Elizabeth Van der Linden*.		T.D.,	July 21, 1677,		73
SWARTWOUT, ROELOFF,		W.,	Mar. 30, 1714,	May 14, 1715,	91
SWYTS, CORNELIS,	Rochester,	W.,	Apr. 13, 1735,	May 2, 1738,	120
SWYTS, JANNETJE (wid. of *Cornelis*).		W.,	Feb. 21, 1737,	June 3, 1746,	127

INDEX TO INSTRUMENTS. 203

T

NAME.	RESIDENCE.	INSTRU-MENT.	DATED.	FILED OR PROBATED.	PAGE.
TEN BROECK, MARIA, or *Maria Ten Eyck*, and her husband, *Wessel Ten Broeck*.	Kingston,	T.D.,	Mar. 7, 1681,		41
TEN BROECK, WESSEL (see above).					
TEN BROECK, WESSEL,	Kingston,	W.,	Sept. 27, 1820,	Sept. 7, 1824,	173
TEN BROECK, WESSEL, SR.,	Foxhall,	W.,	Feb. 14, 1695,	Jan. 6, 1704,	66
TEN EYCK, see *Maria Ten Broeck*.					
TENHOUT, SEVERYN,	Shawangunk,	W.,	Feb. 5, 1708,	Mar. 6, 1717,	95
TEUNISSEN, CLAESJE,		Intestate.		Oct. 30, 1663,	21
TROPHAGEN, WILLIAM,		Deposition,	Aug. 26, 1671,		35
TROPHAGEN, WILLIAM,	Kingston,	W.,	Feb. 16, 1685,		46
TYSEN, JAN, or *Jan Mattysen*, and his wife, *Madelena Blansjan*.		T.D.,	Sept. 25, 1676,		33

V

NAME.	RESIDENCE.	INSTRU-MENT.	DATED.	FILED OR PROBATED.	PAGE.
VAN AALSTEYN, MARTINUS,	Skoherry,	W.,	July 15, 1784,	Oct. 6, 1787,	146
VAN BORSUM, BARENDT, and his wife, *Machtel Van Vlyet*, or *Machtel Adriaensen*.		T.D.,	Nov. 19, 1682,		43
VAN BUNTSCHOTEN, see *Bomschoten*.					
VAN DER LINDEN, see *Theunisse Cornelise Swart*.					
VAN ELMENDORF, JACOBUS, see also *Elmendorph*.		W.,	Aug. 27, 1685,	Nov. 30, 1699,	55
VAN IMBROCK, GYSBERT,		Inv.		Sept. 7, 1665,	21
VAN LANGEDYCK, MARIA, widow of *Cornelis Wynkoop*.		T.D.,	May 16, 1679,		38
VAN LEUVEN, JOHN,	Marbletown.	W.,	Oct. 9, 1781,	Jan. 7, 1791,	151
VAN OSTRANDT, JOHN, or *John Van Vorstrand*.	Hurley,	W.,	1mo., 17, 1822,	June 14, 1827,	178
VAN SLEGHTENHORST, GERRIDT,		T.D.,	Feb. 16, 1682,		43
VAN STEENBERGH, JOHN,	Kingston,	W.,	May 16, 1796,	Sept. 21, 1796,	157

Name.	Residence.	Instrument.	Dated.	Filed or Probated.	Page.
VAN STEENBERGH, THOMAS, see *Jansen*.	West Camp,	W.,	Sept. 7, 1795,	May 4, 1796,	156
VAN STEENWYCK, JAN ALBERTSEN,		Intestate.		Nov. 26, 1663,	21
VAN STOUTENBORCH, JACOB JANSEN,		P.A.,	Nov. 7, 1671,		189
VAN VLYET, see *Van Borsum*.					
VAN VORSTRANT, see *Van Ostrandt*.					
VERMEULEN, JOOST ADRIAENSEN, or *Joost Adryaens*, of Pynacker.		T.D.,	Sept. 2, 1665,		29
VERNOOY, CORNELIS, and his wife, *Annetie Cornelis*.		T.D.,	Feb. 23, 1682,		44

W

Name.	Residence.	Instrument.	Dated.	Filed or Probated.	Page.
WILLEMS, MARIA, or *Marya Schepmoes*, wife of *Dirck Jansen Schepmoes*.		T.D.,	Nov. 1, 1682,		42
WILLEMSEN, DIRRICK,		Intestate,		Sept. 18, 1663,	21
WILLEMSEN, JAN, or *Jan Willemsen Hooghteyling*, and his wife, *Barbary Jans*.		T.D.,	Nov. 8, 1671,		36
WITTAKER, EDWARD,	Kingston,	W.,	Sept. 3, 1694,	Jan. 16, 1694,	50
WYNKOOP, CORNELIUS,	Kingston,	T.D.,	Aug. 11, 1676,		32
WYNKOOP, MARIA (wid. of *Cornelius*).		T.D.,	May 16, 1679,		38

TOPOGRAPHICAL INDEX.

An * indicates that the same name appears more than once on the same page.

Aertsen's, Jacob, land.............130
Albany, 6, 10, 13, 30*, 31, 32, 33, 35, 38, 41*, 46, 54, 58*, 61, 65*, 74, 77, 88, 93, 102, 103, 106, 113, 123, 145, 161, 162, 163, 182.
Albany County, 8, 41, 53, 54, 58, 65, 92, 146.
Almedo, Holland.................30
Almina, Holland 36
Amersfort, Holland 34
Amsterdam, Holland, 24, 28, 36, 43, 46, 54, 57, 65, 88, 92, 121*, 189.
Ancrum, Scotland 128
Anna Salutes Fief, Billeveldt......36
Arme bouwery (poor land).......150
Armentiers, France 31
Artois, France 30, 31, 34, 73

Baarn, Holland 163
Barrevelt 54
Beaver Kill 64, 186
Belgium 99
Bennewater 174
Bergen 43
Bethlehem, Albany Co 54
Bewerwyck 8, 33, 41, 58*, 74, 92
Beyla, Holland 39
Big Meadow 163
Billeveldt 36
Binnekill 173
Blue Hills 120
Bommel, Holland 30
Bonticow 158, 163
Boston, Mass 91
Brabant (Kingston) 30, 123, 179
Beestede, Danmark 32
Brooklyn, N. Y............7, 46, 135
Brunnekill 173
Bruynswick 124
Burned Meadow 125
Bushwick, L. I. 30, 46*

Calais, France 31*, 91
Cale Bergh 31
Callicoone Hooke 34
Catskill 66
Chaumant Bay 178
Churchland 132
Claverack, Albany Co 53, 54
Cline Esopus 56

Columbia County 128
Cocksinck 56, 58
Coonmen, Flanders 88
Corpus Christy fief, Minnen 36
Covelens 41
Cremaker's land 130
Curr Pfaltz, Germany 31

Danmark 33
Delaware 33, 165
Delaware County 6
Delft, Holland 30
Dominie's bouwery 65
Dorsetshire, England............88
Drenthe Province, Holland, 30, 39, 106
Dudley's Plantation 138
Dutchess County, 40, 95, 106*, 131, 133, 134, 135, 139, 165.
Dwarfskill 143, 163

East Friesland 32, 58
Eight Thousand Acres Tract 125
Elburgh, Holland 30
Embden, Holland 43
Embderland 30
England, 31, 34, 42*, 88, 99, 100*, 104, 156.
Esopus, 6, 8, 31, 33, 35*, 40, 42, 46, 58*, 75, 88, 92, 103, 182, 190.
Esopus Creek, 120, 146, 147, 148, 165, 173.
Esopus Kill, 31, 59, 92, 103, 119, 123, 155.
Esopus River 155

"Faith", the ship 35, 42, 44
Five Thousand Acres Tract, 125, 140
Flanders 88
Flatbush, L. I., 39, 41, 44, 59, 169, 184
Flatbush, Kingston 181
Flatlands, Holland 39
Flatts 138
Flounders 149
Flushing, L. I..................82
Fort James 30
Fort Orange, 6, 8, 31, 33, 34, 41, 58
"Fox", the ship 41
Fox Hall......... 5, 6, 33, 42, 66, 75
France, 6, 30, 31*, 34, 49, 73, 91, 93, 111
Frankenthal, Germany 99

206   TOPOGRAPHICAL INDEX.

Gebrande Vley 125
Gelderland, Holland, 30*, 41*, 44, 61, 75
Germany, 31*, 34*, 41, 46, 54, 91, 99, 102, 139, 149, 177, 183, 186.
Ghent 54
"Gilded Otter", the ship, 31*, 34, 73
Gottenburg, Sweden 30
Great Creek 46
Great Ditch 138
Great Kill 46, 71, 72
Great Meadow 40, 163
Great Minnissinck Patent 160
Great Piece 173
Great River 35
Great Spring 72
Green County 6
Green Kill 170
Groningen, Holland 92
Groote Buntecoe 164
Groote Fly 40, 163
Groote fontyn 71
Grootholdt, Holland 57
Groot Stuck Church 159

Hackenberg, Germany 149
Halfmoon 164
Hanover 141, 142, 143
Hanover Precinct 142
Harlem 21, 33
Hassell, Holland 44
Hemelycke, Holland 35
Herfort Prebendary 36
Herwynen, Holland 75
High hill 35
Highlands Precinct 5
Holland, 6, 29, 30*, 32, 34, 35, 36, 38, 39, 41*, 42, 43, 44, 46*, 54, 57, 58*, 61, 65, 75, 81, 88, 92, 102, 106, 163*, 190, 191.
Holstein 35
Hudsons River, 5, 33, 34, 35, 125, 128, 134, 135.
Hurley, 5, 6, 30, 31, 34*, 39*, 40, 43*, 44, 46*, 52*, 59*, 60, 61, 66, 71*, 72*, 73, 74, 75*, 79, 92*, 112, 118, 119*, 120, 123, 124, 130, 135, 148, 168, 169, 170, 178, 183*, 184..
Hurley Great Piece 31, 92, 120
Hycoop, Holland 102

Iceland 27
Ireland 101
Island, the 122
Jacob's Hook 80, 122
Jacomyntj's fly 40
Jan Joosten's land 119
Jansen, Roelof, "Kill" 128
Johannes Jansen's Wey 177

Juffron's Hook 35
Juoner lott 168
Kinderhook 92, 137
King's Farm 65
King's Highway 150
King's Road 147, 158
Kingston, 5, 6, 7, 8, 13, 21, 30*, 32, 33, 34, 35, 37*, 38*, 39*, 40*, 41, 42*, 43*, 44, 46*, 47*, 48, 49, 50*, 51, 52, 53*, 54, 55, 57, 58*, 59, 61, 62, 65, 66, 67, 68, 69, 70*, 71, 73, 75, 76, 77, 79, 80, 81, 82, 83, 84, 85, 91, 92, 95, 97, 99, 102, 103, 105, 106, 112, 116*, 117, 120, 121, 122, 123, 128, 130, 132, 135, 136, 138, 139, 145, 146, 148, 149, 150, 154, 157, 161, 163, 165, 166, 168, 169, 173, 174, 176, 177*, 179, 180*, 181*, 184, 185, 189, 190, 191, 192.
Kished, Germany 149
Kiskatama 155
Kline Kill 162
Knightfield 106
Korcksinck 56
Kroonme Elbow river 35

Lake Ontario 178
Lange stuck kill 129
Leerdam, Holland 30
Lemmichor, (Lemgo), Holland, 35, 36, 46.
Leydenhad 23
Leyden, Holland 30, 42, 81
Lille, Belgium 99
Linlithgo, Scotland 128
Livingston manor 128
Long Island, 7, 30, 39, 41, 44, 46, 49, 59, 82, 169, 184.
Long Reach 35
Long Streak 129
Long Wye Kill 173

Magatt Ramis 35
Manhattan 33
Manhattan Island 65
Manheim, Germany 31*, 34*, 91
Marbletown, 5, 6, 30, 31, 34, 39, 41*, 54, 68, 75, 82, 92, 93, 99, 100*, 101, 102, 104, 120, 130, 132, 141, 142, 143, 151, 155, 161, 162, 170.
Maria Vergina fief, Lemigo 36
Marlborough 161, 174
Marmur 79
Massachusetts 91
Meeteren, Holland 29, 30, 41
Meppelane, Holland 30, 39
Meppelt, Holland 36
Midwoud, L. I. 44, 59, 169, 184

TOPOGRAPHICAL INDEX. 207

Mill Kill 30
Minnen Diocese 35, 36
Moudestadt, Germany 31, 34
Moesel, Germany 41
Moghoonck 35
Moise, France 91
Molen Killitje 70
Mombaccus 118
Mombacus Kill 58, 129
Montgomery 152
"Moseman", the ship 59
Mud Kill 149
Munster, Germany 42
Murderers Creek 5
Mutterstadt, Germany 31

Nescotack 154
New Albany. 31, 32. See Albany.
New Amstel 33
New Amsterdam, see New York.
Newburg 125, 150, 166,
Newcastle, Del 165
New Harlem 93
New Jersey 40, 88, 123
New Marlborough 183
New Paltz, 5, 6, 31, 35*, 41, 46*, 47,
  52, 71*, 72*, 73, 79, 88, 91, 99, 110,
  111, 113, 114, 120, 149, 153, 154*,
  158,*, 160, 161, 163*, 164*, 165, 166,
  167, 168, 169, 170, 176, 178, 183*.
New Rochelle 49
Newstadt, Germany 31
New Windsor 35
New York, 6, 10, 13, 14, 30*, 33, 35, 36,
  41*, 42, 43*, 46, 49, 54, 57, 58*, 65,
  75, 77, 89, 92, 93, 99, 101, 106, 111,
  113*, 114, 121, 125, 129, 145, 189*,
  192.
Nieuwkerk, Holland 44*
Noeville o corne, France 30
North Carolina 65*
North Holland 65
North River 163
Norway 127

Ohio 177
Old Bouery, Hurley 59
Ontario County 179
Oosterbemis, Holland 58
Opymen, Holland 30
Orange County 6, 35, 166
Over-Ysel, Holland 30, 44, 46
Otterspoor farm 121

Pakasek 35
Pakanasink 124
Palatinate 31
Paltz 34, 52, 77, 99, 167
  See New Paltz.

Paltz Creek 112
Paltz Kul 89
Paltz River 125
Pawachta 35
Perth Amboy, N. J...................88
Peter Mour's land 138, 184
Philadelphia, Pa................40, 58
Plaa 173
Platte Beni water 163
Platte Kill, 150, 161, 171, 172, 173, 176,
  179.
Poncknockie 5
Poughkeepsie 65, 95, 165
"The Princess", the ship 65
Pynacker, Holland 29, 30*

Raagh, Germany 41
Rappos Island 35
Raritan River, N. J.............40, 88
Red Hook 65, 135
Renselaerwyck 8, 44, 53, 58, 65*
Rhinish Bavaria 31
Rhinebeck, Dutchess Co............106
Ricame Parish, France 30
Ritsen, E. Friesland 32
Rochester, 44. 99, 100, 101, 118, 120, 124,
  125, 127, 129*, 182*.
Roeloff Jansen's Kill 128
Roundout Creek, 6, 35, 40, 58, 94. 120
Rosendale 132
Rotterdam, Holland 163
Rundale 173
Ruynen, Holland 106
Rvnborch, Holland 38

Saghkill 177
Saintonge, France 91
Salem, N. J........................123
Saugerties, 95, 96, 102, 124, 135, 159,
  160*, 161, 163, 178.
Sawyer's Creek 5
Schagticoke 65
Schenectady, 44, 53, 73, 74*, 79, 121
Shokan 155
Schouwen, Island of 121
Scotland 128
Shawangunk. 95, 96, 102, 124, 135, 159,
  160*, 161, 163, 178.
Shawangunk Church 159
Shawangunk Creek 124, 125
Shawangunk Kill 124, 163
Shawangunk Mountains 125, 160
Shelter Island 49
Ships:
  "Faith" 35, 42, 44
  "Fox" 41
  "Gilded Otter" 31*, 34, 73
  "Moseman" 59

"St. Barbara" 66
"Spotted Cow" 30, 75, 120, 182
"St. John the Baptist" 34
Skoherry Kill, Albany Co..........146
Sloop "St. Barbara" 66
Somerset County, N. J.............40
Southold, L. I....................49
South Holland 30
South River 30
"Spotted Cow," the ship, 30, 75, 120, 182.
"St. John the Baptist," the ship 34
Steenwyck, Holland 46
Sullivan County 6
Sweden 30, 135
Swichtalaer, Holland 39
Swol, Holland 44, 88
Tawaeretagne 35
Tiederwelt 41
Tiel, Holland 30
Trinity Church, New York 65
Turtle Falls 30
Utrecht, Holland 34, 38, 65, 88
Vechten, Holland 88
Vovelens 41

Wagendal 93
Wageningen, Holland 61*
Waghgashkenck 92
Waghkonk 177
Wakankonach 35
Wakaseeck 35
Wallkill 6, 140, 160, 163
Waracahaes 35
Wassemaker's land, 30, 41, 55, 130, 147
Water Kolch 46
Wawarsing 154, 161, 191
Welpe, Holland 41
West Camp 156
West Compensation 174
West Indies 15
Westphalia 43
White Clay Kill 134
Wicres, France 31, 34
Wie, Holland 88
Wiltwyck, 8, 22, 23, 25, 26, 29*, 30, 31, 41*, 75, 92, 182.
Woerden, Holland 32, 65
Wool, Dorsetshire, England 88
Ysselsteyn, Germany 54
Zunderland, Holland 57

INDEX OF NAMES.

Surnames have been indexed as they appear at the beginning of an instrument, as a signature at the bottom thereof, and as they are written in parish registers and public documents, quoted in the historical and genealogical notes, e. g., *Mattysen* under *Mattysen, Tysen, Van Keulen, Van Keuren; Jansen* under *Vermeulen, Van Oosterhoudt, Joosten, Van Steenbergh; Roosa* under *Heymanse; Brinck* under *Lambertse* and *Huybertse,* etc.

Children are indexed under the name of their parents, unless known by some other surname. Married daughters are indexed under the names of their husbands, as well as under the various surnames, by which their parents were known.

Baptismal names have, as a rule, been placed under English headings. Students, who are unfamiliar with Dutch nomenclature, are referred to pages 17-19.

Italics indicate a testator, or an intestate.

An *asterisk* (*) signifies that a name occurs more than once on a page.

Cross references are given where equivalent names are far apart, or dissimilar, or where members of the family were known by several names, as *Aertsen, Van Wagenen, Jacobsen; Alsdorff, Aulsdorff; Slichtenhorst, van Sleghtenhorst.*

Particular attention is called to the fact that it will not be necessary to search the entire index for various spellings of the same surname. Delamater, De Lamater, Delametter, Le Maistre, De la Maistre, will all be found under *Delamater,* etc., cross references under all these headings referring to the general heading.

Negroes have been indexed, by name, under a general heading.

AARTS, AERTS, AERTSEN:
Aart, 93, 94, 95, 190; Abraham, 95; Annatje, 71, 82, 94, 95, 106, 148; Catrina, 95; Clara, 102, 103; Elisabeth, 82, 95, 103; Evert, 94, 95; Gepie, 58; *Gerrit,* 102; Gerrit, 38, 39, 53, 67, 68, 95*, 103, 131, 165, 190; Gertie, 94, 95; Gritie, 32, 38, 103; Henderick, 28*; Hillegond, 95*; Huyberts, 76; Isaac, 93, 94, 95; *Jacob,* 93; Jacob, 40, 48, 50, 55, 70, 71, 79, 93, 94, 95*, 103, 106, 130; Jannetje, 94, 95*; Marytjen, 95; Neeltje, 103, 106; Rebecca, 79, 94, 95; Sarah, 79, 93*, 94, 95*, 103, 106; Symon, 94, 95; see also *Van Wagenen, Jacobsen.*

ABRAHAMSEN:
  Jacob, 192.
ADDISON:
  John, 154.
ADOLPH:
  Jannetie, 43; Peter, 43.
ADRIAENSE, ADRIAENSEN, ADRIANSE, ARYENSEN, ARIAENSE, ADRIAANZ, ARYANCE, ADRIANSEN, ADRYANES, ADRYAENS, ARYENSSE, ADRIEIJANSE, ARIENS:
  Annatje, 45, 71; *Dirck (Van Vliet)*, 41; Elisabeth, 30; Femmetje, 29; Geertje, 41; Gepje, 46; Gheppey, 58; *Hendrick*, 58; Hendrick, 30, 46*, 47; Jannetie, 30; *Joost*, 29; Joost, 29*, 30*, 33, 37, 38, 39, 41; Joost & Co., 30; *Machtel*, 43; Machtel, 41; Mareitje, 29, 30; Sara, 30; *Petter*, 47; Petter, 47*, 191, 192; Willem, 30; Wyntje, 75; see also *Arentse, Arentsen, Hendrick*.
AKEN:
  Appolonia, 121, 127; Jans Thomasen, 121; see also *Van Aken*.
ALBERTS, ALBERTSE, ALBERTSEN:
  Arent, 75; Barent (Bratt), 92; Eva, 49, 92*; *Femmetje*, 45; Femmetje, 29*, 30*, Hendrick, 26*, 28; Jan, 58.
ALDEGONDE:
  24, 28. See *Roosa*.
ALLESSEN:
  Hyman, 37.
AMOYOT:
  Jacob, 31.
ANDERS:
  Edmond, Sr., 190.

ANDRIES:
  Francyntje, 92; Marritje, 106.
ANDRIESEN:
  Albert (Bratt), 92; Anna, 82; Barbara, 44, 57; Eva, 92; Geertruyd, 28, 189; Henderick, 58.
ANDROS:
  Governor, 46, 58, 190.
ANNIS:
  William, 69*.
ANTHONY:
  Aefje (Van Niewenkuyzen), 43; Engeltie, 191; Louis (Van Niewenkuyzen), 43; N., 37, 48; Nicholas, 191.
APOLLINAREN:
  Q., 24.
ARENSE, ARENSEN, ARENTS, ARENTSEN, ARIENS:
  Bennony (Van Hoeck), 74; Gepie (Pier), 46, 58; Gerrit, 59; Gritie, 88; Hendrick, 46, 58, 59; Jacomyntje, 74; Jan, 88; Lysbeth, 44; Margaret, 88; see also *Adriaensen, Cornelisen*.
ASHFORDBY:
  Susanna, 34, 101; William, 37, 42.
AUKES:
  Domine, 74.
BACKER:
  Annah Deamute, 149; Elisabeth, 149; see also *De Backer*.
BAKKERIN:
  Annah Demold, 149; see also *Backer*.
BALDWIN:
  Samuel, 167.
BANCKER:
  Abraham B., 155, 157*, 158, 160, 163, 164.

INDEX OF NAMES.

BANKS:
 Justus, 158; William, 175.
BARCKLAJ:
 J., 24, 28.
BARENTSE:
 Cornelius, 33; Helena, 41; Hester, 41; Lourents, 41.
BARENTSEN:
 Annetie, 32, 33; Annatie (Van de Cuyl), 44; *Cornelius,* 32; Cornelius (Van de Wyck), 40; Cornelius (Van der Cuyl), 44; Cornelius, 48, 189, 190; Hendrick, 32; Jacomyntje, 32, 33; Jan (Kunst), 32, 39; Jan, 58; Lysbet (Van de Cuyl), 44; Matys, 32, 35; Petronella, 32; *Tryntie.* 32; Tryntie, 33, 39.
BARTIANSEN:
 See *Cool.*
BARWEER:
 Carol, 85.
BASTIAESEN:
 Jan, 75; see *Low, Kortright.*
BATTY:
 See *Beatty*
BAYARD:
 Catharine, 82.
BEAMER:
 Adam, 152.
BEATTY, BATTY, BETTIS, BETTI:
 Agnes, 101*; B a t a, 101; Charles, 101; Edward, 101; Henry, 101; James, 101; *John,* 100; John, 34, 101*; Maria, 34, 101; Martha, 101; Robert, 100, 101; Susanna, 34, 100*; Thomas, 34, 101*; William, 101.
BECKER:
 Anna, 149.
BEECK:
 Willem. 191; William P.. 192.

BEECQMAN, BEEKMAN:
 Catrina, 106*; Cornelia, 106, 128; Gerardus, 163; Henry, 39, 49, 52, 59, 60, 62, 64, 81, 82, 87, 94, 106, 128*, 190, 191; Johanna, 190; John, 150; Thomas, 93, 128; William, 23, 25, 26*, 27, 28, 29, 106, 170, 189*.
BELTSNYDER:
 Johannis, 39.
BENSCHOTEN:
 See *Bomschoten.*
BENSON:
 Cornelia, 135; Robert, 135; Tryntje, 135.
BENTHUYREN:
 See *Benthuysen.*
BENTHUYSEN:
 Barent, 134; see *Van Benthuysen.*
BERDINE:
 See *Bodine.*
BERGH:
 See *Van den Bergh*
BERRY:
 Annatje, 133.
BEST:
 Jacob, 134.
BETHLY:
 See *Beatty.*
BETTI:
 See *Beatty.*
BETTIS:
 See *Beatty.*
BETTY:
 See *Beatty.*
BEUTON:
 Barnabas, 176.
BEVIER:
 Abraham, 44, 98, 99*, 157, 158, 160, 164, 165, 166, 168, 169, 183; Andries, 97, 98, 99*, 161;

Anna, 183; Catherine, 99, 160;
Elias, 167; Elisabeth, 91, 99;
Esther, 91, 99*, 127, 183*;
Hester, 98*, 99; Jacobus B.,
183; Jacomyntje, 161; Jean,
97, 98, 99*; Johannes, 154*;
Louis, 77, 91, 99*; Louis, Jr.,
97, 99; *Louis, Sr.*, 97; Louis,
Sr., 99; Magdalena, 99, 154,
183; Margaret, 154; Maria,
99*; Naithen S., 154; Philip
D., 155, 157; Rachel, 44, 99,
154; Samuel, 98, 99*, 114, 116,
154; Sara, 154, 183; Solomon,
99.

BICKER:
Henry, 149.

BIGGS:
Jan, 37, 83; John, 37; Marya,
83; Zara, 120.

BILLOU:
Pierre, 34.

BIX:
See *Biggs*.

BLAN:
See *Le Blanc*.

BLANCHAN, BLANCSAN,
BLANKUN, BLANSJAN:
Annatje, 183; Catherine, 31*,
34*, 44, 48, 91, 154; Cornelia,
154; Elisabeth, 31*, 35*, 48,
95, 106; John, 170; *Magdalen*,
48; Magdalen, 30, 31*, 33, 38,
48*, 82, 99; Margrietje, 31;
Maria, 31*, 48, 73; *Matthes
(Mattys, Matthew)*, 30, 48;
Mattys, 30, 31*, 34*, 35, 48*,
71, 72*, 73*, 101, 106, 183;
Mattys, Jr., 31.

BLEEKER:
Catherine, 145; Ruth, 57, 58;
Rutger, 145.

BLODGOOD:
Judith, 32, 42; Niesje, 93.

BLOEMS:
Mrs., 26.

BLOM:
Hermanus, 22.

BODE:
Marie, 42.

BODINE:
Elisabeth, 140, 141; Jacob, 140,
141.

BOEL:
See *Bode*.

BOGARD, BOGAARD,
BOGAART, BOOGAARD,
BOGART, BOGARDUS:
Aaltjen, 92, 93; Barbara, 57;
Cornelia, 93; Cornelis, 57, 58*,
92, 93; Fannerie, 53, 54; Helena,
58; *Hendrick*, 92; Hendrick,
54, 83*, 93*; Hendrick Cornelis, 53, 54, 64; Jannetje, 54;
Marten, 92*, 93; Mayken, 34,
92, 93; Neeltje, 33, 92, 93; Rachel, 57, 58, 92*, 93; Rebecca,
92; Ruth, 92, 93; Sara, 54, 92,
93; Tanneken, 93; see *Van den
Bogaard* and *Bogardus*.

BOGARDUS:
Anna (Anneke), 65*; An-
thony, 64, 65; Cornelis, 65*,
66; Ephraim, 64, 65*; Ever-
hardus, 65*; Evert, 54, 64,
65*; Hannah, 65; Jonas, 65*;
Maria, 65; Marytje, 66; Notary, 192; *Pieter*, 63; Pieter, 64,
65*, 124; Rachel, 65, 127; Rebecca, 124; Shibboleth, 65;
Tjatje, 54; William, 65*;
Wyntje, 63, 64, 65*.

BOMSCHOTEN, BUNSCHOTEN,
VAN BUNTSCHOTEN:
Anna, 66, 132, 133*; Cathrina,
133; Egbert Hendrikz, 133;
Elias, 34, 104; Elisabeth, 133;
Elsie, 132*, 133*; Gerrit, 66;

Gerretje, 104, 132, 133; Johannis, 104, 132, 133; Maria, 132, 133; Sara, 34, 104, 132, 133*; *Salomon, Sr.,* 132; Teunis, 104, 132, 133*.

BOOKSTAVER:
Mary, 152.

BOOTH:
Elisabeth, 49.

BORDINE:
See *Bodine.*

BORENSEN:
Cornelis, 32.

BORSTIUS:
Jacob, 25.

BORSUM:
Gritie, 35; Margaret, 35; Tymen, 35; see *Van Borsum.*

BOS:
Tryntie, 32; Tryntie Tysen, 32, 73, 191; see *Bosch.*

BOSCH:
Cornelis Teunisse, 65; Maritie, 65; Pieternella, 130; *Tryntie T.,* 32; Wyntje, 65; see *Bos.*

BOTTERWOUT:
Daniel, 27.

BRABANDER:
Jan, 26, 27, 130.

BRADETH:
Elisabeth, 156.

BRADLEY:
William, 170.

BRANNARNE:
Jockein, 48.

BRATT:
Albert Andriessen, 92; Barent Albertse, 92; Eva Andriessen, 92.

BRESTEDE:
Andrew, 43; Annette, 43; Eliza Janse, 32; Engeltje, 106; Jan Jansen, 32, 106; Marritje, 106.

BRINK:
Andrew, 179, 180; Anna, 149, 177, 179, 180; Benjamin M., 136; Cornelius, 113; Cornelius C., 157; Cornelius Lambertse, 133, 182; Egbert, 112*, 113*; Elisabeth, 112; Elsie Lammertsen, 133; Hendrick, 112, 113*; Hendrickjen, 61, 113; Jacob, 112, 113*; Janneken, 112, 113, 182; Lambert, 113; Lambert Cornelisen, 112, 113*; Lambert Huybertse, 8, 60, 61; Marritie Lambertse, 182; Meery, 101; Mynert, 113; Rachel, 112, 113; see *Lambertse, Huybertse, Hendrickse, Pieterse.*

BRINKERHOFF:
John, 135.

BROADHEAD, BRODHEAD:
Charles, 42, 62, 67, 68*, 69, 75, 154, 168; Daniel, 42*, 100, 104, 170; Daniel, Jr., 169; Elisabeth, 156; Gerrit, 170; James, 167; John, 156; John C., 170, 172; Johannis, 170; Magdalena, 34, 104; Maria, 42, 67, 68, 156; Marreganta, 34; Oliver, 167; Richard, 34, 60*, 69, 100, 104.

BROERSENS:
Jan, 192; Jan, 29; Willemtje, 192.

BRONCK:
Hannah, 65; Pieter, 65.

BROWN:
Anna, 171, 172; Benjamin, 171, 172; David, 171, 172; Gertie, 124; Hannah, 171, 172; Henry, 171, 172; Jacobus, 40; Mary, 171, 172; Rachel, 172*.

BRUYN:
Blandina, 145; Catharine, 125*, 127*, 145; Cornelius, 124*, 125, 126*, 127, 161; Gertrude, 96, 125, 127*, 160, 161; Hanna, 125*, 126, 127*; Hester, 127; Ida, 127; J., Jr., 130; *Jacobus,* 124; Jacobus, 95, 96*, 102, 124*, 126*, 127*, 142, 145, 159; Jacobus, Jr., 127, 160; Jacobus, Sr., 127; Jan, 127; Jeannie, 127; Johannis, 124, 125, 126*, 127, 159, 160*, 161, 166, 168; Josias, 127; Maria, 125*, 126, 127*; Peternella, 125*, 126*, 127; Pieternelletjen, 127; Severyn, 95, 124, 125, 126*, 145, 159; Severyn Tenhout, 127*, 160; Tryntje, 96, 124, 126*; see *Tenhout.*

BUNSCHOTEN:
See *Bomschoten.*

BURHANS:
Abraham, 181; Abraham, 181*, 182*; Annatje, 181, 182; Barent, 34, 104, 182; Catherine, 182; Cornelius, 157; David, 182; Deborah, 182; Elisabeth, 130, 182; Gritie, 182; Helena, 46*, 181*, 182*; Hendrick, 80, 182; Hillitje, 50, 82, 182; Isaac, 181, 182*; Jacob, 22, 27, 123, 182*; Jan, 26, 27, 30, 46*, 52, 182; Janneke, 112, 181*, 182*; Johanna, 182; Johannes, 80, 81, 182; Maretje, 123, 181; Margaret, 34, 81, 104, 182*; Maria, 182*; Neeltje, 182; Petrus, 181*, 182; Samuel, 112, 181, 182*; Sarah, 181*, 182; Susannah, 182; William, 122, 182.

BUUR:
Anneke, 34; Jan Hendricks, 34.

BUSH:
See *Bos* and *Bosch.*

BUYR:
Jan, 26.

CAGE:
Rietsert, 27*.

CANTINE:
Catherine, 164; Charles, 171; Elisabeth, 164; Matthew, 141, 163; Moses, 154, 155, 164; Moses, Jr., 157; Nathaniel, 143; Petrus, 154, 164; Pierre, 116; William, 141*; see *Contine.*

CAPITO:
Mattheus, 22*, 25, 26*, 28*, 29*, 30.

CAPPOENS:
Christian, 30.

CARDINAEL:
Sybrand Hansen, 24.

CARLE:
Catherine, 177; Mathew, 177.

CARN:
Mary, 149; Susan Margaret, 149.

CASTLE:
Anne, 178; Joseph, 178.

CHAMBERS:
Abraham, 76; Abraham Gaasbeck, 38, 87, 105, 106, 120, 132, 135; Blandina Gaasbeck, 174; Catherine, 135; Esther, 155, 156; Jacob, 155, 156; Laurentia, 190; Margaret, 33, 38, 190; *Thomas,* 190; Thomas, 5, 26, 33, 38, 39, 42*, 46, 48, 190; see *Gaasbeck.*

CHITTENDEN:
Nathaniel, 175*.

CHRIST, CRIST:
Rachel, 140, 141; Stavennus, 140, 141.

CHROECK:
See *Crook*.
CHURCH:
Caleb, 170.
CLAES:
Aeltje, 22*.
CLAESSEN:
Ariantje, 121; Carsten, 58; Catherine, 49; Claes, 49; Cornelia, 49, 92; Cornelius, 49, 121; Deborah, 49; Elisabeth, 69; Fransyntje, 49; *Hendrick*, 49; Hendrick, 49, 88, 92, 100; Hendrick (Schoonhoven), 92; Ifje, 49; Jannetje (Vechten), 88; Margriet, 31, 49; Nicholas, 49; Tierck, 8, 21, 22*, 26, 27*, 28, 34, 42, 45, 55, 56; see *De Witt, Schoonhoven, Schoonmaker, Vechten*.
CLARKSON:
Mattis, 49.
CLEARWATER:
Alphonso Trumpbour, 5, 163; Elsie, 112; Isaac, 7; Tunis Jacobse, 8, 163; see *Klaarwater*.
CLINTON:
Charles, 127; George, 5, 141, 144, 145.
CLOETE:
See *Clute*.
CLOM:
George, 135.
CLUTE:
Francyntie, 86*, 87, 88; Fredrik, 86*, 87, 88.
COBES:
Lodevicus, 73.
COCK:
Alice, 99, 100; Bregjen, 100; Catrina, 100; Eleanor, 101; Elsje, 100*; *John*, 99; John, 75, 99, 100*; Magdalena, 99, 100; Margaret, 99, 100*; Samuel, 99, 100*; Thomas, 99*, 100*, 101; William, 99, 100, 101.
COCKBURN:
Mr., 188.
CODDINGTON:
Jacob, 168.
COERTEN:
Steven, 39.
COLDEN:
Cadwallader, 125*.
COLE:
Cornelis, 59; John, 173; see *Cool*.
COLLINS:
H. O., 14.
COMELIS:
Ariantje, 121; Geertje, 66.
CONES:
James, 141.
CONKLING:
Frank J., 14.
CONNELLER:
James, 141.
CONNELLY:
Arthur C., 4, 14.
CONSTABLE:
Christopher, 141; see *Konstapel*.
CONTAIN:
See *Contine* and *Cantine*.
CONTANT:
Peter J., 179.
CONTINE:
Petrus (Pierre), 116; see *Cantine*.
COOBES:
Jannetje, 92.
COOK:
John, 69, 108.
COOL:
Anna, 38, 118, 120*; Cather-

ine, 124; *Cornelis,* 118; Cornelis, 38, 52, 60, 61, 91, 113, 120; Cornelis Teunisen, 61, 120; Geertie, 119, 120*; Hendricke, 119*, 120*; Janneke, 38, 118, 119, 120*; Jacob Barents, 28; Lambert, 110, 118, 119*; Margriet, 118, 119*, 120, 177; Sara, 93, 120; Symon, 93; Theunis, 120; Theunis Bartiansen, 120; see *Cole* and *Kool.*

COOPERSLAEGER:
Anna, 36; Johannes Willemsen, 36.

CORNBURY:
Lord, 15.

CORNELIS, CORNELISE, CORNELISEN:
Abraham, 121; Adriantie, 41; Aeltie, 121; *Annatje,* 33, 44; Annatje, 33, 44, 58, 189; Apollonia, 121*; Arie, 59; Barent, 59; Catalyn, 121; Cheiltje, 59, 60, 169, 184; Claes (Van Schoonhoven), 121; Claes (Swits), 121; Cornelia, 44, 53, 54, 121; Cornelius, 35, 44, 53, 54, 121; Elisabeth, 35, 44; Elisabeth (Low), 31, 73, 106; Fannerie, 53, 54; Fytie, 59; Garretje, 59; Gerard, 60; Gerretje, 59, 124; *Gerrit,* 59; Gerrit, 40, 59*, 60, 73, 124, 169, 184; Geertruy, 44, 53; Gilie, 59; Hendrik, 26*, 28, 54; *Hendrik Cornelisen,* 190; Hendrikje, 61; Isaac, 54, 121; Jacob, 44, 54, 121; Jacob Martensen, 53; Jacomyntje, 32, 59; Jan, 30, 59; Jannetje, 44, 54, 121; Johannes, 44; *Marte,* 53; Metje, 75; Neeltje (Van Veghten), 88; *Peter,* 35, 73; Peter, 8, 31, 35, 106, 121, 190; Rachel, 44; Sara, 44, 54; Selie, 44; Susanna, 121; Teuntie, 53; Theunis, 59, 73, 74; Willemtje, 30; see *Ariens, Bosch, Brink, Gerritse, Lambertse, Low, Newkirk, Swart, Swits, Van Schoonhoven, Van Vechten, Vernooy.*

COSENS:
Barnes, 62.

COTTIN:
Catherine, 83; Catherine, 34, 83; Jan, 34, 77, 83, 84, 85; Sara, 84, 85.

COUCH:
Sarah, 42; William, 42.

COUTANT:
Peter, 179*; Peter J., 179*.

COYLER:
Anna, 43*; Henry, 43*.

CRANS:
See *Krans.*

CRAWFORD:
Abigail, 174; Absalum, 175*; Charles, 175; Daniel, 175; David, 175; *Henry,* 174; Henry, 175*; Jane, 175; John, 175; Lowis, 175; Nelly, 175; Phebe, 175.

CRESPEL:
Antoin, 71; Anthony, 73.

CRISPEL:
Anthony, 31, 71, 72, 73, 135, 165; *Antoin,* 71; Aryantie, 71, 72; Elisabeth, 72*, 73*, 165; Geertje, 71, 73; Hilligard, 95; Jan, 71*, 72*; Jannetje, 71, 72, 73*, 135; Jean, 73; Johannis, 71, 72; John, 73; Maria, 31, 71, 73, 184; Mary Magdalena, 33, 71, 72, 73; Neeltje, 43, 73; Peter, 43, 71, 72, 73; Petronella, 73; Sara, 72, 73*; see *Crupel* and *Crespel.*

INDEX OF NAMES.

CROEING:
Lysbeth, 30.
CROM:
Geertrud, 41; Gysbert, 41, 43; Willem, 74, 75; Wyntje, 74, 75.
CROOK, CROOKE:
Catherine, 34, 104, 148; John, 128, 130, 135, 145, 148; John, Jr., 34, 104, 117, 124; Maria, 145, 148.
CROOKSHANK:
Alexander, 156.
CROSWELT:
Bay, 62; Ray, 62.
CRUPEL:
Marya Maddelen, 33; Neeltje, 43; Pieter, 43; see *Crispel* and *Crespel*.
DAMOUR:
Anne, 91.
DAMPORT:
See *Davenport*.
DARETH:
Jan, 92; Ryckie, 92.
DAVENPORT:
Gerret, 152; Humphrey, 47*, 49*, 58, 73*; John, 70, 80, 81; Maria, 81; Richard, 122.
DAVIS, DAVIDS, DAVIDSZ, DAVITS, DAVY, DAVID:
Anna, 155*, 156*; *Christopher*, 155; Christopher, 5, 28*, 156*; David, 190; Deborah, 182; Elisabeth, 155*, 156*; En (Anna), 156; Engel, 156; Esther, 155, 156*; Frederick, 156; Geertruy, 43; George, 37, 190; Isaak, 83, 155*, 156*; Jacobus, 190; Jannetie, 83, 156*; *Johanna*, 190; Johannes, 152; John, 47, 49, 155*, 156*; John C., 156; Joris, 156; Mary, 156*; Rachel, 155, 156*;
Richard (Ritsert), 155*, 156*; Salomon, 110, 156, 190; Samuel, 156, 190; Stoffel, 156; Wyntie, 155, 156.
DEAMUTE:
Annie (Backer), 149.
DE BACKER:
Hendrick, 58.
DEBOIS:
See *Dubois*.
DECKER, DECKERS, DEKKER, DEKKERS:
Amey, 171, 172; Barbara, 118; Cornelius, 67, 68*; Elsie, 67, 68; Geertje, 94, 95, 130; Gerrit, 102; Gerrit Janse, 95, 118; Henry, 129*, 171, 172; Heyltie, 30; Jacob, 94; Jacob Gerritse, 95; Jan Broerse, 30; Jan Gerritse, 118, 129; Johannis, 117; Magdalena, 118; Magdalena Janse, 95, 102; Margaret, 118; Maria, 117, 171, 172; Sally, 171, 172; Willemtje, 30.
DEDERICK:
Geysbert, 146; Jurry Wm., 180.
DE DUYTSE:
Catharine, 127.
DE FEREEST:
Rachel, 23.
DEFFENPORT:
See *Davenport*.
DE GRAAF, DE GRAAVE, DE GRAFF:
Jan Andries, 33; Maria, 31; Moses, 62.
DE GRAU:
See *De Graaf*.
DE HOOGES:
Anneken, 92; Anthony, 92*; Catrina, 92; Eleonora, 92; Eva, 44, 92; Johanna, 182; Johannes, 41, 92; Marichen, 92.

DE HULTEN:
John, 5.
DEIJO, DEIJOU:
See *Deyo*.
DE JONGE:
Weilke, 75; see *Deyo*.
DE JOU, DE JOO, DE JOUW:
See *Deyo*.
DE LAET, DE LALDT:
Johanna, 58, 103.
DELAMATER, DE LAMATER, DELAMETTER, LE MAISTRE, DE LA MAISTRE:
Abraham, 44, 57, 76, 82, 93*, 151; Abraham, Jr., 93; Catharina, 150*, 151*; Christina, 174; Cornelia, 93; Cornelis, 95, 127, 132, 151, 179; *David*, 150; David, 150*, 151*, 174; Dinah, 179; Jacobus, 61, 150, 151*; Jan, 93; Johannes, 128, 132, 137, 151; John, 174; Laurentia, 151; Ruth, 93; Sarah, 93, 150*, 151*; Selia, 44; Seletje, 44; Tanneken, 93.
DE LA MONTAGNE:
See *Montagne*.
DE LANCY:
Stephen, 49*.
DELANDAL:
Eeledt, 36; Johannes, 36.
DELVA:
Annatje, 58, 66; Anthony, 26, 27, 58, 66; Jannetje, 58, 66.
DE MAJER:
See *De Meyer*.
DE MEYER, MEYER:
Benjamin, 76, 96, 188; Cathrina, 82; Elsie, 82; Hendricus, 179*, 180; Mary, 177, 179, 180; Nicholas, 37, 82, 189*; William, 38, 42, 50, 51, 52, 53, 56, 57, 60, 62*, 63, 68, 69, 70, 71, 76, 82, 87, 96, 191, 192.
DE MES:
Benjamin, 93; Rachel, 93.
DEMOLD:
Annah (Backer), 149.
DEMON:
See *Dumond*.
DE MOTT:
Jacob, 58; Maria, 58.
DEO:
See *Deyo*.
DE PRE:
Pieternel, 182.
DEPUY, DEPEW, DUPUIS, DE PUY:
Annatje, 182; Benjamin, 182; Catrina, 127, 182*; Cornelius, 132, 182*; Daniel, 182; Eiche, 182; Elisabeth, 182*; Ephraim, 182; *Jacobus*, 182; Jacobus, 182*; John, 182; Magdalena, 182; Margaret, 182; Maria, 32, 182*; Moses, 32, 118, 127, 182*; Nicholas, 32, 47, 97, 182; Petroneltje, 182; Sarah, 182*; Simon, 182*; Susanna, 182*; Weyntje, 182.
DERRICKSEN:
Teunis, 88; see also *Teunissen*.
DE SILLE:
Nicasius, 65.
DEUNIS:
Antjen, 186; Grietjen, 186; see *Theunis*.
DEUSEN:
John V., 184.
DE VIGA:
Johannes, 24.
DEVOE:
Elisabeth, 186; Michael, 186.
DE WANDELAER, DE WANDELOER:

INDEX OF NAMES. 219

Aefje, 43; Andries, 43; Johannes, 43*; Sarah, 43*.

DE WITT:
Agje, 57, 58; *Andries,* 165; Andries, 45, 56, 58, 118*, 143, 166; Anne, 58, 65*, 66*, 166, 169; Ariantje, 66; Barbara, 44, 56, 57*, 58*, 66, 118*; Bastian, 76; Blandina, 118*; *Boudewyn,* 62; Boudewyn, 50, 62*; Catherine, 66, 132; Charles, 169; Cornelius, 166*; Dieck, 57; Dirck Claessen, 58; Egbert, 127; Eiche, 118, 182; Emmerentje, 57, 73, 135; Geertruy, 57, 58, 82; Grietje, 58; Henry, 166; Ikee, 118; Isaack, 165, 166; Jacob, 44, 58, 118, 130; *Jan,* 118; Jan, 56, 58, 65*, 66*; *Jan Claetz,* 54; Jan Claetz, 55, 58; Jannetje, 45, 57, 58*, 65, 66, 118, 121; John C., 154; Klaes, 58; *Luycas,* 65; Luycas, 57, 58, 66, 132; Maria, 57, 58*, 62, 106; Neeltje, 165, 166*; Peek, 58; Peter, 93; Petronella, 62; Rachel, 57, 58, 65, 118*, 165; Tialie, 54; Tjatje, 34, 57, 58; Tjerck, 56, 58, 88, 108, 165*, 166*; *Tjerck Claesse,* 56; Tjerck Claesse, 8, 21, 22*, 26*, 27*, 28*, 34, 42, 44, 45, 55, 57, 58, 66, 82, 87, 118, 121, 135; Wyntje, 58, 118; see *Claesen.*

DEYO:
Abraham, 110; Abraham, 90, 111, 163*, 170; Agatha, 31, 158; Anne, 31*, 91; Catherine, 165; *Christian,* 31, 47; Christian, 31*, 34*, 47, 91, 154; Christoffel, 183; David, 165; Elisabeth, 31*, 154, 164; Elsje, 110, 111; Jacob, 158; Johannes B., 158*; Jonathan, 163, 164*, 165; Margaret, 31*, 34*, 39, 158; Maria, 31*, 91, 95, 111, 163*, 164*; Peter (Pierre), 31*, 47; Rachel, 165, 166; Wyntje, 111, 170.

DIEDERICK:
Christian, 134.

DIEPPOIS:
Jan Belot, 24.

DIJO:
See *Deyo.*

DINGMANS:
Eva, 91, 92; Jacob, 91, 92.

DINGS:
Hans Jacob, 134*.

DIRCK:
Aeltie, 46; Jannetje (Van Vechten), 86, 88; Michel (Van Vechten), 86, 88; see *Dyrck, Turck* and *Van Veghten.*

DOEJOU, DOIAN, DOIAU, DOIO:
See *Deyo.*

DODGE:
John, 167.

DOLE:
Adam J., 155.

DONALDSON:
Abraham, 168; Abraham, 168; Catherine, 168; Esther, 168; John, 168*; Magdalena, 168; Margaret, 168; Rachel, 168; Samuel, 168*.

DONGAN:
Governor, 5, 30; Thomas, 30, 52.

DOORN:
Aert Martensen, 189; Aert Martensen, 26*, 28, 189; Geertruyd, 28, 189*.

DOW:
Volckert Janse, 92.

DOYAN, DOYEAU, DOYOO:
See *Deyo.*

DUBOIS:
Abraham, 31, 34, 39, 51, 84, 89*; Adam, 137; Annatje, 44, 137, 160, 177*, 178; Anna Margaret, 161, 178; Ariantje, 160; Barent, 123, 124; Benjamin, 115*; *Catharina,* 34; Catharina (Catrintje, Cataline), 31*, 34, 35, 44, 50, 91, 123, 124, 137*, 154, 160, 178; Charles, 178*; Cornelia, 34, 44, 170; Cornelius, 137, 160*, 161*, 162, 178; *Cornelius, Sr.*, 160; Daniel, 112, 114, 154; David, 34, 44, 51, 52, 84, 137; Dina, 159*, 160; Elisabeth, 34, 44, 115, 153, 154*; Gerrit, 123, 124*, 148*; Gerritje, 59, 123, 124, 148; Gertrude, 124, 127, 160, 161; Gieltje, 124; *Hendric,* 158; Hendric, 158, 159*, 160*; Hiskia, 137*; Isaac, 34, 51, 91, 116, 124, 166; *Jacob,* 123; Jacob, 34, 44, 51*, 52*, 59, 80, 81, 84, 87, 119, 124, 137, 148*; Jacomyntje, 123, 160, 161; Jan, 81; Jannetje, 159, 160*, 161, 182; Johannes, 123, 124; Jonathan, 35, 153, 154; *Joshua,* 177; Joshua, 161*, 177, 178*; Josia, 161; Judik, 124; Lea, 159*, 160*, 161*, *Louis, (Lowis, Lewis)*, 34, 46, 50, 51; Louis (Lowis, Lewis), 31*, 34*, 35*, 37, 41, 44, 51, 52, 84, 91, 117, 123, 124*, 125*, 127, 161; Magdalena, 123, 124*, 136; Margaret, 31, 34, 39, 117, 124, 136, 148, 160, 178*; Maria, 34, 91, 115*, 154; Matthew, 34, 35, 51*, 52*, 84, 137, 161, 180; Methusalem, 158, 159*, 160*, 161; Nathaniel, 125, 127, 152, 160, 161; Neeltje, 123, 124*, 166; Petrus, 89, 182; Philip, 116, 129, 159, 160; Polly, 160; Rachel, 34, 35, 115, 125, 127, 159*, 160*, 161, 166; Rebecca, 34, 123, 124, 160; Sara, 34*, 35, 39, 41, 51, 52, 95, 123*, 124, 127, 137*, 148, 160*, 161; Simon, 115, 154, 170; Solomon, 33, 34, 40, 51, 52, 84, 95, 159, 160*, 161; Susanna, 81; Tanneke, 137; Tryntje, 33, 34, 40, 95, 159*, 160*, 161*; Wilhelmus, 160, 161.

DU CONT:
Marytje, 31.

DU JOU, DU JOY:
See *Deyo*.

DUKE:
Jan, 48.

DUKE OF YORK:
42, 50.

DU MOLLIN:
Pieter, 89.

DUMOND, DUMONT, DUMON, DU MON, DEMON:
Catelyntje, 88; Catharin, 88; Cornelius, 184; Femmetje, 88; Francyntje, 86, 87, 88; Grietje, 85, 88; Henderica, 184; Jan Baptist, 85*, 86, 87*, 88; Jannetje, 86, 87, 88*, 182; Johanes, 133; John, 157; Margaret, 86, 87*, 88*; Neeltje, 88; Petrus, 85, 86*, 87, 88*; Petronella, 73; Walran, 26, 27, 28, 31, 47, 71, 72, 86, 87*, 88*, 182; Walran, Jr., 87; *Walrandt, Sr.,* 85, 87; Warren, 46; Weibrandt, 85.

DUNN:
David, 171, 172*; Jeremiah, 171, 172; John, 171*, 172*; Josiah, 172*; Phebe, 171, 172; Sally, 171*, 172.

DYRK:
Catrina, 137, 180; see *Dirck* and *Turck*.

EBBINCK:
Jeronimus, 58, 103; Johanna, 58, 103.

EEN:
Abraham, 164; Abraham, 165*; Annatje, 165*; Catherine, 164, 165*; Elias, 72, 73*, 164*, 165*, 167; Elisabeth, 72, 73*, 165*; Geesjen, 165; Isaak, 165; Jan, 165*; Margaret, 165; Mary, 165; Mary Magdalena, 165; Peter, 164*, 165*; Rachel, 165*; Sarah, 165.

EGBERTZ:
Marytje, 113.

EGBERTSEN:
Jannetje, 58.

EIGN, EIN:
See *Een*.

ELIGH:
Jeremiah, 146.

ELISSE:
Teunis, 38, 62*, 66.

ELMENDORPH:
Anna, 34, 38*, 55, 117, 120, 136; Ariantje, 38, 71, 148*; Blandina, 38, 136*, 145*, 146; Catrina, 127, 145*; *Conrad,* 146; Conrad, 38*, 55, 56, 71, 110, 124, 136*, 145, 148*; Conrad G., 165; Conrad, Jr., 147; Cornelius, 71, 147, 148*; Elisabeth, 145*; Eliza, 145; Engeltje, 71, 148; Gerrit, 136*, 147, 148*; Gertrude, 32, 38*, 55, 56; Grietje, 32, 53*, 103, 148; Helena, 148; Henrica, 136*; *Jacobus,* 37, 55; Jacobus, 32, 38, 53, 55, 56, 72*, 120, 146, 148*; Jacobus C., 103; Janneken, 38, 55, 56, 136*, 148*; John, 145*, 155; Jonathan, 127, 147, 148*; Lucas, 136, 145, 147, 148; Margrietje, 38, 124, 148*; Mary, 145*, 148; Neeltje, 165, 166; Petrus, 165, 166; *Petrus Edmundus,* 145; Petrus Edmundus, 145*, 147, 148*; Sara, 124, 145*, 148*; Tekla, 55; Tobias, 148; *Wilhelmus,* 135; William, 145*, 147, 148*; see *Van Elmendorph*.

ELTINGE:
Aaltje, 39*, 40, 103; Abraham, 137, 159, 160; Bartelt, 39; Blandina, 136; Cornelis, 39, 40*, 41, 88, 97, 136; Dina, 160; Geertje, 39, 40; Henry, 165; Jacomyntje, 32, 33, 39*, 148; *Jan,* 39; Jan, 33, 39*, 40, 60, 71, 72, 131, 136, 137, 148, 191*; Jannetje, 39; Jonas, 136; Magdalena, 136; Maria, 39; Philip, 167; Rebecca, 39, 41; R. Josias, 145; *Roeloff,* 39; Roeloff, 39*, 40*, 90, 97; Sara, 39, 137; Tryntje, 33; William, 39*, 40*, 137, 148; see *Roelofsen*.

ELTON:
See *Eltinge*.

ELYESSEN:
Bastiaen, 75; Metje, 75.

ENTHELBERT:
Joshem, 43.

ENTE:
Jan, 39.

ESSELSTEIN:
Gertrude, 96, 127; Jan Willemse, 96, 127; Willemtje, 96, 127; see *Ysselstein*.

ETKENS:
Elisabeth, 152.

EVANS:
John, 35, 160; Thomas G., 114.
EVERITT:
Esther, 183; Martha, 183; Robert, 183.
EVERTSEN:
Annetje, 189; Jan (Maeter), 189; Saer, 189.
EXVEEN:
Catryntjen, 106; Cornelis, 106.
FALSETT:
Gerret, 112.
FELDEN:
See *Felten*.
FELTEN:
Annatje, 177; Catherine, 176*, 177*; Elisabeth, 17*, 177*; Helena, 177; Jacob, 177; Jacob, Jr., 177; Johannis, 142, 176*, 177*; Lawrence, 176*; 177*; Lena, 177; Margriet, 177*; Maria, 177*; *Philip*, 176; Philip, 176, 177.
FERNOW:
B., 14.
FERRE:
See *Fiero*.
FEVER:
See *Le Fevre*.
FIERO:
Christian, 186, 187; Christian, Jr., 187, 188; Christina, 186, 187; Johannes, 186, 187; Margaret, 149; Stephen, 186, 188.
FISHER:
William, 44.
FOCKEN, FOKKER:
Andries, 103; Elisabeth, 106; Engeltje, 106; Gerrit, 32*, 39*; Gritie, 35; Hillitje, 32*, 97; Jacomyntje, 32*, 33, 39, 97; Jan (Heermans), 106*; Neeltje, 103; see *Heermans*.

FOLANT:
Eva, 182; Philippus, 182; Susanna, 182.
FOWLER:
Caty, 172*, 173; David, 172; 173; Levi, 172, 173; Polly, 172*; Reuben, 172*; *Stephen*, 172; Stephen, 172*, 173*.
FRANCKFORD:
Abraham, 48; Jack, 48; Pearle, 48; Sara, 48.
FRANK:
Sebastian, 24, 28.
FRATSHER:
John D., 4, 14.
FREDRICKSEN:
See *Mourits*.
FREDRIX:
Aeltie, 121.
FRELIGH:
Maria, 149; William, 188.
FRERE, FREER:
Abraham, 78, 114, 183; Aeche, 78; Agatha, 158*; Anna Maria, 158; Antje, 78, 158, 183*; Benjamin, 79; Blandina, 79, 113; Bregje, 158, 183; *Catrina*, 183; Catrina, 79, 95, 113, 154, 164, 183; Elias, 183; Elisabeth, 113, 114; Gerrit, 183; Gerrit, Jr., 183; Hester, 79, 113; *Hugh*, 77, 78, 113; Hugh, 31, 77*, 78*, 79*, 113*, 114, 158*, 164, 183; Hugo, Jr., 154; Isaac, 78, 79, 113*, 114; Jacob, 77, 78, 114, 158*; Jan, 94, 95, 114; Jannetje, 78, 113, 114; Jean, 77, 78; *Johannes*, 158; Johannes, 79, 158, 183; Jonas, 113, 169, 170, 183*; Jonathan, 158*; Joseph, 78; Lena, 183; Magdalena, 183; Margrietjen, 158*; Maria, 77, 78*, 79, 113, 154, 164, 165, 183*; **Maria**

INDEX OF NAMES.   223

Anne, 78*, 183*; Martha, 183; Martinus, 183; Petrus, 183; Rachel, 113, 114; Rebecca, 78, 94, 95, 113, 114; Sara, 77, 79, 113, 158, 183; Simon, 79, 113, 114, 183; Thomas, 173; Wyntje, 169, 170.

FURMAN:
John, 168.

FYNHOUT:
Annatje, 81, 139, 185; see *Vynhout* and *Tenhout*.

GAASBECK:
Margritta, 118, 119; Thomas, 118; see *Chambers*.

GAEMAIR:
See *Guimard*.

GARTON:
Anne, 100; Anne, Jr., 100; Thomas, 49, 50, 100.

GASHERIE:
John, 64, 72, 73; Joseph, 10, 160, 161; Stephen, 55, 71, 72, 116.

GEE:
Benjamin, 175; Joseph, 125.

GEMAAR:
See *Guimard*.

GERLEOGH:
Nicholas, 146.

GERMAN:
Anna Mary, 140, 141; Jost, 140, 141.

GERON:
Daniel, 179.

GERRITSE, GERRITZ, GERRITSEN:
Adrian, 120; Aeltje, 39; Aert, 39; *Albert,* 30; Annatje, 82, 103; Ariantje, 38, 71, 148; Arien, 40, 55, 59, 60*, 61*, 81, 87, 90, 91, 100, 110, 113, 119, 120, 131, 148, 169, 184; Breechje, 61; Cleartje, 61; *Cornelis,* 59; Cornelis, 40, 59, 141; Cornelis Newkerk, 59, 141; Dirrick, 61; Geertje (Decker), 95; Gerretje, 59, 124, 133, 148*; Jacob (Decker), 95; Jan, 59; Jannetie, 59*; Lysbeth, 59, 61, 148, 169, 184; Neeltje, 43, 59*, 73; Teunis, 61; Tryntje, 34, 95, 160, 161; Willemtje, 30.

GEUL:
Johan, 24.

GIDNEY:
William, 176.

GIMAIR:
See *Guimard*.

GODKINS:
Ann, 172; Frederick, 172.

GOMAAR:
See *Guimard*.

GORDONIER:
Lysbeth, 92.

GOVERTSEN:
Albert, 26*, 28.

GRAHAM:
Jeannie, 127.

GRIEKHOLF:
D. L., 149.

GRIGGS:
Elisabeth, 175; Henry C., 175; Verdinant, 175.

GROEN:
Jacob Marieus, 165, 169, 173.

GROENVIS:
Jannetje Claesen, 36, 46; Justje, 46.

GROOT:
Simon, 121; Susanna, 121.

GUDERIS:
Catharina, 69.

GUIMARD:
Anna, 91; Hester, 89, 91; Peter, 72*, 89, 91*.

GYSBERTSEN:
Aeltje, 29; Albert, 21, 22, 28, 29*; Gysbert, 29; Jan, 29; Lysbet, 29.

HAAL:
Marya, 83.

HALE:
George, 83; Joris, 26, 83; Maria, 83; Oeyeke, 83.

HALL:
Elisabeth, 190; Geertje, 39, 40; *George,* 190; George, 189; Marie, 37; Mr., 37; Thomas, 39, 40.

HALS:
Elisabeth, 190.

HAMEL:
Geertrud, 41; Jan, 41.

HANSEN:
Maria, 106.

HARDENBERGH:
Abraham, 143*; Catharina, 127, 143*; Gerardus, 118, 142, 143*; J., 95, 96; Jacob, 125, 127, 167; Janneke, 118; Johannes, 87, 95, 96, 110, 124, 127, 143*; Johannes A., 159, 160; Johannes & Co., 120; Johannes, Jr., 164*; Johannes L., 143; *Leonard,* 142; Leonard, 143*; Margaret, 143*; Maria, 164; Petronella, 125, 127; Philippus, 143*; Rachel, 143*, 160, 167; Sara, 143.

HARDENBROECK:
Johanes, 48.

HARMILIE:
Tomas, 48.

HARRIS:
John, 125; William, 97.

HARRISON:
Francis, 125; George, 140.

HARTGERS:
Fytie, 65; Pieter, 65*.

HASBROUCK:
Abraham, 31, 40, 77, 89, 90, 91*, 95, 125, 126, 127, 170*, 171; Abraham J., 171; Agetta, 158; Andries, 166, 170*; Anna, 31, 91, 165; Benjamin, 91, 165; Catharina, 125, 127, 170; Cornelia, 169, 170*; Cornelius, 161, 171*; Cornelius Dubois, 160; Daniel, 89, 91, 112*, 114, 170; Daniel I., 170*; Elisabeth, 88, 89*, 91, 99, 165, 167, 170, 183; Elsje, 127; Esther, 91, 99, 127; Hester, 89, 91, 98; Isaac, 88, 127, 170*, 171; Isaac, Jr., 170; Isaac S., 171; Jacob, 88, 89*, 90, 91, 98, 99*, 112*, 116, 127*, 154, 161*, 170, 171*; *Jacob J.,* 170; Jacob J., 170, 171*; Jacobus, Jr., 155, 161, 183; Jan, 31, 99, 167; Jannetie, 161; *Jean,* 88; Jean, 90, 91; *Johannis,* 166; John E., 166, 167; Jonathan, 160, 163, 165, 168, 169; Jos., 183; Joseph, 91, 98, 127; *Josaphat,* 169; Josias, 161, 165, 170, 171*, 173*; Louis, 170*, 171*; Margaret, 170, 171; Maria, 31, 34, 88, 89*, 91*, 95, 127; Petronella, 154; Philip, 89, 166; Polly, 166, 171*; Rachel, 35, 90, 127, 159, 166, 167, 169, 170; Samuel, 167; Sarah, 95, 161, 170; Simon, 170*; Solomon, 91, 95, 167; Tobias, 178; William, 158, 169, 170, 171*; William, Jr., 166; Wyntje, 169, 170*; Zacharias, 170*.

HAYNES:
William, 73.

HAYS:
Marya, 30*, 79.
HAYWOOD:
John, 112, 125; Thomas, 125.
HEEREKEUS:
Tialie, 54.
HEERMANS, HERMANS, HEERMANSE:
Andreis, 105, 106; Annatje, 70, 71, 95, 106*, 148; Elisabeth, 64, 106, 135; Engeltje, 70, 71, 105, 106, 148; Focke, 106; Grietje, 106*; Hendrick, 105, 106, 131; Jacob, 70, 71; 105; Jacomyntje, 71; Jan, 53, 54, 55, 64, 70, 71*, 95, 105*, 106*, 148; *Jan, Jr.*, 70; Jan, Jr., 66, 71; *Jan, Sr.*, 105; Jan, Sr., 71; John, 40; Margarieta, 105*; Maritje, 71; Neltje, 106; Philippus, 106; Pieter, 106; Wilhelmus, 106; see *Focken.*

HENDRICKS, HENDRICX, HENDRICK, HENDRICKSE, HENDRIX, HENDERICKS:
Aarian, 59; Anna, 30, 34, 43, 103*, 130; Arrie, 59; Catrina, 59; *Dirck,* 63; Dirck, 63, 75; Egbert, 191, 192; Elsje, 192; Eltje, 43; Engeltie, 83, 191, 192; Femmetje, 29*, 30*; Gepjen, 59; *Gritie,* 75; Gritie, 43, 88; *Hendrick,* 47; Henricus, 28, 47, 59, 63, 103*, 191, 192; Jan, 32, 33*, 34, 55; Jochem, 191, 192; Margaret, 33, 58, 88, 177, 190; *Maycken,* 41; Mattys, 5; Rachel, 59, 61; Roelof, 27, 29*; see also *Hendricksen, Aryance, Van Wegen.*

HENDRICKSEN:
Guert, 28; Jan, 28; Roelof, 29, 30; see *Kortright.*
HERKER:
Meriba, 152.

HERLS:
Cornelis, 24.
HERMANS:
See *Heermans.*
HERMANSEN:
See *Heermans.*
HEXMAN:
Henry, 24.
HEYMANS:
Albert (Roosa), 8, 75; Weyntje, 75.
HEYN:
Piet, 38.
HEYS:
Marritje, 30.
HILL:
Anthony, 125.
HILLEBRANTS:
Femmetje, 29; Jannetje, 58, 66; *Pieter,* 29; Pieter, 27*, 29, 37.
HODGES:
Secretary, 15.
HOFFMAN, HOOFMAN, HOFMANS:
Alida, 135; Anthony, 134*, 135*; Annatje, 135; Catherine, 135; Emmerentje, 58, 73, 135; Henricus, 135; Hester, 127; Ida, 127; Jannetje, 71, 73*, 133*, 135; Lysbeth, 135; Maria, 135*; Marten Hermans, 135; Martin, 45, 58, 73, 134*, 135*; *Nicholas,* 133; Nicholas, 54, 72*, 73*, 102, 135*; Petrus, 134, 135; Sarah, 151; Tryntje, 135; Zacharias, 127*, 134, 135.

HOFSTEDE:
Guiljemus, 39.
HOLLEY:
Catherine, 149.

HOMMEL:
Aantje, 149; Johannis, 149; Jurry, 186*; Margaret, 149; Maria, 149; Peter, 149.

HOOD:
Joseph, 168.

HOOFMAN:
See *Hoffman.*

HOOGEBOOM:
Annatie, 33, 97; Annatie, 33; Bartholomew, 33; Catryn, 33*; *Cornelis,* 33; Cornelis, 33*, 40, 43, 97; Cornelis Pieterse, 33; Janita, 40; Pieter, 33*, 40.

HOOGEN:
See *De Hooges.*

HOOGHTEYLING, HOOHTALEN, HOOGTEELING, HOUGHTEELING, HOOGHTEGLINGH, HOUGHTELLING, HOUGHTALING, HOOGTELING, HOOGHTLYING, HOOGHTALEN, HOOGHTIG:
Anna Margaret, 161, 178; Ariantje, 34, 36*, 82; *Barbara,* 36; Desia, 36, 61; Dina, 36, 184; Hiskia, 36, 61; Jannetje, 37, 74, 75, 160; *Jan Willemse,* 61; *Jan Willemsen,* 36; Jan Willemse(n), 8, 22, 23, 25, 28, 29*, 30, 34, 36, 61, 62, 192; Jan Willemsen, Jr., 37, 61; Kezia, 34, 36, 61; Maria, 64; Philip, 36, 61, 74, 75; Rachel, 143; Samuel, 36, 61; Sara, 133; Tresia, 36; Willem Jansen, 34, 36, 61*.

HOOSTYLER:
Willem, 36.

HOOGHTIG:
Jan W., 37.

HOORNBERG:
Warner, 37.

HOORNBECK:
Anna, 127, 129, 130; Ariantje, 127; Cornelius, 121, 127, 128, 129, 130, 132; Eva, 44; Johanna, 130; Lodewyck, 44, 106, 121; Maria, 127, 128; W., 27; Warnaar, 44.

HORTENBURG:
Gerrit, 43*; Joaptie, 43*.

HOVENIER:
Lysbeth Jacobse (Gordonier), 92.

HOWELL:
John, 176.

HUE:
Anne, 160.

HUME:
William, 156.

HUNTER:
Matthew, 152.

HUTTEMAN:
Albert, 24, 28.

HUTTERIS:
Albert, 24, 28.

HUYBERTSEN:
Eve, 61; Hendrick, 61*; Hendrickje, 61; Johannis, 61; Lambert, 60; Lambert, 8, 26*, 27*, 51, 59, 61*, 113, 120, 169, 184; Roeloff, 61; Thomas, 61; see *Lambertse* and *Brink.*

HYMANS:
See *Heymans* and *Roosa.*

HYSELSTEIN:
See *Esselstein* and *Ysselstein.*

HYSER:
John, 157.

IN:
See *Een.*

INDIANS:
35.

JACOB:
Long, 26.
JACOBS:
Gritie, 102; Heyltje, 30; Willem, 46; Willemtje, 30, 192.
JACOBSE:
Lysbeth (Hovenier), 92; see *Jacobs.*
JACOBSEN:
Aert, 8, 38, 82, 95, 103; Annatje, 103; Annatje (Van Wagenen), 82, 103; Grietje, 38; Ruth, 26; Theunis (Klaarwater), 8, 163; see also *Pietersen* and *Van Wagenen.*
JACOBUS:
Jannetje, 92.
JAN, THE SMITH:
28, 37.
JANS, JANZ, JANSSE, JANSZ:
Anneke, 43, 45, 65, 82; *Barbara,* 36; Catrina, 65, 148; Diewertje, 82; Elsie, 32, 82, 191, 192; Fytie, 65; *Gritie,* 45; Grietje (Roosa), 73; Grietje (Schut), 102; Hester, 41; Hillitje, 60; Jacobje, 45; Jaepje, 45, 58; Jan, 65; Johannes, 43; Joost, 34, 39, 51, 52; Margaret, 182; Maria, 101; Maria (Langendyk), 32, 38, 39; Mattys, 82; Mattys (Van Keuren), 33; Pieter, 58; Pieterje, 45; Rebecca, 39; Roeloff, 65; Sara, 34, 51, 52, 65; Thomas, 64, 157; Volckert, 92; Willemtje, 96, 127; William (Schut), 102; see *Jansen, Ryckman, Schutt, Van Steenbergen, Decker, Langendyk, Van Keulen, Joosten, Brestede, Kortright, Roosa.*
JANSEN, JANSSEN, JANZEN:
Aeltje, 29; Albert, 26*, 27*, 28*, 36; Albert v. S., 29; Anna (Anneke, Anne), 34, 38, 117*; Anna (Van Oosterhout), 30, 130; Arent, 26; Catherine, 34*, 41, 104, 117; Claes (Van Heyningen), 95; Cornelius (Cortright), 75; Cornelius, 116, 117; David, 34, 104, 117; Derrick, 39; Dirck, 43; Dirck (Schepmoes), 42, 43, 73; Elisabeth, 41, 117; Elsie, 32, 191, 192; Geertruy, 189; Geesje, 45, 61; Gritie, 45, 116, 117; Gysbert, 41; Hendrick, 34, 104, 117, 165; Hilligond (Van Heyningen), 95; Jacob (Slicoten), 189; *Jacob (Van Stountenborch),* 189; Jacobus, 116, 117; Jan, 29, 32, 34*, 41, 104*; Jan (Brestede), 32; Jan Mattysen), 8, 31, 38; Jan (Schepmoes), 43; Jan (Slicoten), 189; Jan (Van Amersfort), 26*, 27; Jan (Van Oosterhout), 26, 29, 30, 31, 130; Janneken (Van Heyningen), 95; Jannetie, 33; Johannes, 116, 117*, 120, 177; Joost, 41; Laurens, 75; Lubbert, 29; Magdalena, 31, 34, 38, 104, 116*, 117; Margaret, 33, 34, 58, 104, 117; Maria, 34, 75, 101, 116, 117; Mayken, 34, 92, 93; *Mattys,* 116; Mattys, 22, 34, 38, 58, 104; Rachel, 34, 116*, 117*; Rebecca, 41; Sara, 34, 41, 102, 104; Sara (Schepmoes), 43; Theunis, 43; Thomas, 34, 92*, 93, 104*, 116, 117*, 157; Volckert (?), 64; Willem, 36*; Willem (Schutt), 102; Willem (Slicoten), 189; see *Jans, Fransen, Hooghteyling, Joosten, Mattysen, Oosterhout, Pruyn, Van Keuren, Van Steenbergen, Schutt, Schepmoes, Van Heyningen, Van Osterhout, Brestede,*

228 INDEX OF NAMES.

Kortright, Decker, in this and the second volume.

JARRET:
Allen, 35.

JAY:
Augustus, 49.

JELLES:
Annetjen, 30.

JENKINS:
Albert, 167; Brijet, 167; Catherine, 167; Crines, 167*; Elener, 167; Hannah, 167; James, 167*; John, 167; *Lambert,* 167; Margaret, 167; Mary, 167; Rachel, 167*; William, 167.

JOCHEMSEN:
Christina, 30; David, 30; Elsie, 32; *Hendrick,* 192; Hendrick, 8, 22, 27, 32, 191, 192*; Marritje, 30.

JOHNSTON:
William, 152.

JOIRE, JOORE:
Magdalen, 30, 31, 48; *Magdalen,* 48.

JOOSTEN:
Adriaentie, 41; *Jacob,* 40; Jacob, 41*; *Jan,* 41; Jan, 23, 25, 26*, 27, 28, 30*, 37, 39, 40, 41*, 42, 43, 119; John, 40; *Maycken,* 41; Maycken, 37, 41; Neeltje, 41; Rebecca, 41; Simon, 43; see *Jansen.*

JORISE:
Catalyntje (Rapalie), 88; Jeronimus, 88; Maddalen, 31, 48.

KAMP:
Jan & Co., 124.

KANTAIN:
See *Contine.*

KEALET:
John, 141.

KEATOR:
Claes, 93; Engeltje, 129, 130; Nicholas, 129, 130.

KEECH:
David, 176.

KEGEL:
Philip, 25.

KELLENAER:
Laurentia, 42*, 66, 67, 190.

KETCH:
Alexander, 176; Aney, 176; Benjamin, 176*; Daniel, 176; *David,* 176; Deby, 176; Henry, 176; John, 176; Maria, 176; Peter, 176; Phoebe, 176*; Ruth, 176; Stephen, 176*; William, 176*.

KETCHAM:
Titus, 168; William, 168.

KETELKAS:
Aeltje, 43; Jan Evertz, 43.

KETTLE, KITTLE, KETTEL:
Catharine, 69; Elisabeth, 68*; 69*; *Jeremy, Sr.,* 68; Jeremy, 68, 69; Richard, 68, 69*; Susan, 68, 69; Susanna, 69.

KIEFT:
Director, 33.

KIERSEN:
Janneken, 95.

KIERSTEDE, KEERSTEDE, KIERSTEDER:
Aldert, 119, 148; Anghe, 58; Anna, 32; Blandina, 38, 136, 145; Christopher, 159, 160; Eyke, 32, 38; Eyke Albertse Roosa, 38; Hans, 65, 91, 98, 120; Ikee, 58, 75; Ilke, 75; John, 65; Lea, 159, 160; Luke, 166; Roelof, 32, 37, 38, 58, 75, 192; Sara, 33, 46, 65*, 184; Wyntje, 58.

KIP:
Antie, 86, 87; Henderick, 44,

131; Jacob, 22, 23, 26, 40, 91, 92*, 131, 182, 190; Lea, 182; Marytje, 182; Rachel, 91, 92*; Tryntje H., 32; Tyntie, 41.

KITTLE:
See *Kettle*.

KLAARWATER:
Abraham, 162; Abraham, 162*, 163*; Daniel, 162*; David, 163; Esther, 162*; Eva, 162*, 163; Frederick, 162*, 163; Hester, 163; Isaac, 162*, 163; Jacob, 162, 163*; Joseph, 162*, 163; Lisabeth, 163; Mary, 162*, 163*; Theunis Jacobsen, 8, 163; Thomas, 162*, 163; Wyntje, 162*, 163; see *Clearwater*.

KLUN:
Joisg, 135.

KLUTE:
See *Clute*.

KNICKERBACKER:
Cornelis, 133, 134.

KOECH:
Sarah, 42; William, 42.

KOOL:
Beeletjen, 139; Catherine, 124, 182; Cornelis, 59; Hendrickje, 148; Jacob, 81; Margriet, 177; Sara, 81, 93; Symon, 93; Willem C., 128; see *Cool*.

KORTRIGHT:
Catrina Hansen, 58; Cornelis Jansen, 75; Hendrick Hendricksen, 58; Hendrick Jansen, 58; Marritje, 58; Metje, 75; see *Low*.

KRANS:
Adam, 142*; Catherine, 142; Christeen, 142; Elisabeth, 142*; Hendricus, 142; Jacobus, 142*; *Johannis,* 142; Maria, 142*; Petrus, 142*; Stofel, 142; Susannah, 142*; Wilhelmus, 142*.

KROM, KRUM:
Elisabeth W., 30; Geertje, 41; Guisbert, 41.

KRYPEL:
See *Crispel*.

KUNST:
Barent, 32; Jacomyntje, 32, 39, 60; Jan Barentsen, 32, 39, 60, 192; Jannetie, 32, 59*, 60; Jannetje Jansen, 33.

LABONTE:
Christina, 158.

LA CHAIR:
Jan, 87.

LAFAVER:
See *Le Fevre*.

LAKE:
Wells, 176.

LAMATER, LA MAISTRE:
See *Delamater*.

LAMBERTSE, LAMBERTSEN: LAMMERSE, LEMBERTSEN, LAMBERT, LEMMERTSE, LAMBERTZ:
Abraham, 44; Antje, 45, 61; Breecje, 61; Claertje, 61; *Cornelius,* 112; Cornelius (Brink), 60, 61*, 112, 120, 133, 182; Dirrick, 61; Elsie (Brink), 133; Gerrit, 37, 61*; Geesje, 45, 61; Gritie, 45; Helena, 61; Hendrik, 61*; Hendrickje, 61, 91, 92*; Huybert, 60, 61*, 91, 92*; Jan, 45; Janneken, 38, 61, 120, 182; Johannes, 61; Lambert, 61*; Lysbeth, 59, 61*, 148, 169, 184; Marytje, 112, 182; Matthew, 61; Pieter, 61*; Teunis, 61; see *Brink, Huybertse*.

LAMETTER:
See *Delamater*.

LA MONTAGNE:
See *Montagne*.

LANGEDYK:
Cornelis, 66; Geertie, 66; Jannetje, 66; Maria Janse, 32, 38, 39; Pieter Janse, 66.

LAMESINK:
Abraham, 44.

LANSING, LANSYNCK, LANSINGH, LANSINCK:
Aeltve, 43; Gerrit, 44*; Gysbertje, 44; Hendrick, 44; Hillitie, 44; Johannis, 44.

LARUAH:
John, 146; Peter, 146.

LATTING:
Elisabeth, 179; John, 179.

LAUCK, LAUCKS, LAUKS:
Eva, 46; Hans Jurian, 46.

LAUW:
See *Low*.

LAWRENCE, LOURENS, LOURENSE, LAURENSE, LAURENSEN, LOUWERSEN:
Blandina, 69*, 70; Claes (Van de Volgen), 74*; Claes (Van Purmerend), 74*; *Jan*, 69; Janneke, 69, 70; Johanna, 69; Johannis, 69; Laurence, 69, 70; Marytje, 74; Mettje, 69.

LE BLANC, BLAN:
Andre, 99; Maria, 99*.

LE CONT:
Moyse, 71, 72; see *De Graaf*.

LEENDERSEN:
Arriaentjen, 41; Marckes, 41.

LE FEVRE, LAFAVER, LEFEVER, LEFEVRE, LE FEVER, FEVER, LE FEBRUE:
Abraham, 154; *Andries*, 153; Andries, 98, 114, 154*; Catherine, 153, 154*, 163, 164*; Cornelis, 153, 154; *Daniel*, 163; Daniel, 164*; Elisabeth, 31, 153, 154*, 163, 164*; Isaac, 154, 158, 164*; Isaac, Jr., 164; Jacob, 164; Jan, 154; Janneke, 164; Jean, 154; Johannes, 164, 167; John, 167; Magdalena, 153, 154; Maria, 153, 154*, 163*, 164*; Margriet, 143, 154*; Matthew, 153*, 154*, 163, 164*; Moses, 164; Nathaniel, 154; Peter, 163*, 164*, 166, 167; Peter, Jr., 158, 165; Petronella, 154; Philip, 164; Rachel, 153, 154, 167; Ralph, 35, 77, 113; Sarah, 153, 154, 164; Simon, 31, 153*, 154*, 164*.

LEGG:
Annatje, 81, 139, 184, 185*; Barent, 122*, 123; Beeletjen, 139; Cornelis, 139, 184, 185*; Elisabeth, 185; Geesje, 81, 123*; Helena, 139, 184, 185*; Jan, 123, 139*; *John*, 138; John, 63, 80, 81, 138*, 139*, 185*; John, Jr., 138; Margriet, 81, 122*, 123, 182; Maria, 81, 122, 123*, 185; Neeltje, 138*, 139; Samuel, 81, 122*, 123, 139, 184, 185*; Sara, 80, 81, 123, 138*, 139, 184, 185; Susanna, 80, 81*, 138, 139*; *William*, 80, 184; William, 50, 62, 75, 76*, 80*, 81*, 122*, 123*, 138*, 139*, 192, 184, 185*; *William, Jr.*, 122.

LE MAISTRE:
See *Delamater*.

LEMBERTSEN:
See *Lambertse*.

LENDT:
Elisabeth, 74.

INDEX OF NAMES.

LEONARDS:
Albert, 121; Ariantje, 121.
LE ROY:
Anna Maria, 158; Maria Anne, 79, 183.
LE SEUR, LESUER:
Elsie, 39; Hillebrand, 39; Jannetie, 39.
LESTER:
Albert, 179.
LEWIS:
George H., 65.
LIEVENS:
Marritje, 43.
LIEUW:
Marritje, 30; Philip, 30.
LIVINGSTON:
Alida, 128*, 129, 135; Allada, 106; Catherina, 128, 129; Cornelia, 106, 120, 128; Cornelius, 128, 129; *Gilbert*, 128; Gilbert, 105, 106*, 110, 117, 120, 128*; Gysbert, 128; Henry, 120, 128*, 129; Jacobus, 129; James, 128; Joanna, 128*, 129; Margaret, 128*, 129; Philip, 128*, 129, 135; Robert, 53, 128*, 134; Samuel, 128, 129; Wilhelmus, 129.
LIVIUS:
Titus, 24.
LLOYD:
Thomas, 124.
LOCKWOOD:
Abby, 171, 172; Cornelius, 171, 172*; David, 171*, 172*; Gilbert, 171, 172; *Henry*, 171; Henry, 171*, 172*; Jeremiah, 171; Josiah, 171; Patience, 171, 172; Rachel, 171; Robert, 171, 172; Sally, 171*, 172; Samuel, 171*, 172*; Uriah, 171, 172.
L'HOMMEDIEU:
Benjamin, 49; Benjamin, Jr., 49; Elisabeth, 49; Hosea, 49; Martha, 49; Patience, 49*; *Peter*, 49; Peter, 49; Silvester, 49; Susan, 49.
LOOMAN:
Hendrik Jansen, 21, 22.
LOPERS:
Johanna, 190.
LOUKS:
See *Lauck*.
LOUNDERT:
Philip, 134.
LOURENCE:
See *Lawrence*.
LOUW:
See *Low*.
LOVELACE:
Governor, 31, 41, 58, 92.
LOVERIDGE:
Margaret, 86, 87, 88; William, 86, 87, 88.
LOW:
Abraham, 35, 154, 155; Antje, 35, 154; Benjamin, 155; Catherine, 154; Cornelius, 35*; Cornelis Pietersen, 73; David, 161*; Elisabeth, 31, 73, 95, 106, 154*; Geertruy, 44; Helena, 177; Hendrikje, 119, 120, 148; Jacob, 35, 154; *Jacobus*, 154; Jan, 132; Janneken, 44, 148, 154; Johannis, 35; John, 154*; Johannis A., 177; Laurens Jansen, 75; Magdalena, 35; Margaret, 35; Maria, 35, 95; Mattys, 35, 75; Peter, 35, 44, 95, 188; *Pieter Cornelisse*, 35, 73; Pieter Cornelisse, 8, 31, 35, 43, 73, 106; Rachel, 154, 155; Timotheus, 113, 119, 120, 131*, 132*, 148; Zara, 132; see *Cornelisse, Kortright*.
LUBBERS:
Aeltje, 30.

LUBBERTSE:
Abraham, 92.
LUBBERTSEN:
Francyntje, 92.
LUCAS:
Daniel, 188.
LUCASSE:
H., 99.
LUCASZ:
Willem, 81.
LUSENA:
Jacob, 37.
LUYCK:
Neeltje, 138*, 139; Pieter, 138*, 139; Willem, 81.
LYNCH:
Frances, 173*; Francis, 173; George W., 173.
LYNDRAEYER:
Hendrick Cornelisen, 26*, 28.

McDONALD:
William, 167.
MACKEY:
John, 172.
McKINSTRY:
John, 152.
MACKLIN:
See *Maklin*
McPIKE:
Eugene, 14.
MAETER:
Jan Evertsen, 189.
MAKLIN, MACKLIN:
Cornelis, 82; Grietje, 106; Jan, 58, 106*, 151; Marritje, 58*; Sarah, 82.
MARET:
Susanna, 81, 139.
MARKEL:
See *Merkel*.
MARRID:
Susanna, 81, 139.

MARSTON:
John, 82.
MARTINSEN, MARTENSEN, MARTENZ, MARTISSEN, MARTENSE, MARTENS:
Aert (*Doorn*), 189; Aert (Doorn), 26*, 27*, 28, 189; Cornelia, 54; Cornelis, 54*; Cornelis (Van Buren), 38; Fannerie, 54; Geertruy, 189; Jannetje, 54; Marritje, 54; see *Cornelisse*.
MARTESTOCK:
Diederick, 135.
MARTIN:
James, 175; John, 53; Phebe, 175; Selah Tuthill, 175.
MARVEN, MARVIN:
Anna, 172; Augustus, 172.
MASTEN, MASTON:
Aart, 82*; Abraham, 34, 82*, 117; Catherine, 82; *Cornelis*, 82; Cornelis, 58*, 76*, 82*, 103, 151; Deborah, 82*; Diewertje, 82*, 95; Elisabeth, 82*, 103, 180; Ezekiel, 82; Gertruy, 76, 82*; Grietjen, 82; Johannis, 82*; Margaret, 178; Marytje, 82*; Pieternella, 82.
MATTHEWS:
Peter & Co., 125; Vincent, 100.
MATTYSEN, MATTHYSEN, MATTHEWSSEN:
Anna, 34, 38; Catrina, 34; Cornelis, 36; Geertruy, 61; *Jan*, 33, 103; Jan, 8, 31, 34*, 38, 40, 54, 82, 117, 182; Kesia, 36; Magdalena, 31, 33, 34, 38, 82, 103; Margriet, 182; Mattys, 33, 34*, 35, 38, 57, 58, 82, 87; Mattys, Jr. (Van Keuren), 33; Sara, 35; Tjatje, 34, 57, 58; Tjerck, 95; Trezia, 36; Tryntje, 33; see *Jansen, Tysen, Van Keuren*.

INDEX OF NAMES. 233

MAURITS:
See *Mouritz.*
MEERMANS:
Aeltie (Dirricks), 36, 46.
MERKEL:
Frederik, 170.
METSELAER:
Maria Adams, 157.
MEYER:
See *De Mayer.*
MYNDERSEN, MEYNDERTSE, MEYDERSEN, MEINDERTSE, MEYNDERTSZEN, MEYDERSE, MYNDERSE:
Eghbert, 45; Eghbert, 58; Femmetje, 45; Jacobje, 45; Jaepje, 45, 58; Jannetje, 45, 58; Marritie, 113; Mayken, 45; Myndert, 45.
MIDDAGH:
Batha, 101; Brechje, 100; Jan, 83; Johannis, 101; Joris, 83*, 92, 93, 101, 102; Magdalena, 93, 102; Martha, 101.
MIDLER:
Christopher, 185.
MILLER:
Gavin, 144; Johannes, 157; Moses, 182.
MILSPAUGH:
Jacob, 142.
MINGAEL:
Thomas, 65.
MOLE:
See *Moull.*
MOLINEJ:
Petrus, 25, 28.
MONE:
Marytjen, 102; Paulus, 102.
MOORE, MORE, MOURE, MOOR:
Governor, 15; Peter, 138, 184.

MONTAIGNE:
Catherine, 99; Jan Money, 23; Johannes, 22, 23, 58; Rachel, 22, 23; Wm. de la, 23*, 24, 26, 31, 35, 37, 44*, 45, 48, 192.
MORRISON:
Geo. A., Jr., 14.
MOULL:
Christopher, 142.
MOURE:
See *Moore.*
MOURITZ, MAURITS, MOURITSE:
Elisabeth, 83*; Engel, 83; Engeltie, 82, 83*, 156; *Fredrick Pietersen,* 82; Fredrick Pietersen, 83, 156; Geertruid, 83*; Hendrick, 83; Jannetie, 83*, 156; Marya, 83; Mouritz, 83; Oeyke, Oetje, 83*; Peter, 83*; Pieter Jacobsen, 192.
MOWRIS:
See *Mouritz.*
MYER:
See *De Meyer.*
MYNDERSE:
See *Meyndersen.*
NEGROES:
Abram, 166; Anna, 150; Benjamin, 135; Bet, 163, 166*; Bette, 135; Bishe, 134; Carlyn, 118; Charles, 153; Cuffe, 139; Dejaen, 150, 163; Dick, 150; Dien, 136; Dina, 84, 156; Floor, 186; Fortune, 134; Fredrik, 71, 72; Gerrit, 88; Harry, 165; Herry, 136; Jack, 154, 164; James, 88, 154, 166; James York, 175; Jan, 163; Jane, 160; Jenny, 106, 110; Joe, 135, 166; John, 138; Judy, 153; Kieser, 61; Margriet, 71, 163; Mary, 135; Mingo, 150; Molly, 89; Pegge, 134; Peter,

75; Phill, 140; Phillis, 168; Rachel, 84; Rose, 160; Samson, 63; Sera, 84; Seser, 153; Sime, 160; Susan, 153; Susannah, 118; Tom, 81, 153, 166, 175; Yanna, 175.

NEWKERK, NEWKIRK, NIEUWKERK, NOUKERK, NUKERCK, NEWKIERK, NIEUWKIRK, NUKIRK:
Aaltje, 93; Adam, 140, 141; Adrian, 60, 93, 141; Andries, 168, 169; Anne, 168, 169*; Ann Mary, 140, 141; Arian Gerritsen, 148, 184; Ariantje, 148, 183, 184*; Ary, 169, 184*; Barent, 60, 106; Benjamin, 169; Blandina, 168, 169; Charles, 168, 169; *Coenradt*, 169; Conrad, 168, 169*, 184; *Cornelis*, 183; Cornelis, 40, 60, 61, 113, 124, 183, 184*; Cornelis Gerritse, 60, 141; Dina, 183, 184; Dorothea, 141; Elisabeth, 140*, 141, 169, 184*; Gertrude, 112; Gerrit, 60, 113, 131, 141, 148, 183, 184*; Gerrit B., 169*; Gerrit Cornelissen, 73; Gerretje, 168, 169; Ghilje, 184; Gilles, 60; Gritie, 148; Hendericus, 112, 140, 141*; Hendrikje, 73, 183, 184*; Jacomyntje, 60; Jacob, 140*, 141; Jan, 60, 141, 184; Jannetie, 40, 60, 119*, 136, 148, 169, 183, 184; Jannetie (Gerritse), 60; Johannes, 112; *Johannis*, 140; Johannis, 59, 140, 141*, 169; John, 168; J. M., 180; Lea, 183, 184*; Margaret, 168, 169; Maria, 168, 184; Meyndert, 141; Neeltjen, 73, 124, 141; Onmary, 112; Petrus, 184; Philippus, 183*, 184; Rachel, 140*, 141, 184; Sara, 184; Trineke, 149.

NICKOL, NICHOLLS, NICOLL:
Agatha, 31; Col., 42; Governor, 31, 32.

NIEHOSEN:
Johannes, 36.

NOBLE:
John, 69.

NOLAND:
Philip, 181.

NOORTRYCK:
Joosje Wilemsen, 36, 46.

NOTTINGHAM:
Mr., 37; William, 69, 72*, 75*, 81, 82, 83*, 88, 90, 91, 93, 98, 100, 102, 105, 106.

NOUE:
Margaret, 88; Pierre, 31, 61, 88.

NOXON:
Thomas, 40, 70, 71.

NUEE:
See *Noue*.

OLIVER:
James, 164.

OOSTERHOUT:
Abraham, 181; Aldert, 129*, 130*; Annatje, 129, 130*, 182; Appolonia, 130; Ariaan, 130; Ariaantje, 66, 130*; Cornelis, 185, 186; Elisabeth, 112, 130, 185, 186*; Engeltje, 129*, 130*; Geertie, 130; Gysbert, 66; Helena, 130, 149, 182; Henry, 82, 129*, 130*, 181; Hendricus P., 152; Heyltje, 182; Jacob, 129*, 131; Jan, 112, 129*, 130*, 132, 182; Jannetje, 82, 182; Jan Pietersen, 123; Johanna, 130; Johannes, 130*; Kryn, 80, 129, 130*; Lawrence, 182; Margaret, 127; Maria, 66, 123, 129, 130*, 131, 132, 186; Petrus, 80, 81*, 129, 130*; Pieter Jans, 182; Pieter-

INDEX OF NAMES.

nella, 130; *Teunis,* 129; Teunis, 53, 130, 182; Tryntje, 82; see *Van Oosterhout.*

OSTRANDER:
Cornelis, 172; Geesjen, 132; Harmanis, 132; Huybert, 184; Jacob, 132*; Jonathan D., 179; Levi, 173; Marytje, 132*; Petrus, 91; Wilhelmus, 172; see *Van Ostrandt.*

OSTRANDER & SUDAM:
171.

OTTERSPOOR:
Aerdt Aerdtsen, 190, 192; Petronella, 190, 192.

OVERBAGH:
Mary, 149.

PAREE:
Ambrosius, 24.

PARSON:
See *Persen.*

PARYS:
Everdt, 37; Everdt, 37.

PATTISON:
Michael, 185.

PAULDING:
See *Pawling.*

PAULUS:
Hendrikje, 73.

PAWLING, PAULDING:
Aagje, 58; Albert, 106; Anne, 166; Catherine, 106; Henry, 27*, 28*, 33, 40, 58, 59, 75; Jacomyntje, 33, 40; Jan, 58; Marie, 34; Neeltje, 58, 75.

PEARTREE:
William, 163.

PEARS:
Mattys, 85, 136, 137.

PEARSON:
See *Persen.*

PEELE:
Tryntje, 46.

PEERS:
Mattys, 85; see *Persen.*

PELS:
Clara, 103, 106; Evert, 22*, 26, 27, 95, 103*; Jannetie, 103; Sara, 79, 95, 103, 106.

PERSEN, PERSON, PEARSON, PEARSE, PIERSON:
Abraham, 82; Adam, 136*, 137*; Alida, 137, 180; Anna, 137*, 179, 180*; Catrina, 82, 137*, 179, 180*; *Cornelius,* 179; Cornelius, 136, 137*, 157, 180*, 186; Deborah, 137; Elisabeth, 179*, 180*; Jan, 136, 137*; John J., 185; Margaret, 179, 180*; Maria, 137, 179, 180*; *Matthys,* 136; Matthys, 85, 180; Sara, 137*; Tanna, 137; Theunis, 180.

PETERS:
Annatje, 65; Margaret, 171.

PETERSON:
See *Pieterson.*

PHILIPPSE, PHILIPP, PHILIPS, PHILIP:
Adolphus, 163; Cornelius, 172; Fredrick, 140; Henry, 172*; Mary, 172; Widow, 143.

PICK, PIK:
William, 143.

PIER:
Gepje, 46.

PIERSON:
See *Person.*

PIETERS:
Sarah, 42, 43.

PIETERSON, PETERSON, PIETERSEN, PIETERSE:
Adrian Van Alcmaer, 32; Antje, 61; Cornelis, 61; Cornelisen, 33, 73; Elsie, 32; Engeltie, 83; Fredrick, 83; Gerrit, 61; Grietje, 63; Helena, 61;

Henderik, 61; Johannes, 61; John, 73; Lambert, 61*; Lysbeth, 61; Matthew, 61; Pieter, 46*, 71, 72; Rebecca, 46*; see *Jacobsen, Cornelisen, Lambertsen* and *Mouritz.*

PLOEG, PLEEGH, PLOEGH, PLOEY:
Abraham, 123; Arent, 112; Barbara, 82; Catharina, 157; Elisabeth, 182; Geertruy, 123; Geesje, 81, 123; Helena, 139, 185*; Jan, 182, 185; John, 185; Rachel, 112; Wilhelmus, 82.

POPINGE:
Rachel, 34, 117.

POST:
Catrina, 179, 180; Elisabeth, 167; Hendrick, 123; Isaac, 179, 180*; Margaret, 123; Samuel, 180.

POULSE:
Gommen, 53; Gommert, 38.

POULUSSEN, POWLISSEN:
See *Poulse.*

PRAA:
Marya, 30*; Peter, 30*.

PROVOOST:
Benjamin, 37*, 39, 41; David, 125.

PRUYN:
Hendrick, 110.

PULING:
See *Pawling.*

QUACKENBOSS:
Neeltje, 118, 182.

QUYNELL:
Mr., 37.

RADEMAKER:
Claes (Swyts), 121.

RAINEY:
Christian, 143; David, 143; Esther, 143; Hesia, 143; *James,* 143; Mary, 143; Martha, 143; Ruth, 143; Samuel, 143; Sara, 143; Susan, 143.

RAPELYEA:
Catalyntje Jorise, 88; Jeronimus Jorise, 88.

RAY:
Cornelius, 145; Elisabeth, 145.

RECHTINGER:
Jurry W., 186*.

RELYA:
Denie D., 161; Lucas, 172; Sally, 171, 172.

RIGHMEYER:
Mary, 149.

RIKER:
Abraham, 34; Mary, 34.

ROE:
John, 170.

ROELANDSEN:
Adam, 65.

ROELOFSEN:
Elting, 39; Elting, 33*, 41, 103; *Jacomyntje,* 39; Jacomyntje, 32; Jan, 58, 65; Sarah, 65; Willemtje, 39; see *Eltinge.*

ROGGAN:
Peter, 163.

ROMEYN & VAN BUREN:
180.

RONK:
George, 172; Polly, 172.

ROOSA, ROSA, ROSE, ROOS:
Abraham, 130, 132, 136; Albert Heymans, 8, 58*, 75; Aldert, 75, 110, 130, 131*, 132; Alldert, 74, 75*, 131*; Anghe, 58; Anna Margriet, 42, 75; Antjen, 130, 131, 132; Arie, 75, 131*, 132, 182; Ariaantje, 130; Barbara, 66; Benjamin, 184; Cathrina, 66, 130, 131,

132*, 149; Claes, 75; Cornelia, 135; Dirck, 136; Eiche, 32; Elisabeth, 132; *Evert,* 130; Evert, 66, 131*, 132; Eyke Albertsen, 38; Geertje, 71, 73; Geesjen, 132, 165; Gritie Janse, 73; Guert, 75; Gysbert, 74, 75*; Hilligond, 66, 75; *Hyman,* 74; Hyman, 42*, 51, 52, 58, 75; Hyman Aldersen, 28, 75; Ikee, 58; Ilke, 75; Jacob, 130, 131, 132, 149; Jannetje, 37, 74, 75*, 148, 184; Johanna, 182; John, 108, 147, 176; Lea, 74, 75*, 130, 131, 132; Maria, 75, 130, 131*, 132, 176; Neeltje, 58, 75*, 124, 182; Nicholas, 74, 75*; Petronella, 75; Rachel, 42, 74, 75*, 127, 130, 131, 132, 148; Rebecca, 130; Sarah, 75, 130, 131, 132; Tietje, 66, 130, 132; William, 176; Wyntje, 40, 74, 75*, 182.

ROSEBOOM:
Guysbertje, 44; Hendrick, 44.

ROSENKRANZ, ROOSEKRANS:
Antje, 66*; Appolonia, 130; Ariantje, 130*; Harmon, 130; Helena, 130; Hendrick, 66; Herman, 130*; Jacobus, 152; Sara, 62.

ROSEVELT:
Ann Margriet, 42, 75.

RUTAN:
Abraham, 89; Abraham B., 50.

RUTGERSEN:
Jacop, 43.

RUTS, RUTZ, RUTSE:
Elisabeth, 132; Jacob, 37; Jacob, Sr., 106; Sara, 75.

RUTSEN:
Alida, 128, 129; Allada, 106; Catherine, 106*, 127; Hendricus, 106; Jacob, 40, 52, 53, 54, 56, 57, 58, 60, 82, 96, 100, 106*, 120, 128, 129; Jacob, Jr., 129; Johanna, 106; Johannes, 125; *John,* 106; John, 93, 97, 110, 124.

RYCKE:
Hendrick, 35.

SALAEME:
Maria (Metselaer), 157.

SALAMONSE:
Jacob, 64.

SAMUELS:
Ariaentie, 34, 36.

SAMUELS-DOGHTER:
Ariaentie, 36.

SANDTVOORDT:
Jacob Abrahamsen, 192.

SARCHARSON:
Johan, 24.

SCHAETS:
Dom., 74.

SCHELLINCK:
Willem, 36.

SCHEPMOES:
Abraham, 43*; Aeltie, 43*; Anna, 43*, 107, 108, 109, 117; Ariante, 43, 107, 108, 109, 110; Catharina, 32, 178; *Dirck,* 106; Dirck, 30, 33, 38, 43*, 46, 52, 59, 62*, 75, 82, 87, 91, 109; *Dirck Jansen,* 42; Dirck Jansen, 32, 43*, 73, 191; Dirck Willemse, 43, 109; Geertruy, 43; Jan, 43; Jan Janszen, 42, 43*; Joaptie, 43; Jobje, 43; Johannes, 43, 73, 96, 109; Lea, 43, 103, 109; Maregrietie, 43, 106; *Maria,* 42; Maria, 103; Maria Willems, 43, 73; Neeltje, 43, 73; Rachel, 43, 92, 109; Sarah, 42, 43, 109; Tryntje, 43; Wesel, 43; Widow, 147; William, 43, 82, 107, 108, 109, 110.

SCHERP:
 Pieter, 188.
SCHMIDT:
 See *Smith.*
SCHOONHOVEN, SCHOOHOVEN:
 Catharine, 49; Claes, 49; Cornelia Claessen, 49; Cornelis, 49, 92; Deborah, 49; Francyntje, 49; Henricus, 49; *Hendrick Claessen*, 49; Hendrick Claessen, 92; Ifje, 49; Margriet, 49, 141; Nicholas, 49; see *Schoonmaker* and *Van Schoonhoven.*
SCHOONMAKER:
 Annatje, 34, 133; Aryantje, 82; Barbara, 81, 82; Benjamin, 127, 182; Catrina, 81, 82, 127, 182; Daniel, 117; Edward, Jr., 185; Egbert, 81, 87; Egbert Hendricksen, 133; Elisabeth, 163, 182; Elsie, 32, 81, 82*, 127, 133; Gertruy, 58, 81, 82; *Hendrick*, 81; Hendrick, 81, 82, 112; Hendrick Hendricksen, 58, 82, 122; Hendrick Jochemse, 8, 32*, 58, 82; Heskia, 81, 82; Jacobus, 81, 82; Jannetie, 81, 82*; Jochem, 32*, 82, 129, 133; Jochem Hendrikse, 32, 127, 182*; Johannes 81, 82*, 106, 145, 157; John, 121, 130; Màgdalena, 117; Margaret, 182; Maria, 81, 127; Peter, 180; Petronella, 32, 127; Philip, 166, 167*; Sara, 81, 82*, 182; Theodosia, 82; Thomas, 163, 182; Thomas, Jr., 182; Tjerck (Tyrk), 81, 82, 185; Tyrick, 82, 138; Tryntje, 82, 96, 127.
SCHOUTEN:
 Jannetie, 70; Johanna, 70; Johannis, 70; Mettje, 70.

SCHRIVER:
 Jacob, 151.
SCHUTT:
 Abraham, 102*; Ephraim, 102; Geerthen, 102; Gritie, 102*; Heyltje, 102; Jan, 102; Jan Willem, 102; Jannetje, 102; Magdaleen, 95, 102*; Marytje, 93, 102*; Menasses, 102; Myndert, 102*; Neyltie, 102*; Salomon, 102*; Sara, 102; *Willem Jansen*, 102.
SCHUYLER:
 Alida, 128; Geo. W., 35; Philip, 49; Philip & Co., 125; Philip Pieterse, 92.
SEALE:
 Esther, 162, 163; Jacob, 162, 163.
SEBA:
 Wm. Jansen, 21, 22.
SEEBRINCK:
 Jan, 39.
SEELEY, SEALE, SEELY:
 Esther, 162; Hester, 163; Jacob, 162, 163.
SELLECK:
 David, 172.
SELLICK:
 Abby, 171, 172.
SEMONS:
 See *Symons.*
SESUMS:
 See *Tysen.*
SHARPS:
 William, 140*.
SHEVER:
 Johannis, 133, 134.
SHEW:
 Martinus, 134.
SHOE:
 Martinus, 134.

INDEX OF NAMES. 239

SHUART:
John, 172*.
SILVESTER:
Nathaniel, 49; Patience, 49.
SIMS, SYMS:
Lancaster, 125.
SLECHT, SLEGHT, SLEGT:
Anna, 32, 33*, 133; *Annitie Cornelissen*, 33; Anthony, 33, 93; Cheiltje Cornelis, 59; Cornelis, 26, 27, 33*, 191; *Cornelis B.*, 32, 191; Cornelis Barentsen, 21, 22, 33, 36, 39, 60, 73, 189*, 190, 191*; Elisabeth, 33; Elsie, 32, 191*; *Hendrick Cornelisen*, 190; Hendricus, 32, 33, 190, 191; *Jacomyntie*, 39; Jacomyntie, 32*, 33, 39, 60*, 91; Jan, 33; John, 147; Madleen, 64; Mattys, 32, 52, 64, 71, 72*, 73, 76, 191*; Mattys Cornelisen, 32, 33, 35; Maria Magdalena, 32, 33*, 71, 72, 73; Neeltje, 33, 93; Petronella, 32, 127, 191; Petrus, 33; Sara, 33; Tryntje, 33, 34, 191; Tryntje Tysen Bosch, 32, 73.
SLICOTEN:
Geertruy, 189; Jacob Jansen, 189; Jan Jacobsen, 189; Jan Jansen, 189; Willem Jansen, 189; see *Slykkoten*.
SLIMER:
Mathise, 112.
SLINGSLAND:
Teunis, 92.
SLICHTENHORST:
Aeltye, 44; *G. V.*, 44; see *Van Sleghtenhorst*.
SLUYTER:
Daniel, 158.
SLYKKOTEN:
Geertruyd, 28; Jan Jacobs, 28; see *Slicoten*.

SMEDES:
Benjamin, 35, 102, 117; Catrina, 124, 148; Elisabeth, 33; Helena, 148; Magdalena, 35; Peter, 124, 148; Rachel, 117.
SMITH:
Abraham, 141*; Daniel, 141; Elisabeth, 152; Fallen, 141; Henry, 141, 152*; Hezekiah, 170; Jan, 141; Jan Cornelisen, 27; *Johannis*, 141; Margaret, 141, Marrslye, 141; Nelly, 141; Petrus, 141; Thomas Gibson, 168; *William*, 152.
SNYDER, SNIDER, SNEYDER, SCHNEIDER:
Abraham, 149*, 186; Antjen, 148, 149*, 186*; Annah Deamute, 149; Benjamin, 149*, 157*; Catherine, 132, 149*, 186; Ceeletjen, 186; Christian, 148, 149; Christina, 185, 186*; Cornelia, 186; Elisabeth, 149, 186*; George, 186; Grietje, 149, 185, 186*; Helena, 149; Henry, 149*; Isaak, 148, 149*; Jacob, 151, 173; Jeremiah, 148, 149, 180; Johanna, 186*; *Johannes*, 185; Johannes, 148; 149*, 151, 186*; Johannes, Jr., 186; Jury, 186; Lea, 186; Margaret, 149*; *Martinus*, 148; Martin, 148, 149*; Maria, 149*, 185, 186*; Petrus, 186; Rachel, 186*; Seletje, 186; Susan Margaret, 149; Trineke, 149; Willem, 134, 148, 149; Zacharias, 148*, 149*.
SOPER:
William, 170, 176.
SPROEDT:
Harmen, 36.
STAAT:
Abraham, 54.

STEENBERGH,
  STEENBERGE:
  Maria, 157; Thomas, 157, 188; Thomas J., 157; see *Van Steenbergen.*
STEVENSE:
  Geertruy, 83; Joseph, 83.
STEVENSEN:
  Goert, 39.
STOL:
  Jan, 191, 192.
STYLES:
  James J., 177; William J., 177.
STOKER:
  Catharina, 183.
STRAHAN:
  James, 144.
STRYCKER:
  Jan, 39.
STUYVESANT:
  Director, 58; Governor, 92.
SUDAM & OSTRANDER:
  171.
SUYLANDT:
  Huybert, 72, 73*; Johannes, 184; Rachel, 182; Sara, 72, 73*.
SWAAN:
  Jacob, 62*.
SWACHENHALS:
  37.
SWART:
  Adam, 71, 74; Baartjen, 182; Catharine, 117, 137; Cornelius, 74, 85, 150; *Cornelisse Theunis,* 73; Elisabeth, 73, 74; Esais, 74; Femmetje (van Middle), 88; Jan Teunissen, 88; Frederic, 74; Gertruyd, 103; Jacomyntje, 71, 74; Janneke, 164; Jesias, 74; Johanna, 186; Marytje, 74, 82; Metje, 71; Rachel, 186; Teunis, 74; William, 106; see *Cornelisse, Theunissen.*
SWARTWOUT, SWARTWOLT:
  Anthony, 91, 92*; Ariantje, 92; Bernardus, 43, 92*, 110, 119; Cornelia, 49, 91, 92*; Elisabeth, 92; Eva, 49, 91, 92*; Francyntje, 92; Hendrikje, 61, 91, 92; Jacobus, 92; Jacomyna, 92; Jannetje, 92; Rachel, 43, 91, 92*; *Roeloff,* 91; Roeloff, 22*, 26, 27*, 28*, 29, 31, 37, 40*, 49, 55, 60, 92*, 189*; Rudolphus, 92; Thomas, 91*, 92*.
SWITZ, SWYTS, SWITS,
  SWETTS, SWITSER,
  SWITZART:
  Abraham, 121; Aeltie, 121; Apolonia, 121*, 127; Arientje, 121; Claes Cornelissen, 121; Cornelia, 121; *Cornelis,* 120; Cornelis, 57, 58, 118*, 121*, 127; Cornelis Claessen, 121; Isaac, 121; Jacob, 121*; *Jannetje,* 127; Jannetje, 57, 58, 120, 121; Pieter, 121; Susanna, 121.
SWITZLER:
  Eva, 182.
SYBRENDE:
  Wyntje, 65.
SYMONS:
  Ariantje, 92; Jannetie, 103.
SYMS:
  See *Sims.*
TACK:
  Aart Pietersen, 22*.
TAFFIN:
  Jan, 25.
TAPPEN:
  Barber, 127*; Barbara, 34; Catharina, 43; Charles, Jr., 171, 172, 178; Christ, 149;

Christopher, 120, 141; Corn., 165; Elsie, 39; Geo., 166, 177; H. & Co., 177; Jheunes, 110; Maragritie, 43; Pieter, 34, 110, 171; Teunis, 66.

TAPPER:
See *Tappan*.

TELLER:
Helena, 58.

TEN BROECK:
Abraham, 174; Benjamin, 181*; Blandina, 174; Catherine, 106, 127, 145, 148; Conrad, 42*, 67, 68; Cornelia, 32; Cornelius, 173, 174*; Dirck Wesselse, 32, 65, 106, 128; Elisabeth, 42; Elsie, 42, 66, 67, 68; Geertruy, 42, 66, 67*, 68*; Henry, 173, 174; Jacob, 42, 67, 68; Jacomyntje, 42; Johannis, 67, 75, 105, 127, 148; John, 42*, 173, 174*; Laurentia, 42, 66, 67, 151; *Maria*, 41; Maria, 42*, 44, 66, 67, 68; Rachel, 42, 75, 127, 148; Sarah, 42, 44, 66, 67*, 68*, 150; W., 105; Wessel, 32*, 33, 34, 42*, 44*, 50, 59, 61, 66, 67*, 68*, 173, 174*, 191, 192; *Wessel*, 41, 66, 173; Wessel, Jr., 42; Wessel, Sr., 42, 46.

TEN EYCK:
Abraham, 148; Conrad, 42; Grietje, 148, 182; Hendrick, 62; Janneke, 75, 148*; *Maria*, 41; Maria, 34, 42, 44; Matthys, 42, 75, 148, 169, 182; Petronella, 62.

TENHOUT:
Catherine, 148; Cornelis, 103; Gertrude, 95, 96, 127; Leveryn, 41; Neeltje, 103; *Severyn*, 95; Severyn, 40, 41, 96, 127, 148; see *Bruyn, Fynhout, Vynhout*.

TER BOSCH, TER BOS:
Catrina, 88; Marytje, 102.

TERPENNING:
Breechje, 158, 183.

TERWILLIGER, TERWELGER, TIRWILLIGER:
Maria, 129, 130; Mattheus, 129, 130; Salomon, 132.

THEUNISSEN, TUENISSEN, THEUNIS, THEUENIN, THUNJUN, TEUNISSE, THONISSEN:
Adam (Swart), 74; Antjen, 186; Arent, 27*, 47, 58*, 192; Christina, 186; Claesje, 22; Claesje (Swart), 74; Cornelis (Cool), 120; Derick, 88; Esaias (Swart), 74; Femmetje (Van Middle Swart), 88; Frederic (Swart), 74; Geertruy, 61; Grietjen, 186; Jacomyntje (Swart), 74; Jan (Swart), 88; Jan, 116; Jannetie (Cool), 120; Maria, 58, 74; Sweer, 22, 74, 105; Teunis (Swart), 74; see *Bosch, Cool, Derriksen, Klaarwater, Swart, Van Middle Swart, Van Vechten*.

THOMASSE:
Jan, 64.

THOMPSON:
Beekman, 177; Elisabeth, 177; William A., 168.

THEUNGAS:
Annatje, 186.

THUNJUS:
See *Theunissen*.

TILSON:
Hannah, 179*; Paul, 179.

TITSOORT, TOETSOO:
Abram, 68; Aeche, Willem, 79; Elisabeth, 50.

TRAPHAGEN, TRAPHEGEN, TROPHAGEN:
Aaggien, 46; Aarent, 46; Aeltie, 36, 46*; Alida, 46; Anna, 36; Anthony, 36; Catryn, 36, 46; Eelet, 36*, 46; Elsebus, 36; Eva, 46; Eycke, 46; Geesje, 46; Gepje, 46; Helen, 46*, 182; Hendrick, 35, 36, 46*; Jannetie, 36, 46*; Johannes, 36, 46*; Jonathan, 46; Joosje, 36, 46; Josie, 46; Justje, 46; Lucas, 46; Rebecca, 36, 46*; Roeloff, 46; Sara, 46; Tryntje, 46; *Willem*, 35, 46; William, 35, 36*, 46*, 63, 76*, 182; William Jansen, 46.

TRIMPER:
Andrew, 142; Elisabeth, 142.

TROMMELS:
Ariantje, 121.

TROPHAGEN:
See *Traphagen*.

TRUMPOR:
See *Trimpor*.

TUNISSEN:
See *Theunissen*.

TULP:
Nicholas, 24.

TURCK:
Catrina, 95, 137, 180; Jacob, 95; Jannetje, 94, 95; Johannes, 94, 95.

TUTHILL:
Jonathan, 49.

TYNHOUT:
See *Tenhout*.

TYSELL:
Jan, 53.

TYSEN:
Jan, 33; Jan, 105; Jannetje, 102; *Matelen*, 33; Magdalen, 34; Marreganta, 34; *Tryntie* (*Bosch*), 32; Tryntie (Bosch), 73, 191*; see *Mattysen*.

TYSON:
John & Co., 34.

UIN:
See *Een*.

UYTHOFF:
Elisabeth, 74; Wouter, 74.

VALLEOU:
Steven, 49*, 51.

VAN AALSTEYN:
Isaac, 146; *Martinus*, 146.

VAN AKEN:
Abraham, 118; Catrina, 182; Cornelius, 182; Isaak, 118; Jannetje, 118; John E., 180; Maria, 177; Martinus, 182; Pieternel, 182; Rachel, 118; Samuel, 177; see *Aken*.

VAN ALCMAER:
Adrian Petersen, 32; Elsie, 32.

VAN AMERSFORT:
Jan Jansen, 26*, 27, 28.

VAN BENSCHOTEN:
See *Bomschoten*.

VAN BENTHUYSEN:
Barent, 81, 103*, 134, 182; Catryntje, 95; Janneke, 81, 103*, 182; Margriet, 81, 182.

VAN BERGEN:
Deborah, 137.

VAN BOMMEL:
See *Van Bone*.

VAN BOMSHOTEN:
See *Bomschoten*.

VAN BONE, VAN BOME, VAN BOMMEL, VAN BUMMEL, WAMBOMEZ:
Deborah, 182; Pieter, 95, 182.

VAN BORSUM:
Aefje, 43; Annatje, 43*; *Barendt*, 43; Barendt, 190; Cor-

nelis, 65; Egbert, 43*; Gritie, 35, 43; Hermanus, 43; Hendrick, 43; Jannetie, 43; *Machtel,* 43; Margaret, 35; Neeltie, 43; Sarah, 65; Tyman, 35, 43.

VAN BROUGH:
Catherine, 65; Johannes, 65; John, 65.

VAN BRUGH:
See *Van Brough.*

VAN BUNTSCHOTEN:
See *Bomschoten.*

VAN BUREN, VAN BEUREN:
Anneke, 133; Ariantje, 38; Cornelius, 133, 178, 179, 180; Cornelius Martinsen, 38; Elisabeth, 179, 180; Gerrit, 133; Henry, 180; John, 180; Sara, 133; Tobias, 106.

VAN BUYTSCHOTEN:
See *Bomschoten.*

VAN CLECK:
Johannes, 113; Tryntie, 113.

VAN COVELENS:
Adriaentie, 41; Jacob Joosten, 41.

VAN CURLER:
Jonkheer, 121.

VAN DAM:
Kip & Co., 125; Rip, 163.

VAN DE CUYL:
Annatje, 44; Cornelis Barentsen, 44; Lysbet, 44.

VAN DEN BERG:
Ariantje Gerritse, 38, 71; Divertje, 82*, 95; Deborah, 82*; Elisabeth, 95; Guysbert, 82*, 95, 136; Marytje, 58.

VAN DEN BOGAARD:
Catrina, 59; see *Bogaard.*

VANDERHEUL:
Abraham, 32; Femmetje, 32; Tryntje, 32.

VAN DER LINDEN:
Elisabeth, 73, 74.

VAN DER MERKEN:
Geesjen, 130.

VAN DER VOLGEN:
Claas Lourense, 74; Claes (Laurense van Purmerend), 74; Marytje, 74.

VAN DER WYCK:
Cornelis Barentse, 40.

VAN DER ZEE:
Hillitie, 44; Storm, 44.

VAN DEUSEN:
Jan, 136; Joh., 184.

VAN DE WATER:
Hendrick, 42.

VAN DYCK, VAN DYKE:
Jacobus, 110.

VAN ELMENDORPH, VAN ELMENDORF:
Anna, 38*, 55; Ariantje, 38; Blandina, 38; Conrad, 38, 55*, 56; Geertje, 38*, 55, 56; *Gertie,* 55; *Jacobus,* 55; Jacobus, 38*, 53, 55, 56; Jenneke, 55, 56; Margaret, 38, 53; Tekla, 55*; see *Elmendorph.*

VAN ETTEN, VAN ETEN, VAN NETTEN:
Catharine, 182; Jacobus, 75, 182; Jacobus G., 177; Lea, 182; Petronella, 75; Tietje, 66, 130, 132.

VAN FLIET:
See *Van Vliet.*

VAN GAASBECK:
Abraham, 157, 163, 190; Dom., 42; Jacobus, 173*; Jacomyntje, 42, 190; John, 174; Laurentia, 42*, 190; Laurentius, 42, 190; Maria, 190; Peter, 174; Thomas, 173, 174.

VAN GISEN:
Aeltie, 43*; Johanes, 43*.

VAN HEYNINGEN:
Claes Jansen, 95; Hilligond Jansen, 95; Janneke Jansen, 95; Marytje, 103.

VAN HOECK:
Bennony (Arents), 74; Jacomyntje, 74.

VAN HOOGHTEGHLINGH:
Sara, 133; see *Hooghteyling*.

VAN IMBROCK:
Gysbert, 23; Gysbert, 22*, 25, 26; Lysbeth, 22.

VAN KEULEN:
See *Van Keuren*.

VAN KEUREN, VAN KEULEN:
Barbara, 34; Benjamin, 34; Claes, 34; Cornelius, 34, 36; Gerardus, 34; Hasuel, 34; Hendrick, 34; Kesia, 34, 36; Lea, 34; Maria, 34*; Mattys, 34; Matys Jansen, 33; Mattys Matthysen, 58; Nicholas, 34; Sara, 34; Tjatje (Mattysen), 58; Thomas, 34*; Tjerck, 34*; Tjerck Mattysen, 34; Trezia, 36; Tryntje, 34; see *Matthysen*.

VAN LEUVEN:
Andries, 139; Angenietjen, 152; Annatie, 158*; Barbara, 66; Catrina, 152; Daniel, 151, 152*; Dina, 152; Elisabeth, 152*; Hanna, 152; Johannes, 66; *John,* 151; John, 152; Margaret, 152; Mary, 152; Meribah, 151, 152*; Peter, 139*, 151, 152*; Rachel, 152.

VAN MEETEREN:
Emanuel, 24; *Jan Joosten,* 41; Joost Jansen, 39, 41; Maycken, 41; Rebecca, 39; Sara, 39, 41.

VAN MIDDLE SWART:
Femmetje, 88.

VAN NAMEN:
Joshem Enthelbert, 43.

VAN NEECK:
Lambert, 58.

VAN NETTEN:
See *Van Etten*.

VAN NEWKERK:
See *Newkerk*.

VAN NIEVENKUYZEN:
Aefje, 43; Louis, 43.

VAN OOSTERHOUT:
Anna Janzen, 30, 130; Jan Janse, 26, 29, 30, 31, 130; see *Oosterhout*.

VAN OSTRANT,
VAN VORSTRAND:
Anna, 178; Dinah, 179; Elias, 178; Elisabeth, 179; Frederick, 178; Hannah, 179; *John,* 178; Lewis, 178, 179; see *Ostrander*.

VAN PURMEREND:
Claes Laurense, 74.

VAN RENSSELAER:
Alida, 128; Elisabeth, 145; Rev. Nicholas, 128.

VAN SCHOONHOVEN:
Catalyn, 121; Claes Cornelisen, 121; Margrietje C., 31; see *Switz* and *Schoonhoven*.

VAN SLICHTENHORST,
VAN SLEGHTENHORST:
Aeltye, 43; Brandt Arentse, 44; *Gerrit,* 43; Gerrit, 33, 44; Gouda, 44; Hilligond, 44; Ragel, 44.

VAN SLYK:
Alida, 137, 180; Angenietjen, 152; Metje, 71.

VAN STEENBERGH(EN):
Abraham, 156*, 157*, 158*;

Alida, 157; Annatje, 136, 157, 158*; Aries, 182*; Baartjen, 182; Benjamin, 182*; Catharine, 157*; Christina, 156*, 158; Cornelis, 156, 158; Elisabeth, 157, 158; Geertruyd, 157; Helena, 156*, 157, 158, 181, 182; Henderikus, 156, 157; Jane, 157; Jannetje, 158; Johanna, 182; Johannes, 157*, 181, 182; *John*, 157; John, 156, 158, 165, 168, 169; John T., 158; Margaret, 156, 157*, 168*; Maria, 157; Matthew, 156, 158; Paul, 156, 157; Petrus, 158; Rachel, 182; Sara, 136*, 182; *Tobias*, 156; Tobias, 156, 157*, 158*; Tobias Jansen, 157; see *Steenbergen.*

VAN STEENWYCK:
Albert Jansen, 25, 29; Jan Albertsen, 22.

VAN STOUTENBORCH:
Jacob Jansen, 189.

VAN TWILLER:
Governor, 65.

VAN VEGHTEN,
VAN VECHTEN:
Jannetje, 88; Johannis, 65*; Maria, 65; Michael Dirk, 88*; Neeltje Cornelis, 88; see *Theunissen, Vechten.*

VAN VENETIEN:
P. Paulus, 24.

VAN VELPEN:
Adriaentie Cornelis, 41.

VAN VLERK:
Isaac, 192.

VAN VLIET:
Anna Andriesen, 71, 82; Annatje, 71; Arry (Arie, Aerry), 82; Catharina, 151; Dirck, 71, 82, 120; Dirck Aryensse, 41; Geertjen (Gritie), 41, 43, 82;

Gerrit, 62; Jan, 76, 191, 192; *Machteld,* 43; Machteld, 41.

VAN VOVELENS:
Jacob Joosten, 41.

VAN VORSTRAND:
See *Van Ostrand.*

VAN VREDENBURGH:
Cornelia, 54.

VAN WAGENEN
(WAGENINGEN):
Aart, 35, 39, 71, 82*, 95, 103*, 114; Abraham, 95; Aeltje, 103; Aeltje Gerritse, 39; Aert Jacobsen, 8, 38, 82, 95, 103; Anna, 70, 82, 103; Annatje Aertse, 71, 95, 103, 106*, 148; Barent, 103*, 110; Benjamin, 95; Catherine, 95, 165; Clara, 103, 106; Elisabeth, 82, 95; Evert, 70, 95, 103*; Gerrit, 40, 95*, 103; Gerrit H., 14; Gerrit Aartsen, 106*; Gertrud, 95, 103; Gritje Aartsen, 32, 38, 148; Goosen, 103*; Hannah, 127; Hillegard, 95; Hillegond, 95; Isaac, 95; Jacob, 103*, 182; Jacob Aartsen, 71, 79, 95*, 106; Jannetje, 81, 95*, 103*, 182; Lea, 103; Maria, 35, 95, 103*; Neeltje, 103*, 106; Rachel, 167; Rebecca, 79, 95, 103, 160; Sara, 95*, 127; Sara Aartsen, 79, 95, 106; Simon, 95, 103*, 127, 147; Solomon, 127, 167; see *Aartse, Aartsen, Jacobsen.*

VAN WEGEN, VAN WAYEN,
VAN WYAN, VAN WEYEN:
Annatie, 79.

VAN WOLPEN:
Arriantie, 41.

VAN WYCK:
135.

VAN ZUTPHEN:
  Bernard, 24, 28.
VAS:
  Dom. Petrus, 93, 117.
VAUGHAN:
  Sir John, 5.
VECHTEN:
  Hendrick Claessen, 88; Jannetje Claessen, 88; see *Van Veghten*.
VELLE:
  Mary, 79; Louis, 79.
VELTEN:
  Max(imilian), 177; Philip, 177.
VERBEEK:
  Jan, 54.
VERBRUGGE:
  Old Michael, 27*.
VERKINDEREN:
  Jan, 46; Joosje, 46.
VERMEULEN:
  Elisabeth, 30; Femmetje, 29, 30; *Joost A.*, 29; Joost A., 41; Marietje, 29, 30.
VERNOOY:
  Anna, 58; *Annetie*, 44; Conrad, 154; Cornelia, 34, 44; *Cornelis*, 44; Cornelis, 42, 44, 58, 81; Cornelius, Jr., 81; Elisabeth, 34, 44, 164; Geertruy, 44; Grietje, 44, 58; Hendrick, 163; Jacob, 44; Jenneke, 44; Johannes, 44; Margriet, 154; Maria, 44, 162, 163; Petrus, 162, 163; Rachel, 44, 99; Sara, 42, 44, 164; Selia, 44; Seletje, 44.
VER PLANCK:
  Wm. Gordon, 14.
VERSCHEUER:
  Arriaentjen, 41.

VERSTEEG:
  Diederick, 28.
VIELE:
  Antje, 35; Arnold, 135; Jacomyntje, 74; John, 128; Philip, 35; Philip, Jr., 122; Petrus, 74, 134; Pieternella, 82.
VLECHT:
  Mellysen, 55.
VLIET:
  Arie, 82; Geertie, 82; Volckert, 64; see *Van Vliet*.
VOSBURGH:
  Jan, 134.
VREDENBERGH:
  Antje, 66.
VROOMAN:
  Elisabeth, 74; Jacob Meese, 74.
VYNHOUT:
  Cornelis, 74; Jacomyntje, 74; see *Fynhout* and *Tenhout*.
WALDERON, WALDRON:
  Isaac, 163; Niesje, 93; Ruth, 92*, 93; Samuel, 93; Sarah, 163.
WALRAVEN:
  38.
WANBOOM:
  See *Van Bone*.
WARD:
  Jan, 49, 51; John, 39, 55, 104.
WARRING:
  James, 171, 172; Patience, 171, 172.
WEBBER:
  Catrina Hansen, 58.
WELLS:
  A. J., 92; Mary, 82.
WELLES:
  Philipps, 31, 34, 59, 92.
WEMP:
  Jan Barentsen, 22.

INDEX OF NAMES.

WESSELSE:
Dirck, 65; see *Ten Broeck*.
WEST:
John, 135, 139; Petrus, 146; William, 94.
WESTBROECK:
Johannis, 72, 106.
WESTPHAEL:
Blandina, 118; Jurian, 27, 31, 118; Neeltje, 118, 182*; Symon, 118, 182.
WEYEN:
Antje, 158.
WHEALER:
Joseph, 106.
WHITAKER, WITTIKER:
Benjamin, 177*; Catherine, 177*; *Edward*, 50; Edward, 50*, 80, 81, 82, 182; Edward James, 122; Elisabeth, 50; George, 177; Hannah, 50; Helena, 182; Hillitje, 50, 82, 182; James, 50*, 80, 81, 181; John, 122, 123; Lawrence, 177*; Peter S., 177; Philip, 177; Sawney, 177*; Theodosia, 82; Tjerck, 177; Zacharias, 177.
WIBAU:
Janneke, 79.
WIDDIGER:
See *Whitaker*.
WILEMAN:
Henry, 124.
WILLIAM, WILLEMS, WILLEMSE, WILLEMSEN, WILLIAMSEN:
Aeche (Titsourt), 79; *Barbary*, 36; Catherine, 142; Dirrick, 21; Elisabeth, 30; Hilligondt, 75; *Jan*, 36; Jan, 8, 26*, 27*, 28, 30, 36, 189; Jannetie (Claes Groenvis), 36, 46; John, 48, 142; Joosje (Noortryck), 46; Justje (Claes Groenvis), 36, 46; Maria, 43, 73.
WILLEMSEN:
See *Schutt*.
WILLEMSDOGHTER:
Maria, 43.
WILLKIN:
John, 144*, William, 144.
WINEKOOP:
Johannes, Sr., 112; see *Wynkoop*.
WINNE:
Aagje, 46; Anna, 137; Livinus, 53; Peter, 54, 188; Tanna, 137; Teuntie, 53.
WIRTSUNGH:
24.
WITTIGERT, WITTIKER:
See *Whitaker*.
WOLF:
Maria, 185.
WOLVEN:
Edward, 138; Frederick, 163; Jan, 52; Jonathan, 172; Maddeleen, 100; Margriet, 152; Thomas, 163.
WULFIN:
Anna Margaretta, 149; Johannes, 149; Sara, 185.
WYGERT:
Aeltje, 22, 29.
WYNKOOP:
Annetie, 32, 97; Benjamin, 32, 38; Catherine, 32, 38; Cornelia, 32; *Cornelius*, 32; Cornelius, 32, 36, 38*, 39, 42, 124, 161, 182; Cornelius D., 161; D., Jr., 181; Dirck, 120*, 136, 141, 146, 148, 149, 151, 152, 155, 160, 162; Elisabeth, 42; Evert, 32, 38, 64, 81; Femmetje, 32; Geertjen, 38, 56,

120*; Gertrude, 32; Hillitje, 32*, 40, 97; Janneke, 127, 128; Johanes, 32, 38, 42*, 47, 52, 62, 64, 112; John D., 145; Judith, 32, 42, 124; Lea, 160*, 161, 162; *Maria,* 38; Maria, 32, 38*, 39, 182; Maria Janse Langedyk, 32*, 38, 39; Mattyse, 56; Nicholas, 32; Tobias, 122.

YATES:
Peter W., 161, 162.

YEA:
August, 49.

YORK:
Elias, 173*.

YSSELSTEIN:
Gertrude, 96, 127; Jan Willemse, 96, 127; Willemtje, 96, 127; see *Esselstein.*

ZALOME:
Maria (Mestelaer), 157.

ZOUT:
Eva, 46.

ZUYLANT:
See *Suylant.*

ZWITS:
Cornelis Claesse, 121; see *Swits.*

www.ingramcontent.com/pod-product-compliance
Lightning Source LLC
Chambersburg PA
CBHW030547080526
44585CB00012B/295